Getting
Oriented

Getting Oriented

What Every Christian Should Know about Eastern Religions, but Probably Doesn't

Paul Alan Laughlin

Getting Oriented: What Every Christian Should Know about Eastern Religions, but Probably Doesn't

Published in 2005 by Polebridge Press, P.O. Box 6144, Santa Rosa, California 95406.

Interior illustrations by Karen Hanke of PinkLime Design

Library of Congress Cataloging-in-Publication Data

Laughlin, Paul A., 1946-
   Getting oriented: what every Christian should know about Eastern religions, but probably doesn't.
      p. cm.
   Includes bibliographical references.
   ISBN 0-944344-54-2
   1. Christianity and other religions--Asian 2. Asia--Religion. I. Title.

   BR5128.A77L38 2005
   200'.95--dc22

                                                    2004058636

Table of
Contents

Acknowledgements

Were I to express appreciation and gratitude to everyone who contributed directly and indirectly to the content of this book, there would be much less room for treating its subject matter. The list would certainly include my parents, Frank and Edna Laughlin, whose noble and sincere efforts to ensure that I would grow up a devout, mainstream Christian went terribly wrong and fairly early on, but who kept me in their wills anyway. It would contain the names of a host of teachers from my youth in both public and Sunday schools; but in particular, Ted Clingner, a high school English teacher whom I never had for class, but who opened my sophomoric eyes to historical criticism in religious matters when in a casual conversation he averred that he would have been a Christian himself if only the faith had stuck with Jesus and not been ruined by the Apostle Paul. I would also have to list every minister of my Methodist youth, including the many Southern pietists among them, but especially Paul Royster, a progressive Christian pastor who recommended to me (then a curious and skeptical teenager) stimulating and liberating books like *Honest to God* and *The Christian Agnostic*. I also appreciate all of my professors throughout college, seminary, and graduate school, but especially those at Emory University who most taught me to think theologically: Manfred Hoffmann, Brooks Holifield, Theodore Runyon, and Justo Gonzalez. I am also indebted to the authors of all of the books I have ever read in the fields of religion and philosophy, but particularly to Aldous Huxley for *The Perennial Philosophy*, W. T. Stace for *Mysticism and Philosophy*, Huston Smith for

Forgotten Truth, Frithjof Schuon for *The Transcendent Unity of All Religions*, Richard E. Friedman for *The Hidden Face of God*, John Hick for *God Has Many Names*, and Masao Abe for *Zen and Western Thought*.

The more immediate contributors to this volume constitute a more manageable company—at least after I get past the thousands of students who have endured my "Human Nature in the World's Religions" course at Otterbein College over the past quarter century, including those brave souls among them who pressed me toward ever greater clarity about the various exotic faiths and their relevance. The folks at Polebridge Press have been most helpful and gracious, especially Char Matejovsky, Wendell Bain, Tom Hall, and Robaire Ream. I am particularly beholden to those who read and commented on various drafts of *Getting Oriented*, all of them excellent scholars and even better friends: Paul L. Redditt of Georgetown College, Dell deChant of the Univeristy of South Florida, Thomas P. Kasulis of The Ohio State University, Glenna S. Jackson and William O. Amy of Otterbein College, Bob Garrett of Unity Church in Dallas, and Henry C. Galganowicz of Holy Innocents St. Paul Episcopal Church in Philadelphia. I hereby duly absolve all of these wonderful folks of responsibility for any good advice that I ignored and mistakes of fact and interpretation that I made despite their advice.

My friend C. Grey Austin, formerly of The Ohio State University (retired) and his lovely (and eagle-eyed) wife Barb truly deserve to share an Iron Person Award for having read every draft of every version of this book that evolved over four years until (as the Shakers would have put it) "it came round right." In addition to being a wonderful proofreader, Grey has long been a valued friend, adviser, confidant, and supporter, not to mention the most widely-read person I know in the area of spirituality; and our weekly lunches have always stimulated my thinking, sharpened my vision, elevated my spirits, and reassured me as to the worth of my theological and literary ventures. My dear and longsuffering wife Randy, to whom I dedicated *Remedial Christianity* and who has been just as marvelously supportive and understanding this time around, is therefore perfectly happy that I dedicate this volume to him—as long as I direct any royalty checks from it to her.

Introduction

Turning and Traveling East

> "I realized that I had joined a pilgrimage to the East, seemingly a definite and single pilgrimage—but in reality, in its broadest sense, this expedition to the East was not only mine and now; this procession of believers had always and incessantly been moving towards the East, towards the Home of Light."
> — Hermann Hesse, *The Journey to the East*

In the year 635 CE, a band of white-robed Christian monks from Persia arrived in the Chinese city of Chang-an (now known as Xian). They had traveled eastward via the already venerable but still difficult trade route known as the Silk Road. They bore not only crosses and icons, but a body of Christian teachings to share with the inhabitants of this distant and exotic land. Either *en route* or after their arrival, but certainly as a result of Chinese Taoist and Buddhist ideas that they had encountered along the way, these missionaries produced a novel and curiously Oriental rendering of the core teachings of and about Jesus. The written form of these was called *The Jesus Sutras* (*sutra* being a Sanskrit term used by both Hindus and Buddhists to mean "lesson" or "scripture"), which constituted a tenuous, yet bold synthesis of traditional Christian teachings and such Eastern notions as *karma*, reincarnation, and *Tao* (or *Dao*). These writings and the ideas they contained, became in turn the core of a Chinese Christianity called "The Luminous Religion," which thrived for nearly three centuries in the Tang dynasty

(618–907). These texts and the hybrid faith they represented apparently fell into disfavor with the later Sung regime (960–1279). As a result, not long after the year 1000, manuscripts containing *The Jesus Sutras* were hidden along with many non-Christian writings and sealed in a cave near the town of Shachou (now Dunhuang), where they were discovered late in the nineteenth century. The eight *sutras* that survive provide ample evidence that the foreign-born faith being newly promulgated in this ancient Oriental land had been deeply affected by the established religious beliefs and philosophical notions there in not only intriguing but often compelling ways.

Retracing an Ancient Route

The itinerant Christian monks who spawned this remarkable historical turn of events seem to have "gotten Oriented" as a result of their eastward journey in two senses of that phrase. First, they had intentionally encountered and engaged the prevailing faith traditions of the Far East in a way that made them not only deeply aware but profoundly appreciative of the exotic spiritual treasures that lay therein. Second, they had laid claim to some of these precious legacies and with them enriched not only themselves, but the faith that they had brought with them. This was neither the first nor the last time that committed Christian missionaries were bedazzled and transformed by the beliefs of the foreign people they had come to serve and perhaps convince.

This book seeks to follow in the footsteps of these noble ancient travelers, taking professed Christians to the East and exposing them—some perhaps for the first time—to a panorama of the alien yet profoundly captivating spiritual beliefs and ancient religious practices that flourish there. The stated purpose will be to get ourselves "Oriented," figuratively speaking, in at least one and perhaps both of the ways our Persian-Christian forerunners did. At the very least, we shall become more knowledgeable about and, one would hope, respectful of the major faith traditions that originated in the farther reaches of Asia (that is, beyond the "Near" or "Middle" regions of that continent), and particularly in India and China. (Some would say that the very fact that Christianity emerged in Asia makes it Oriental from its inception; but as we shall show in the following chapter, most modern scholars of comparative religion draw the East-West line much farther to the east of ancient Palestine.) More than merely becoming informed, however, we shall also be open to the distinct possibility that some or perhaps much that we find there will be valuable, useful, and—as in the case of those brave monks long ago—capable of being incorporated into the Christian faith in salutary ways.

A New Journey Eastward

We propose, then, to embark upon something of a journey, one that will follow to a great extent the route of its seventh century prototype, albeit with a different goal and purpose. It will admittedly be more figurative and mental than geographical and physical in nature: we shall be traveling in our imaginations rather than actual caravans. But its direction will be nonetheless eastward—toward *the* East, in fact, and a great light that is said to be there, a light whose various refractions and reflections may be found in the great religious traditions (especially Hinduism, Buddhism, Taoism, and Confucianism) that thrive there. Likewise, it will be as much a spiritual journey as was its predecessor, and one that will similarly result in a reconceiving of the Christian faith in light of the major Eastern religious and spiritual traditions. But while the blending of West and East that we shall eventually propose in these pages is in the spirit of our ancient predecessors, our goal will be to surpass their well-intentioned but tentative results with a much better informed and more thoroughgoing synthesis. The major difference between our work and theirs is that our purpose will not be to propagate our faith among Eastern non-Christians, but rather to enrich and enhance it for Westerners who already profess it—or once did. Nevertheless, like them we seek and expect outcomes that will be luminescent and therefore enlightening.

The trip I propose, then, is designed mostly for Christians and former Christians who may know little or nothing about the great Eastern faiths, but who are at least open to new ideas, however exotic they may at first appear. Such a journey is bound to take travelers into unfamiliar and perhaps even threatening territories. My primary purpose, like that of any experienced guide, is to help these travelers find new illumination and enrichment in the traditional Christianity they were born into or at some point adopted. I especially hope that this journey will benefit those who have become disaffected with their Christian faith, or even deserted it altogether. Our shared goal will be to explore the great Eastern religions and to obtain from them some Eastern light that will illuminate the standard variety of Christianity familiar to most Catholic, Protestant, Orthodox, and sectarian followers.

The Urgency of Our Trip

The traditional Christianity that we hope to elucidate by our journey to the East is characterized first by its monotheism, and second by its cardinal doctrines: the Holy Trinity, the Incarnation with its consequent humanity and divinity of Christ, the radical sinfulness of humanity, and the atoning death of Jesus as the sole source of salvation. These distinctive and definitive tenets were the focus of my previous book, *Remedial Christianity: What Every Believer Should Know about the Faith, but Probably Doesn't* (Polebridge Press, 2000). Though by no means presupposing the present reader's knowledge of the contents of that earlier work, *Getting Oriented* is intended to supplement it.

From all over the world, readers of *Remedial Christianity* have expressed their appreciation for the book, and especially for the way in which it critically—by which I mean carefully, contextually, and comparatively—analyzed and correlated the central doctrines of the faith. Of particular interest, it appears, was my treatment of the traditional Christian understanding of sin and salvation, a doctrine that posits a humanity so deeply flawed as to be helpless to restore its broken relationship with God, and thus to require a vicarious, atoning sacrifice of an Incarnate God-Son. My views on such matters seem to have confirmed and validated misgivings and suspicions that these readers already had about the mainstream expressions of the Christian faith, reservations that had led them either to question it deeply or abandon it completely. Yet it also seems to have alleviated nagging doubts and even guilt and shame, both for some who had managed to tough it out and stay in the church and for others who had given up on it and left. Many of these good people also expressed gratitude for the constructive "bright spots" contained in that book. They seem to have appreciated most of all its offering of alternative ways of viewing Jesus as the Christ and its reconsideration of the relatively little-known mystical sub-tradition of Christianity.

Not only the number, but the sincere and often passionate tone of such responses indicated to me that a journey like the one on which we are embarking was sorely needed. Its urgency, in fact, can hardly be overstated. That is especially true for those Christians who consider themselves moderate, mainstream, liberal, or progressive in their thinking about religious matters; for it is these who most often find themselves beleaguered by stridently conservative individuals and groups. For at a time when the American public's interest in religion may be at an all-time high, conservative, evangelical, and fundamentalist expressions of the Christian faith are flourishing, while mainstream churches and denominations appear to be floundering. Their memberships are not merely declining, but in some cases virtually hemorrhaging. Many liberal and progressive believers who manage to remain committed and active Christians are either mildly dissatisfied or seriously disaffected with the faith; not a few find themselves barely hanging on out of a sense of nostalgia or in despair over the apparent lack of meaningful and acceptable alternatives.

Nonetheless, clear signs of hope for Christianity are evident in the excellent work of such progressive thinkers and authors as Karen Armstrong, Bishop John Shelby Spong, Marcus Borg, Matthew Fox, and Lloyd Geering. Still, it was not until the publication of *Remedial Christianity* that I became aware of a loose network of organizations committed to bringing a sometimes hopelessly outdated Christianity into currency and making it more plausible and credible to thoughtful people. I am speaking about groups like Spong's Christians for the Third Millennium, the Center for Progressive Christianity, the FaithFutures Foundation, and the Westar Institute, home of the Jesus Seminar and Polebridge Press. Like *Remedial Christianity* before it, *Getting Oriented* stands in this nascent but promising progressive Christian tradition and picks up where its predecessor left off by providing further constructive suggestions for a new and exciting understanding of the faith. The ultimate objective of the present volume is indeed ambitious; it is to rebuild Christianity by retaining the key components of the faith, but reformulating them in light of insights drawn from the great religious and spiritual traditions of the East. Specifically, we can expect to find Christianity enriched by Hinduism, Buddhism, Taoism, and to a lesser extent, Confucianism.

The Journey Motif

The image of the spiritual journey that lies at the heart of this book is a recurring theme in the world's religions, both Eastern and Western. The ancient Hinduism of India, for example, has long offered three spiritual *margas* or "paths," while the very name of the equally venerable Japanese religion Shinto means "the way of the gods." The Buddha called the spiritual discipline that he taught "The Middle Way," and Ultimate Reality in both Taoism and Confucianism is dubbed the *Tao* or "Way." The history of Judaism begins in earnest only with the Exodus, a forty-year trek by the Israelites from Egyptian captivity toward the Promised Land. The Jesus of John's gospel refers to himself as "the

Way," and this became the earliest appellation for the faith he spawned before anyone thought about calling it "Christianity." For their part, Muslims mark the beginning of both their faith and their calendar as the *hijrah*, a pivotal migration that Muhammad and his followers made in 622 CE from Mecca to Medina. They also call their *Qur'an*-based code of conduct *Shari'a*, the root meaning of which is "road," and refer to their central body of tradition as *Sunna*, yet another term that connotes "way."

These are but a few of many examples that point to the widely shared sense that whatever else it is, faith is a journey. To be sure, the world's religions are far from unanimous about the nature of the destination, and agree even less upon the precise route to follow. Still, there seems to be a tacit agreement that the whole point of a religion is to move a person from an unsatisfactory spiritual situation to a more salutary one. As one of my young students recently put it, "Religion's a trip, man."

The Journey's Motives

The root purpose of our proposed trip to the exotic East is to gain knowledge. We expect to find and bring home treasures of wisdom, mainly in the form of information and ideas that can be used by active and alumni Christians who wish to get a new slant on their faith. But there are other good reasons for making a trip like this, and many outside the Christian fold can also profit from such an excursion. Some travelers, for example, may wish simply to satisfy their curiosity or fill gaps in their stores of historical and other factual information about the world's great religious traditions, on the sound premise that it is useful and pleasurable to know things. Indeed, an extensive cache of general and seemingly extraneous knowledge is one of the marks of a liberally educated and well-informed person. As an added benefit for such mildly curious or seriously inquisitive folks, new information about Eastern faiths may lead to better success with crossword puzzles and trivia competitions. It might even win them some big money on a popular TV game show!

Perhaps a more important reason for non-Christians to make a journey like this is that religion—however one may feel personally—is beyond question one of the most significant human phenomena. Whether directly or indirectly, it has throughout history played a dominant role in most people's lives and nearly all societies. And despite predictions of its inevitable decline and disappearance, it continues to have an enormous effect—sometimes for better and sometimes for worse—not only on individuals, but on politics, economics, literature, the arts, and virtually every other aspect of human life and culture. For that reason alone, it should be clear that no one who is ignorant of the world's great religious traditions can be considered truly educated or even well-informed. In addition to the merely curious, therefore, I shall welcome on this journey those who want to expand their awareness of the world. Further, as we shall see shortly, such an excursion will offer us Americans a deeper understanding of our nation's history and changing religious complexion.

Still other potential recruits for our merry band of fellow-trekkers include the many who today find themselves searching for a viable religion of their own. Our survey of the major Eastern religions will be objective, balanced, non-judgmental, respectful, and even appreciative; and for that reason it should at least help these seekers to clarify their choices and discover some hitherto unknown options. This group will no doubt include the increasing number of individuals who identify themselves as *spiritual* rather than religious because of the institutional connotation of the latter term. They may well find some useful raw materials from which to shape satisfying systems of spiritual belief and practice—if necessary, creating a patchwork quilt. Some may even elect to settle into one of the Eastern faiths we visit and not, so to speak, return home with us.

Such a decision, if based on solid information and careful deliberation, should not be discouraged, for it might well be the best possible outcome for people with certain dispositions and life experiences. Given the difficulties and challenges of adopting an exotic religion wholesale, however, we should expect such felicitous defections to be rare. In any case, people who embrace other faiths or no faith at all, those who are searching for faith, and those who are merely curious about faith are alike welcome to join our company and may equally expect to benefit from our explorations. Still, the primary objective of this journey of discovery will be to enrich and enhance the faith experience of thoughtful Christians in the Third Millennium.

Americans and the East

The kind of turning East proposed in this book is hardly new for Americans; indeed, a fascination with Eastern spirituality and thought is deeply ingrained in our history. The framers of our U. S. Constitution, for example, knew of Confucius and in some ways emulated his vision of the ideal state. One of these, Benjamin Franklin, is said to have modeled his famous *Poor Richard's Almanac* after the *Analects* (that is, the

collected sayings) of the ancient Chinese sage. The Transcendentalists of
the early 19th century were quite taken with Hinduism. Ralph Waldo
Emerson, for example, wrote a controversial poem entitled "Brahma"
that was based on a passage from the Hindu *Upanishads*. And in the
American classic *Walden*, his friend Henry David Thoreau wrote, "In
the morning I bathe my intellect in the stupendous and cosmogonal
[cosmic-origins oriented] philosophy of the Bhagavat-Geeta [*Bhagavad
Gita*], since whose composition years of the gods have elapsed, and in
comparison with which our modern world and its literature seem puny
and trivial. . . . The pure Walden water is mingled with the sacred water
of the Ganges." The later years of that same century saw the founding of
the Theosophical Society in New York by Madam Helena P. Blavatsky,
an occultist and world traveler with aristocratic Russian ancestry and
strong ties to Eastern religions, notably Buddhism. Due in part to her
work and influence, by the 1880s Buddhism was popular in Boston
among the educated, and especially with the relentlessly unorthodox
Unitarians. Toward the very end of that century, there appeared on the
American religious scene the New Thought movement (the major institutional expressions of which are currently Unity and Religious Science),
among whose founders many if not most were greatly influenced by
Eastern religions and philosophies.

What truly opened the floodgates for the influx of world religions into
America, however, was the first World Parliament of Religions, which was
convened in Chicago in conjunction with the Columbian Exposition and
World's Fair of 1893. For the first time in human history, spokespersons for
all of the world's major religions were invited to and particpated in a grand
and well-publicized dialogue. As a result, many articulate foreign teachers,
in particular Hindus from India and Buddhists from Japan, gained followings in America, and established such important religious organizations as
the Vedanta Societies and, later, the Buddhist Church of America.

America's popular interest in the world's religions continued to grow in
the early twentieth century and increased dramatically in the 1950s and
1960s. Many of the luminaries of the so-called "Beat Generation," including novelist Jack Kerouac and poets Gary Snyder and Allen Ginsberg, were
powerfully influenced by Zen Buddhism and other Eastern spiritualities.
Hinduism became very fashionable in the mid-1960s, especially after the
Beatles visited India and met Maharishi Mahesh Yogi, the founder of Transcendental Meditation. Not long afterward, actress Shirley MacLaine
included her affirmation of previous lives and the Hindu doctrine of reincarnation in her first autobiography, *Don't Fall Off the Mountain*, and she
openly discussed her experiences and views on radio and TV talk shows. The

music of Indian sitarist Ravi Shankar became widely known in the United States during these years; and American jazz guitarist John McLaughlin converted to Hinduism, explored musical modes and styles drawn from the traditional music of India, and gave both himself and his *avant-gard* orchestra the spiritual name "Mahavishnu." A phalanx of Eastern gurus like Meher Baba, Mahara Ji, and Satya Sai Baba attracted American followers; and there arose a spate of transplanted Asian religions, such as Subud, Tibetan Buddhism, the Sivananda Yoga Society, and Nichiren Shoshu, to name but a few. D. T. Suzuki, Alan Watts, and Ram Dass (Richard Alpert) also advanced the cause of Eastern religions with their popular interpretations of Buddhism, Taoism, and Hinduism. Clearly, the East was attracting the attention of Americans and speaking to them in engaging ways.

The East in America

The American population itself changed drastically during this same period, and especially after the relaxation of U. S. immigration laws in the last third of the twentieth century generated (and continues to produce) waves of newcomers from other lands and cultures, including those where the Eastern faiths dominate. These new neighbors have made us increasingly aware of the richness and variety of previously unknown religious traditions. Even in medium-size Midwestern cities, Americans increasingly find themselves driving past Buddhist and Hindu temples. More important, they increasingly avail themselves of such meditative techniques as *yoga*, whose roots are in Hinduism; *vipassana*, a by-product of Theravada Buddhism; and *zazen*, a Zen Buddhist technique. Others are undergoing acupuncture for their medical complaints, employing *feng shui* to produce more agreeable living and working environments, or practicing *t'ai chi* as a martial art or exercise regimen—all practices that are rooted in Chinese religion. Most of us, in fact, find that we now have neighbors, business associates, physicians, storeowners, clerks, fellow students and teachers—and perhaps even family members—who profess an Eastern faith, sometimes in emulation of a favorite recording, TV, or movie star. All of this is a part of what Diana Eck of Harvard has rightly called "the changing landscape of American religion," a transformation that is producing an increasingly eclectic and pluralistic society and a wider range of religious and spiritual options than ever before.

It should come as no surprise, then, that coinciding with this influx of religiously diverse people, Americans have demonstrated a heightening interest in Eastern faiths. One unmistakable indication of this trend is the considerable number of bookstore shelves devoted to Eastern religions and alternative spiritualities fueled by them. Also, more and more Americans are familiar with the Hindu *Upanishads* and *Bhagavad Gita*, the Buddhist *Dhammapada*, and the Chinese *Tao Te Ching*. Increasingly visible are the *Om*, a Buddha, the *Ta'i chi* (*yin-yang*), or some other Chinese or Sanskrit symbol worn on neck chains and T-shirts, and even sported as tatoos. Americans are also enjoying movies like *The Karate Kid, The Golden Child, Little Buddha, Seven Years in Tibet,* and *Kundun,* all of which have Buddhist themes; *The Kama Sutra*, which is an adaptation of the ancient Hindu erotic classic; *Crouching Tiger, Hidden Dragon,* which brims with Chinese spirituality; and a seemingly endless string of films featuring the martial arts, all of which are grounded in Eastern spirituality and philosophy. Not so many years ago, PBS ran the Hindu epic *Mahabharata* as a TV miniseries, and cable channels continue to rerun episodes of the original *Kung Fu* series, which conveys at least a hint of Eastern spirituality despite its wildly stylized characters, philosophically suspect concepts, and downright hokey plots. When added to our nation's historical fascination with the East, such pop-culture phenomena make our proposed trip seem nearly as American as baseball, hot dogs, and—well—Jesus.

Getting Our Bearings

The urge to understand more clearly such exotic threads in our social fabric and their potential relevance to our spiritual lives should make us eager to get started. Before we set out, however, we first need to determine more specifically the direction we shall be heading—to get our bearings on this East that we are going to explore. One would think that would be an easy task. After all, "East is East, and West is West," we are told in story and song. If only it were that simple! An elementary course in geography will inform you that on the basis of landmasses, the Western Hemisphere consists primarily of the Americas, while the rest of the inhabited world—including Africa, Asia, Australia, and Europe—are in the Eastern Hemisphere. But if you walk next door to a course in Western Civilization, you'll find that "Western" includes Europe and in some cases even such portions of the Middle East as the Mesopotamian cradle of civilization (modern Iraq), both of which the geographer had placed in the Eastern Hemisphere. A subsequent visit to the classroom across the hall may cause you even more confusion, especially if it is hosting a course on the world's religions. For the scholars of that field of study long ago drew yet a different East-West dividing line to suit their particular purposes.

For religionists, the rule of thumb is this: if a religion was born in or west of Persia, it is a Western religion. The major world religions that meet that criterion are Judaism, Zoroastrianism, Christianity, Islam, and Baha'i—all of which emerged in the geographic Middle *East*. Likewise, if the religion originated in or east of India, it is an Eastern religion. Thus Hinduism, Buddhism, Taoism and Confucianism are Eastern religions, as are the less familiar Jainism, Sikhism, and Shinto. The imaginary line between Iran (Persia) and India—running, as chance would have it, through Afghanistan—is not arbitrary, but as we shall see in Chapter 1, typological. It is based on the fact that for all of their mutual differences, the Eastern religions look more like one another than any one of them resembles any Western religion, and vice versa, especially in their conceptualizations of an Ultimate Reality. Subsequent voluntary and forced migrations of most of the Western religions took them both westward and in an easterly direction (the exception being Judaism), with the result that most Zoroastrians today live in India (as Parsees), Indonesia is the world's most populous Muslim country, and Australia is predominantly Christian. The Eastern faiths, by contrast, remained and expanded mostly in or near their points of origin for the better part of their histories, touching the West significantly only in the past century or so. Our eastward excursion, therefore, will take us to India, China, and—where else?—points east.

Checking Our "Head" Lights

As already suggested, we expect to gain some sort of *enlightenment* as a result of our metaphorical journey to the East and our encounter with the major faiths there, particularly Hinduism, Buddhism, and Taoism; and we expect to see the Christian faith enriched as a result. As we shall see, the images of light and enlightenment are commonplace in Eastern religious discourse, and carry a distinctive connotation not generally found in the West. This is not to say, however, that we shall be departing or traveling in complete darkness. For as Westerners, we are already heirs of one Enlightenment: the eighteenth-century Western European movement that presented the dynamic duo of the mind and sensory experience as the final path to and arbiter of truth. As a result, we undertake this journey as an inquisitive people who are open to unfamiliar ideas and committed to rational and empirical thinking.

It is impossible to overestimate the impact of the Western Enlightenment on the history of ideas and the shaping of modern Western thought. Indeed, it is the source of the prevailing (and still relatively young) scientific worldview that undergirds our implicitly shared, conventional, and commonsensical understanding of a reality that functions in accordance with natural law. This worldview employs verifiable evidence and reasonable explanation to arrive at knowledge that is worthwhile and trustworthy. Some Christians and other religionists have rejected part or all of this Enlightenment and its worldview as inimical to faith, revealed truth, and scripture. By contrast, an Oriented Christianity, along with all liberal and progressive expressions of religious faith, will enthusiastically embrace the Western Enlightenment and its by-products, even when these appear to have a negative impact on matters of religion and spirituality. It will not, however, absolutize this modern mode of thinking. It will instead recognize that however durable and persistent worldviews are, they are transitory and destined to be refined and even replaced. It will also acknowledge that perfectly valid alternative understandings of reality co-exist even now, including the animism of tribal peoples and, more to the point here, the philosophies generated by Eastern religions.

Unlike the Western philosophical tradition, Western religions like Christianity rarely if ever use the term "enlightenment," preferring instead the notions of *revelation* to characterize knowledge that comes from God and *salvation* to describe the ultimate goal for humans. To be sure, light is sometimes a metaphor for the divinity that "shines" from above, as we see in the traditional (and, unfortunately, gender-exclusive) blessing: "May the Lord lift up the light of His countenance and make His face to shine upon you." Christians often sing hymns about walking in the light of God or God's Word. Nor is it uncommon for biblical authors to use the image of light to describe God's presence or activity (recall Moses' shining face in Exodus 34:29–35). Indeed, light is said to be the first thing created by God in the very first chapter of the Hebrew Bible (Genesis 1:3). The word "light" is also prominent in the first chapter of the Fourth Gospel, where Jesus is referred to as "the Light of the world" (John 1:9) and later portrayed as claiming that title for himself (John 8:12). Matthew's version of the event in Jesus' ministry traditionally referred to as the Transfiguration (Matt 17:19) makes explicit what the parallels in Mark and Luke only imply: that his face radiated light akin to that of the sun. Paul's reported encounter with the risen Jesus on the Damascus Road entails a light so bright it blinds him (Acts 9:1–9). Yet despite such important scriptural references and many others like them, traditional Christianity has never added the word "enlightenment" to its vocabulary.

By contrast, Eastern religions and the philosophies they have generated use the notion of "enlightenment" a great deal, but in a very different sense from that of Western philosophy. In Hinduism and Buddhism, for example, the idea of enlightenment tends to emerge not in the context of popular devotional piety, which directs attention to deities or other quasi-divine entities, but in the more esoteric mystical expressions, in which spiritual attention is directed to some sort of Power within. In that context, enlightenment is generally understood as trans-sensory and trans-rational, for the mind has to go beyond the senses and even itself to experience it. This sort of enlightenment entails a much deeper spiritual Wisdom than the intellectual knowledge so valued in the West, and implies a Sacred Light that does not shine upon one from an outside Source above, but radiates from an abiding Force within. We can express this distinction with a metaphor: a person enlightened in an Oriental way does not aspire to walk *in* such a Light, but yearns instead to walk *as* that Light—inwardly aglow, as it were. Again, this important distinction reflects a basically *mystical* attitude, which will be explained in greater detail in Chapter 1, and posited in Chapter 5 as the very foundation of a transformed, enlightened Christianity.

So it is that we begin our journey already enlightened in a Western sense, yet seeking further enlightenment of the kind found in the great religious traditions of the East. It will not be predominantly intellectual or rationalistic, as is its Western counterpart, but rather more *intuitive*. It will be empirical, therefore, but in a different way: the experience on which it will focus is the sort that goes beyond the five senses and eventually the rational mind. This is not sensory but *spiritual* experience, and since it involves profound inwardness and unity, it will be inherently mystical in nature and will provide light of a different hue from that with which we are familiar.

Mapping Our Itinerary

This book addresses the major Oriental religious traditions and their potential for enlightening Christians and Christianity in five chapters. A very busy Chapter 1 provides some useful tools and supplies for our journey. First it provides a descriptive working definition of religion that conveys a sense of its complexity as a human enterprise, as well as a widely used schema for recognizing and correlating seven distinct aspects of religion. It then proceeds to clarify and correlate such tricky terms as "religion," "spirituality," "theology," "philosophy," "school," and "sect."

Next the chapter presents a brief overview of the history of religions as a good starting point for understanding the sometimes bewildering array of religious traditions that will be encountered in subsequent chapters. It concludes with an even more revealing typological model that discloses the contrasting patterns of thought about Ultimate Reality—what most Westerners call "God"—that distinguish Oriental from Occidental religions and reflect two very different types of spirituality.

Our journey proper comprises the next three chapters. Chapter 2 examines Hinduism, the broadly inclusive and highly complex majority religion of India, while Chapter 3 treats one of its offshoots, Buddhism, in its many and varied forms. Chapter 4 deals with the seemingly contradictory but ultimately complementary Chinese religions, Confucianism and Taoism, and identifies the latter as more promising as a source of Christian "Orientation" and the sort of enlightenment it needs. In my treatment of each of these Eastern religious traditions, I have organized the material under the headings Overview and Origins, Scripture and Beliefs, Historical Developments, and Distinctive Practices (including the role and status of women). And I have concluded each discussion with brief indications about what Christians should know about that particular religion. These suggestive tidbits will be fleshed out in the fifth and final chapter, in which we come home to Christianity bearing the radiant treasures that we have found in the East. Here the reader will find specific suggestions about how the major Christian doctrines might be enriched and even transformed in the light of what we have found in the Eastern religious traditions into a working model of what we shall term an *enlightened* Christianity. This capstone chapter further suggests how an enlightened Christian faith might be better poised to meet the daunting challenges of the young millennium and an emerging global worldview, and closes by inviting the reader to join in what promises to be a lengthy, challenging, and rewarding enterprise of further construction.

As connected as these five chapters are, each stands quite nicely on its own as well. If a reader should have a particular interest in Buddhism, for example, he or she might want to proceed directly to Chapter 3, leaving both the first, preparatory chapter and the second, on Hinduism, for attention at a later date. Returning eventually to digest the skipped chapters would still be advisable, however, since both provide important historical-contextual and other useful background information for Buddhism. Likewise, the desire to see the end result of our journey—the Christianity envisioned in this book as the end-result of our engagement with the East—might prove irresistible. In that case, the reader would do well to jump all the way to the last chapter—to take the Orient Express to the end of the line, as it were, without stopping to pass GO (that is, the "Getting Oriented" process in Chapters 1 through 4). Still, she or he would also be well-advised to return thereafter to the starting point of the trip, to gear up, and make the trip by foot, so to speak, plodding through all of the chapters and reaping the rewards that engaging directly in the process of enlightenment delivers. For those who do make a leap of faith ahead, the extensive glossary at the very end of the book should help to fill in any informational gaps that the by-pass has caused and to clarify any strange terminology that may be encountered.

Adjusting Our Attitudes

To fully appreciate a book like this and the journey it offers, the reader would be well advised to suspend disbelief while we travel together, as well as to relinquish any prejudices against religion as a whole or any particular religion. For the sake of the learning process, the reader is further encouraged while en route to hold in abeyance—to pack and store, as it were—any religious or spiritual creed, beliefs, or practices that she or he may hold dear. That does not mean, of course, abandoning, renouncing, or otherwise compromising one's personal faith existentially or permanently. What it does entail is shelving it momentarily for the sake of expanding one's intellectual horizons and conceptual boundaries. Such a mental discipline is not unlike that of a political scientist who sets aside a personal perspective or allegiance in order to understand more fully and assess more fairly another view or system. It likewise resembles the methodology of an historian who puts modern standards and values aside temporarily, the better to appreciate past eras on their own terms. For only when we accept that sane, intelligent, and well-intentioned people might plausibly believe and conscientiously do what we shall encounter in these "strange" Eastern traditions can we begin to give unfamiliar religions a fair reading. Only by walking a mile or so in the shoes, slippers, and sandals—or in some cases, the bare feet—of their followers can we truly understand and appreciate other faith traditions.

One thing that has always helped me in this respect is the recognition that I am what I am, religiously speaking, largely by accident of birth. Statistics and sociological studies confirm what our own experience and common sense tell us: that people born in the United States have a high statistical likelihood of being Christians, just as the natives of India tend to be Hindus, those of Japan are inclined to be Buddhists, and those of Saudi Arabia are almost certainly Muslims. More than that, those who are most enthusiastic about their Christianity in Iowa or Ireland would probably have been just as enthusiastic about their Hinduism if they were natives of India, or their Islam if they had been born in Iran. Such a realization does more than humble us; it also encourages our openness to and appreciation of others and their faiths.

As its subtitle suggests, *Getting Oriented* aims to inform Christians about the great faith traditions of the East. Its purpose in doing so is not to promote any particular Eastern religion or to undermine Christianity, but rather to assist its adherents (including the discontented among them) in clarifying and enriching their faith. Indeed, even dogmatic Fundamentalists might benefit from the information contained in these pages. So might those at the other end of the religious spectrum, namely, agnostics and doctrinaire atheists, if only to get a clearer picture of some options of which they may not have been aware or knowledgeable enough to consider previously. I would hope for all of these folks that they might finish the trip a bit more tolerant of views they do not personally embrace. The book is aimed primarily, however, at those who stand somewhere between these extremes, and is intended to shed new light on Christianity and to make some suggestions about how at least some of its followers might benefit from such an exercise. While it is certainly not my purpose to drive such folks into the arms of another faith tradition, I know from experience that when Eastern religious traditions are presented with clarity, enthusiasm, empathy, and respect, they all manifest attractive and sometimes downright seductive features. As a result, an open-minded reader cannot help but be affected by them, almost invariably in positive ways.

A Reassurance and an Invitation

Despite some challenges and apparent dangers and threats that we shall encounter along our itinerary, we expect no casualties on this trip. Everyone who completes the journey will not only survive but thrive. Over the past three decades, of the thousands of students I have led on similar treks to the East in the classroom, I have not had a single one lose her or his faith as a result of exploring the religions there in a fair and even-handed way. A few—but *only* a few—have converted from one faith to another or switched denominations within their own tradition as a result of what they learned from the adventure. But many more have declared that in the exploration of these seemingly exotic faiths, they had discovered a context and terminology for what they had always believed in their heart of hearts. The problem was that they had hitherto been unable to grasp or articulate their intuitions or beliefs within the context of their professed religious tradition. Still more have insisted that engaging the world's many religions in an objective and comparative way simply confirmed them in their existing faith by bringing it into sharper focus or giving it a new spin. As already noted, the attractive ideas found in Eastern religions should not threaten or undermine one's Christian faith—or for that matter, any other belief system—but serve to enrich it.

Therefore, on the basis of my deep conviction that the Eastern religions are not only fascinating but edifying, I invite you to join in a great adventure. There's a very good chance that you, too, will be edified and inspired, as others have been who have gone before. I feel certain that you will be at least interested and perhaps fascinated by what you encounter in the following pages. You may even be entertained and surprised. Whatever your response, you will not be unaffected. The subject matter is just that compelling.

Enjoy the trip!

Recommended Reading

Ian Gillman and Hans-Joachim Klimkiet, *Christianity in Asia before 1500*. Ann Arbor: University of Michigan Press, 1999.

Samuel Hugh Moffitt, *A History of Christianity in Asia: Beginnings to 1500*. 2d ed. New York: Orbis Books: 1998.

Martin Palmer, *The Jesus Sutras: Rediscovering the Lost Scrolls of Taoist Christianity*. New York: Ballantine: 2001.

Ray Riegert and Thomas Moore, eds., Jon Babcock, trans. *The Lost Sutras of Jesus: Unlocking the Ancient Wisdom of the Xian Monks*. Berkeley, CA: Seastone, 2003.

John M. L. Young, *By Foot To China: Mission of the Church to the East, to 1400*. Lookout Mountain, GA: Grey Pilgrim Press, 1991.

Chapter 1

Preparations and Provisions

for the Trek

Objectives of this Chapter

- to acknowledge and explain the difficulty of defining the term "religion," and to provide a useful working definition

- to recognize and illustrate the seven dimensions of religion posited by scholar Ninian Smart, and to suggest an eighth

- to define "spirituality," "theology," and "philosophy" and clarify their roles with respect to Eastern and Western religions

- to distinguish between schools, sects, and denominations as they apply to Eastern and Western religions

- to provide an overview of the history of religions that identifies four periods and their distinguishing characteristics

- to examine the marked differences between Western and Eastern religions with respect to how they view Ultimate Reality, the cosmos and time, as well as humanity's nature, predicament, and prospects

Before embarking on the kind of journey proposed by this book's title and Introduction, we might do well to get a sense of the lay of the land, and then map out a trail to follow—or at least a tentative one. Since it is clear by now that the general area in which we shall be traveling is *religion*, it might be a good idea to begin by examining the meaning of that word. The first part of this chapter addresses that important issue, and will take us to a working definition of religion. This in turn will lead us to recognize the complexity of the subject and to generate a helpful schema for putting things in order. After that we shall examine a number of closely related issues and terms, and then move on to a brief historical survey that will provide a temporal framework for the several religions to be treated in detail. Finally, a detailed contrast of Eastern and Western religions will help us better understand both Christianity and the other religions that we shall encounter in this book.

The reader should be forewarned that as with any journey, our provisioning will be diverse. After all, even a well-planned vacation trip requires the packing of such varied items as toiletries, clothes, travel documents, and sometimes bedding and tents as well. Surely the same is true for a serious intellectual or spiritual excursion. If the contents of this chapter seem to be something of a jumble of this and that, therefore, just remember the suitcase or duffel bag you took with you the last time you traveled. Or to switch the metaphor slightly, think of the many bits of information in this chapter as a sort of spiritual trail mix of terminology, history, and typology that will provide sustenance when the going gets rough. And it is bound to, given the complexity of the terrain that we intend to cover. A still more apt metaphor for this chapter, perhaps, would be the tourbook one carries to a foreign country: it is chock full of tips on such divergent topics as itineraries, hotels, restaurants, points of interest, regional history, and more. Whatever the comparison, this chapter's variegated contents should provide some useful mental preparation for the trek ahead. Let's start by getting a fix on the general landscape ahead: the realm of religion.

Scoping Out "Religion"

One of the most difficult things about understanding religion in general is getting a handle on the subject matter. All objects of inquiry pose their own unique problems, of course, especially when they involve matters of human belief and behavior. None, however, is more daunting than religion. There are a number of reasons for this. First of all, the derivation of the word "religion" presents ambiguities. It comes ultimately from the Latin word for "tying" or "binding," but the connection between that sort of task and what we recognize as religion is far from clear. It might, for example, connote any or all of such diverse objectives as connecting, restricting, or securing. Another source of difficulty is that religion comprises a multifaceted complex of phenomena, a veritable kaleidoscope of beliefs, concepts, myths, rituals, ethics, experiences, institutions, and literary, visual, and musical expressions. Since many of these are at odds with one another (such as vegetarianism and animal sacrifice, celibacy and ritual sex, ecstatic worship and silent meditation), it appears that almost any form of human behavior can be subsumed under the term "religion." Yet another problem in defining "religion" is that it often implies the existence of extraordinary or even unique beings, realms, events, experiences, and mental states—to say nothing of its attachment to such slippery terms as "belief" and "faith." Also problematic is the fact that virtually all of us were born into and reared within a particular religious environment that includes family, social circle, culture, and era. The power of such influences, especially in our formative years, makes it highly likely that unless we undertake significant investigation and thought, we shall define "religion" in terms of our own limited experience of it, and thereby ignore much that needs including.

A Working Definition

Given these problems, no one definition of "religion" will be completely satisfactory. I offer the following, therefore, merely as a useful working definition that encompasses the phenomena that we shall encounter in the following chapters: *Religion is the sum total of what individuals and/or groups experience, feel, think, say, do, produce, and hope for relative to whatever they believe or perceive to be an Ultimate Reality or Truth.* To be sure, some religions (such as animistic, polytheistic, Jainist, and Shintoist) appear to have no concept of an Ultimate Reality, but only a mysterious realm filled with such extraordinary beings as spirits and gods. But although the above is hardly an all-purpose definition, it certainly works for the Eastern religions that we shall explore as well as for the Christianity that we seek to enrich.

The five that are the main focus of this book have different understandings of Ultimate Reality. For Christians, of course, it is a single, supernatural, personal, creator God, a view that puts them into general agreement with Jews and Muslims, whose religions also descended from Abraham. By contrast, the great Eastern religions cast the Ultimate as non-personal, something more like a spiritual essence than a superior entity. Hindus commonly identify it as *Brahman,* the Supreme Spirit or simply the Absolute; Buddhists (at least in the Mahayana branch) conceive it as *Shunyata*, the infinite Emptiness or Void; and Confucianists and Taoists both honor it as *Tao*, the powerfully inactive Way—three views of Ultimate Reality that, despite their peculiarities, are cut from pretty much the same cloth. Given this pattern of similarity and difference, therefore, an important part of our task will be to clarify the images of Ultimacy inherent in the world's great religious traditions.

The Subjective and the Objective

Our working definition raises a number of issues, but for now, let us focus on its subjective and objective components. The subjective portion of the definition is everything prior to the "whatever," and embraces the human side of religion. The phrase "sum total" and the list of activities that follows it serve to remind us that religion is a very complex phenomenon—or better, a complex of phenomena. The first half of the definition, therefore, reflects the multifaceted nature of religion as a human enterprise. The second half points in a different direction, to the presumed focus or "object" of religious experience and expression in the world's great faith traditions: the Ultimate that evokes the varieties of beliefs and behaviors suggested in the first part of the definition. In this and the following chapters I shall have much to say about the diverse conceptions of this center of attention; but for now suffice it to say that the existence of this Reality cannot be proved. Fortunately, we don't have to; the definition requires only what is obviously true: that individuals and/or groups "believe or perceive" that there is such a One.

As an aid in sorting out the multiplicity of religion's subjective side, scholar Ninian Smart developed a very helpful and widely used interpretative scheme that identified at first six, and ultimately seven dimensions of religion (See Figure 1-1). The *doctrinal* dimension focuses on the beliefs, doctrines, creeds, affirmations of faith, theologies, and all other conceptual aspects of any religion. The *ritual* dimension involves the sorts of symbolic ceremonial actions that a religion engages in and finds meaningful. The *experiential* dimension comprises the kind of inner emotional or psychological states and changes that a religion values and seeks to engender. The *ethical* dimension has to do with the standards of conduct and morality established as normative by any religion. The *mythical* dimension refers to the traditional stories that a religion treasures for the truth or meaning that they convey to the faithful. The *social* dimension involves the special communities that a religion generates, as well as the relationship that it establishes to the larger, surrounding societal setting. The *material*—perhaps better called the *artistic*—dimension was the important aspect that Smart at first overlooked, but finally came to

Figure 1-1

Laughlin's Spin on Ninian Smart's Seven Dimensions of Religion*

1. Artistic—includes all of the material or physical "stuff" produced by any religion as expressions of any or all of the other dimensions (e.g., visual art, architecture, literature, music, dance)
2. Doctrinal—includes creeds, doctrines, dogmas, philosophies, theologies (i.e., products of intellectual activity)
3. Experiential—includes any experience that a religion deems important (e.g., conversion, meditation, mystical union, ecstasy)
4. Ethical—includes the behavioral expectations of a religion (do's and don'ts)
5. Mythical—includes all of the stories and symbols that a religion finds spiritually or doctrinally significant
6. Ritual—includes all of the ceremonies a religion might include as an expression of myth or doctrine, or as a means of eliciting a particular experience
7. Social—includes both the way a body of believers group and organize themselves as well as how they (or any particular believer) relate to the larger society or humanity as a whole

*I list the dimensions in alphabetical order here in order to indicate that no one is more popular than another. Westerners may well think that the doctrinal dimension, which is to say, the belief system, is the most important. But some of the world's religions are much more about behavior (either ritual or ethical) than belief. Moreover, even religions that appear to emphasize doctrine may in fact be more about practice than beliefs. All of this is to say that not all religions exhibit or emphasize any or all of these dimensions to the same degree.

recognize and appreciate rather late in his life. It refers to the visual art, architecture, music, literature, drama, dance, and all tangible objects produced by religions for symbolic, ceremonial, inspirational, or devotional purposes.

All religions have these seven dimensions, said Smart, though with varying degrees of emphasis. Some religions are more intensely ritualistic, while others are more heavily ethical; some are more interested in doctrines (teachings, beliefs, and so forth), while others place more weight on experience or personal growth. I would suggest yet another dimension that Smart seems to have overlooked, but that greatly affects all religions of any longevity: the *historical* or *evolutionary.* This eighth aspect acknowledges the fact that religions change over time and in response to new cultural settings and worldviews, and that such transformative processes, far from being tangential to a faith tradition, often help it to survive and thrive. With or without this emendation, however, Smart's schema both underscores the multifaceted and complex nature of religion and affords a convenient tool for sorting through the unfamiliar religions that we shall encounter—to say nothing of our own.

What is Spirituality?

Though it doesn't appear in our working definition, the word *spirituality* deserves our attention if only because it has become a buzz word in American popular culture in the past decade. But here is yet another case of a human phenomenon that is much easier to identify than to define. The truth is that until very recently, Jews and most Christians rarely used the word, either in congregations or in seminaries. Only in Roman Catholicism was the term employed at all, and then mostly in a narrowly technical sense, denoting the relatively obscure mystical sub-tradition within the faith and the type of theology that it produced. That changed when Twelve-Step recovery programs and New Age (or New Alternative) religions began to make their presence felt in bookstores, movies, and discussions on television talk shows, for both of these approaches employ "spirituality" as a key part of their working vocabularies. Arguably the most influential person in this regard in recent years has been Oprah Winfrey, whose TV show has frequently addressed the issue of spirituality, mostly in non-traditional ways, and made it a part of the consciousness and discourse of millions of devoted viewers.

Given the variety of contexts in which it is currently used, the term "spirituality" can refer to one or more of the following: (1) any expression of the essential, innermost aspect or facet of every person—what theologian Paul Tillich called "the depth dimension in human life"; (2) the particular manner in which a person or group experiences, expresses, and enhances that aspect; or (3) a person or community's fundamental orientation toward life, the cosmos, and any perceived Ultimate Reality. In none of these senses does spirituality necessarily entail a belief that human beings have an eternal spirit or immortal soul that survives death, though that is commonly and perhaps usually a part of the picture. Indeed it is quite possible for an atheist or a secular humanist who believes that nothing survives the life of the body to exhibit spirituality or be spiritual. I have known some who obviously did and were. Spirituality is not *necessarily* religious, then, though more often than not it is framed in religious terms. (See Figure 1-2.) At root, spirituality is simply the drive and the striving to achieve a healthy, productive, comfortable, and satisfying orientation toward life and the cosmos—a

Figure 1-2

Spinning Spirituality

One of the challenges of studying religion and spirituality objectively is that some of the most important terms one encounters there are ambiguous. Consider, for example, how many ways we talk and think about "spirit".

purpose, as it were, or what mythologist Joseph Campbell liked to call one's "bliss." I like to refer to spirituality as a person's center or axis, around which all of life's other concerns revolve and take on meaning, at least ideally.

Of course, spirituality *may* be religious. In fact, it is almost certain that all religions begin as a particular spirituality, one that can thus be regarded as their basic impulse and, ideally, their sustaining energy. In this regard, I sometimes refer to religion metaphorically as "a house that spirituality builds." Yet, I think it must be painfully obvious that religions can and often do lose touch with their formative spiritual energies, stray from the original intentions and visions of their founders, and in some cases evolve into empty (albeit durable) institutional shells. For that reason, I usually add to the image of religion as "a house that spirituality builds" the phrase "and often abandons, sooner or later." (In my more skeptical moments, "often" becomes "more often than not" or "usually"; when in an especially cranky frame of mind, I say "inevitably.") In fact, it seems to be a recurring historical pattern that religious movements lose their initial spiritual impetus and drive. It is noteworthy that the reformation and restoration movements that spring up from time to time in any religion's history are always efforts to recapture an original spiritual impulse or principle now seen as lost or obscured. It could be argued, on the other hand, that at least some religions have deviated from their original spirituality over time precisely in order to adopt other, equally valid forms of spirituality more appropriate to later settings and situations. In either case, the relationship between spirituality and religion remains, ironically, both important and ill-defined.

Theology or Philosophy?

As we shall see later in this chapter, Western and Eastern religions differ at many points. That is particularly true when it comes to the question of the relationship between religion, theology, and philosophy. Western religions prefer to use the word "theology" when they speak of ideas, concepts, or theories concerning their Ultimate Reality, God. That term comes from two Greek nouns, *theos* (god) and *logos* (word, concept), which means that theology is thought and talk God or gods. At the simplest level, any meaningful statement about a deity would be a theological one. In truth, however, the term is generally reserved for thought, discourse, and writing about God that is formal, systematic, learned—and *Western*. Eastern religions, by contrast, seldom if ever "do theology." Even with respect to Hinduism, which has a huge pantheon of gods and goddesses, rarely if ever does one see or hear any reference to "Hindu theology." Perhaps this reflects the fact that these deities are much more objects of devotion and worship than of speculation or conceptualization. When the Eastern religions deal with Ultimate Reality, however, the ideas that they produce are regarded as *philosophical*, precisely because they do not concern a god or God. Thus, analyzing the concepts of Eastern religions, as we shall be doing in several of the chapters of this book, is by nature a philosophical pursuit.

"Philosophy," which also derives from two Greek words—*philos* (love) and *sophia* (wisdom)—refers to the discipline that uses reason to explore and determine the nature of reality, the source and validity of knowledge, and the basis and bounds for ethical action. The fact is that any subject, issue, or phenomenon is fair game for philosophical speculation, whose purview is all of reality, including the Ultimate. In the West, then, the difference between philosophy and theology is *not* that the latter deals with God, while the former does not. Both fields may deal with God, but insofar as possible philosophy will wrestle with the *idea* of God in a secular way, on the basis of reason and logic alone. For its part, theology is generally much more open than philosophy to claims of revelation and religious experience made within a given religious tradition, and it presumes to subject to rational examination the nature of God that emerges from such sacred sources.

In the Western world, religion and philosophy have taken largely separate tracks. For example, most formal religious thought in the West has been done under the banner of theology rather than that of philosophy, though over the centuries some theologians have relied on the work of non-religious philosophers in formulating their own systems. And for their part, Western philosophers have been known to scrutinize such fundamental religious ideas as the Christian concept of God. Despite such cross-fertilization, however, Western philosophy and religion have remained for the most part parallel traditions. Accordingly, it is rare indeed to encounter the phrases "Christian philosophy," "Muslim philosophy," and "Jewish philosophy," though there certainly have been a number of outstanding Christian, Muslim, and Jewish philosophers. By contrast, the Eastern religions—in which deities are either non-existent or subordinate to a greater Absolute—have produced *philosophies* rather than theologies. (See Figure 1-3) In fact, unlike the overwhelmingly secular philosophical tradition of the West, virtually the only philosophies that South Asia and the Orient have given to the world have been religiously inspired and spiritually grounded.

Because we shall be rethinking Christianity's traditional beliefs at the end of our journey East, we should be prepared to engage in some theology. In fact, *the reader would do well to think of this entire book as an exercise in constructive Christian theology*, despite its comparative religions approach and appearance. To the extent that we shall be exploring Eastern religions, however, the reader may expect to encounter some philosophy along the way. But a fair warning is in order here: what we shall discover in Eastern philosophies won't be much like anything that one finds in Plato, Aristotle, or most of the rest of the Western philosophical tradition. It will have a different look and feel, mostly because it is spiritually grounded and has an essentially mystical foundation. For that reason, it will not be discursive, linear, logical, or neat; rather it will likely appear metaphorical, cyclical, paradoxical, and even obtuse to the

Figure 1-3

The Relation between Religion & Philosophy (West Versus East)

The movement of history from mid-1st century CE to the present

The Western Pattern

Religion

Philosophy

Note: The downward arrows indicate theologians looking to various philosophical traditions for useful concepts or frameworks of thought, while the upward arrows indicate the attention – often but not always critical – paid by philosophers to concepts produced by religions.

The Eastern Pattern

Religion

Philosophy

Note: The intertwined lines indicate that religion and philosophy in the East are not two separate traditions, but inextricably interwoven. Indeed, all of the great philosophies of the East arose out of spirituality or religious experience rather than reason itself. This has led some Western philosophers to the rather provincial opinion that the great Eastern philosophies aren't really philosophies because they do not obey the same rules of linear reasoning and logic.

Western mind; but therein lies its uniqueness and, as we shall see, a major part of its value for enriching the Christian faith.

Schools and Sects

It sometimes seems that any religion that has lasted more than two weeks has undergone a schism (that is, a major rift) of some kind. That is an exaggeration, of course, but only a slight one, for the history of religions strongly indicates that the human tendency to disagree about important matters is all but inevitable, and the urge to part ways over such differences of opinion virtually irresistible. In the life of a religion with an identifiable founder, such disagreements usually begin in the very first generation after that person's death, and often focus first on the question of who the successor should be. Eventually, however, the pivotal issue almost always becomes how closely the words and ways of the founder or founders should be followed. The broad options in this regard are but two: (1) strictly and perhaps even to the letter and (2) in principle, but with freedom and flexibility to grow and change. The former, of course, is the conservative or orthodox religious stance; the latter is the liberal or progressive position.

All of the major Eastern religions have generated factions. For convenience, Western scholars usually call the large divisions (typically two or three) "schools," and refer to any subdivisions of these as "sects," though most practitioners of the faiths in question make no such distinction. For example, we speak of the Theravada and Mahayana *schools* of Buddhism and the many *sects* that the latter contains, like Zen, Nichiren, and Pure Land. Taoism is generally treated as having two major schools, the one philosophical and the other religious, but rarely are sects within these specified. The opposite is true of Hinduism. That ancient, founderless faith seems never to have had an original coherence that led to subsequent schism into large schools. Instead, it was from the start a conglomeration of small groups with diverse religious beliefs and practices, a few of which—Buddhism, Jainism, and Sikhism—spun off to become neither schools nor sects of Hinduism (though some Hindus persist in seeing them as such), but religions in their own right. Since Hinduism experienced no major historic fracture like the ones that occurred in the founded faiths that followed, the word "school" is not generally used with reference to Hinduism's many religious divisions, but only with respect to its competing *philosophical* traditions. The many relatively small *religious* groups that comprise Hinduism are, however, dubbed "sects." The term "sect" is used to identify relatively small and new Christian groups as well, but the word "school" is rarely if ever applied either to them or to the other Western religions (Judaism, Zoroastrianism, and Islam). Their major expressions are usually referred to as "divisions," "branches," "denominations," or something of that sort.

Historical Overview

Since we shall be encountering a number of schools and sects in the course of our journey to the East, it might be helpful to set Hinduism,

Buddhism, Confucianism, and Taoism into some sort of historical context before plunging headlong into the business of analyzing them individually. By doing so, we will establish that we are dealing with at least two types of religion here. On the one hand, there is Hinduism, which is ancient, has no nameable founder or unifying principle or practice, and—except for a few isolated philosophical concepts and spiritual exercises that it has managed to export successfully—has remained for the most part culturally bound. The remaining three, on the other hand, are much younger, claim a specific founder and focal idea, and have proven themselves archetypal and transcultural if not universal in appeal. Our overview will also help us to establish important connections, influences, similarities, and divergences not only among the four, but between them and Christianity as well.

Periodization Per Se

The first thing to know about history, both general and religious, is that it does not fall naturally or neatly into periods. Rather historians *arrange* contiguous events, years, decades, and centuries into periods according to some chosen set of criteria. Ideally, the resulting organizational system generates a wide acceptance and perhaps even a consensus that a particular segment of time has a certain character and coherence that distinguishes it from the centuries that preceded and followed it. Because historians do not always agree on the criteria, however, they often divide history variously, arrive at different threshold dates for the resulting segments, and even characterize and label those periods differently.

I shall follow here a fairly common pattern among contemporary scholars of dividing the history of religions into four major periods (See Figure 1-4.): (1) the Prehistoric-Animistic (100,000 to 3000 BCE), (2) the Polytheistic-Ancient (3000 to 700 BCE), (3) the Perennial-Archetypal (700 BCE to 700 CE), and (4) the Prolific-Alternative (700 CE to the present). My terminal dates are all quite approximate and always subject to tweaking; and my labeling is rather idiosyncratic, though nicely descriptive of the kind of religions that each period has produced. For clarity, I have adopted the practice of capitalizing the descriptive names of the periods, and leaving them lower case when they refer to the religions that emerged therein.

Approximate though it may be, this particular pattern of periodization is useful. But it really works only for the Eastern hemisphere, for two reasons. First, in the Americas, human prehistory and early history reflect

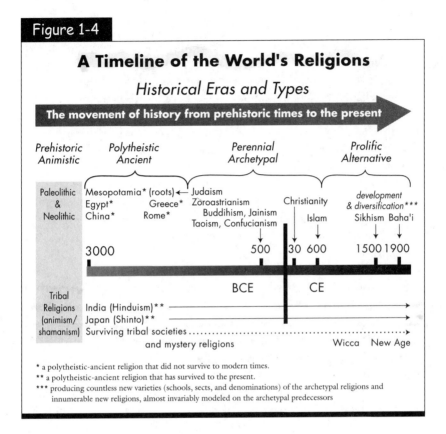

Figure 1-4

A Timeline of the World's Religions

Historical Eras and Types

The movement of history from prehistoric times to the present

Prehistoric Animistic	Polytheistic Ancient	Perennial Archetypal	Prolific Alternative

Paleolithic & Neolithic

Mesopotamia* (roots) ← Judaism
Egypt*   Greece* Zoroastrianism   Christianity   development & diversification***
China*   Rome*   Buddhism, Jainism
                           Taoism, Confucianism   Islam   Sikhism Baha'i

3000   500 30 600   1500 1900

BCE   CE

Tribal Religions (animism/ shamanism)

India (Hinduism)** ————————————————————→
Japan (Shinto)** ————————————————————→
Surviving tribal societies ....→
and mystery religions   Wicca   New Age

* a polytheistic-ancient religion that did not survive to modern times.
** a polytheistic-ancient religion that has survived to the present.
*** producing countless new varieties (schools, sects, and denominations) of the archetypal religions and
innumerable new religions, almost invariably modeled on the archetypal predecessors

the relatively late migrations of Asian peoples. The result was that the first two periods—what I call the Prehistoric-Animistic and the Polytheistic-Ancient—occurred here two millennia or more later. During this time many of the so-called Native Americans or American Indians continued to live in a purely tribal pattern, while others—most notably the Aztecs, Incas, and Mayans—evolved into full-fledged civilizations. Second, the further historical development of these comparatively late civilizations was interrupted by European invasion, conquest, and colonization, thereby preventing their religious traditions from evolving into or producing anything like indigenous forms of what we are calling "perennial-archetypal" religions—the likes of Buddhism and Islam, to give but two examples. Instead, beginning in the late fifteenth century, an existing foreign religion of this type, Christianity, was imposed upon the hapless native peoples by conquistadors, missionaries, and colonialists.

The Prehistoric-Animistic Era

The first period in the history of religions is the Prehistoric-Animistic, the epoch prior to both the invention of writing and the emergence of the concept of deity, both of which occurred around 3000 BCE. Our earliest reliable information about this era comes from the portion of it called the Stone Age (which preceded the Bronze, Iron, etc.) and is therefore largely archeological, since, in the absence of writing, no primary documentary evidence exists. To an overwhelming degree, the meaning of the unearthed or otherwise discovered evidence—burial sites, artifacts, cave paintings, megaliths, and the like—must be inferred. These inferences can, however, be supplemented and reinforced by the findings of anthropologists studying contemporary tribal people who are still, in effect, living in the Stone Age, and who can explain their practices and beliefs to researchers.

The religion of prehistoric tribal peoples used to be called "primitive," but now is more accurately and appreciatively termed "primal" or "basic." It appears uniformly to have been based upon *animism* (from the Latin *anima,* "spirit"), the belief or assumption that the world is full of (nature) spirits, that they can bring good or cause harm, and that they can be influenced, at least to some extent. The person in the tribe charged with wielding this influence—the witch doctor and medicine man of old jungle movies and TV Westerns—is now called generically a *shaman,* originally the Siberian tribal title for such a practitioner. In fact, these figures were so nearly universal among tribal animists that "animism" and "shamanism" are today practically synonymous. Depending on the tribe and the region of the world involved, a shaman might be either male or female. In either case, this key person was born to the position, probably distinguished by certain bodily marks or signs that we would regard simply as congenital birthmarks or abnormalities. In that era, these marked her or him as specially gifted. As a youth this charismatic person would apprentice to an older shaman, and learn not only to deal with spirits, but to control an a-personal, amorphous, and awesome spiritual power, now generically called *mana.* Named after the Melanesian word for "numinous power," this *mana* could invade and possess, for a long or short term, persons, places, or things, thereby making them *taboo* (i.e., spiritually charged, potentially dangerous if mishandled, and therefore off-limits) to the average person. The shaman would often be regarded as thus possessed, especially during rituals.

In order to manage and manipulate the spirits and the *mana*, the *shaman* would use various forms of *magic*. In this context the word means not the sleight-of-hand of modern entertainers, but all of the means and methods believed to be available and effective in influencing the various forces that threatened human life and well-being. In other words, the earliest magic constituted the tools rather than the tricks of the trade—though to be sure, thinking of the shaman's vocation as a "trade" stretches that word. Among these tools was *divination*, which entailed the reading of patterns in such things as the flight of birds, cracks in animal bones or tortoise shells heated on a fire, or tossed sticks or stones; its purpose was to discern the direction of current events. Also at the shaman's disposal was *imitation*, that is, the performance on a small scale of a desired subsequent result on a large scale. War dances and cave paintings of successful animal hunts, for example, were apparently done *beforehand*. Two more important kinds of magic were *fetishism*, the use of various special objects (like amulets, talismans, bones, feathers, and pipes) to influence the spirits; and *totemism*, the identification of a tribe or clan with a *totem*, i.e., a "power animal" such as a bear, lion, or buffalo. The fetish would be jealously guarded and protected, and the totem would not be hunted for food, though its body and blood might well be ritually consumed for spiritual renewal and strength.

If there is a ring of familiarity in that last observation, do not be surprised. For although such beliefs and activities strike us as extremely primitive and far removed from life in a world ruled by reason and science, for several reasons they are not. First, the so-called "developed" civilizations of the Western world have produced such subcultural movements as ancient Greek mystery religions and medieval European Wicca that carried on the nature worship of the pre-historic, tribal animists. More recently, the always eclectic and sometimes eccentric spiritual expression known as "New Age Religion" has found inspiration in the beliefs and practices of tribal peoples (particularly Native Americans), and has woven these together in various patterns with Wicca, mystery religions, and other (especially Eastern) spiritual traditions. Second, scholars of both religion and anthropology have recognized that many of the components of these prehistoric religions survive today in the form of superstitions, such as the belief in lucky charms and the identification of sports teams with powerful animals. But they also endure in such sophisticated religious rituals as Christianity's Holy Communion, in which the "body" and "blood" of a "Lamb of God" are consumed for spiritual nourishment.

Third, these scholars also have come to appreciate the complexity and imaginativeness of these early religions, and have even argued that they represent religion at its purest, when it was both the prevailing worldview *and* a way of life.

The Polytheistic-Ancient Era

The religions that give the next era its name are those associated with specific empires and civilizations that flourished in the Eastern hemisphere between about 3,000 and 700 BCE, though some endured beyond that latter date. Sometimes called "ancient culture," "ancient civilization," or simply "ancient" religions, these include the earliest beliefs and practices in Mesopotamia, Egypt, India, China, Japan, and Greece—and of course Rome, whose culture was essentially an extension and imitation of that of the Greeks it conquered. As already indicated, ancient cultures and their religions arose much later in the Americas with the Mayans, Incas, and Aztecs. Historians disagree about exactly what it takes for a society to qualify as a formal culture or civilization, but almost all include at least (1) cities, (2) writing, (3) specialization of labor, and (4) a centralization of political power, usually under a monarch and a ruling class. The religions produced under such circumstances have no nameable founders, and likely emerged over time as the product of a communal consciousness rather than of a single genius.

What is perhaps most remarkable about these religions is their striking resemblance to one another despite the fact that they were produced by cultures that were for much of their formative history quite distant and relatively isolated from each other. For one thing, all were *polytheistic*—with gods and goddesses numbering from a few score (in Greece and Rome) to thousands (in Mesopotamia) to hundreds of millions (in India). All were also characterized by *ritualism*, mostly in the form of sacrifices to appease their pantheons (councils) of gods and goddesses. These rituals were conducted by trained *priests*, whose status and function were sanctioned not by the possession of innate charismatic credentials, but by the occupancy of a formal office. The ceremonies, furthermore, were not so much expressions of affection or devotion to the various deities as duties performed out of a sense of fear, obligation, and necessity. *Temples* were constructed for the requisite sacrifices and sacred *scriptures* were produced, mostly to provide formal instructions for the conduct of specific ceremonies.

These ancient cultural religions were civilization-specific—that is, Mesopotamian religion was for Mesopotamians, Egyptian religion was for Egyptians, and so forth. Lacking the urge to convert people of other cultures, they had no missionary impulse or zeal. As a result, when the ancient cultures themselves died out or were displaced—as when the Egyptian culture was first Christianized, then wiped out completely by Muslim Arabs—their religions disappeared, leaving only some stone and literary monuments, visual art, artifacts, and fascinating mythologies. The only exceptions were Hinduism in India and Shinto in Japan, which have survived to the present day. Hinduism endured because India was not conquered and colonized until well after that faith had imprinted itself indelibly on the culture, while Shinto persisted because the first and most effective foreign religion that invaded Japan, Buddhism, did so peacefully and gently, making no exclusive claims or conversion demands.

The Perennial-Archetypal Era

The period that produced what we are calling the perennial-archetypal religions extends from around 700 BCE to 700 CE or thereabouts. These religions—often termed "classic" or "classical"—are *perennial* in the sense that unlike most of their polytheistic, ancient predecessors, they did not die out with the cultures that produced them, but have survived and prospered to modern times. They are *archetypal* for two reasons. First, they have become what amounts to the gold standard of religions, providing the broad range of Eastern and Western options in spiritual belief and practice that any informed modern person would recognize as the kinds of things that the word "religion" connotes. Second, they have provided the basis and inspiration for virtually all of the innumerable religions of that era that followed, which in many respects are but themes, variations, extensions, and syntheses of these classic models.

German philosopher Karl Jaspers coined the term "axial" for the early part of this Perennial-Archetypal period (c.700–300), with 500 BCE as the specific "axis" around which all of the rest of the history of religions revolved. He intended such imagery to underscore the extraordinary, unprecedented, and as yet unequalled burst of spiritual creativity that the world experienced during these centuries. In just over a millennium, no fewer than eight major world religions were founded, at least four of them within a single century, the sixth BCE, including three explored in this book—Buddhism, Confucianism, and Taoism. The religions of this

Perennial-Archetypal period are sometimes referred to as "universal," reflecting the fact that directly or indirectly their impact has transcended geographical and cultural boundaries and changed the world's religious landscape in significant and sometimes profound ways. Unlike their polytheistic-animistic ancient predecessors, most of these religions did have missionary zeal and widespread appeal: they not only traveled, but traveled well. (A glaring exception is Jainism, which endures to modern times despite its remaining largely disinterested in proselytizing and pretty much confined to its native India.) Most, in fact, faired better outside their particular countries of origin than they did within them, and in some cases, it is by traveling that they survived at all.

The first of the perennial-archetypal religions to appear was Zoroastrianism, which claims to be a monotheistic religion, though it appears to posit two deities. By most accounts, it was promulgated in the late seventh century BCE by the Persian prophet Zarathustra, who is better known today by his Hellenized name, Zoroaster. In the following, very busy century, Jainism and Buddhism emerged in India, and Taoism and Confucianism in China. At about the same time, Judaism, whose roots extend back to the Polytheistic-Ancient Era, was becoming the religion we would recognize by that name today. (This happened largely as a result of the destabilizing effects of a military defeat and exile that forced the Jewish people to define their religion over against that of their conquerors and captors.) Greek philosophy was also coming into its own during this century under the Pre-Socratics. About half a millennium later, the early-to-mid first century saw the founding of Christianity, and some six hundred years after that, Islam was created by the Arab messenger-prophet Muhammad—or, as Muslims would put it, by Allah's working through him. That event brought to an end the extraordinary Perennial-Archetypal Era.

Like their polytheistic ancient counterparts, these perennial-archetypal religions had many things in common. First, they had nameable founders, though to be sure the lives of all these figures are clouded with legendary elements and historical problems, some of the latter being quite serious and daunting. Second, all of these religions displayed a narrowing of focus with respect to the object of faith, devotion, and worship. That is, attention was no longer directed to many spirits (animism) or multiple gods (polytheism), but to a Divine Unity—a single personal God (monotheism) or a non-personal Absolute, Supreme Something (monism). Finally, these religions are marked by the emergence of *canons* of scripture: carefully defined collections of focal, authoritative, and widely if not universally accepted sacred writings—for example, the

Tanakh of Judaism, the *Tripitaka* of Buddhism, the Bible of Christianity, and the *Qur'an* of Islam.

In part because they survived to *have* a history and in part because they spread to various new cultures, these religions also seem to have followed a common pattern in their historical development. (See Figure 1-5.) First there was a founder with relatively simple teachings. With his passing, his disciples sought (and sometimes struggled) to understand and articulate what his precise identity and purpose had been, and then to follow as best they could (and to their own satisfaction) his example and directions. Beginning with them, and increasingly thereafter, the primordial simplicity gave way to complication. Doctrines and institutions became more and more complex, racked with controversy, then fixed in

Figure 1-5

The Typical Pattern of Evolution in Universal Religions

Founder	Later Generations
• personal charisma, genius • revolutionary but relatively simple message • relatively simple organization: community, fellowship → • localized geographically & culturally	• definition of identity & message of founder • doctrinal formulations • doctrinal disputes • creation & multiplication of schools, sects • determination of canonical scripture • institutionalization • creation of formal offices, hierarchies • schisms over differences in belief, practice • migration/missionary activity • adaptation of message to new audiences • new cultural elements/emphases

Note: All of the things listed under "Later Generations" happened concurrently, beginning with the very first generations of disciples after the passing away of their founder. Ever thereafter, the increased urge to define and organize the faith inevitably led to dispute after dispute and schism upon schism, a tendency that was only exacerbated by the enormous impact of new cultures being encountered.

creeds. Disagreements resulted in schisms (splits) that produced schools and sects (in the East), branches (in Judaism and Islam), and denominations (in Christianity), as well as sub-divisions of these. As the religions traveled from culture to culture, they picked up new beliefs and practices, wrinkles and twists—including much that in retrospect appears extraneous or even contradictory to the message, mission, and self-image of their founders. As a result, all of the perennial-archetypal religions are today variegated, fragmented, and downright messy, usually in direct proportion to how long they have been around. The convictions and claims of their practitioners notwithstanding, it is most doubtful that the founder of any of these faiths would recognize most of what is being professed and performed in his name.

The Prolific-Alternatives Era

The period from around 700 CE to the present has seen the emergence of a plethora of both new religious traditions and branches, schools, sects, or denominations of existing religions. It is for this reason that we define this period—which is sometimes deprecated with the label "post-classical"—in terms of the *prolific alternatives* that it produced. Most Western textbooks on the world's religions present only two of these: Sikhism, whose founder sought to synthesize two of the classic religions, Hinduism and Islam; and Baha'i, which grew out of Islam, but claims to consummate and supercede not only its parent faith, but all preceding religious traditions. Both of these new religions continued the religious theme of the Unity of the Ultimate found in the religions of the Perennial-Archetypal Era. Both have also remained small, though in very different ways. Sikhism has remained more or less geographically and culturally limited to its native Punjab region of northern India, showing little missionary impulse and thus contacting the rest of the world mostly through individual and family emigration. Baha'i, by contrast, had within a century of its founding spread itself (though very thinly) across many countries of the world—more, in fact, than any other religion except Christianity.

In addition to these two, which seem of special interest to Western scholars, a staggering number of other prolific-alternative religions have emerged in this period, including some that are numerically significant. The modern Korean religion, Juche, for example has three times the followers as Baha'i; and both Cao Dai in Vietnam and Tenrikyo in Japan are effectively competing with the venerable religious traditions of their respective countries in terms of numbers of adherents. Japan alone has around 3,000 so-called "New Religions" (*Shin Shukyo*) that are two centuries old or less; and a few of these—such as Sukyo Mahikari, Sekai Mahikari Bunmei Kyodan, and Seicho-no-ie—have established missionary centers in North America.

The emergence of the innumerable new religions has not been the only thing happening with respect to religion in this period, of course. The process of development in the perennial-archetypal religions has continued apace, taking each through its own distinct medieval period or beyond, and producing an ever-growing, evolving, elaborate, and often eclectic tradition and a mind-boggling proliferation of splinter groups (sects, denominations, and the like). Equally important and far more threatening to religious traditions in this era has been a seemingly extraneous phenomenon: the emergence in the European West of our prevailing modern scientific worldview. The seeds for this widely shared yet largely tacit way of understanding reality had been planted by the European Renaissance of the fourteenth and fifteenth centuries and its spirit of inquisitiveness, freedom, and humanism. But this new perspective began to grow in earnest in the seventeenth and eighteenth centuries with the Enlightenment, an intellectual movement that proclaimed the inductive investigation of sensory evidence by human reason to be the only valid path to knowledge and the final arbiter of truth.

The result was a new and determined adherence to the findings of *empiricism* and *rationalism* that amounted to a frontal assault on the treasured presuppositions, stories, beliefs, and practices of the great religious traditions, all of which were grounded in a pre-scientific worldview. First to be challenged were miracles, myths, revelation, and therefore scriptural authority. But it was only a matter of time until the light of modern scrutiny fell upon the very existence of such religious staples as the human soul or spirit and Ultimate Reality—whether that be God, *Allah, Brahman,* or *Tao*. The end result is that while it remains possible for a modern scientifically-minded person to be religious, to do so certainly takes more energy and thought—and perhaps a suspension of disbelief and other exertions of the will—than it did in past eras.

The addition of this new worldview and the later prolific-alternative religions to the constellation of faith traditions surviving from earlier eras points to another challenge facing religious people in modern times. It is the simple fact of a plurality of religious traditions, all with their own claims to truth and authenticity. Our awareness of Eastern religions in particular is rather recent in the West, coming mostly in the late nineteenth and twentieth centuries, but the resulting smorgasbord of faiths has already led some to give up entirely on religion as purely a matter of opinion, acculturation, and wishful thinking. Those who still elect to be religious have their own challenge: to decide whether to follow the faith of their birth alone, or to remain committed to it but open to insights and inspirations from other religious perspectives, or to abandon it completely in favor of another religion. Yet while the variety of available religious traditions may further increase the quandary facing religious people in the empirically grounded twenty-first century, I hope to show in this book that it also affords the opportunity for the available faiths to enrich one another.

The Fork in the Road

As indicated in the Introduction, scholars place the dividing line that separates Eastern from Western religions somewhere between Iran and India—that is, in the vicinity of Afghanistan. They do so because the perennial-archetypal religions that arose to the west of that demarcation resemble one another in profound ways, and likewise for those that originated to the east of it. Let me be more specific: despite their differences, Western religions hold such remarkably similar views concerning Ultimate Reality or Truth as make them resemble one another more than any of them resembles an Eastern religion—and vice versa. The East-West distinction, therefore, involves two fundamentally different religious and spiritual perspectives, for though agreeing in principle that there is an Ultimate Reality, they are diametrically opposed on how to envision that Reality and relate to it. In terms of our journey imagery, the divergence of East and West constitutes a fork in the road of religious history following the surprising uniformity of the Polytheistic-Ancient Era, and offers us the opportunity to explore what is for us the less traveled route.

A Typing Lesson

What I am doing here is a *typology*, which in this case is simply a logical distinguishing between different kinds of related things—something that in the sciences might be called a "taxonomy." Before proceeding, however, I should issue some caveats about the sort of typing that I shall be doing here. First, any typology is a generalization; and as a wise person once said, "One who generalizes generally lies." That means that as soon as one identifies something as a type, a handful or host of exceptions that seem to belie the validity of the type will quickly come to mind or be called to one's attention. Of course, enough such exceptions will utterly scuttle any typology; yet as long as they are well focused and not considered absolutely definitive or final, typologies can be useful teaching and learning tools.

In the present case, I shall be focusing first on the differing Eastern and Western views of Ultimate Reality, a notion that, as we asserted earlier, lies at the heart of all the major living religions. We shall set aside Confucianism for the time being, because although its ethical system, like that of Taoism, is based on an Ultimate called *Tao*, that concept remains rather far in the background. In fact, Confucianism's major contribution to this book and its figurative journey East will be to bring the more useful Taoism into sharper relief. That leaves us with a "Big Three" to exemplify Eastern thinking about Ultimate Reality: Hinduism, Buddhism, and Taoism along with their respective notions of *Brahman*, *Shunyata*, and *Tao*. Representing the West will be its own impressive trio of Judaism, Christianity, and Islam together with their respective central concepts: Jahweh, God, and Allah.

One Who or What? (Monotheism versus Monism)

When it comes to thinking about Ultimate Reality or Truth, the three major Western religions embrace a theology of *monotheism* (often shortened to *theism*), while Eastern religions opt for a philosophy of *monism* or something resembling it. (See Figure 1-6) The reason for the divergence is that while the West treats the Ultimate Reality as a God, the East sees it as an Absolute Something—a Power, Presence, or Principle, perhaps, or a Force, Source, or even a Spirit, but not a god or even an entity *per se*. Any thought about such a One, then, must be philosophical rather than theological in nature. As it turns out, that philosophy is of necessity some variation of *monism*, which literally means "one-ism" or "one-something-ism." Specifically, it will be some variation of what philosophers call *idealistic monism*, which in a religious context may also be termed "spiritual monism." The opposite position, materialistic monism, holds that the "one something" that constitutes reality is matter. That is, of course, a plausible view and one remarkably hospitable to our empiricism-grounded modern scientific worldview; but it is not the monism found in the Eastern religions.

It is all too easy and way premature, however, to get bogged down in such arcane philosophical terminology. First we need to narrow our focus to the two dominant conceptual models in the history of religions, Western monotheism and Eastern monism, to examine them one at a time, and to see what makes each tick, as it were. To do this, however, we must come to terms with the most basic and crucial distinction

Figure 1-6

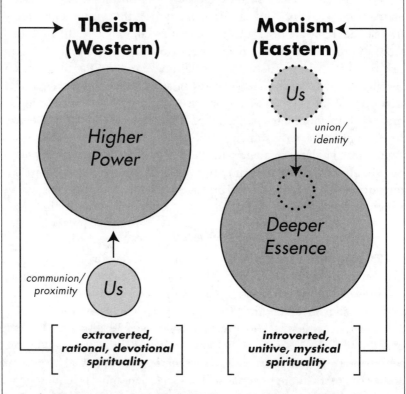

Transcendence and Immanence:

The Views of Ultimacy that Reflect them,
and the Spiritualities that Generated Them

**Theism
(Western)**

**Monism
(Eastern)**

*Higher
Power*

Us

union/
identity

*Deeper
Essence*

communion/
proximity   *Us*

*extraverted,
rational, devotional
spirituality*

*introverted,
unitive, mystical
spirituality*

In the Western pattern, the believer directs attention to a Higher
Reality, usually identified as God, and hopes to grow closer, and
perhaps even to spend eternity in the company of this Other. In the
Eastern pattern, the devotee blissfully realizes his or her essential
oneness with the One, and looks forward to the ultimate bliss of total
and eternal absorption into it.

These spiritualities and matching theologies dominate the respective
hemispheres of the entire world as defined by historians of religion
(as opposed to geographers, for whom Europe, a Western continent
by our standards, is actually in the Eastern hemisphere). But, as we
shall see in later chapters, particular religious experiences and concepts
in both religious hemispheres actually reflect the pattern that
dominates in their counterparts. For example, the mystical Sufism of
Islam, a Western religion, is Eastern in type. Likewise, the devotion to
particular gods and goddesses in Hindu popular piety reflects, or at
least resembles, the Western pattern.

underpinning and in truth defining all theologies and every philosophy that posits an Ultimate Reality. Indeed, it is no exaggeration to say that not only monotheism and monism, but all conceptual models involving a Supreme One are but a play upon and admixture of these two key ideas: *transcendence* and *immanence*.

Transcendence and Immanence (High Octane)

Simply put, *transcendence* means "otherness" and *immanence* means "within-ness." In formal theological and philosophical reflection about God or Ultimate Reality, these are by far the two most important concepts. (Not coincidentally, they are the controlling factors in Figure 1-6.) Unfortunately, they are also the most difficult to define and understand, for both have various shades of meaning and are often used in vague, equivocal ways, and with no indication of exactly what is intended. To ensure that we are, so to speak, all on the same page with these terms, let me sort out the various meanings of both. This is an important task, because—as already suggested—all theological and philosophical models designed to delineate the nature of God or the Ultimate are built upon these two concepts.

Transcendence, used in its strongest sense, refers to the quality of being prior to, above, beyond, or other—or to any combination of those. Philosophers call this strong kind of transcendence "ontological," a term that always implies that we are talking about the very being, the basic nature, or the defining essence of something. When attributed to God, as it often is in the West, this variety of transcendence generally incorporates the ideas that God (1) predates the universe, (2) is in some sense a "higher" kind of being or power, and (3) is other than the natural, physical, spatial-temporal universe and anyone or anything in it. Less sophisticated persons may understand such transcendence in the ancient or medieval spatial sense, as connoting a God who is "up there" or "out there" somewhere. In any case, this Deity dwells in (or simply *occupies*) a realm external to the cosmos (usually called "Heaven"), and partakes of a totally different sort of reality from anything found in nature, including humanity. A truly transcendent God is, quite simply, "something else"—or, more precisely, Someone Else—and thus by definition *supernatural* (literally, "above nature").

Immanence, on the other hand, when used in its high-test, ontological sense, denotes the quality of "within-ness." The word is derived from the Latin *immanere*, "to indwell." When applied to the Ultimate Reality, as it generally is in the East, it connotes an Absolute One that in contrast to the God of the West is not an Other, much less "up there" or "out there." On the contrary, a truly (ontologically) immanent Ultimate Reality permeates, saturates, or infuses the cosmos and everything and everyone in it *as their very essence*. In other words, the Ultimate is *coextensive* with the universe, though not necessarily identical to it. This is a very different conceptual approach from that of the West, which begins by thinking of the supernatural God and the cosmos as two different things, and is therefore inherently and profoundly dualistic. The East tends to think instead in terms of a single closed system, albeit with two aspects: an outer (material, physical) modality that is essentially but not necessarily completely one with the One, and an inner (spiritual, psychical) essence that *is* one with the One. Of course these two aspects introduce a kind of dualism that can be avoided only by denying either the reality of, or any significant difference between, matter and spirit— which is often done. But compared with that of monotheism, the subtle dualism found in monism is comparatively mild—and, some would add, benign.

Ontological Immanence Made Simple?

Because such an immanence-based concept of Ultimacy has been entertained only rarely by religions and philosophies of the West, it is quite literally foreign to most people in this part of the world. It therefore requires extra attention simply to make it intelligible, much less plausible. Yet we only have to turn to the popular *Star Wars* movies for a convenient example. "The Force" that the characters spoke about and related to was immanent, for it seemed to infuse everyone and everything, and even to empower those who knew how to tap into it. "Use the Force, Luke" meant that he should shun external technological devices and look to his innermost self for that abiding immanent Power. It is hardly surprising that the Jedi Masters in those films were intentionally modeled on Eastern spiritual Masters, particularly of the Zen variety.

A couple of other images might be useful here. If you were to ask someone whether she believes in God, and if the answer were "yes," a logical next question would be "Of what sort?" Suppose the answer were this: "I believe that just as you and I talk about having a soul or spirit that is not the same as our physical self and yet intimately connected to it, I take God to be the inner soul or spirit of the universe." That would be a description of an immanent God, one whose body, in effect, is the cosmos. (Unlike the *Star Wars* example, this would be *pantheism* rather than monism, simply because of the use of the term "God," but as we shall see, there is no essential difference between those two conceptual models.) Suppose further that same person should come to you later and declare that she has since modified her theology because the terms "soul" and "spirit" had finally struck her as too vague and ambiguous. It seems that she now regards God as the Inner Consciousness of the universe, bearing the same relation to the cosmos that the mind does to the brain in human beings. That would be a shift of thinking, certainly, but only a slight one; for the operative theological model would still be pantheism, and the God thus described would still be an immanent One. This deity would be very different from the traditional Western God, who may *have* a mind or perhaps even *be* a Mind, but must impact the universe from beyond it *through* creative acts, rather than *as* an abiding, inherent, indwelling intelligence.

In short, talking about transcendence versus immanence in their strongest theological and philosophical senses means distinguishing between Ultimate Reality as an *Other Entity* versus an *Inner Essence*. Theologians and philosophers sometimes put it this way: an ontologically transcendent God is *discontinuous* with the cosmos, for the two do not share in the same essence or being; while an ontologically immanent God is *continuous* with the universe, sharing in and indeed serving *as* its very being and essence. In a perfect world, that would be that: "transcendence" and "immanence" would each have a single, univocal meaning, and it would be in this high-octane sense. In fact, however, there is another less potent, but still important set of connotations for both terms.

Transcendence and Immanence (Low Octane)

As difficult as it may at first be to grasp the distinction between transcendence and immanence in the strong or ontological sense, the problem is further complicated by the fact that both terms are also used in theology and philosophy in much weaker senses. Yet, these weaker definitions are also important, for they too serve as building blocks in the construction of theological and philosophical views of God.

The weaker meaning of "transcendence" has to do not with the nature of God or the Ultimate, but with the inaccessibility of that One to human perception and conceptualization. To say that God is transcendent in this sense simply means that God eludes (or "is beyond") our five senses and finite minds: we cannot see, hear, or touch God, nor can we finally understand God. Even an ontologically (strongly) transcendent Deity or

Absolute will likely be transcendent in this weaker sense as well. The only exception would be an Ultimate Reality that was totally comprehensible and available to sensory perception. (Most of us would consider someone who believed they saw, heard, and completely understood God to be stupid, insane, comical, or a televangelist.) But a God or Ultimate Reality that is ontologically immanent (that is, *really* within us) can also be—will almost certainly be—transcendent in this weaker sense, because this Inner God or Ultimate is likewise bound to be "beyond" ordinary human awareness and intellect. A good example is the nineteenth century American Transcendentalists' God, who—or more properly, which—was *really* immanent, indwelling nature and human nature. (In fact, Ralph Waldo Emerson often referred to God as the Cosmic Soul.) But this Deity remained nonetheless beyond sensory reach or conceptual grasp. By rights, then, Emerson and his circle should have been called "Immanentalists," for their Ultimate Reality *really was* within everyone and everything, however elusive to the senses and reason it might be. In other words, their movement was misnamed—in large measure because they were not concerned with being clear to themselves or others about their basic theology, and were seldom if ever philosophically rigorous in expressing their beliefs.

Just as immanentalists can affirm a weak transcendence that involves limitations of awareness or conceptualization (or both), those who espouse a truly (ontologically) transcendent God may well assert that that God is immanent in the world, but only in a manner of speaking: *as an agent acting upon it*. "Immanence" in its weak sense, then, refers to the *activity* of the transcendent Ultimate, especially in human affairs. Most believers in a transcendent God (in the strong ontological sense of "Other") nonetheless believe that their God is "in" the world and their lives, in the sense of impinging upon historical events and personal experiences. (If they didn't, they would be deists, that is, believers in a remote, aloof Creator God who is no longer interested or involved in the world.) But that weaker sort of immanence does not allow for God to *become* the world or anything in it. In other words, the profoundly (ontologically) transcendent God may be "in" the world in a manner of speaking (as an Active Presence), but cannot really be *in* the world (as its Abiding Essence). That would make God immanent in the strong sense, and would require of mainstream Jews, Christians, and Muslims either a thorough modification of their historic faiths or a complete abandonment of them in favor of a truly immanentalist system of belief—in other words, a real turning East.

A Mild Disclaimer

Now that we have clarified the basic dynamics of the Western monotheistic and Eastern monistic conceptual types as emphasizing *transcendence* and *immanence*, respectively, it is necessary to admit both are to be found in all religions to some extent. Western religions, for example, though *predominantly* theistic and transcendental in their thought about their Ultimate (God or equivalent), nevertheless contain some traces of the Eastern type, particularly in their relatively small mystical subtraditions, which always aim and sometimes claim to experience the profound presence of the immanent Ultimate within themselves. The reverse is true: Eastern religions, though *predominantly* monistic and immanental in conceiving the Ultimate, exhibit strains of monotheism (or something very much like it), specifically in their devotional practices. Hinduism, for example, almost hopelessly complicates things by having a profusion of deities, none of whom is the Ultimate Reality—that designation being reserved for the non-personal, supreme, universal, and *immanent* spiritual Essence called *Brahman*. Yet as individuals lock on to one or another of these deities and make them objects of devotion, the result appears for all practical purposes to be something akin to monotheism (though as we shall see in Chapter 2, it is really *henotheism*.) Despite such exceptions, however, one can safely say that *when it comes to the way the world's religions envision Ultimate Reality, East really is East, and West truly is West*, and *in that context* they exhibit two different and distinct patterns of belief, practice, thought, and spirituality.

Whenever the Eastern monistic model has been adopted and employed in the West as an alternate, variant way of conceiving of God—and the instances have been quite rare—it should come as no surprise that it has garnered only a small following and been treated as suspect and even subversive. That is because monism essentially violates the dominant presuppositions of the prevailing monotheism, and in particular the fundamental notion of transcendence. Given the familiarity of their traditional language about the Ultimate, however, the Western monists generally retained the term "God," thus transforming the philosophy of monism into a variant theology called *pantheism* ("everything-is-God-ism"). That is because the only discernable difference between pantheism and the idealistic or spiritual monism of the East is a semantic one. Still more recently, some Western theologians have been exploring and advocating a kind of hybrid of monotheism and monism called *panentheism* (literally, "everything-in-God-ism"). This model holds that God and the cosmos mutually contain each other in such a way that God exhibits a profoundly (ontologically) immanent aspect *and* an equally transcendent aspect as well. It remains to be seen whether panentheism is a well-founded theological synthesis, or merely an esthetically attractive compromise by Western theologians who are drawn to the Eastern view, but reluctant for some reason to embrace it fully.

Now that the appropriate exceptions have been noted and the basic meanings of "transcendence" and "immanence" are perhaps reasonably clear, it is possible to move on to the next step and elaborate upon the basic distinction between Western and Eastern ways of conceiving of the Ultimate Reality. What follows here is, in effect, a fuller explication of the contrast sketched above and depicted in Figure 1-6. We shall start with the conventional Western view of Ultimate Reality and the closely related notions of the *cosmos, time, humanity,* and *spirituality,* and then proceed to the less familiar Eastern understanding of these matters. Throughout we shall see in the two perspectives differences sufficiently pronounced and profound as to constitute a diametrical opposition.

The Western Route

Briefly stated, the major Western religious traditions—Judaism, Christianity, and Islam—view Ultimate Reality as a single, largely transcendent, personal God of the theistic type. Accordingly, the cosmos is a finite creation of this God, and secular (not sacred) in nature. Time is understood as linear, with an absolute beginning and an equally absolute culmination. Humanity in this schema is the handiwork of the Creator God, intended to have a positive relationship with—and even to bear some kind of (unspecified) resemblance to—the Deity. (Some literalists persist in regarding this similitude as physical, though most theologians have long interpreted it as spiritual in some sense.) But human beings are essentially distinct from the Supreme Being. More than that, they are profoundly predisposed to become alienated from this Other, and are therefore in need of a way to mend the awful rift—Christians call it "salvation." Now let's unpack that very full suitcase of ideas.

Ultimate Reality: The One God

The Ultimate Reality in the West is generally identified as a single god, which means that Judaism, Islam, and Christianity are monotheistic (from two Greek words for "single" and "god"). Christians, of course, merely capitalize the generic word "god" and use it as a name: God. Similarly, Muslims add a definite article to the Arabic word for "god" and call their Ultimate *Al-lah,* which literally means "the god" or simply "God."

Judaism takes another tack: it has a proper name for God: *Jahweh* (pronounced and sometimes spelled *Yahweh*), which most Orthodox Jews especially, and even others less strict and devout, avoid using. They employ instead the euphemism *Adonai* ("Lord") in deference to the commandment about taking the name of God "in vain" (Exodus 20:7).

Called by whatever name, this God is personal, and is traditionally imagined, depicted, and addressed as male in gender—an assumption that modern feminist and liberal Jewish and Christian theologians are properly challenging. This masculine personification of God leads to specifically personal images and metaphors, including such traditional and popular ones as King, Lord, and Father. It also suggests a God who is subject to human emotions like jealousy and anger, and leads inevitably to anthropomorphism—the portrayal of God in human form, possessing a face and hands and being able to walk, talk, sit on a heavenly throne, and keep his eyes on sparrows.

As Figure 1-6 indicates with its separate large circles for God and the Universe on the left, the God of monotheism is not to be confused with the universe or anything in it, including the world and humanity shown by the smaller circles as being contained in the universe. Again, philosophers and theologians sometimes speak of this relationship between God and the cosmos as one of "ontological discontinuity," meaning simply that the being or essence of God is separate and distinct from that of the universe. The universe and its contents constitute nature, and God is above nature, that is, *supernatural.* This is precisely what it means to say that monotheists believe in a profoundly transcendent God, one whose very existence and essence are above, beyond, and other with respect to the cosmos and its contents.

Given this clear line of demarcation between divinity and humanity, to treat anything or anyone in the natural world as though it were divine is *idolatry*, a grievous sin indeed in Western religions, since it mistakes (that is, mis-takes) for God what in monotheism, at least, clearly is not God. Traditional Jews, Christians, or Muslims, for example, might admire sunsets or trees as God's handiwork, but would not worship them. Yet the Christian doctrine of the Incarnation maintains that the man Jesus was also divine— "God in the flesh," as it were; and many Christians consider him worthy of worship. To the more strictly monotheistic Jews and Muslims, this belief appears to be a clear and unacceptable violation of the ontological discontinuity that must be maintained between God and nature, including human nature. In effect, they believe, the idea of Incarnation invites and indeed constitutes a kind of idolatry. Given the non-negotiable status of their monotheistic distinction between God and the world, Jews and Muslims find Christianity's insistence that Jesus was a unique case—the exception that proves the rule, perhaps—unconvincing and heretical.

Although the God of monotheism is—or is supposed to be—Wholly Other, this profoundly transcendent Deity, while necessarily in some sense remote, is not completely aloof. No, this God is also *immanent*, in the relatively weak but nonetheless important sense of "active." This God is, after all, the Creator of the universe, whose primordial act of Creation, however conceived or depicted, stands as the first instance of divine immanence-as-activity. But that is not all. The God of monotheism is also a *providential* God who continues to be involved in the affairs of the world—most notably in human events and history—and this ongoing involvement amounts to a recurring and indeed ongoing immanence-of-activity. This kind of immanence is of the weaker sort. It permits God to *use* nature and human nature for divine purposes, and even allows the Deity to be active in human lives. But it does not allow God to *become* them or anything in them; that is, it does not spill over into the more profound immanence-of-being. God may have spoken to Moses out of a burning bush, but God was not that bush and Jews did not afterward become Bush-worshippers—or for that matter, Moses-worshippers! (There is an almost irresistible joke about Republicans lurking in that last sentence, but I shall mercifully refrain from spelling it out here.)

It is impossible to overstate the theological importance of monotheism's fundamental insistence on God's ontological transcendence. In fact, every other Christian theological issue and topic, including the understanding and treatment of the cosmos, time, and humanity, must begin with this fundamental presupposition and continue to honor it, in order to maintain the basic monotheistic framework of the faith, at least as traditionally understood. Of course, it is the intention of this book to push the envelope of this traditional Christian understanding, including its insistence upon transcendence and monotheism. Oddly enough, mainstream Christianity inadvertently has provided us a precedent in this endeavor in one of its key doctrines, none other than the Incarnation.

The Exceptional Incarnation

Earlier we briefly noted the one important exception to the rule that the God of the Western theistic religions is transcendent with respect to the natural world. The Christian doctrine of the Incarnation, officially formulated by the Council of Chalcedon in 451 CE, asserted that Jesus was unique in being one person but having two complete natures, one

Figure 1-7

The Mystery of the Christian Incarnation

Illustrated in Art and Explained (but Not Proven)
through Geometry and Set Theory

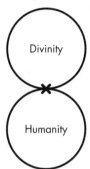

Divinity

Humanity

Classic paintings of Jesus often show him making this symbolic hand gesture, which signifies two natures, perfectly united in one person. We have no reason to believe, of course, that Jesus ever made—or would have understood—this gesture.

Set theory in mathematics often uses circles to indicate qualities or types of things. Geometry tells us that a circle consists of an infinite number of points, and that two circles may share a single point. Combining these two, we can let the top circle stand for divinity, the bottom one for humanity, and the one point they share for the Jesus Christ of the orthodox Christian doctrine of the Incarnation. *In Eastern religions, the two circles would coincide, for all humanity (and the cosmos itself) incarnates divinity.*

human and one divine. (See Figure 1-7.) His divine nature was none other than the Second Person of the Trinity, God the Son—or the Word (*Logos*) that according to John's Gospel *was* God (John 1:1). Thus Jesus, as the Incarnate (embodied) Word of God (John 1:14), though completely human in every way—body, mind, soul, and spirit—was wholly God as well. That belief, so central to traditional Christianity, clearly denies the discontinuity between God and Creation that a strict monotheism demands. For traditional Christians, of course, the exceptional status of the case underscores its miraculous quality, and most would not see it as a theological compromise, simply because of its unique, once-and-for-all character. But again, from a Muslim or Jewish perspective it is a clear and reckless violation of the very heart of monotheism, the ontological transcendence of God.

The Christian idea of the Holy Spirit would likewise appear to be at least a compromise if not an utter violation of the ontological transcendence of God, especially when the New Testament repeatedly proclaims that a person may be filled with it. But the New Testament Greek word for "spirit" is *pneuma*, which also means breath or wind, which Jesus is quoted as saying "blows where it will" (John 3:7–9), that is, unpredictably. Acts 2 depicts the Spirit as coming upon people at Pentecost, showering them with charismatic powers, and then leaving them; it does not become a permanent part of them, much less their very essence. Thus Pentecostals, who emphasize the indwelling of the Holy Spirit more than any other Christian group, would never dream of claiming that they become divine when they are "filled with the Holy Ghost." What they do affirm is the profound experience of God's *presence* within them, an endowment that, like their breath, they may lose. Nor would they ever think of bowing to one another in a gesture of prayer or offering a salute to one another's inner divinity. Hindus, however, do just that; for they believe that the Absolute, Ultimate, Supreme Spirit indwells everything and everyone as their *essence*. To put it another way, Hindus and all true Immanentalists believe that all of nature is inherently divine and thus "incarnated."

In a similar vein, the recurrent theme of mysticism in Christianity and the other Western religions has tended to extend the idea of Incarnation—always unofficially and at its own peril—to the individual believer. For mysticism is precisely the search, usually through some kind of practice of contemplation or meditation, for the Divine Within. Although prevalent in Eastern religions, mysticism has typically and perhaps predictably been treated as at best an orphan child in Christianity, Islam, and Judaism. After all, it goes against the dominant theological type, monotheism, and its insistence on strong transcendence—that is, a God whose primary trait is Otherness. Little wonder that mysticism has never been more than a sub-tradition in the Western religions, always suspect as a deviant and potentially subversive approach to the God on High.

The Cosmos: A Profane Place

In monotheism, then, the created order and its inhabitants are not to be confused in any way with the Creator. They are *natural, secular,* and even *profane* in the original sense of that word, which comes from the Latin meaning "outside the temple or holy place." In other words, the cosmos, though divinely constructed, is *unsacred.* By contrast, God (and only God) is supernatural and sacred. Thus God is God, and the cosmos is the cosmos; and while the two entities do encounter one another in monotheism, they can never coincide, or coextend, or be identified with each other without compromising the basic structure of theism.

Medieval Christian theologians reached a consensus that underscored this distinction with their doctrine of *creatio ex nihilo,* "creation out of nothing." Some among them had toyed with the idea that God had used pre-existing chaos or stuff as raw materials for the cosmos; but the idea that something might have been uncreated and thus coeternal with God was unacceptable. Others speculated that God had taken a part of "His" own divine substance, and fashioned it into "the heavens and the earth" of Genesis 1. But that made the universe in some sense divine, and thus blurred the distinction between Creator and Creation in a way that threatened the transcendence that was so basic to monotheism. The solution was to declare that God simply spoke everything into existence out of nothing (or nothingness), using no raw materials at all.

This view of the origin of the created order has an important practical consequence: as purely secular stuff, all of creation is at humanity's disposal. In fact, Genesis 1:28–30 has God turning the whole world over to the primordial couple to "have dominion over" and "subdue," making them, in effect, resident managers for an Absentee Landlord. And subdue it their alleged descendants have done: with reckless abandon we have used (and sometimes used up) natural resources for our own purposes, often with such dire consequences as the pollution and depletion of earth, skies, and waters. One can only wonder how much differently we Westerners might have treated the environment had we thought of it as sacred—as divine Mother Earth or Mother Nature. Some years ago an anti-litter TV commercial depicted an old, traditionally attired Native American man sitting on a horse, looking down upon a highway that was being carelessly littered by passing motorists (monotheists, no doubt), and shedding a tear at the sight of his sacred earth being so woefully abused. Some ecologists have in fact suggested that many if not most of our environmental problems can be laid at the feet of the secularizing monotheistic mindset that has dominated that part of the world most responsible for those problems, which is to say, our own Western Civilization.

Time as a Fine Line

In the Western world time is perceived as linear. That is, it is regarded as a non-repeatable succession of events (labeled "history" in retrospect) that proceed from an absolute beginning to a definite end. The beginning, called "Creation," is regarded as the start of the universe and its history. Its culmination is variously envisioned as a series of events triggered by the Second Coming of Christ, the arrival of the Messiah (Judaism), or the advent of a Mahdi (in Shi'ite Islam, the equivalent of the Messiah). This view of time is a kind of corollary to monotheism, which likes to retain infinity as a divine trait and thus assigns both a *terminus a quo* and a *terminus ad quem* (which is to say, finitude) to the created order.

Although this linear view of time prevails in the West and affects our thinking about almost everything, it seems to be largely subliminal and unconscious. Quite simply put, we Westerners are used to thinking in terms of lines rather than circles. We name our years with numbers in a strictly linear and unrepeatable sequence: 2003, '04, '05, and so on. We draw time-lines, as I myself did earlier in the chapter. Our reasoning and logic move from point A to point B to point C; we criticize people for talking in circles or engaging in circular arguments. We stand in lines, we sit in rows, we march in rank and file. We mostly construct houses with straight sides, and whenever possible we draw our property lines and borderlines straight and lay out streets that are not only straight, but parallel and perpendicular to one another. We square dance and line dance. We admire straight shooters and people who get straight to the point. We tell each other that we "only live once," for most people in our culture believe that life proceeds in a straight line, beginning with birth and ending in death. We say that people who cheat on their partners are "running around" on them, and we encourage them to walk "the straight and narrow." We hate to be given the run-around. The most popular sports in the Western world today, American football and soccer, are played, not in circles, but on rectangular fields defined by straight-lined boundaries and marked with straight lines, which dictate the course of the game. Even the boxing ring is really a square!

Western religions are likewise linear: Christians and Jews generally worship in rows of pews, or seats, or chairs; Muslims in a mosque kneel in straight lines to pray. Symbols and even gestures in these religions tend to be built of straight lines (e.g., the Jewish Star of David, the Christian Cross, the Muslim's extended index finger tapping out the oneness of God during prayer), the crescent of Islam being a notable exception. The word "circle" appears only three times in the entire Bible—all in the OT—and in some English translations not at all. To be sure, some of the readings in the so-called Wisdom literature of the Old Testament—which include Job, Psalms, Proverbs, Ecclesiastes, and Song of Solomon—do suggest a cyclical view of existence. In the book of Job, for example, the plot follows a cyclical pattern with the main character being restored to his original good fortune after his ordeals. The book of Ecclesiastes displays an ongoing cyclical theme: "The sun rises, the sun sets, and the sun rises again . . . and there is nothing new under the sun." (1:5–9) Likewise, some of the parables of Jesus either use the cyclical imagery of planting and reaping, or like the Prodigal Son involve the return of the central character to his original home or place or status. But such examples are few and far between. For the most part Jews, Muslims, and traditional Christians see the universe and its history as having one definite beginning at Creation, and as proceeding in a straight line, event after event after event, to some kind of end-time consummation.

Humanity's Place, Plight, and Prospects

The place of humanity in all of this is quite clear. Because God is transcendent, then human beings—like everything else in the cosmos—are not divine, however much they may be in God's "image" or "likeness" or both. Put quite simply, with the one exceptional and controversial Christian doctrine already noted, we humans are *creatures*, and as such are no more to be confused with the Creator than a portrait—even a self-portrait—is to be confused with the person it depicts.

Further, humanity is seen to be not only *other than* God, but also *alienated from* God—a condition summed up in the word "sin." To be sure, the three great Western religions put different spins and emphases on sin, with orthodox Christianity taking the most radical position. As Judaism and Islam would have it, sin is simply a bad deed, or at most an accumulation thereof. In Christianity, however, and thanks largely to the New Testament writings of Paul, it is first and foremost *an innate and universal human condition*, one inherited from Adam and inevitably producing actual sins. Despite this remarkable difference of interpretation, all three religions agree that sin connotes a broken relationship between the Deity and humanity, and indeed see its mending as their main purpose.

Extraverted Spirituality, External Salvation

This Western view of divinity and humanity sets the stage for how spirituality is to be understood and practiced. For if God is a transcendent Other whose being is vastly and qualitatively different from humanity's, then all that can be hoped for is a healthy *relationship* between them. This sort of *relational spirituality* is inherently *extraverted* and *devotional*. For it is oriented toward an Other, whom it strives in a heart-felt and often emotional way to love, honor, obey, and otherwise please. The expected rewards are further blessings, revelations, and ultimately salvation. The teaching of mainstream Christianity in this regard is that all such benefits accrue from and are assured by the atoning death of Jesus, and that believers need only avail themselves of them.

From the Western perspective, the divine-human relationship is characterized by *communication* and *communion*, both of which suggest a relationship and a desire for ever more closeness—as in the hymn, "Nearer, My God, To Thee." This relationship is enhanced by acts of devotion and worship directed to a personal God or Higher Power, in hopes of *receiving from above* spiritual well-being and growth in addition to religious comfort and assurance. The staple practice of such a relational spirituality is *prayer*, which is communication with the Deity to which one is devoted. For Christians, prayer is rivaled in importance only by—what else?—Holy Communion. One of the best metaphors for this kind of spirituality is the mountaintop experience, the meeting of the "upward bound" believer and the exalted Other who "descends" from a lofty dwelling place for a face-to-face encounter. Another would be the familiar praying hands pointed heavenward, like a spiritual dish antenna (but with only one available channel whose only consistently reliable signal is an uplink!). Even the Christian vision of eternal life is shaped by notions of *communion* with God as a being-in-the-divine-presence (as opposed to an absorption into the divine essence forever, which would bespeak the ideals of unity and union in the mystical paradigm).

In this picture, humanity is anything but self-sufficient with respect to wisdom, but rather stands ever in need of divine assistance in the form of revelation. The same is true for salvation, which in all monotheistic faiths entails realizing a closer relationship with God, which in turn depends on God's grace. In Judaism and Islam, the grace comes precisely *as* revelation, in the form of scripture, by means of which the faithful may be guided toward the achievement of righteousness. In Christianity, the grace is much more radical: Jesus Christ is seen as the quintessential divine revelation, whose atoning death offers the free gift of salvation to a humanity too profoundly sinful to earn by its own efforts that eternal reward. That primary revelation underwrites the witness of scripture, whose revelation is important, certainly, but finally derivative from and secondary to the Lord that it proclaims and portrays.

The Eastern Route

In stark contrast to the Western view, the major Eastern religions—Hinduism, Buddhism, Taoism and Confucianism—regard Ultimate Reality as an eternal, immanent, non-personal Something. They take the cosmos to be the uncreated and infinite expression or emanation (out-pouring) of this Something's essence, and therefore inherently sacred, precisely because the Ultimate is immanent within it (as indicated in the right-hand portion of Figure 1-6). Time is seen as cyclical, with no absolute beginning or ending, but rather marked by periodic transformations within an overall pattern of eternal recurrence. Humanity is another expression of the Supreme Something, and is essentially one with that One. Humans are therefore inherently divine, but since they suffer from ignorance about their true identity, they are in need of ever-deeper awareness and actualization of their essential nature.

Ultimate Reality: The One Something

The basic Eastern view of Ultimate Reality is in most respects the polar opposite of that of the West. As already indicated, the Oriental religions view the Ultimate not as a god, but rather as an Absolute One. This One is called *Brahman* in Hinduism, *Shunyata* in Buddhism, and *Tao* in Taoism. Though these three permutations of the Ultimate differ somewhat in the way they are conceived and explained in their respective traditions, they exhibit a profound formal similarity as well.

To be more specific, as opposed to the God of the West, who is a transcendent, personal, and self-revealing Supreme Being, the Ultimate of the East is an immanent, non-personal, and hidden Deeper Presence. It is more like Being Itself than a being, and so mysterious that, paradoxically, it is finally closer to Nothingness than to Being. Hinduism's *Brahman*, for example, presents anywhere from one to 330 million personal aspects or faces to humanity. In and of Itself, however, *Brahman* is actually beyond any distinctions, including that between personal and impersonal. Still, Hindu philosophers tend to prefer impersonal pronouns and metaphors for this transpersonal Ultimate, ostensibly because personal imagery would be even more misleading. At its deepest, *Brahman* has no qualities at all, which is about as close to Nothing as one can get.

We shall examine this view of Ultimate Reality in greater detail in chapter 2. For now, suffice it to say that the ancient Hindu scriptures called *Upanishads* tell us that *Brahman* is hidden in everyone and everything as cream is hidden in milk and salt in salt water—note the impersonal images—and is finally an unknowable Mystery.

In Buddhism, the equivalent of *Brahman* is *Shunyata*. That name means "Nothingness," "Emptiness," "Void," or "Zilch." We shall explore this notion in depth in Chapter 3. Here it is enough to point out the obvious: *Shunyata* looks nothing whatsoever like the always personal and often anthropomorphic Jahweh, God, or Allah of traditional Western religion. Neither does the Ultimate Reality proferred in ancient Chinese (folk) religion as well as the later perennial-archetypal Taoism *and* Confucianism: the *Tao*. In fact, according to the *Tao Te Ching*, this "Way" is really unnamable, unknowable, and—like its Buddhist counterpart, *Shunyata*—empty and formless, but nevertheless the Source of all that is.

In all these cases the Ultimate—whether designated *Brahman*, *Shunyata*, or *Tao*—is conceived not as a transcendent reality in the sense of being above, beyond, or other than the cosmos, but as immanent, which is to say, indwelling, permeating, saturating, and infusing all existing things and beings. Hinduism, Buddhism, and Taoism all assert that this Absolute is finally indescribable but nonetheless experientially knowable; still, they treat it less as a "Higher Power" than as a "Deeper Presence." If it is said to be transcendent at all, it is only in the weak sense of being beyond immediate human perception and mortal powers of conception. In other words, this Ultimate really and truly (i.e., ontologically) is the very essence of all humans whether or not they are able to feel, realize, acknowledge, understand, or articulate it. They are indeed and profoundly one with the One.

A fair and almost inevitable question is why the Eastern concept of Ultimate Reality is so different from the Western. The most plausible answer is that the former is much more grounded in *unitive* mystical experience, which always connotes a spiritual journey to some mysterious depth within the believer. Mystical experiences typically yield either sketchy reports of a blissful encounter with an unspeakable Mystery or, more commonly, an awe-struck and reverent silence. Mystical experience, while not unknown in the West, will naturally be rarer where one's connection to God is commonly understood and described in terms of a relationship with a transcendent Other. Of course, that explanation begs another question: Why is the unitive mystical experience more intentionally cultivated and frequently realized in the East? The great mythologist Joseph Campbell suggested that the Eastern mystical view was grounded in the experience of farmers whose experience of the life-giving earth, the cyclical seasons, and so forth led them to posit a Spirit that infused nature. The Western view, by contrast, arose among tribal nomads who needed a Warrior-King to watch over them and protect them against the environments and enemies that threatened their well-being. That is a plausible, but hardly universally accepted explanation.

A Devotional Deviation

Just as I noted earlier that the Christian doctrine of the Incarnation constitutes a strong exception to the monotheistic pattern, so I must now acknowledge a similar case with respect to Eastern religions. The simple fact is that many and perhaps most people in the East do not relate very well to the Ultimate Reality presented by their religions. Perhaps because it is so non-personal and abstract (and therefore difficult to conceive of, much less identify with), many Hindus, Buddhists, and Taoists choose to direct their attention—or more correctly, their hearts—to one or another deity or quasi-deity. Instead of focusing on *Brahman*, the Supreme, most Hindus choose to devote themselves in prayer and worship to one or another of the 330 million gods or goddesses. Likewise, many Buddhists eschew *Shunyata* and put their faith and hope in one or another celestial Buddha or *bodhisattva* (a compassionate, helpful being one step removed from Buddhahood). Modern Taoists likewise leave the *Tao* to the religious and philosophical professionals and turn their attention to a myriad of deities and spirits, some distant, aloof, and disinterested, but others local, familiar, and beneficent, upon whom they can put their trust. The result in all such cases is a religious practice approaching and resembling Western monotheism, despite the persistent monistic theoretical conviction that at root all is really One.

The fascinating irony of this is that in theory the Eastern faiths universalize the Christian doctrine of the Incarnation by affirming that not only Jesus, but all sentient beings and perhaps everything that exists "enflesh" divinity. But at the same time, they adopt a Western style of spirituality by devoting themselves to one or another personal manifestation and embodiment of their own non-personal Ultimate. To put it another way, while a few Westerners adopt the more typically Eastern spirituality of mysticism and seek the Divine within, many Easterners adopt the Western model of devotion that addresses itself to an external divine entity. This is an ironic situation, one that suggests the possibility of a universal affective need or yearning in the human condition. It also illustrates the tenuous nature of typologies and underscores the wisdom of caution in employing them. For our present purpose it is important to remember that our East-West distinction is based on differing views of Ultimate Reality rather than the sentiments and practices of popular piety, which tends to focus on more proximate entities (lesser gods, saints, and the like).

The Cosmos: Running Sacred

The fact that in the East the Ultimate is understood as fundamentally immanent naturally has important implications for how the universe itself is conceived. For whereas in the transcendentalist West the cosmos is seen as secular or profane, in the immanentalist East, it is essentially divine and profoundly sacred. It is nothing less than an essential expression or manifestation of the Ultimate. It is also eternal and uncreated, at least in the sense of an absolute creation, for Eastern thought does allow for successive mini-creations or recreations of the world as well as recurring culminations, but in a process that itself has no beginning or end. In other words, the cosmos always existed in some shape or form, because there was never a time when the Ultimate was not self-manifesting.

As already suggested, that self-manifestation is generally treated in the East as being not so much the creation of a separate reality as an *emanation* or *outpouring* of the Divine. This way of conceiving of the origins of the cosmos means that the Ultimate Source remains an integral part—indeed the very essence—of the resulting cosmic stuff. Westerners, of course, might well maintain that everything *has* to have a beginning—a necessity that somehow has escaped the Eastern non-linear mind. Having made that bold assertion, however, they generally turn around and attribute the cosmic beginning to a Deity who is said to be eternal, and who is therefore apparently exempt from the rule. To the Oriental mind, it makes more sense simply to cut to the chase, so to speak, by attributing eternality to the universe itself.

Eastern Standard Time?

The Eastern view, then, is that the cosmos had no absolute beginning. It likewise will have no absolute end, though it may collapse upon itself from time to time in preparation for one of those occasional re-creations. That makes time in the East cyclical rather than linear, at both the macro and the micro level. Hinduism, for example, sees the world as passing through incredibly long *yugas* (ages), which combine to form even longer *mahayugas* (aeons), which in turn succeed one another in a definite pattern that returns everything to the beginning of a brand new aeon with its ages, and so on *ad infinitum*. That macrocosmic pattern is reflected on the microcosmic scale as cycles within cycles, producing among other things the notion of *samsara* or the endless reincarnations (or transmigrations) of a spirit into one physical form after another, human or otherwise.

While such a conception of time appears strange in the West, to the Eastern mind it simply reflects the patterns of nature. The shapes and routes of the heavenly bodies, for example, are far closer to circles than to lines. Seasons follow one another and recur again and again like clock-work. (Come to think of it, even in the West clocks and sundials have usually been round, but now that technology makes it possible, they are rapidly being replaced by digital readouts of linear-sequential numbers.) Winds also blow in circular patterns rather than straight lines, a fact that we only tend to notice when it blows really hard, as in tornadoes or hur-ricanes. Birds' nests and beehives are rounded rather than flat-sided. Even the horizon is curved rather than straight. Modern astrophysicists are now telling us that the shape of the universe resembles the outer sur-face of a balloon—and an expanding one at that. Why should we Westerners imagine that time itself does not follow this obviously perva-sive natural pattern?

It should come as little surprise that the cyclical-temporal mindset of the East is reflected in its symbols, nearly all of which are circular. Taoism con-structed the *T'ai Chi* symbol (better known as the *yin-yang*) so as to suggest cyclical movement. Likewise the eight-spoked wheel of Buddhism implies a cyclical rotation. Lesser known, perhaps is the *enso* or empty circle of Zen calligraphy, which symbolizes not only the cyclical pattern of time, but the Emptiness (*Shunyata*) within that is ironically the Unrealized Source of all possibilities. Perhaps this is the reason that it was chosen as the logo for a well-known technologies company, though one of its former employees told me recently that the symbol now looked more like an indication of that business's net worth and future prospects.

Affinities with the cyclical orientation of the East can be found in the most unlikely places. Among our Native Americans, for example, traditional homes like *tipis*, *hogans*, and *igloos* had circular floor plans, as did the *kivas* used for ritual purposes by the Pueblo Indians and their forerunners. Native Americans have typically fashioned their arts along circular patterns, and, of course, danced not in lines and squares, as Westerners do, but in circles. An interesting exception to the prevailing Western linearity can be found within Christianity itself: the Shakers, who built their barns in the round, frequently danced in concentric circles, and wrote and sang hymns about "coming out right" only after "turning, turning." (See Figure 1-8.) Perhaps the fact that both tribal peoples and the Shakers lived close to the land and nature made them especially attuned to the cycles of nature and thus strange bedfellows not only with one another, but with Eastern thinkers as well. Another Western exception to the prevailing linear pattern is found in the Sufi tradition of Islam and its so-called "whirling dervishes," who are famous for their simultaneous spinning *and* rotating in circles in meditative dance. (Even their flaring robes form circles at the hem.) This practice, however, seems to have little to do with nature, but stems purely and simply from the mysticism of the Sufis, who—unlike the majority of Muslims—seek Allah at their individual spiritual centers; and centers imply circles and cycles, rotations and revolutions.

These notable exceptions aside, Eastern thought about time and cosmic processes has taken a different direction from that which has

Figure 1-8

The Shakers' Eastern Tilt

Best known for their celibacy for all members, their beautiful but simple furniture and architecture, their unique hymnody and use of dance in worship, the Shakers were one of many, mostly homegrown Christian communitarian groups that populated the 19th century American religious landscape. Ironically, perhaps, many aspects of their life, and particularly their appreciation of simplicity, make them appear almost Taoist. Their most famous hymn certainly reflects their affinity for simplicity, flexibility, and cyclical thinking. Not surprisingly, it was often sung as (what else?) a round.

"Simple Gifts"

(composed in 1848 by Shaker Elder Joseph Brackett, Jr.)

'Tis the gift to be simple, 'Tis the gift to be free,
'Tis the gift to come down where we ought to be,
And when we find ourselves in the place just right,
It will be in the valley of love and delight.

When true simplicity is gained,
To bow and to bend, we will not be ashamed.
To turn, turn, will be our delight,
'Til by turning, turning, we come round right.

generally prevailed in the West. A possible explanation for this divergence may again lie in the thoughts of Joseph Campbell about East and West. He suggested that the Western linear view of time was conceived by nomadic herders whose yearly migrations tended to take them from point A to point B, and thus in linear patterns rather than around in circles. The people who shaped Eastern thought, by contrast, were more agrarian and thus naturally attuned to the cyclical successions of the seasons, and that experience shaped their thinking about time as it had about the inherently sacred or divine earth.

A Divine Humanity

The East sees humanity, like everything else in the cosmos, as an expression or emanation of the One Supreme Something, and therefore as essentially—which is to say, spiritually—one with it. As we have seen, of the three great Western religions, only Christianity posits an incarnation or enfleshment of God in human form, and then only in one person (Jesus), but the Eastern traditions effectively regard everything and everyone as an incarnation of the Supreme Sacred Source. And being essentially divine, humanity shares this One's eternality; hence, the pervasive belief in reincarnation in the Oriental traditions.

The Eastern religions do not define the human predicament in terms of sin, a notion that connotes alienation and therefore implies two parties, but as humankind's ignorance of its own essentially divine nature. This blindness is both corporate and individual, pervasive and persistent. That is, humanity is pictured as having lost a sense of its inherent divinity, and the resultant ignorance inevitably leads to evil thoughts and deeds. But since the root problem is ignorance rather than sin, what is needed and sought for is not salvation but *enlightenment*, which in turn leads to bliss. Predictably, perhaps, sin is not much of an issue in Eastern religions. At best, it would connote the bad things that accrue as a result of spiritual ignorance: we *are* one with the One, but not knowing that (at least in a way that counts for anything), we don't act like it and behave badly. Overcome the ignorance and the "sins" will take care of themselves.

Introverted Spirituality, Inner Self-Realization

Any specific view of human nature all but dictates a particular understanding of spirituality and revelation. As we have seen, the Western model proffers a *relational* spirituality in which two parties, one human and one divine, seek communication and communion. By contrast, the

Eastern pattern presents a *unitive spirituality* that assumes an essential oneness of the individual with the immanent One, and looks for nothing short of an experience of total and absolute *union* and *identity* with it. This Eastern style of spirituality, pursued (or at least prepared for) by meditation and other spiritual disciplines and exercises, finds its corollary in a particular view of revelation. In such a system the source of Divine Truth is not the word or will of an Other received from the heavens above, but the believer's mystical experience of an essential spiritual identity. Revelation then amounts to one's self-realization *as* none other than the Inner Ultimate within. That mystical experience itself *is* the Truth, the whole Truth, and nothing but the Truth.

The Eastern type of spirituality, then, is *introverted*, for it concentrates on inner states of being for evidence of a Deeper Presence or Self Within. It is also *unitive* and aims at a *Self-realization* that amounts to *self-dissolution*, for the believer strives for no less than the blissful experience of the utter absorption of the individual self-identity into the Oneness. The process starts with the obliteration of the ego-self that we in the West spend so much time and effort discovering, analyzing, developing, and guarding. The most common practice underwriting this kind of spirituality and spiritual goal is *meditation*, which in its Eastern form is not "thinking about things," but clearing the mind and the senses in order to smooth the way to an experience of profound interiority and identity. The best metaphor for this sort of spirituality might well be plumbing the depths of a cave in search of the undiscovered mineral vein or hidden treasure that is at once one's truest self *and* the Deepest Divinity—spiritual spelunking, as it were.

Conclusion

We have moved rather quickly in this chapter from fashioning a generic working definition of religion, to the raising of important issues and the clarifying of related terms, to an overview of the history of religions, and finally to a detailed exposition of the great East-West religious divide. In so doing we have encountered again and again religion's variegated character: its many dimensions, its wide variety of beliefs and practices, its many individual and group expressions, and its profound connections to both spirituality and thought. To get a handle on the dizzying complexity of religion as a human enterprise we have also discovered and tucked away some helpful tools: Smart's seven dimensions (plus one of my own), a typical periodization of religious history, and an East-West typology.

All of this information will stand us in good stead for the journey ahead. As much as anything can, it will prepare us for the rich diversity of experiences, institutional expressions, values, beliefs, and practices to be encountered in the faiths that we will soon be exploring. As we have amassed this array of useful provisions, perhaps we have begun to recognize that far from being a weakness to be regretted and overcome, the diversity within and among religions (including Christianity) is a trait to be celebrated. For it allows a faith to speak to a wide variety of individual dispositions and needs, as well as to people of different cultures. It may well be this very diversity, in fact, that ratifies Christianity—along with other similarly multiform world-class faiths—as a truly universal religion.

The primary goal of this book is, in fact, to both draw upon and add to that diversity in a salutary way. The intention is to uncover the many treasures of the East and to use them to provide yet another perspective—what we are calling an "Oriented" one—on the Christian faith that will enlighten it enough to make it more plausible and compelling, especially to those who abandoned it because it no longer had the ring of truth. As it turns out, what we have done in this preparatory chapter is more than merely stock up on provisions for our figurative journey East. We have also, in effect, backtracked along the Western route as far as the fork in the road that occurred at the dawn of the Perennial-Archetypal Era, when religious experience and thought left the surprising unanimity of the Polytheistic-Ancient religions and parted ways to head in opposite directions. In the following chapter we shall begin to traverse in earnest the less familiar Eastern route in order to see what new and valuable things we can discover at the various stops along that way. Fear not of getting lost or stranded. We shall return to our more familiar road and surroundings eventually. But do take a deep breath, for it's going to take a while and we may encounter some heavy going along the way.

Questions for Reflection and Discussion

1. Suggest some senses in which the religion with which you are most familiar is in accord with the Latin root for "religion," which means *binding*. Which one of these makes most sense to you? Why? In your own experience of religion, does the "binding" have more of a positive or a negative character? How do you account for your answer? Why do you suppose that some people might see it otherwise?

2. Because we will never know the answer, this chapter has not addressed the question of where religion came from in the first place. What

would you imagine to be the origins of religion in human history? What would be your evidence, and how might you test your theory? Can you think of any alternative explanations? How do you account for religion's (1) persistence in history and (2) apparent evolution through distinct phases?

3. What do you think of the idea that the pre-historic, tribal religions represent religion in its purest form—the real "old-time religion"—and that modern religion pales by comparison? Explain your answer. What do you think about the idea that modern superstitions and other practices (like naming sports teams) are really fossil behaviors left over from pre-historic times; or that certain favorite beliefs and rituals of your own faith tradition may be derivative from those of the tribal Stone Age? If they are, how would you account for the apparent longevity of pre-historic religious elements?

4. What do you make of the fact that different halves of the world view Ultimate Reality so very differently? Can you think of any reason or reasons why that may have happened besides those suggested in this chapter?

5. All thinking about Ultimate Reality or God is ultimately metaphorical. Traditional images used in the Christian West are Lord, King, Shepherd, Father, and even Rock. One set of metaphors for the distinction between "transcendence" and "immanence" might be butterflies soaring in the sunlight (*illuminated* from without) versus fireflies cavorting on a dark and cloudy night (*illuminating* from within). Think about those images and try to explain transcendence and immanence to a family member or friend on the basis of them. Can you think of another metaphor or set of metaphors for these two difficult concepts?

6. Does either the Eastern or the Western view of Ultimate Reality make more sense to you, or come closer to resonating with your personal experience of the world? Which one? Why? How does your preferred view fit with the religious tradition in which you were reared or in which you find yourself now? If it is an awkward fit, what might you have to do to make it smoother or more comfortable? To put it another way, do you consider yourself a religious person, a spiritual person, both, or neither? If you consider yourself a spiritual person, which of the two spiritualities (relational versus unitive) delineated toward the end of this chapter comes closest to capturing your personal style? If you do not think of yourself as spiritual, do you tend to be a self-reliant person, or are you inclined to lean on family, friends,

or others for your strength? What do you think about the possibility that a person can be spiritual, but in a purely secular or humanistic way? How might you benefit from finding or founding a community of people like you?

Recommended Reading

Michael Barnes, *In the Presence of Mystery: The Nature and Evolution of Religion*. Mystic, CT: Twenty-Third Publications, 1990.

Joseph Campbell, with Bill Moyers, *The Power of Myth*. New York: Anchor Books, 1990.

Denise Lardner Carmody, *Women and World Religions*. 2d ed. Englewood Cliffs, NJ: Prentice-Hall, 1989.

Mircea Eliade, *The Sacred and the Profane: The Nature of Religion*. Trans. William R. Trask. New York: Harcourt, Brace & World, 1959.

Robert S. Ellwood, *Introducing Religion: From Inside and Outside*. 3d ed. Englewood Cliffs, NJ: Prentice Hall, 1993.

Winston L. King, *Introduction to Religion: A Phenomenological Approach*. Rev. ed. New York/Evanston/London: Harper & Row, 1968.

Ursula King, *Women in the World's Religions: Past and Present*. New York: Paragon House, 1987.

James C. Livingston, *Anatomy of the Sacred: An Introduction to Religion*. 3d ed. Upper Saddle River, NJ: Prentice Hall, 1998.

Lucinda Joy Peach, *Women and World Religions*. Upper Saddle River, NJ: Prentice-Hall, 2002.

Ninian Smart, *Worldviews: Crosscultural Explorations of Human Beliefs*. 3d ed. Upper Saddle River, NJ: Prentice Hall, 2000.

Ninian Smart and B. Srinivasa Murti, *East-West Encounters in Philosophy and Religion*. Long Beach, CA: Long Beach Publications, 1996.

Huston Smith, *The World's Religions: Our Great Wisdom Traditions*. San Francisco: HarperSanFrancisco, 1991.

Wilfred Canfield Smith, *The Meaning and End of Religion: A New Approach to the Religious Traditions of Mankind*. New York: New American Library, 1964.

Paul Tillich, *What is Religion?* Trans. James Luther Adams. New York, et al.: Harper and Row, 1973.

John C. Wilson and W. Royce Clark, *Religion: A Preface*. 3d ed. Englewood Cliffs, NJ: Prentice Hall, 1997.

Chapter 2

The Many Paths of Hinduism

Something for Everyone

Objectives of this Chapter

- to present Hinduism as an ancient religion of extraordinary diversity, inclusiveness, and tolerance

- to provide some of the history of India as a background against which to view the Hindu religion

- to explore the Indian caste system as the traditional social context within which Hinduism operates

- to examine Hinduism's complex scriptures and belief system and the key roles that deities, Ultimate Reality, reincarnation, and *karma* play

- to provide an overview of popular piety and practice in contemporary Hinduism, with special attention to the deities most venerated today

- to explain the traditional life goals and life stages recognized by Hinduism, and their functions in the spiritual scheme of things

- to examine the variety of spiritual paths regarded as valid in Hinduism, and to show how successive historical periods have emphasized certain ones

- to indicate the impact that Hinduism has made on the West, especially in the last century or so

The first stop on our journey of spiritual exploration is India, which has been a fertile seedbed of spirituality for at least 3500 years. No fewer than four major religions sprang up there over the centuries—Hinduism, Jainism, Buddhism, and Sikhism—as well as a host of minor ones, most of which either died out or were absorbed into the wonderful conglomeration that is Hinduism. Jainism is a monk-focused religion with a system of individual salvation based on a more or less ascetic discipline dating to the sixth century BCE and derived from Hinduism, while Sikhism is a five-century-old, lay-oriented, monotheistic, devotional faith whose main emphases are worship and acts of loving kindness. Neither of these generated a missionary impulse, and except for the comparatively small number of their followers who have emigrated, both remain largely culture-bound to the land of their birth. The former offers no clear concept of an Ultimate Reality, while the latter derives largely from Muslim theology with some Hindu concepts mixed in. Therefore, our time on this trip will be better spent attending to the far more original and increasingly influential Hinduism, which is the subject of this chapter, and the well-traveled and widely embraced Buddhism, to which we shall turn in the next.

Overview and Origins

Hinduism is as old as India itself and has roots that are older still. It is therefore arguably the most enduring of the major living religions of the world. It originated in the same historical period as the religions of ancient Mesopotamia, Egypt, Greece, and Rome, and is one of only two among the polytheisthic-ancient religions to survive (the other being Japan's Shinto). Most of the religions of that era met their demise because they were too closely tied to their respective cultures and lacked any missionary impulse. Thus, when the civilizations crumbled under military and political conquest at the hands of adherents of younger, more aggressive religions like Christianity and Islam, their religions died out as well. Hinduism, however, endured the inevitable social, political, and cultural upheavals, foreign invasions, and colonizations that have marked India's long history. As a matter of fact, it was largely defined and in the long run strengthened under pressure from such challenges, and remains a living and vibrant faith today.

Complexity, Diversity, Inclusiveness, and Tolerance

Due in large part to its longevity, Hinduism is incredibly complex and diverse, and in that respect reflects the very nature of India, which is a mind-boggling pastiche of sub-cultures, races, languages, and customs. Indeed, it is not too much to claim that almost anything that can conceivably be believed or practiced religiously by human beings has been believed and practiced at some time and in some way by Hindus. Hinduism has embraced, for example, such divergent views as polytheism (worship of many personal deities), monism (belief in a single non-personal and all-pervasive-and-inclusive Ultimate Reality), and henotheism (devotion to one god or goddess without denying the existence or importance of other deities). It has also included such disparate practices as *asceticism*, which is the denial, deprivation, and even destruction of the physical body ("the flesh") for spiritual reasons; and *Tantrism* (also known as *Shaktism*), which indulges the bodily appetites (including sensuality and sexuality) for the purpose of spiritual advancement. Most remarkable of all is the fact that Hinduism has managed to incorporate such diverse beliefs and practices *simultaneously*.

Longevity alone does not account for Hinduism's complexity and diversity. Equally important are its attitudes of tolerance, inclusiveness, and openness to innovation and assimilation. Hindus have always recognized not just the existence of many valid spiritual paths, but indeed the necessity of them. In this regard, Hinduism acknowledges the obvious: all people are not the same in psychological makeup, disposition, temperament, and tastes; and therefore no one spiritual path or style could possibly be right for everyone. This is perhaps a novel and strange attitude for Westerners, who are probably used to hearing religious folks claiming their views and activities to be the only true way. Hinduism, by contrast, has managed to accommodate and affirm—or failing that, simply to tolerate—all kinds of spiritual expressions as valid alternative ways to be religious. Hinduism has developed over the centuries, therefore, a variety of spiritual paths (*margas*) or disciplines (*yogas*), one of which can be expected to be tweaked and tempered into a good fit for any particular individual.

While the tolerance of the Hindu faith itself is self-evident and has been articulated again and again by many of its leading lights from ancient to modern times, certain Hindu individuals and groups over the centuries have opposed (and sometimes fiercely) other religions and their adherents. For example, while most Hindus have recognized the three independent religions that their faith spawned—Jainism, Buddhism, and Sikhism—as merely idiosyncratic sects within it, some have found occasion (usually under political pressure) to treat adherents of these faiths as outright enemies. Likewise, while most Hindus have affirmed the validity of the other great faiths of the world, and even regarded sincere practitioners of them as Hindus in the broadest sense, there have arisen quasi-fundamentalist Hindu voices in protest to the perceived threats of foreign religions and their practitioners. This is especially true with regard to Muslims and Christians, who between them colonized and ruled India for the better part of five centuries, thus generating an understandable resentment and hostility among the natives. More than that, these Western monotheistic faiths forcefully attacked Hinduism in all of its forms as a false religion, each offering itself instead as the one true faith. Faced and threatened with such exclusivist claims, the ever inclusive and tolerant Hinduism was forced into the ironic defensive position of becoming intolerant, not of monotheism *per se*, but of the intolerance common to advocates of that theology. Hinduism, therefore, is no exception to the rule that when any religion mixes with nationalism and politics (as it invariably does) and is confronted by colonial aggression and occupation (as is often the case), its purest principles and impulses are inevitably compromised.

An Incredible Inventory?

Such exceptional circumstances and cases notwithstanding, Hinduism has clearly exhibited a remarkable internal tolerance and, as a consequence, nothing short of a wild diversity. For that reason, it has been aptly likened to a very old antique shop, one that for its entire existence has collected curiosities, rejecting little and selling, discarding, or giving away almost nothing. Over time, therefore, it has become more and more crowded and cluttered—and yes, even messy—so that today's casual browser is likely to be quite overwhelmed at the quantity and variety of its inventory. This old store has changed the display in the front window from time to time, but has only moved what used to be there to a different part of the premises—an attic or basement, perhaps.

According to some, even that image sells Hinduism short; they would see it as resembling more a panoply of little specialty shops crowded together in a very busy mall—or, more in keeping with India's culture, a host of independent vendors' stalls jammed together in a huge, crowded street market. Even to call it "Hinduism" may be misleading, for that suggests a unity and coherence that simply do not exist. The name is, after all, a fairly recent Western invention, one imposed (depending on which source you believe) either in the sixteenth century by India's Muslim conquerors or in the early nineteenth by the British colonialists who then controlled the country politically. But the Indian people have long had their own Sanskrit name for their "shop" or "mall." They call it *Sanatana Dharma*—the "Eternal Doctrine" or "Perennial Truth"—thereby suggesting that they see at least some coherence in their faith, despite its often chaotic appearance.

I sometimes tell my students, in fact, that if they have read an assignment on Hinduism—an encyclopedia article or chapter in a textbook on world religions, for example—and have wound up a bit puzzled or downright perplexed, they have probably done it right. It is nevertheless possible to do an inventory of that large and messy religious shopping center. The place to start is with the historical background and origins of Hinduism and the social structure that emerged from these roots. Taking stock of these will provide a backdrop against which the whole religion may be better examined and understood.

Aryans and the Indus Valley

By most accounts, both India itself and the conglomeration of spiritual traditions we call "Hinduism" are the result of a 3500-year-ago invasion and conquest—or rather a series of invasions and conquests—of what was then northwest India (but is now mostly Pakistan) by an ethnic group called the Aryans (literally, "the noble ones"). The Aryans—contrary to what Adolf Hitler believed—were from the vicinity of modern Iran (whose name literally means "land of the Aryans"), and therefore anything but blonde, Nordic types. They were, in fact, a swarthy, tough, unsettled, nomadic people with a rugged lifestyle and what might justifiably be regarded as a high testosterone society.

The people they defeated and subjugated (or perhaps merely superceded) are variously called "Dasyus," "Dravidians," and "Harappans." They were an indigenous people living in and around cities in the Indus River valley. These people were agrarian, settled, and peaceful, bearing all the makings of a true civilization, including cities, a written language, and specialization of labor. They were also polytheists, but with a strong inclination toward goddess-worship, which was typical of ancient peoples who lived close to the soil and its fertility and had to be attentive to the seasons (and their cyclical patterns). Such folks were, of course, no match for the fierce, aggressive, equestrian invaders, whose polytheism was dominated by male deities and was ritualistic in an intensely and sometimes brutally sacrificial way. This defenselessness would be especially true if, as some now contend, the fledgling Indus civilization was already in serious decline and perhaps had largely or completely collapsed before the Aryans arrived.

Whether at the peak of their powers or on the wane, the gentle Indus Valley people were, to put it briefly and mildly, subsumed by the invaders. Thus, although both India and Hinduism bear the name of this river valley and, by extension, that of its inhabitants, the country and its spiritual traditions actually came—at least early on—to reflect much more the preferences and practices of the Aryan invaders. Yet even as the vanquished were being incorporated into the emergent society of India, their beliefs and practices became assimilated into Hinduism, a development that may well have set in motion the dynamic—and dizzying—diversity that characterizes the faith to this very day.

The Caste System

The Aryan invaders apparently brought with them their own traditional social structure, a three-tiered, descending hierarchy of *Brahmins* (priests and scholars), *Kshatriyas* (rulers and warriors), and *Vaishyas* (merchants and farmers) that formed the basis of what would become the Indian caste system. (See Figure 2-1.) They then grafted onto this system the conquered Indus Valley people as the lowest social level, and called them *Shudras* (servants or commoners). The resulting four-tiered social structure affected almost every aspect of life, including diet, social interactions, dress, vocational choices, and selection of mate, the last of which is for Hindus traditionally a matter of family arrangement rather than individual choice. Each of the four constituent strata is called a *varna* ("caste," but literally, "color") and includes hundreds of *jati* ("sub-castes," but literally, "births"), which makes it a hopelessly complicated social system not only to foreigners, but to many Indians as well. Beneath these four tiers there also developed a social sub-stratum of outcastes or untouchables (variously dubbed *avarnas*, *candalas*, *dalits*, and *pariahs*), so-called because they performed such ritually unclean and defiling tasks as those that required the handling of dirt, excrement, blood, and the dead.

In fact, it is likely that India's entire caste system was originally based on vocations, and that at first it was possible for a person to change vocations—say, from worker to warrior—and therefore castes. But the system gradually became hereditary, dictating rather than merely reflecting vocations, and thus affording little chance for significant individual social mobility, especially upward. The upshot is that a Hindu in India has simply no way to work, earn, buy, or win his or her way into a higher caste within a lifetime. For example, one born a *Vaishya* can expect to die a *Vaishya*. The only possibility for positive social mobility is offered by

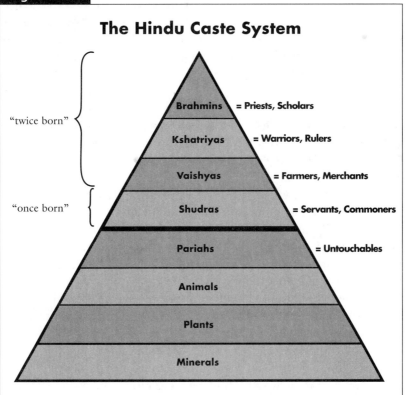

Figure 2-1

The Hindu Caste System

"twice born"

"once born"

Brahmins = Priests, Scholars

Kshatriyas = Warriors, Rulers

Vaishyas = Farmers, Merchants

Shudras = Servants, Commoners

Pariahs = Untouchables

Animals

Plants

Minerals

The sharp dividing line in this caste (*varna*) sytem is between the four human castes and the nearly sub-human untouchables. While there is a theoretical possibility of coming back as an animal, plant, or rock, hardly anyone expects that or worries about what the duty (*dharma*) of these three clearly sub-human castes might be. All you need to know is your own station in life and duties that accrue to it.

their doctrine of reincarnation (or transmigration) of spirits from physical form to physical form, a concept that will be discussed in detail below. Suffice for now to say that one can aspire to a higher status within a caste or a higher caste, but only in a future incarnation. Each caste has its specific *dharma*, a set of duties or expectations, the fulfillment of which builds good *karma*. This latter term refers to the merit earned from one's deeds, a sufficient accumulation of which can lead to a higher station in life next time around.

Thus the caste system of India differs in two important ways from the social class structure of the West: the lack of upward social mobility and the fact that the whole system is spiritually rather than economically based. In America, for example, people are lower class if they are poor and upper class if they are rich; and a poor person may aspire to be and actually become rich, and thus attain a higher social status through hard work. One can even rise from the lowest to the highest class literally overnight, just by hitting a big super lotto or a casino jackpot. In India, however, those at the top of the social heap are not the wealthy—who are more likely to be found among the political and business castes—but the most spiritual: the *brahmin* or priestly caste. One of the poorly paid automobile drivers that my wife and I hired in India was a *brahmin* who, on the job at least, was deferential to the mostly *kshatriya* and *vaishya* guides who established the day's itinerary and directed him where to go next. Likewise, one of these guides told us that the untouchables who by family tradition have managed the funeral fires over eons are extremely wealthy because of the huge tips that loved ones give them to do right by their dear departed.

Over the centuries and particularly in modern times, the entire caste system has become evermore complex with the emergence and proliferation of new vocations and their concomitant social roles, most of which have failed to fit neatly into the ancient schema. It also became increasingly oppressive, especially to those born outcastes. Efforts to reform or abolish the system have come and gone within Hinduism, the most notable being that of Mohandas ("Mahatma") Gandhi, who referred to the outcastes as *harijans* ("children of God") as a way of raising consciousness of their worth as human beings. In fact, the caste system was formally outlawed in the late 1940s, yet for many Hindus it still functions as an unofficial, but nonetheless binding arrangement.

Exceptions and Endurance

Not everyone in India fits into this structure, however. For example, persons who have done something terribly heinous or unclean can be ejected from their caste and thus become outcastes (rather than members of another caste). Some ascetic holy men effectively bypass the caste system of their own accord by renouncing, usually early in life, all social ties in order to pursue the ultimate spiritual liberation (*moksha*) in a focused, vigorous, even physically rigorous way. (See the discussion of the *sadhu* below.) Also, those of non-Hindu religions—like Jains, Sikhs, Zoroastrians, and Muslims—are similarly self-excluded from and often oblivious to the caste system and its exigencies. For example, a young Parsee (Zoroastrian) man from Mumbai (Bombay) in one of my world religions classes claimed that he had learned more from me about the caste system in an hour than he had from twenty years of living in India. That was less a tribute to my pedagogical skills than an admission that as a non-Hindu, he had been completely isolated from the whole institution of castes, and thus clueless about how they actually functioned. In modern times, even many Hindus have chosen to renounce or simply ignore their caste of birth in favor of living a more secular life. For the majority of India's more than one billion people, however, the caste system is as much a fact of life (and sometimes an onerous burden) as it was three thousand years ago.

The tenacity of this system and its attendant expectations have had a great impact upon Hinduism. In fact, it could be said that Hindu spiritual and religious beliefs and practices can be fully understood only within this framework. For the explicit goal of all pious Hindus is to rise through the social ranks incarnation after incarnation, achieving an ever-higher spiritual position in the grand scheme of things in pursuit of the spiritual liberation that is their goal. Most, however, envision this as an incredibly long process played out in an infinity of time, and thus have a deeply ingrained appreciation for delayed gratification in the spiritual realm and low expectations for any given lifetime.

Scripture and Beliefs

As already indicated, Hinduism is a complex and diverse religion. Those traits are certainly reflected in its scriptures, which are numerous and dissimilar in age, genre, substance, and vocabulary. They are also evident in its belief system, which includes both an Ultimate Reality and a myriad of deities that together have not only suggested but actually produced nearly every philosophical and theological "ism" that humanity has ever conceived with respect to religion. We turn first to the writings of Hinduism, which—with the possible exception of Buddhism—boasts the richest and most variegated body of scripture of any religion we know of, living or extinct.

Revealed and Remembered Writings

Unlike Christianity and Islam, each of which has only one canonical scripture, Hinduism has many beloved holy writings. The oldest and most venerable by far are the *Vedas*, many if not most of which date back to the non-literate Aryans, who had preserved them in oral form. The *Vedas* (literally "Wisdoms") are four in number, with each divided into four parts. They are mainly hymns and other literature related to ritual. Hindus put the *Vedas* in a class by themselves called *shruti* ("revealed"), and regard them as written by the gods and channeled through anonymous authors. So important are these *Vedas* that for some the only authentic definition of "Hindu" is "one who acknowledges the authority of the *Vedas*." That does not mean, however, that all Hindus consult or heed the *Vedas*. As is often the case in any of the world's religions, this scripture is probably far more revered among the faithful than actually read.

The *Vedas* offer us a wealth of information about the deities that were most important to the Aryans and thus to early Hinduism, chief among them Indra, the god of sky and thunder, and Agni, the god of fire, sacrifice, and hearth. We also find philosophy in the form of the mystical *Upanishads*, which were probably the work of ancient seers called *rishis*. Their mystical orientation and practice gave the *Upanishads* their recurring monistic theme: the fundamental spiritual unity of all things. Because early Hinduism was primarily ritualistic and polytheistic rather than philosophical and monistic in nature, these *Upanishads* appear to have been tacked on to the end of the ritualistic material rather as an afterthought and generally disregarded for centuries. Nonetheless, as we shall see shortly, they became more important, and even achieved an identity of their own apart from the *Vedas*, at a later stage of Hindu history in which ritual fell on hard times in the face of a burgeoning attention to mystical and philosophical pursuits.

Rounding out the basic scriptures of Hinduism is a set of scriptures referred to as *smriti* ("remembered" or "tradition"), a term that connotes a lower level of inspiration than the *shruti* of the Vedas. Yet these writings have been very important in the development of the Hindu religion, and one has even eclipsed the venerable *Vedas* in popularity, if not in status. Among these *smriti* is the epic poem, *Ramayana* ("Rama's Deeds"), which relates the adventures of King Rama, who is one of the *avatars* or incarnations of the god Vishnu. The equally epic and poetic *Mahabharata* ("The Great Bharata Tribal War"), with nearly 100,000 stanzas, is the longest poem ever written in any language and looks a bit like an ancient "soap opera from hell." For it tells the tale of a long and fierce family feud, fought on such a grand scale that even the gods become involved in the action. Eighteen chapters of the *Mahabharata* were eventually extracted and became the *Bhagavad Gita* ("The Lord's Song"), which—like the *Upanishads* before it—has taken on a life of its own. The *Gita* tells of Krishna, another of the manifestations of Vishnu, who appears incognito (despite his blue skin!) as the charioteer of Prince Arjuna, whom he engages in a philosophical conversation on a battlefield prior to an impending, internecine fray. Yet another set of *smriti* are the eighteen *Puranas*, which focus on the three gods who eventually became the focus of devotional (*bhakti*) Hinduism: Brahma, Vishnu (and his ten incarnations, but especially that as Krishna), and Shiva. Added to this interesting mix of scripture are numerous *Sutras* ("lessons," but literally "threads"), such as the philosophical *Brahma Sutra* and the erotic spiritual classic, the *Kama Sutra* ("Pleasure Lessons").

Given their diversity, it should come as no surprise that these writings have combined to generate and underwrite a very complicated belief system. Indeed, as was observed earlier, it is possible to find in Hinduism almost every conceivable theological and philosophical expression. (See Figure 2-2) We have, for example, a *polytheism* comprising 330 million gods and goddesses, a mind-boggling number whether taken literally or understood figuratively as connoting innumerability—something like "a zillion." That number is sometimes either reduced to a mere 33 million or inflated slightly to 333 million, again suggesting that it is probably not to be taken literally. We also find *henotheism*, the devotion to one among a number of deities, and the closely related *kathenotheism*, which is the serial worship of a single deity at a time, one after another. Henotheism and kathenotheism are sometimes called "theistic Hinduism" or even "monotheistic Hinduism," despite their lack of the kind of theological exclusivism—with one God and no others—found in truly monotheistic religions like Judaism and Islam. Hinduism does include a theme of divine unity, but in the form of *monism* rather than monotheism, for it posits a single, non-personal Absolute and Supreme Spirit called *Brahman* behind the many deities, each of whom represents a facet of the Ultimate Singularity.

The Trimurti

The three most prominent deities of popular Hindu devotion today are not those who figured so prominently in the ancient *Vedas*, but those featured in the later *Puranas*: Brahma, the Creator; Vishnu, the Preserver; and Shiva, the Destroyer. (See Figure 2-3.) For no apparent reason, the first of these has hardly any followers and only two temples dedicated to him, while the other two command large numbers of devotees and temples. Still, together they are called *Trimurti*, which means "the three forms" (with "of *Brahman*" understood). Rather than being a repudiation of the pantheon of 330 million deities mentioned above, the preeminence of these three

Figure 2-2

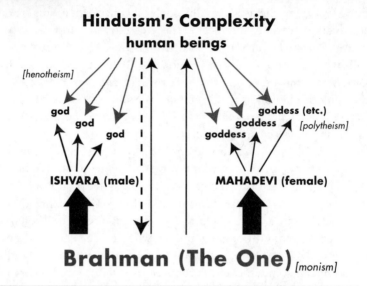

Hinduism's Complexity
human beings

[henotheism]

god
god
god

goddess (etc.)
goddess
goddess
[polytheism]

ISHVARA (male)

MAHADEVI (female)

Brahman (The One) [monism]

Note: The solid black lines represent emanations of the Ultimate as deities and humans. The broken line reflects mystical meditation as the way to direct experience of *It*. The gray lines represent devotional focus on this or that deity, each of which represent only a single personal facet of *Brahman*-as-manifested.

Hinduism manages to be monistic, polytheistic, and henotheistic all at the same time. It is monistic in that it teaches belief in *Brahman*, the Ultimate, Absolute, Supreme Spirit (not a god) that is the source of everything. It is polytheistic because this non-personal *Brahman* first emanates (gives off, exudes, radiates) two primal, personal manifestations: *Ishvara* (male "Lord") and *Mahadevi* (female "Great Goddess"), who in turn manifest as the millions of gods and goddesses, respectively. It is henotheistic because individual people (who are also manifestation of *Brahman*) may choose to worship one or another of these deities.

gods is more of a concession to popular piety on two grounds. For one thing, the Ultimate Reality, *Brahman*, is almost too abstract and non-personal to conceive of or discuss, much less relate to affectively. On the other hand, 330 million gods and goddesses constitute such a huge throng as to

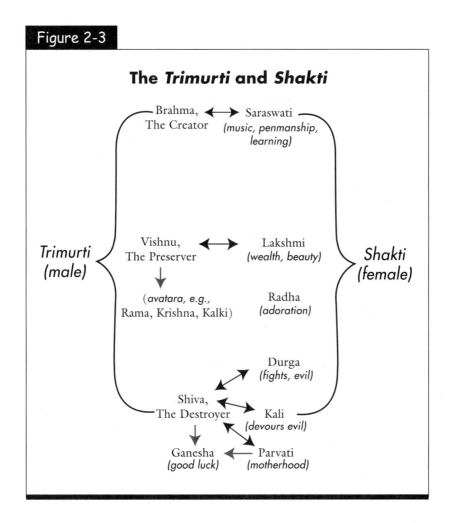

Figure 2-3

The *Trimurti* and *Shakti*

Brahma, The Creator ←→ Saraswati *(music, penmanship, learning)*

Vishnu, The Preserver ←→ Lakshmi *(wealth, beauty)*

(avatara, e.g., Rama, Krishna, Kalki) — Radha *(adoration)*

Durga *(fights, evil)*

Shiva, The Destroyer — Kali *(devours evil)*

Ganesha *(good luck)* ← Parvati *(motherhood)*

Trimurti (male)   *Shakti (female)*

be mind-numbing and overwhelming for the worshipper. A happy compromise, it seems, was to focus upon three gods and their relatively small number of mates, children, and other attendant deities as objects of devotion.

Brahma the Creator—not to be confused with *Brahman*, the Ultimate Supreme Spirit already mentioned and to be treated in earnest below—is responsible only for the creation of our world. (According to one Hindu visualization, the universe itself is a dream of Vishnu.) Like all the gods and goddesses, and unlike *Brahman*, Brahma is finite or mortal. He does live a very long time, however, something like 432 trillion human years, at which point he is replaced by a replica or clone, in a never-ending process that has been going on eternally. As long as Brahma's eyes are open, our world remains intact, going through various ages and stages of progress and decline. But even a long-lived god has to blink occasionally, and when Brahma does, our world is destroyed, with another coming into being when his eyes open again. As seen in artistic renderings of him, Brahma's primary symbols are his omnidirectional four heads (representing his omniscience) and the swan that he supposedly rides.

Vishnu is the Preserver, and is responsible for the continuity found in nature. That means that you have Vishnu to thank if you are able to recognize the tree in your yard as the same entity whether it is budding and flowering in spring, full of green leaves in summer, shedding brown ones in the fall, or barren of foliage in winter. Likewise, if you can identify yourself as the same person in the photos on successive driver's licenses over twenty or thirty years' time, despite the fact that they show you evermore fat, gray, and wrinkly, then again it is because of Vishnu's good graces. Vishnu's symbols are the conch shell, mace, and discus, and he is often pictured holding these and, in his fourth hand, the ever-popular symbol of spirituality, the lotus flower. He is also depicted as at least slightly androgynous, a gender-bender reminiscent of Michael Jackson or Boy George.

As gods go, Vishnu is a kind of chameleon, for he likes to enflesh himself from time to time as one or another *avatar*, which means "incarnation." Ten of these appear in any given world cycle (that is, between Brahma-blinks), some animal, some human, and two animal-human composites. The three most popular are: (1) King Rama, star of the aforementioned ancient epic *Ramayana*, which depicts the abduction and, after many adventures, the recovery of his queen; (2) Krishna, the blue-skinned, flute-playing darling of the pastoral maidens as well as the charioteer in the *Bhagavad Gita*; and (3) Kalki, the horse-headed, human-bodied tenth and final incarnation who will usher in the end of the present world's cycle and thus make way for a whole new one. Of these three *avatars*, the most popular by far is Krishna, whose devotees are fond of artistic portrayals of him as a child stealing butter or a youth cavorting with beautiful young female cowherds in pastoral settings, often playing his flute to charm them. Hinduism regards the Buddha as one of Vishnu's avatars, and thus, in a striking example of the faith's penchant for assimilation, refuses to recognize Buddhism as anything other than another of its own countless quirky sects.

The third of the Big Three deities is Shiva, who has by far the most interesting job description of any deity in any religion in world history. He is, of course, the Destroyer, which makes him responsible for the discontinuity in nature. He is therefore the god of disease, death, and decay. That does not make him evil in Hindus' eyes, however, for those three things are all a part of the natural process, and without them the new could not emerge. If not for death, for example, the possibility of reincarnation and ultimate spiritual liberation would be negated. So far so good in consistency; but here is where Shiva gets really interesting: he is also the god of dance, music, sex, and—of all things—asceticism, which almost invariably means giving up all physical comforts, including sex, for spiritual pursuits. Shiva's main symbols are the serpent, the trident, and the *linga*, which is a stylized phallus cradled in an equally stylized *yoni* (vagina), representing thereby his powers to oversee life as well as death. *Shivalingas* (as they are called) of various sizes and styles are found in temples and homes, are honored with pouring rituals and hanging devices that keep them moist, and are often covered or surrounded with offerings of flowers, fruit, or incense. Temples dedicated to Shiva often have an overtly phallic shape and occasionally an explicitly phallic name, and—unconsciously in the spirit of Freud, perhaps—are sometimes inhabited by serpents.

Shiva's most popular manifestation in art is as *Nataraja*, the royal dancer, who plays in one hand a drum that beats the rhythm of the universe, while in another, he holds the blazing fires that will destroy that same cosmos. In yet a third hand, he gestures reassurance, while the empty fourth hand points down to the dwarf *Avidya* ("Ignorance"), upon which Shiva has planted his pivotal foot, with the other suspended gracefully in the air. Shiva is not the only Indian deity portrayed as a dancer, but the chances are that if you see a dancing god, it will be Shiva. Another popular portrayal of him is as *Ardhanarishvara* (literally, "Lord Half-Woman"): male in physique and attire on the right side and female on the left.

As definitive as their job descriptions appear to be, each of these three gods—Brahma, Vishnu, and Shiva—is often claimed by his followers to possess all three powers: creating, sustaining, and destroying. Such an assertion results from what is called "holy exaggeration" (*mahatmya*) and is justified in part because all of the traits and powers of these three deities (as well as all the rest) derive finally from *Brahman*, and therefore cannot be the exclusive domain of any single god-manifestation. Each is but a form (*svarupa*) of which *Brahman* is the substance or essence (*svabhava*), and however imperfectly, that same essence infuses all three of the *Trimurti* (and presumably us as well) with all aspects of its infinite power. Thus Hindus are not prone to be exclusivists; and if they show monotheistic tendencies in their intense devotion to one particular deity, it is nearly always tempered intellectually by their recognition that each divine manifestation is best understood as complemented and reinforced by those worshiped by their neighbors. It is that very attitude that qualifies modern Hindus as henotheists, even if in their devotional fervor they sometimes sound like monotheists.

Shakti and Other Pop Devas

The gods *(devas)* of the *Trimurti* have their corresponding female consorts or mates. These are called *Shakti*, a collective name for the feminine divine principle that is said to reflect the power of *Brahman*. Brahma's partner is Saraswati, goddess of music and penmanship, and thus the patron deity of school children. Often depicted playing a sitar (an Indian lute) and riding her consort's swan, she is celebrated in school festivals all over India. Vishnu's mate is Lakshmi (or Laxmi), gentle goddess of fertility, wealth, beauty, and luck. She is usually pictured as having gold coins cascading from the palms of her hands, and during the annual festival of Diwali, people keep their houses clean and leave their doors unlocked and open so that she may easily enter and bless them. Vishnu's most popular *avatar*, Krishna, has the playful Radha as his favorite, and the two are sometimes depicted in a standing embrace, or sharing the seat of a swing, or riding a giant bird in flight. Shiva, being the god of sexuality, has multiple mates. First there is the sweet, gentle, and lovely Parvati, mother of Shiva's children. Then there is the fearsome Durga, armed with sundry weapons, wearing a blood-red dress, and riding a lion or tiger as a warrior into battle against evil. Finally, there is the jet-black-skinned, bloody-tongued, and utterly terrifying Kali, a devourer of evil bedecked with human skulls and often shown holding the severed head of a man and standing upon a prone (and sexually aroused) Shiva. Though very different in appearance and disposition, these three are widely regarded as one and the same goddess (*Shakti* or *Mahadevi*), and sometimes as manifestations of the feminine side of Shiva himself.

Rounding out the list of most popular traditional deities in India today are Ganesha (also known as Ganapati) and Hanuman, both of whom bear the likenesses of animals. Ganesha (which the modern Hindi language shortens to Ganesh) is the elephant-headed son of Shiva, a remover of obstacles, and therefore the god of good fortune. He is the patron saint of business people, and can be found in little shrines overlooking the cash registers in most traditional Indian shops. In temples dedicated to other deities, a Ganesha shrine is often the first stop just inside the entrance, for prayers to him are believed to facilitate or enhance subsequent ones to all other deities. Hanuman is the monkey general who assisted King Rama in the rescue of his kidnapped wife in the classical epic *Ramayana*, and was ostensibly promoted to the status of god for his successful efforts. He is therefore forever associated with Rama, Krishna, and the god they embody, Vishnu, and is a model of both devotion and protection against evil. Neither Ganesha nor Hanuman has generated a distinct sect of followers, yet both are held in esteem by all pious Hindus.

Still another deity, the goddess Ganga, belongs in a category all her own. She is most often associated with Shiva, but she is also regarded as a consort of Brahma and Vishnu as well. She is so highly valued for her powers of purification that the river in northern India named after her, the Ganga or Ganges, is the most sacred in the entire country, and the holiest Hindu city, Varanasi (also known as Banaras, Benares, and Kashi) sits on her banks. Ironically, the Ganges is chemically one of the most polluted rivers in the world. In places, it literally bubbles with methane generated by untreated sewage dumped into it; and on top of that, whole or partial decomposing dead bodies of humans or animals can occasionally be seen floating downstream. But to the eyes of Hindu faith, the Ganges is absolutely pure, and the throngs of people daily frequenting— and during festivals, thronging—her banks use her waters for bathing, drinking, cooking, and clothes washing, ostensibly without harm. Some even do this downstream of the relentless funeral fires, where the ashes of the newly cremated dead are thrown into her waters to hasten the liberation of the recently departed souls. The guide in Varanasi who took my wife and me on an idyllic morning rowboat ride on the surprisingly (and deceptively) pleasant Ganges is a case in point. He was nearly thirty at the time, but looked a good ten years younger, and he swore that his youthful appearance was due to the fact that, having always lived in Varanasi, he had drunk the water of Mother Ganga every day of his life. A highly educated and very practical young man, however, he was careful to warn us visitors to drink only bottled water, since that same holy water would likely kill anyone not used to it.

Perhaps the most unusual of all the objects of popular devotion is Sai Baba, a modern Indian saint who died in 1918, and whose image is often displayed next to the more venerable deities in homes, shops, and even temples in India. When I feigned ignorance and asked one shop-keeper in Agra, the city of the Taj Mahal, who that was in the photo taped to his display case, he answered quite proudly and reverently, "He is our god!" Sai Baba is not to be confused, however, with the still-living Satya Sai Baba (born in 1926), another widely acclaimed and controversial Indian holy man best known for his alleged miraculous ability to produce large quantities of holy dust from his bare hands. So deeply revered is this latter Sai Baba that within a decade of his eventual death he will certainly be promoted—informally, since there is no institutional authority or mechanism for doing so—to the status of deity. Indeed, some of his followers already worship him as a living god.

Brahman, the Elusive Essence

The kind of philosophy found in the *Upanishads* is *monism*. Monism is what philosophers call a *metaphysics*, which is to say, a systematic view of what constitutes reality. Western philosophies have generally produced four kinds of metaphysics: (1) *materialistic monism*, which says that reality is basically and essentially *matter*; (2) *idealistic monism*, which says that reality is essentially *Mind* or *Spirit*; (3) *dualism*, which says that what constitutes reality is the interplay between *matter* and *mind-spirit*; and (4) *pluralism*, which claims that reality is made up of not just one or two sorts of things, but of a multiplicity of constituent elements—though pluralists rarely agree on what or how many there are. Eastern religions, however, typically reflect an altogether different metaphysics, one that is closest to idealistic monism. It might better be called a *neutral monism*, however, since it claims that the Ultimate Reality is neither matter certainly *nor* mind exactly (though it may manifest as either), but an indescribable, indeed inconceivable Supreme Something.

Formally speaking, as we shall see in the chapters that follow, all the major Eastern philosophies point to this same, or at least a strikingly similar, Ultimate. Buddhism calls It—rather than He or She—*Shunyata* ("Emptiness," though with a surprisingly positive spin, as we shall see in the next chapter). Taoists dub It *Tao* ("Way"), though the most famous Taoist scripture, the *Tao Te Ching*, asserts that It is really nameless and unnamable. When Hindus refer to It as *Brahman*, the final "n" denotes a neuter gender and thus distinguishes this Absolute not only from the male god, *Brahma*, but from any and all of the other 330 million deities as well. Like *Shunyata* and *Tao*, *Brahman* is not God or even *a* god, but merely the Supreme, the Ultimate, the Absolute, the Source, the One, the All. Hindus sometimes call it "God" and "Supreme Being," but largely in deference to Westerners who are used to thinking about

Ultimacy in such terms. *Brahman*, however, is much closer to Being-Itself than *a* being, and as such doesn't so much exist as just incorporate "is-ness."

Because Hinduism's philosophy is monistic rather than dualistic, this *Brahman* cannot be thought of as an Other above and beyond the cosmos, that is, transcendent with respect to Its being or nature. Rather, in good Eastern fashion, *Brahman* is profoundly *immanent* ("indwelling") or infused in nature, including human nature, in such a way that all things share the very same spiritual essence. To be sure, *Brahman* can be described as transcendent, but *only* in the weaker sense of being hidden and "beyond" our ordinary powers of perception and conception; for the fact of the matter is that, metaphysically speaking, *Brahman* is really and truly immanent, whether or not we see or comprehend it. It is upon the recognition of the presence of *Brahman* within human nature, however, that Hindu spirituality is built. *Brahman* is not just *at* an individual's spiritual center but serves *as* that center. It is innate and permanent: it cannot come or go. It is this recognition of the inherent divinity of human beings that sets the stage for a supremely mystical (that is, introverted and unitive) spirituality.

Hinduism recognizes two aspects of *Brahman*. First, there is *Brahman nirguna*, which literally means "without qualities" or "lacking attributes." This is the mysterious depth of *Brahman*, which may be pictured as an infinite Spiritual Sea, shoreless and unfathomable. (See 2-4.) About this most profound level of the Ultimate, we are clueless; we can know and say nothing accurate or worthwhile. We had best remain silent, as we would have to if we were in a rowboat in the middle of the Atlantic Ocean and asked to describe its bottom on the basis of our unaided vision. No adjective used to identify or describe qualities or attributes of *Brahman* will suffice, because even the most well intended and seemingly complimentary one will be inadequate and at best will disparage the Ultimate with faint praise. If, for example, I try to honor *Brahman* as "great," I have just used an honorific that I might apply to a tasty pizza, and thus have inadvertently put the Absolute on a par with a conglomeration of pepperoni, cheese, and bread. Yet, *Brahman* has another, more accessible aspect called *Brahman saguna*, which means "with qualities" or "possessing attributes." That aspect of Brahman is comparable to the *surface* of the sea, about which we can observe and utter some things, though they will be necessarily and intrinsically superficial.

Hinduism in fact recommends that if one is to speak about *Brahman* at all, it is best to do so obliquely, by using *neti neti* language, the negative approach of saying "not this, not that"—a strategy sometimes used

Figure 2-4

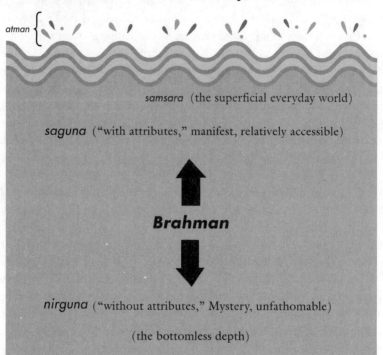

Brahman as a Great Spiritual Sea

atman {

samsara (the superficial everyday world)

saguna ("with attributes," manifest, relatively accessible)

Brahman

nirguna ("without attributes," Mystery, unfathomable)

(the bottomless depth)

Brahman is metaphorically and aptly called the great Spiritual Sea. With an actual ocean, what goes on at its depths is utterly inaccessible to a typical person staring over the rail of a boat. This is even more true of *Brahman*, which—being infinite—has no bottom . . . or shore, for that matter. Its depths remain a mystery. With unaided senses, a seafarer may be able to observe and describe some things about an ocean being sailed, but only with respect to its surface. So it is with *Brahman*, whose surface is none other than the world of *samsara*, whose ever-changing elements and events are represented in the diagram as churning ocean waves. Waves are real, all right. They can engulf a ship, in fact. Yet they are not substantial: you can't take one home in a bottle, for example. They are simply the playfulness of the ocean's surface and superficial, therefore, by definition.

in Christian theology and called the *via negativa*. In English, that would mean using "in-" and "un-" words, like infinite, invisible, inaudible, intangible, unimaginable, unspeakable, unbounded, and (my favorite because of its depth reference) unfathomable. When *Brahman* does begin to manifest Itself as *saguna* (Again, see Figure 2-4.), it is in both personal and non-personal forms. One of its principal personal forms is *Ishvara*, which literally means "Lord." Another is *Mahadevi* ("Great Goddess," a virtual synonym with *Shakti*). These two constitute what one might think of as the two primordial personal faces of *Brahman*, one male and one female; and they in turn diffract, as it were, into the 330 million specific personifications that are the gods and goddesses. Indeed, the sun's pure white light that produces a full spectrum of colors when passed through a prism is a good analogy for Brahman's generation of multiple forms (deities and all existing beings and things) when its spiritual energy passes through the dense medium of *samsara*.

Atman, the Incarnate Infinite

The individual inner spiritual energy-essence of everyone and everything—what Western religions would call the "soul" or "spirit"—Hindus call *atman*. With respect to humans, *atman* is the deep Self, in contrast to the ego-self. There are several remarkable things about this *atman*, not the least of which is that, like *Brahman*, it is neuter and non-personal. Furthermore, it is not merely immortal, but indeed eternal, having always existed in one form or another. It is also recyclable, for Hindus believe not only in reincarnation, which would allow for successive human embodiments of an *atman*, but *transmigration*, which holds that theoretically the *atman* may assume any form: human, animal, vegetable, or mineral. In truth, however, most Hindus do not pay much attention to the spiritual life of bees, bushes, or boulders—or even bovines, since cows are venerated and protected as sacred in India, but not really worshipped. The fact of the matter is that to the Hindu mind all animate beings and inanimate things are sacred precisely because they embody *atman*. By far Hinduism's most radical (and to Western minds outrageous) claim about *atman*, however, is that it is none other than *Brahman*, the Absolute Ultimate. *Atman* is not in the image and likeness of *Brahman*, mind you, nor merely similar in appearance or substance, but one and the same as *Brahman*.

The identity of *atman* and *Brahman* has some interesting implications. One of several nicknames for *Brahman*, for example, is the Sanskrit word

Tat, which means simply "That" or "That One." A Hindu may proudly assert "*Tat tvam asi*," which means "That is you" (or, more precisely, "That you are"), a bold declaration of the hearer's unity with *Brahman*. They may also declare on their own behalf *aham Brahmasmi*—that is, "I am *Brahman*." Of course, such a seemingly impious and arrogant assertion really makes sense only in a truly monistic framework, in which all is One; or as one modern sage put it: "I am That. You are That. All this is That. And That's all there is." No wonder, then, Hindus routinely greet one another with a bow, hands palm-to-palm and pointed toward one another in a gesture of prayer, and utter the word *Namaste* or *Namaskar*, both of which mean "I reverently acknowledge the divine in you."

An equivalent claim would be unthinkable in Western religions. Imagine, for example, someone announcing "I am God" in either a Jewish synagogue or a mainline Christian church service. The congregation would probably want to get that person professional psychiatric help. Or consider the consequences of proclaiming "I am Allah" in a Muslim mosque at a Friday prayer service. You would be lucky to make it to the door unscathed—or even alive in some parts of the world. Declare the equivalent in a Hindu temple, however, and folks would fault you only for stating the obvious, and perhaps wonder why you bothered. "So what's your point?" they might ask.

To return to our marine imagery, one might say that *atman* is a drop in the Spiritual Sea, which after all is but the sum of its drops. Conversely, the drop is identical to the ocean. For those who might wonder where all the extra "drops" may have come from that are enfleshed in the four billion additonal human bodies that populate the earth today compared with a mere half century ago, two things may be said. First, many plants and animals that once inhabited the earth have died, and some species have disappeared altogether, thus freeing up countless *atmans* to be embodied elsewhere and elsewhen. Second, and more to the point, the Spiritual Sea is truly infinite, and therefore has an infinite number of drops—far more than enough to go around, both now and in the future.

Samsara, Cycles, and Superficiality

Quite naturally, Hindus are far more interested in the *atmans* that are currently in circulation than those that are not, and are especially concerned with their own. These are embodied in the everyday world, which is called *samsara*, a word that is also used to designate the reincarnation or transmigration process that recycles *atman*. In other words, *samsara* connotes not only the nearly endless cycles of rebirths, lives, and deaths, but also the temporal setting in which these are played out—the process *and* the place, as it were. *Samsara* may thus be thought of as the moving and sometimes roiling surface of the ocean, the waves that kick up the droplets (little *atmans* all), sometimes repeatedly. (See Figure 2-4.) These droplets appear to be individuals that are separate from the ocean, at least for a time. But appearance it is, for it should be obvious to even a casual observer of the surf that the drops, waves, and ocean are all parts of the same reality. So it is with *atman, samsara*, and *Brahman*. As in any good monistic system, everything must finally be one and the same.

So both the surface motion of the sea (*Brahman*) and the recurring but mistaken appearance of the droplet (*atman*) as a separate entity constitute *samsara*. As such, both are called *maya*. Often translated as "illusion," *maya* does not mean that our everyday (what philosophers call *conditional* or *phenomenal*) reality is unreal, but rather that it is *insubstantial*, by which they mean *not enduring*. In an actual ocean, a wave is certainly real. It can knock you down, drag you out to sea, and even drown you. But you still cannot bring a wave home in a bottle, because it is not a substantial thing. It is instead a movement or process—something the surface *does* rather than something that actually *is*. The same is true of everyday reality: it is real in the sense of being a process, but finally insubstantial. The only "illusion" involved, then, is our mistaking it for something substantial and apart, when the fact of the matter is that there is only one "thing" that is truly substantial: the eternal, unchanging *Brahman*. The cause of such an illusion is *avidya*—that is, our ignorance of our real essence as *atman*, our incomprehension of our profound oneness with the One, and thus our not-so-blissful unawareness of our true identity *as* the Sea that is Brahman.

In the same vein, *samsara* is also called *lila* ("frivolity" or "play"), which is to say superficial and a mere "going through the motions," a kind of role-playing that is fun and entertaining, perhaps, but finally pointless. This is the frivolity one sees in children at play, who become cops, robbers, cowboys, Indians, and space cadets, and take their roles very seriously, as though they really were these characters. We may smile at them and say, "How silly and cute!" Hindu philosophy, however, says that about the personal, vocational, and social roles we all assume, perform, and take so seriously in life, but which are finally no more meaningful or substantial than what the little ones are doing at play. It's all *lila*.

All of this, of course, flies in the face of what we in the West regard as substantial. We regard things in our world like chairs as substantial because we can trust them to support the weight of our bodies. In other words, we take the material world to be substantial. From a typically Hindu (Eastern) perspective, however, the material world is the reflection of a transitory process and therefore insubstantial. (Oddly enough, Western physics of the last half century or so has arrived at much the same conclusion, as when it insists that atoms, which were formerly envisioned as built of tiny particles, are more like clusters or waves of energy.) By contrast, the Ultimate Reality that we in the West—at least the majority of us still living in the mechanistic-materialistic world of Newton— regard as insubstantial because it is purely (and *merely*) spiritual, they see as enduring and indestructible and therefore the most substantial entity imaginable.

Perhaps another metaphor will help to clarify the Hindu view of *samsara* as *maya* and *lila*. Our position relative to *samsara* (the everyday world and our endless recyclings into it) is not unlike that of the hamster in a cage. The hapless little animal has a wheel for exercise, but it takes him nowhere and produces nothing really. Yet the indefatigable runner always has a look of intensity, earnestness, and determination on his furry little face, as if he were doing something useful or important. But no progress is made and nothing is accomplished. The hamster simply tires out, gets off the wheel, and rests for a while; then awakes and goes through the same seemingly pointless routine again . . . and again . . . and again. For Hinduism, we humans are that hamster; and our "wheel" is a treadmill called "life." Our delusion is that all of our efforts are yielding something worthwhile or durable—that we are getting somewhere. In fact, our busyness is no more productive than that of the rodent on the rotating wheel. We simply tire ourselves out (grow old) and get off the wheel (die) for a rest from time to time . . . only to get back on and do it all over again (reincarnation).

Getting Off the Treadmill

What Hinduism promises its adherents is that it is possible to get off the treadmill once and for all time—or to use the other analogy, for the drop to return to the oceanic depth (of the Absolute) so that its identity with that figurative Spiritual Sea is unambiguous. This desired state of affairs is called *moksha*, which means "liberation" or "release." What are we liberated or released from? First, the *avidya* (ignorance) of our true natures and of reality as a whole that has helped to keep us suspended like a drop or busy like a hamster; and second, from our bondage to *samsara*. But *moksha* also frees us from the other thing that has kept us "up in the air" or "on the wheel" of *samsara*: our *karma*.

Karma is one of those many Sanskrit words that have several layers of meaning. Its most basic definition is "deed," but it also means the unavoidable spiritual consequences that accrue to the doer of any deed. *Karma* guarantees that no good deed will go unrewarded nor any evil deed unpunished, though it may take one or more future lifetimes for justice to be realized. (A child who dies in a house fire, for example, may well have been an arsonist in a previous life.) Finally, *karma* connotes the spiritual law (*not* an overseeing deity) that ensures that it all balances out in the long run. The overall sense of *karma*, then, is that sooner or later "What goes around comes around." Or, in the imagery of the Christian New Testament, in the long run "You reap what you sow."

This idea of *karma* is bound up in Hinduism with the notion of *dharma* or duty; and *dharma* is determined largely by one's caste and gender. As we have seen, each caste has certain expectations for its men and women that are different from the rules and demands of the other castes. Every member of every caste learns these in childhood from the family and society by simple acculturation, quite as easily and naturally as people everywhere learn to understand and speak their native languages. Once one's *dharma* is absorbed and understood, merely *doing* what it calls for will build good *karma*.

In Hinduism, the belief in transmigration of a spiritual essence (*atman* or "soul") allows the law of *karma* time to work. This is very different from the common notion among Westerners who have begun to entertain the possibility of reincarnation, for many of them presume that the experience of successive lifetimes is all about "learning lessons." Now that may be true, but it is certainly not the view of those who have longest believed in multiple lifecycles. For Hindus, reincarnation does not exist for the purpose of learning lessons, but involves doing one's duty in the present circumstances in order to move in the great chain of being toward oneness with the One. To be sure, ignorance is overcome in the process; but that happens via a self-realization experienced within a single capstone lifetime, rather than through an accumulation of little insights along the way. It is for that reason that Hindus show no interest in learning about—much less *from*—past lives. It simply does not matter whether one is a Vaishya because of having failed as a Kshatriya or succeeded as a Shudra in a past life. Whether one ascended or descended to his or her present rank, what's done is done. The only thing that really matters is that you know where you now are in the scheme of things, and what specific expectations your present position or rank entails. For it is in this present context that you are to build good *karma* by doing your *dharma*, and thereby—perhaps—find the bliss of *moksha* or, failing that, move a step closer to it.

Historical Developments

The mind-boggling complexity of Hinduism is due in large part to its tremendous longevity and capacity for assimilation. Quite simply, it has been around so long that virtually every conceivable belief and practice has arisen and been added to the mix, and the result often appears to Hindus as well as non-Hindus as a clutter, if not complete chaos. Fortunately, however, Hindu history has unfolded in a definite pattern in which specific types of religious orientation and practice arose and dominated for various periods of time. These religious types are usually seen to be three in number and are called *margas* ("paths"). Aside from the important role they play within Hinduism itself, they are extremely useful to outsiders trying to come to grips not only with the history of that religion, but with its rich diversity as well. (See Figure 2-5.) They will help us understand not only the origins of the polytheistic, monistic, and henotheistic beliefs reviewed above, but the surprisingly comfortable way in which such divergent beliefs systems apparently coexist in a single religion.

Three Margas ... or Four (or Five) Yogas?

The three distinct spiritual *margas* ("paths") recognized by most Hindus are most clearly articulated in the devotional classic, the *Bhagavad Gita*, but certainly predate that scripture. The first, *karma marga* ("the way of the deed") originally referred to the *Brahmana* ("priestly") tradition of ritual sacrifice to the gods, but was later extended to include ethical action and duty (*dharma*) as well. The second, *jnana marga* ("the way of insight"), entails the intellectual understanding of scriptures and doctrine and the divine truth they contain, but also includes the employment of the non-rational, mystical capacities of the mind to transcend its own limits. The third, *bhakti marga* ("the way of the heart"), focuses on faith or love, and invariably involves devotion directed toward one or another personal deity (usually Vishnu, Shiva, or one of the *Shakti*). Implicit in the recognition of these *margas*—as it were, religion of the *hands*, *head*, and *heart*, respectively—is the understanding that people will be drawn to different spiritual paths depending

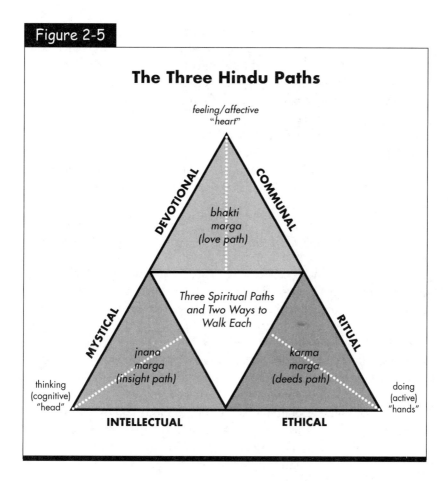

Figure 2-5

The Three Hindu Paths

feeling/affective
"heart"

DEVOTIONAL

COMMUNAL

bhakti
marga
(love path)

MYSTICAL

RITUAL

Three Spiritual Paths
and Two Ways to
Walk Each

jnana
marga
(insight path)

karma
marga
(deeds path)

thinking
(cognitive)
"head"

doing
(active)
"hands"

INTELLECTUAL

ETHICAL

on their individual dispositions or natures. Each of these paths thus has its own integrity and validity, and none of them is regarded as better than the others, much less final.

Other Hindus assert that rather than three *margas*, we should recognize four *yogas*: *karma yoga, bhakti yoga, jnana yoga,* and *raja yoga.* The word *yoga* connotes a spiritual discipline or practice, but literally means "yoke"—a reference to the desire to connect (or reconnect, actually) the individual *atman* with the universal *Brahman.* Advocates of the *yoga* (as opposed to the *marga*) typology arrive at the number four by removing mysticism from the umbrella of *jnana*, and designating it as a separate and distinct style, *raja yoga* ("the royal discipline"). There are perhaps good reasons for doing this. For one thing, though all forms of Eastern mysticism originate in the mind, they use the intellect in ways quite foreign to rationality, and eventually abandon or transcend it in favor of pure, unitive experience, which they further claim to be incomprehensible in ordinary ways. Second, as the regal name of this particular *yoga* suggests, Hindus grant mysticism an extra measure of prestige and respect that would seem to make a new category of spiritual endeavor almost a necessity. Finally, this alternate *yoga* typology comports with Hinduism's fascination with the number four: four castes, four vedas (each in four parts), four life goals, and four stages of life.

Missing from this list of *yogas* is the one with which Westerners are most likely to be familiar. What is widely taught in community and fitness centers and even churches is what is known in India as *hatha yoga*, a physical discipline designed to prepare one physically for the ultimate realization of *raja yoga*. In other words, *hatha yoga* is the elementary level of what is ultimately a spiritual discipline. It is based on the idea that seven spirit-centers called *chakras* are located along the spine from the cranium to the base of the spine: crown, brow, throat, heart, solar plexus, visceral-genital, and root (though these are known by a variety of names). Each center is a locus of spiritual energy that affects the organs immediately surrounding it. In addition, some *yogis* (practitioners) claim that an additional source of potential spiritual energy called *kundalini*, often pictured as a coiled serpent or spring, is located at the base of the spine. The purpose of *hatha yoga* is to release these energies and bring them into alignment, thereby facilitating the journey toward realizing true, mystical *raja yoga*, which links *atman* (one's individual spiritual essence) to *Brahman* (the Absolute Spirit). Ideally, the *kundalini* would also be uncoiled, thus releasing its power to flow up the spine and connect the *chakras* from bottom to top.

Whether there are three, four, or (counting *hatha*) five spiritual disciplines, and whether they are best thought of as *margas* or *yogas*, depends on which Hindu practitioner or pundit you care to believe. Most prevalent, however, seems to be the three-*marga* system, and for our purposes it proves to be the most useful. For Hindu history seems to have fallen into three periods thus far; and these correspond to the three *margas*, each of which characterizes a particular era. (See Figure 2-6.) All of this helps to explain the earlier comment about the changing displays in the front window of that ancient "shop." An examination of successive historical periods and their distinguishing characteristics is a useful way of sorting out its inventory, including the polytheism, monism, and henotheism—and the scriptures and practices reflecting and supporting them—that we encountered in the preceding section of this chapter.

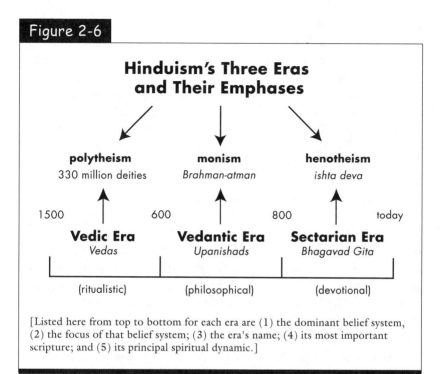

Figure 2-6

Hinduism's Three Eras and Their Emphases

polytheism	monism	henotheism
330 million deities	Brahman-atman	ishta deva

1500	600	800	today
Vedic Era	**Vedantic Era**	**Sectarian Era**	
Vedas	Upanishads	Bhagavad Gita	

(ritualistic)   (philosophical)   (devotional)

[Listed here from top to bottom for each era are (1) the dominant belief system, (2) the focus of that belief system; (3) the era's name; (4) its most important scripture; and (5) its principal spiritual dynamic.]

...and Three Periods

The first period of Hindu history ran roughly from 1500 to 600 BCE, and is called the Vedic Era after the *Vedas*, the most ancient of Hindu scriptures. Both these scriptures and this period were heavily polytheistic, ritualistic, and sacrificial in focus, largely because of the tremendous impact of Aryan religion at this early stage of Hinduism. This time span of nearly a millennium thus clearly reflects a *karma marga* type of religion. It is this tradition that attests 330 million gods and goddesses and names as chief among them Indra, the sky-thunder god; Agni, the god of fire (and therefore of sacrifices and the hearth); and Varuna, god of cosmic order (an eternal principle called *Rita*). That these dominant deities were male also bespeaks Aryan influence.

Around 600 BCE, the dynamic of Hinduism began to shift to monism—that is, the belief in one Ultimate Absolute Reality, *Brahman*—and to the kind of mystical philosophy that would both articulate and facilitate the experience of that One. This era, which has a decidedly philosophical (*jnana marga*) emphasis, lasted until about 800 CE.

During this time the *Upanishads*—which had been contained in the venerable *Vedas*, but as appendices seemingly tacked on as an afterthought—rose to prominence as the key scriptures. Because of their philosophical character, they had hitherto been downplayed or ignored; now they gained a much higher status. Indeed, whereas the *Upanishads* originally had been called *Vedanta* ("end of the *Vedas*") because of their placement and lowly status, that appellation now came to connote the completion, culmination, or capstone of those most ancient scriptures. And that term, *Vedanta*, with its positive new spin, gives this period its name: the Vedantic Period. It might as aptly be called the Upanishadic Period, since *Vedanta* and *Upanishads* are synonymous.

To say that Hinduism's dynamic shifted in this period does not necessarily mean that a new mystical-philosophical emphasis suddenly became popular. In whatever religion they have appeared, philosophy and mysticism have been minority expressions; and that holds true even in Hinduism, where these endeavors seem to have been appreciated and developed to the highest degree. Since history rarely records the lives of the masses, we can say only that while not demonstrable, it is likely that the polytheistic and ritualistic Vedic religion remained very popular during this period. But Hindu intellectuals and mystics who had lost interest in that tradition came to envision a single Ultimate Reality and produced a monistic philosophy to account for it.

The third period runs from about 1000 CE to the present. It is sometimes subdivided into medieval and modern phases, but because of the consistency of the religious type throughout, it may be considered as a whole and called the Sectarian Era. That name reflects the fact that this period has been dominated religiously by henotheism (the commitment to one deity among many) and devotionalism (*bhakti marga*), and thus has seen the rise of unorganized and unstructured but nonetheless distinct and influential sects that love and worship particular gods and goddesses. Fortunately (and perhaps mercifully) for everyone concerned, the number of deities was whittled down from millions to a relative few—mainly the *Trimurti* and their consorts, the *Shakti*, all of whom have been treated in detail above. As we have already seen, it is usually but not always the case that a person relates to one of them as his or her *ishta deva* (personal deity). The scripture that has best captured the tone of this period is the aforementioned *Bhagavad Gita* (*Song of the Lord*), which presents Lord Krishna, an *avatar* (incarnation) of the god Vishnu, as the appropriate object of faith and devotion. In fact, some Hindu scholars argue that for all practical purposes, the *Bhagavad Gita* has now eclipsed the venerable *Vedas*, not only for the devotees of Vishnu and his incarnations, but (because of its decidedly *bhakti* tone) for followers of other deities as well.

It is worth remembering, however, that Hinduism never discards or otherwise rids itself of anything, but rather manages to incorporate in some way virtually everything it has ever acquired. Earlier I compared Hinduism to an antique store or street market; let me now use a more dynamic and thus more appropriate image. Let's think of Hinduism today as a slowly cooking stew, in which the oldest ingredients from the Vedic era have long since settled to the bottom of the pot. Those of the Vedantic period are suspended the middle, leaving the most recent and still prevailing devotional emphasis of the millennium-old Sectarian Period close to the surface. All of these constitute and flavor the stew, though what is on the surface is most visible and probably provides most of the flavor to those who sample it. As a result, travelers to India today will encounter the dominant Hindu devotionalism (*bhakti*) in public expressions of adoration of this or that god or goddess at the many temples. They will surely see the buying and selling of small statues and pictures of the various deities and other devotional paraphernalia, and may well experience the excitement of one or more of the many festivals and pilgrimages dedicated to this or that god or goddess. They might have to search a bit to find a real *pundit* (scholar) of the philosophical (*jnana*) tradition, or priests (*brahmanas*) chanting the ancient *Vedas* in the performance of a traditional Vedic ceremony (*karma marga*). The diligent seeker of such expressions would probably not be disappointed, however, for like everything else in Hinduism, they can be found somewhere in that ever-simmering pot.

Of the three historic types of Hinduism—the priestly polytheistic-ritualistic Vedic, the mystically monistic-philosophical Vedantic, and the piously henotheistic-devotional Sectarian—it is the mystical and philosophical that has had the most impact upon the West and is therefore most likely to contribute to Western spirituality (including Christian) in the future. Westerners are not likely to buy into a polytheism with a huge pantheon of foreign deities that require ritual sacrifices. (Some might justifiably argue that whatever deep human need polytheism satisfies is currently filled for many Americans by their worship of movie and TV stars, musical idols, sports icons, and other celebrities.) Nor are they likely to embrace a henotheism that introduces a smaller number of divinities from which to choose. But many Westerners have shown considerable interest in the practice of the mystically-based Hindu discipline of yoga, and in the ideas that underpin it. Most American bookstores of any size stock a variety of translations of the philosophical *Upanishads*; certain Sanskrit philosophical terms—like *karma* and *yoga*—have found a permanent place in Western vocabularies; and such Eastern ideas as reincarnation are increasingly finding favor in America and other Christian-dominated cultures.

Three Great Philosophers

Hinduism embraces six major philosophical traditions, called *darshanas* ("viewpoints"). By far the most influential and revered among philosophers and other scholars is the Vedanta, which, like the second historical period noted above, was named after the *Upanishads* (aka *Vedanta*). As its name suggests, the Vedantic tradition drew upon that most philosophical of ancient Hindu scriptures as its chief source of inspiration. But it also employed the *Brahma Sutra* (also called *Vedanta Sutra*), which was a first or second century BCE aphoristic distillation of the *Upanishads* around the notion of *Brahman* (rather than the god Brahma, its title notwithstanding). To a lesser extent, the Vedanta tradition also managed to derive inspiration from the devotional *Bhagavad Gita*, which does indeed have its philosophical moments. All of these scriptures assert *Brahman* as the fundamental reality, but philosophically they remain highly diverse, and thus allow for a variety of interpretations concerning the nature of *Brahman* and its relation to the world and individual selves. In fact the Vedanta tradition developed three great schools: (1) Advaita, whose leading light by far was Shankara; (2) Vishishtadvaita, proposed and promoted by Ramanuja; and (3) Dvaita, founded by Madhva.

Shankara (788–820 CE) is far and away the best-known and among the intelligentsia of India the most influential—not only of the Vedantists, but indeed of all Indian philosophers; accordingly, he has often been dubbed "the Aquinas of Hinduism." Indeed, most of what has been said above about common Hindu belief in *Brahman, atman, samsara, karma, moksha,* and related concepts bears his imprint, and so need not be repeated in detail here. Suffice it to say that in his thought and that of the Advaita school he founded one finds the highest expression of monism. For Shankara declared that *Brahman* alone is ultimately real and without (*a-*) any duality (*dvaita*). (To emphasize his point, Shankara sometimes added the word *Kevala*, which means "Absolute," to *Advaita*.) Thus devoid of duality, *Brahman* is properly understood as *nirguna* (without qualities or attributes), which renders thought and language about it utterly impossible, and leaving mystical experience as the only effective avenue to true "knowledge" or wisdom about *Brahman*. Shankara, then, conceived of but one Reality, of which all particular entities and indeed the cosmos itself were manifestations. In this context, he did indeed refer to the phenomenal world of space, time, and differentiation as *maya*. As already suggested, that term is usually translated as "illusion" and taken to imply that Hinduism holds the phenomenal world to be unreal. For Shankara, however, the phenomenal world *was* real precisely as a process, and therefore illusory only in its appearance of substantiality and trustworthiness. As a true mystic, Shankara was persuaded that one must go behind the derivative and transitory everyday world and seek the unitive experience of oneness with the One.

Ramanuja (1017–1137; and yes, that is 120 years) was the next major philosophical innovator after Shankara. His philosophy, like Shankara's, was based on a reading of the *Upanishads* and *Brahma Sutra*, but consciously and explicitly rejected certain of his predecessor's key ideas. Perhaps because Ramanuja was not a mystic focused on *Brahman* but rather a devotee of the god Vishnu, the system he produced differs sharply from Shankara's in that it introduces a measure of transcendence and personality to the Ultimate—just the sort of otherness and objectification that devotion (*bhakti*) requires. Ramanuja's viewpoint was called *Vishishta Advaita*, which literally means "Qualified (or Complex) Non-dualism," as opposed to Shankara's *Kevala Advaita* ("Absolute Non-dualism"). Like his predecessor, Ramanuja wanted to maintain that *Brahman* is the only Absolute Reality; but he insisted—perhaps because of Christian or, more likely, Muslim influence in the India of his day—that *Brahman* is best thought of as God (called either *Brahman*-God or *Ishvara*). He rejected Shankara's *Brahman nirguna* as an empty abstraction, and asserted that *Brahman*-God *has* qualities (*saguna*), including personhood (and, ostensibly, masculinity); and that stipulation is what "qualified" or mitigated Ramanuja's non-dualism. Matter and souls are ultimately as real as God, and being created out of "His" eternal substance, are not independent of *Brahman*-God. They are, in fact, the body of which *Brahman*-God is the soul. Thus *Brahman*-God is in them, but they are likewise in "Him" and indeed in a way *are* "Him." Yet souls are eternal and similar to, but not precisely identical with, *Brahman*-God; and their goal is to love God and to enjoy communion (versus union) with "Him" forever.

Vedanta turns out to be a kind of philosophical spectrum, with Shankara providing the radical end, Ramanuja the moderate middle, and

Madhva (1238–1317) the opposite, conservative pole—the one that is the least monistic. Like Ramanuja, Madhva was a devotee of Vishnu in the person of his *avatar* Krishna, but unlike Ramanuja, he was a confirmed dualist, as indicated by the name of his philosophy: *Dvaita* ("dualism"). Madhva argued that all reality consists of two irreducible principles: one independent, eternal, and unitive (Divinity, which he called "Lord Sri Hari"); and the other dependent, created, and plural (finitude). The distinction between these two realities, and particularly between God and the individual self (*jiva*), is absolute and eternal. The spiritual goal, however, is the same as in the *Vishishtadvaita* of Ramanuja: the enjoyment of God-as-Krishna. That, for Madhva, is bliss and the experience of *moksha*. It is also a clear example of the kind of devotional dynamic whose demand for an object of devotion—an Other—is bound to compromise the immanence of pure monism, perhaps to the point of nullification.

It should be obvious from this brief overview that there was much difference of opinion among the philosophers of the Vedanta tradition, with Shankara staunchly maintaining the total immanence and non-personality of the Ultimate, Madhva arguing for Its complete transcendence, and Ramanuja trying to hold onto both qualities. Yet, amazingly, they were in enough agreement with one another—for example, on the importance of metaphysical speculation—to constitute a single philosophical school (*darshana*) and to distinguish themselves from the other five Indian philosophical traditions. (Most of these have either waned in influence to near oblivion or been absorbed into Vedanta, and therefore need not concern us here.) So it is that in philosophy as in everything else in Hinduism, the appearance of diversity often masks an underlying unity.

Three Modern Sages and Their Motley Styles

In the twentieth century, Hinduism gained more attention and had more influence in the West than it had in its entire prior history, a trend that promises to continue in the third millennium. This emerging awareness began in earnest in 1893 with the first World Parliament of Religions, which was attended and addressed by the dynamic and charismatic Swami Vivekananda, a student of the venerable sage Ramakrishna. Vivekananda's efforts permanently opened the spiritual doors of the West, and especially America, and gave an opportunity for a number of important and influential Hindu figures to make a significant impact on the beliefs and practices in this part of the world. Three bear special attention: Mahatma Gandhi, A. C. Bhaktivedanta, and Maharishi Mahesh Yogi.

Certainly the best known of these three is Mohandas Karamchand Gandhi, who late in life was better known by his spiritual title "Mahatma" ("Great-Soul"), which (with its masculine ending) is a common appellation for holy men in India. Gandhi is best remembered for his opposition to the British colonial rule there and his advocacy of political independence for his native land through non-violent means. His activism was both fueled and shaped by the philosophical principle of *satyagraha*, which literally means "truth force." By that he meant the non-violent application of the inner Absolute Truth that everyone embodies, and that will therefore eventually appeal to the consciences of those practicing or supporting social injustice or any other kind of evil, however stubborn and cruel they may be. Also important in his thinking and actions were the Hindu-Jainist concepts of *ahimsa* (non-injury to life forms, the meaning of which he broadened to include compassion) and *tapas* ("self-restraint"), gently mixed together with a touch of ascetic simplicity thrown in. (One of Gandhi's famous aphorisms was: "Live simply that others may simply live.") Largely because of his unswerving adherence to such principles, the mighty British *Raj* ("Rule") was toppled and India gained independence in 1947. That same year Gandhi was assassinated by a fellow Hindu, an extremist upset with the sage's conciliatory attitude toward the Muslim minority in India and his support of the partitioning of India to form the Muslim state of Pakistan.

Less known in the West than Gandhi, but perhaps no less influential, was Abhay Charan De, who is better remembered by his spiritual name, A. C. Bhaktivedanta, and his title, Swami Prabhupada. Though he was a philosopher of great acumen and renown, Bhaktivedanta's real claim to fame, however, is that he founded the International Society for Krishna Consciousness (ISKCON), which is better known as the Hare Krishna movement. His devotion to Lord Krishna was introduced to the West during a 1965 trip to the United States. He died twelve years later, but his organization lives on, with centers all over the world. Hare Krishnas are known for their communal living, renunciation of material things, strict discipline and ethics, distinctive dress (saffron robes and sandals) and hair style (shaved heads for men with a small ponytail-like topknot), vegetarianism, and rhythmic and joyous dancing and chanting of "Hare Krishna" and "Hare Rama." They are quite deliberate and sometimes assertive in propagating their faith, routinely distributing their literature in public places, especially Bhaktivedanta's impressive and illustrated commentary on the *Bhagavad Gita*.

Mahesh Prasad Varma was born in India in either 1911 or 1918, and was educated as a physicist. Early on he took up the study of Vedantic philosophy and developed an interest in yoga, which he synthesized, simplified, and largely secularized into a technique he called Transcendental Meditation (TM). Adopting the spiritual name Maharishi Mahesh Yogi, he promoted his new system in a series of trips to the United States in the late 1950s and early '60s. During this period, he came to the attention of the Beatles, who quickly adopted him as their *guru*, a connection that not only raised his own profile and promoted interest in TM, but also stimulated public awareness and curiosity about Hinduism. Today he has many followers in the United States and worldwide who insist upon the efficacy of his approach. Most recently, the Maharishi has promoted the traditional Indian system of holistic medicine called *Ayurveda*, a program widely and effectively championed by physician and best-selling author Deepak Chopra.

Of particular interest about this trio of sages is that each reflects one of the three *margas* treated earlier in this chapter, at least in his public persona and major contribution. As a political activist, Gandhi employed a hands-on, social-ethical, and therefore *karma marga* approach. A. C. Bhaktivedanta, by contrast, represents *bhakti yoga* in his promotion of Krishna Consciousness devotion and worship. Maharishi Mahesh Yogi, in turn, reflects the more mystical and meditative *jnana marga* style. In fairness, however, it must be acknowledged that none of these men can be regarded as one-dimensional. Gandhi also expressed devotion to Krishna; Bhaktivedanta (as this title implies) had a great affinity and affection (*bhakti*) for philosophy (*vedanta*); and the venerable Maharishi has shown an ever-increasing practical concern that his individual meditative techniques should make a positive contribution to society, the environment, and the world.

Distinctive Practices

The distinctive practices of the vast majority of Hindus today revolve around the worship of the *Trimurti* and *Shakti* and their attendant deities, rather than abstract contemplation of *Brahman, atman,* and their essential unity or the even older sacrificial ceremonials of Vedic times. In other words, except for the relatively few practitioners who devote their lives to meditation and a study of the mystical-philosophical *Upanishads* and some others who in times of special need call upon priests to perform ancient rituals, contemporary Hinduism is far more devotional than mystical or ceremonial. Simply stated, throughout India *henotheism* has all but eclipsed monism and polytheism, and the *bhakti marga* has over-shadowed both the *jnana* and the *karma*.

Bhakti and the Ishta Deva

As already suggested, in Hinduism, personal devotion (*bhakti*) revolves around the notion of *ishta deva*, which literally means "chosen deity." Typically, an Indian devotee will hold one such god or goddess in a special place of reverence in his or her heart, but more likely as a result of family tradition than a personal choice. In general practice, Hindus are usually quite ecumenical: in good henotheistic fashion, they neither deny the existence or importance of other deities, nor disparage them, nor try to convert someone who worships a different deity. However, he or she may well engage in what is called *mahatmya*, which literally means "praise," but connotes overstatement or exaggeration as well. Thus *mahatmya* (which should not be confused with the honorific title *Mahatma*) may even lead a devotee to declare his or her deity as "the one and only," much the way a passionate woman might declare her lover as "the only man in the world." Such a statement often leads writers about Hinduism to call this style of devotion "monotheistic." The fact is that since most devotees would no doubt recognize and admit their own enthusiastic and seemingly exclusive declarations to be a bit overblown, they would be better regarded as henotheists.

Further, a person's special connection to one chosen or inherited deity (*ishta deva*) does not mean that he or she ignores the other gods and goddesses. A good example is an engaging, intelligent, and university educated young man named Mahesh, whom I accompanied on a visit to a large *mandir* (temple) in New Delhi. By family tradition, Shiva—his namesake, since Mahesh is another name for the Destroyer—is his *ishta deva*. Yet, after paying his initial respects to Ganesh (for good luck), he made *pranam*, the bowing gesture of reverence, hands with palms prayerfully together, not only to Shiva, but to each and every deity in the place. That included (as he put it) "Lord Buddha," "Lord Mahavira," and "Lord Nanak Dev," the founders of Buddhism, Jainism, and Sikhism, respectively, all of whom Mahesh regards as Hindu divinities misinterpreted by followers who needlessly render themselves schismatic by their own particularism. He further explained to me that he devotes respective days of the week to Hanuman, Vishnu, the Shakti (or Mahadevi), and so forth, and adjusts his devotions and diet daily to accommodate the various expectations of each deity. (As noted earlier, the technical term for this is *kathenotheism*, the worship of one god after another.) In observing and listening to this young man, I could not help but think of the Western term "ecumenical" as a way of describing his attitude. Nor did I get the impression that in his inclusiveness, Mahesh was at all hedging his bets on which deity might do him good. Rather he seemed to be acknowledging in a simple and straightforward way the awesomely multi-faceted omnipresence of the One that was hidden in the many divine forms and their images—the One attested by the great philosophers of India.

The devotion to *ishta deva* is expressed in two ways. The first is the easier for Westerners to understand. It is *puja*, which entails either the private or public worship of a deity, whether one's *ishta deva* or another god or goddess—with prayers, offerings, and other devotional expressions. The other is *darshan*, which literally means "viewing" or "seeing," and entails a kind of mutual gazing: one sees the deity in the image, but at the same time is also beheld by the deity. (Hinduism even includes ceremonies designed to open the eyes of a deity's statue.) *Darshan* is perhaps the most moving spiritual experience that a typical Hindu can have. It can happen at home or in a local temple, but its effect is most powerful at a place of worship that is a pilgrimage site. Wherever it occurs, one is literally blessed through the eyes by the very sight of the image in which the deity is believed in some sense to reside. The fact that there are thousands upon thousands of images of the same deity all over the country is no problem to the believer. For the presence of every deity, reflecting the all-pervasive ubiquity of *Brahman*, is polycentric, and thus able to inhabit innumerable (and disposable!) physical representations simultaneously. One can tell by the demeanor and facial expressions of worshippers engaged in *darshan* that it is an experience they do not take lightly.

Life Goals and Stages

Hindu religious practice occurs within the traditional pattern of life goals and stages. (See Figure 2-7.) The life goals (*purusharthas*) are four in number, arranged in an ascending hierarchy of importance, and roughly parallel to the four successive life stages (*ashramas*). Traditionally, these goals and stages applied only to adult males of the top three castes, who are called the "twice-born" because of a ritual of rebirth undergone by boys at puberty. In recent times, however, such observances have been emulated by some women and low caste (*Shudra*) people as well. The lowest goal, that of pleasure (*kama*), is especially appropriate for someone at the *student* stage, which

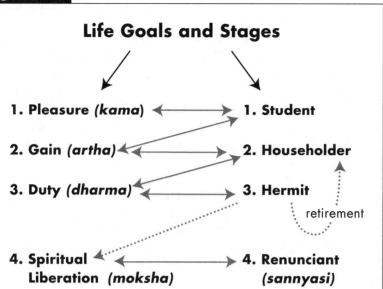

Figure 2-7

Life Goals and Stages

1. Pleasure *(kama)* ⟷ 1. Student

2. Gain *(artha)* ⟷ 2. Householder

3. Duty *(dharma)* ⟷ 3. Hermit

retirement

4. Spiritual ⟷ 4. Renunciant
   Liberation *(moksha)*   *(sannyasi)*

The traditional life goals and stages in Indian society roughly parallel one another. For example, while pleasure is certainly to be expected of one at the student stage (ages 12–24), eventually a person who is there must begin to think about earning a living that will support the next stage. It is possible to get stalled out at a stage, particularly the householder, at which point one may spend a lifetime merely making ends meet and never achieving the kind of financial security that would allow for spiritual retirement. Likewise, a hermit who has hit the proverbial wall in his spiritual pursuits may simply return home to retirement and his grandchildren. If successful, however, he will achieve *moksha* and move on to Stage 4

begins around age twelve and focuses on the ancient *Vedas*. (Presumably, pleasure is an important part of childhood as well, but childhood and whatever secular schooling is received therein do not factor into the stages schema.) As a man nears adulthood (age 24 or so), attention should normally turn toward the higher goal of gain (*artha*), which is the main preoccupation of one at this second, or *householder* stage, especially early on. But as he proceeds toward mid-life—assuming that he has managed to be a successful householder and to provide for the needs of the family—the householder should turn his attention from gain to the next higher goal, duty (*dharma*). This goal will ultimately require leaving home and embarking upon a kind of spiritual retirement as a *hermit* (or forest-dweller) during which one adopts a simple life of non-attachment in pursuit of the fourth and highest of the life goals. This, of course, is liberation (*moksha*), a spiritual state of perfect union with the Supreme One or Ultimate Spirit (*Brahman*).

If a hermit reaches the limit of what he can accomplish spiritually in the present lifetime and fails to reach *moksha*—"hits the wall," as it were—he may return home to resume his profession or vocation and family life. More likely, he will simply enjoy retirement and his grandchildren. If successful in reaching *moksha*, however, he will embark on the fourth and final stage as a *sannyasi*, a wandering beggar or renunciant (that is, one who has renounced). As such, he will forever forsake his name, profession or vocation, family, possessions, religious observances, society in general, and even his own personal identity and name; and he will live henceforth a life of blissful detachment while awaiting death. A *sannyasi* is said to be beyond even the gods, for they can do nothing for the man who, spiritually speaking, already has everything.

Self-Denial or Sexual Indulgence?

The *sannyasi* is not to be confused with the *sadhu*. A strikingly colorful figure, the *sadhu* is a person (usually male, though there are a comparatively few female counterparts called *sadhvis*) who very early in life and sometimes in childhood renounce society, including the caste system, in order to pursue a life-long ascetic path. Asceticism is found to some extent in all religions, usually as a minor expression. It is based on the conviction that spirit and flesh are mutually exclusive and in such tension with one another that the elevation or enhancement of the former demands the suppression of the latter, often by extreme measures. Typical ascetic practices include celibacy, fasting, and poverty; but some devotees adopt such extremes as self-inflicted pain and bodily mutilation. Such is the case with the *sadhu*, who probably will take upon himself a specific, demanding physical discipline. These may include extreme bodily piercings (sometimes accompanied by heavy weights to stretch the affected body part (e.g., the tongue or the genitalia), sleeping on thorns, or refusing to sit or lie down for years or even decades on end, even to sleep. (Those who adopt this last rigor generally rest and sleep with their elbows in a large, chest-high sling hung from a tree.) One *sadhu* became quite famous for cutting off a little more of his arm each year. Some *sadhus* also smoke *ganja* or hashish to achieve advanced mental or spiritual states (and perhaps to alleviate pain as well). Many *sadhus* bear on their foreheads the distinctive horizontal white lines that are the mark of a *Shaiva*, a devotee of the god Shiva—who among his many other duties is the god of ascetics. Some *sadhus*, however, are Vaishnivas rather than Shaivas, and so bear instead the vertical "U"- or "V"-shaped mark of Vishnu. The *Shaivas* also typically sport a huge mane of uncut and matted hair, and often cover their nude or nearly-nude bodies with the ashes of the cremated dead. In other words, *sadhus* make the old *sannyasi*, who appears so self-denying by Western standards, look like a spiritual slacker.

Tourists headed to India should perhaps be forewarned that not all *sadhus* are genuine. Especially at the major historic and scenic stops, a number of fellows dress up to emulate *sadhus* in order to make a fairly decent living by soliciting tips for mugging for photographers. (A purported "ascetic" soliciting anything material should be a tip-off.) It's really all in good fun, though. The costumes (another giveaway) and make-up are often very colorful and the poses downright humorous, and yield some interesting photos and stories to share with folks back home. A real *sadhu* might, if politely asked, pose for a photo, but would be reluctant to accept as recompense more than a few coins for a little food.

The *sadhu* affords a good opportunity to illustrate the inclusiveness of Hinduism. For at the other end of the spectrum from these renouncers of the flesh stand practitioners of Tantrism, who believe that spirit and flesh not only are not at odds, but are in fact in continuity. They hold that indulging the flesh—for example, by extreme sexual practices—is actually a path to spiritual realization. This attitude is reflected in the *Kama Sutra*, an ancient Hindu sex manual that is famous even in the West. Its underlying premise is that sexual intercourse, when done correctly (which means, among other things, intensely and imaginatively), is an effective path to spiritual realization. Tantrism is also seen in the architecture of the millennium-old Hindu temples at Khajuraho in north-central India, the facades of which are literally covered with carvings of gods and goddesses engaged in every conceivable (and sometimes utterly incredible) manner of sexual activity, including (but not limited to) intercourse. Some of them, for example, depict autoeroticism. Others depict creative and occasionally downright comical sexual *menages* of various sizes and configurations. The mere fact that a single religion can contain such extremes as the asceticism of the *sadhus* and the sensuality of the *Kama Sutra* and Khajuraho is a testimony to both its inclusiveness and its recognition that many valid paths are available to fulfill human spiritual needs.

Women in Hinduism

As is the case in every major world religion, the issue of the role and status of women in Hinduism is not only complex and ironic, but nearly impossible to distinguish clearly from more general traditional and cultural expectations. It is unclear whether Hinduism itself defined the place of women in Indian society or (more likely) functioned primarily to reinforce an already hopelessly patriarchal system. But the fact is that for at least the past two and a half millennia, the vast majority of Indian women have found themselves in subservient roles and worse. (A notable exception, of course, is Indira Gandhi, who served two terms in India's highest political office in the 1970s and '80s, something that no woman has managed to do in an advanced, Christian-dominated America.) The four stages of life and life goals, for example, applied only to males of the top three castes, and only they were formally initiated into adulthood with the triple string of the "twice-born" placed on their shoulders. Furthermore, the strong tradition of *pativratya*, which literally means "husband worship," dictated that women achieve meaning, fulfillment, and even spiritual realization by serving their husbands. The most extreme and alarming expression of this subservience has been the ancient practice of *sati* (or *suttee*), in which a woman—supposedly voluntarily, but often under coercion—would throw herself on the funeral pyre of her husband and be consumed by his cremation fire. Though outlawed in modern times and rarely practiced today, it is still known to occur, especially in rural India.

On the positive side and quite ironically, Hinduism has always demonstrated great reverence for the feminine. Numbered among the earliest Vedic deities, for example, were such important goddesses as Usas (Dawn), described as both "the brightness of the Godhead" and "Mother of the gods." In a later myth, the primordial goddess Adi Shakti created not only the world, but the *Trimurti* (Brahma, Vishnu, and Shiva), and *Shakti* continues to be regarded as the awesome power of *Brahman* Itself as well as Its personal-feminine manifestation (*Mahadevi*), which diffracts into the various goddesses. Nor are these goddesses—the likes of Saraswati, Lakshmi, and Kali—seen as inferior companions to their male consorts, but rather as complementary partners without whom the gods would be powerless, not to mention less interesting and attractive. It is also noteworthy that in Vedantic (philosophical) Hinduism, an individual's spirit has no gender (the word *atman*, you may recall, is neuter), so that at the deepest level a person is neither female nor male, but all are essentially and absolutely the same, and therefore equal. Finally, some argue that the devotional type of spirituality that dominates Hinduism today calls upon the worshipper of male deities to emulate the corresponding goddess—for example, male devotees of Lord Krishna are expected to assume the *pativratya* role of his adoring female consort, Radha. Hinduism would thus appear to afford ample potential for a feminist movement of monumental (if not cosmic) significance, if only such precedents could be tapped.

Conclusion

Many aspects of Hinduism could never be acceptable to most Christians, particularly its perpetuation of the personally restrictive and socially stifling caste system, its continuing subordination and suppression of women, and its apparent inability to speak to the dire problems of overpopulation and abject poverty in its own land. Nevertheless, Christians might take some valuable lessons from a religion that, as arguably the oldest and certainly the most complex of the living religions, has "seen it all." At the practical level, for example, Hinduism teaches that a religion can not only persist over millennia, but actually thrive without a central authoritative figure or governing body or even an institutional structure—subsisting, for all intents and purposes, solely in the hearts and minds of its followers. In fact, this is very likely the feature that has led to both a rich diversity of spiritual paths and religious forms and a laudable degree of tolerance for diversity, even when that diversity has resulted in apparent or actual contradictory views and divergent practices. Simply put, Hinduism is a prime example of an inclusive and accepting faith, offering the proverbial "different strokes for different folks" in spiritual pursuits and religious activities.

But Hinduism has much more to offer Christians at the conceptual level than it does at the practical. It opens up, for example, the possibility of an Ultimate Reality that is non-personal and fully immanent in being, that inheres pervasively in material reality, and that emanates not only as deities, but as the entire cosmos, including, of course, human beings. This monistic view might well prove a useful option to the increasing number of Christians who find the transcendent, personal, and heavenly creator God of traditional monotheism either problematic or altogether unacceptable. Likewise, the Hindu notion that the multitudinous deities are manifestations, forms, or aspects of the Ultimate might provide Christians with some useful conceptual handles for reformulating the perpetually troublesome doctrine of the Trinity, which continues to be framed in ancient Greek philosophical terms that outlived their usefulness long ago.

In the same vein, Hinduism's view of the universal incarnation of *Brahman* in all extant beings and things, might challenge Christians to rethink their own concept of a specific, unique Incarnation in the person of Jesus. It might also shed light on the biblical notion that after him, God's Holy Spirit was somehow let loose in the world—an image by no means incompatible with an incarnation that affects all of reality and the inhabitants thereof rather than one unique individual. Another boon to Christianity might be its strong feminine dynamic, which is evident not only in the many beloved goddesses, but in the notions of *Shakti* and *Mahadevi* as discrete aspects and powerful manifestations of the Supreme Ultimate. Finally, the Hindu belief that humans are fundamentally divine and merely in need of paths to the discovery and existential realization of that fact might prove attractive to Christians who can no longer accept their faith's traditional claim that humans are inherently sinful and in need of a vicarious atonement. Such Hindu notions would, of course, have some practical applications for Christians as well, such the need to cultivate meditation and other techniques for accessing the Power or Presence that allegedly resides within us all.

These and other related ideas will be much more fully developed in Chapter 5. For now, we proceed on our journey of Orientation in order to visit another great Eastern religion, Buddhism, which sprang from Hinduism in much the same way that Christianity emerged from Judaism. As we shall soon see, it also has much to offer Christians who are struggling to rethink, reaffirm, and in some cases recover their own faith.

Questions for Reflection and Discussion

1. List the ways in which Hinduism is inclusive and tolerant. Why do you suppose that other religions behave just the opposite in claiming exclusive validity for their God and their views of God? Which attitude comes closer to reflecting your views? What do you think has shaped your thinking in this regard? What, if anything, would make you reconsider your stance or change your mind?

2. Describe the Indian caste system in your own words, and compare and contrast it with the social system with which you are most familiar. What advantages does the caste system have? What arguments would you use in a debating contest in order to demonstrate its superiority?

3. What view of the relationship between spirituality and the material world is implicit in asceticism? How does it differ from Tantrism's presupposition in this regard? Which do you find more persuasive or compelling? Why?

4. What do you think about the idea that rather than a single way (or Way), a variety of valid spiritual paths or disciplines exist to accommodate such various personality types as thinkers, feelers, and doers? Which of the three *margas* or the four *yogas* would be most suitable for you? Is there a niche in the religion with which you identify or with which you are most familiar that would fit or at least come close to your preferences in this regard? Which one and how?

5. Of the Hindu deities described in this chapter, which one do you find most appealing? Why? Is there any character or figure in the religion in which (or near which) you were reared that is in any way similar, or that meets the same human spiritual need in another way? Whether there is or is not, how do you account for that fact? What do you think about the notion that all gods and goddesses in every religion are essentially reflections of aspects of human nature, spirituality, or psychology?

6. What do you think of the Hindu view of Ultimate Reality as *Brahman*? How difficult would it be for you to relate to a non-personal Ultimate Reality? What are the strengths and weaknesses of the notion that human beings and nature itself are essentially divine? What would it take to allow you to say "I am Ultimate Reality, the Supreme Spirit" with a straight face?

7. What do you think about the related terms—*atman, samsara, moksha, karma,* and *dharma*—and the system they comprise? Is this little constellation of ideas at least internally consistent? If not, where does it go wrong? If so, is it at all plausible to you? Why or why not? What is the likelihood that it actually represents the way things are? Do you think your views in this regard would be different if you had been born into a Hindu family in India?

8. How do you account for the growing popularity of Hindu ideas like reincarnation and Hindu practices like yoga in the West? Do you think these are fads, or are they are meeting spiritual needs that Western religions cannot? Why? If there is a Hindu temple where you live (or should you hear of one being built), how do you (or would you) feel about that? Why? What would its existence say about the common claim that the United States of America is "a Christian nation"? What rights do you believe that Hindu Americans have (or should have) under the Constitution? Why?

Recommended Reading

A. L. Basham, *The Origins and Development of Classical Hinduism*, ed. Kenneth G. Zysk. Oxford: Oxford University Press, 1991.

Deepak Chopra, *How to Know God: The Soul's Journey into the Mystery of Mysteries*. New York: Crown Publishers, 2000.

Ram Dass, *Be Here Now*. New York: The Crown Publishing Group, 1971.

Diana L. Eck, *Encountering God : A Spiritual Journey from Bozeman to Banaras*. Boston: Beacon Press, 1994.

Gavin D. Flood, *An Introduction to Hinduism*. Cambridge: Cambridge University Press, 1996.

Stephen P. Huyler, *Meeting God: Elements of Hindu Devotion*. New Haven, CT: Yale University Press, 1999.

David R. Kinsley, *Hinduism: A Cultural Perspective*. Englewood Cliffs, NJ: Prentice Hall, 1982.

Klaus K. Klostermaier, *A Short Introduction to Hinduism*. Oxford: Oneworld Publications, 1998.

Kim Knott, *Hinduism: A Very Short Introduction*. Oxford: Oxford University Press, 1998.

Juan Mascaro, trans. *The Upanishads*. New York/London/et al.: Penguin Books, 1963.

Swami Prabhavananda and Christopher Isherwood, trans. *The Song of God: Bhagavad Gita*. New York/London/et al.: Mentor (Penguin), 1954.

Ed Viswanathan, *Am I a Hindu? The Hinduism Primer*. San Francisco: Halo Books, 1992.

Chapter 3

The Middle Way of Buddhism

Nothing is Real

Objectives of this Chapter

- to introduce Buddhism as the product of a reform movement within Hinduism

- to examine the life of Siddhartha Gautama, the fountainhead of the Buddhist faith

- to trace the history of Buddhism in terms of two distinct schools that gradually became concentrated in two different regions of Asia

- to explore the four divergent sects of the Mahayana School of Buddhism that have had a significant impact upon the modern West

- to present the Zen tradition as the form of Buddhism that has the most to offer as a corrective to the Western spirituality

- to explore the Four Noble Truths as well as key terms and concepts in Buddhist philosophy, with prominent attention to the seemingly nihilistic notion that Ultimate Reality is Emptiness

- to give a brief account of the history of Buddhism in the West, and particularly in American religious history

The next stop on our spiritual journey is Buddhism. That means that initially, at least, we have not traveled very far from Hinduism, for both religions claim India as their place of birth. We shall see, however, that because Buddhism was a deliberately and very successful missionary religion, it not only spread far and wide, but assured its survival by doing so, for it virtually died out in its homeland eight centuries ago. In this chapter, therefore, we shall find ourselves in such diverse places as Southeast Asia, Japan, and Tibet, where each exotic culture made its own distinctive and lasting impression on the migrant and pliable Buddhist faith.

Overview and Origins

Buddhism is one of three expressions of a spirit of dissatisfaction that arose within Hinduism in sixth-century BCE India. As we saw in the preceding chapter, Hinduism had previously been characterized by polytheism and ritualism and had been under the dominant influence of the priestly Brahmin caste and their narrow interpretations of the ancient *Vedas.* We also noted Hinduism's movement at that time toward the more mystical and philosophical emphasis and an increased interest in the *Upanishads* that resulted in Vedantic Hinduism. This was a revolution in itself, but one that Hinduism managed to absorb and nurture. This same busy century, however, saw the emergence of two other movements that could not be similarly contained and therefore became separate religious traditions in their own right: Jainism and Buddhism. The former of these exhibited very little missionary spirit, and thus has remained pretty much culturally and geographically bound to India. Buddhism, however, actually survived and thrived better outside its country of origin than it did within it—so much so that the only reason for anyone interested in Buddhism to go to India today is to visit the historic sites associated with its founder. He was a man who discovered and mapped out for his followers a "Middle Way" between the luxuriant self-indulgence of his upbringing and the ascetic self-denial of his middle years.

From Before Birth to the Big Break

In contrast to Hinduism, Buddhism originated with a nameable historical founder: Siddhartha Gautama, who is also known as *Shakyamuni,* "Sage of the Shakya Clan"; *Tathagata,* "Way Shower"; and above all as *The Buddha,* "The Enlightened One" or "He Who Awoke." Despite the fact that his biography was first presented in a coherent form several centuries after his death and many of the events and deeds attributed to him

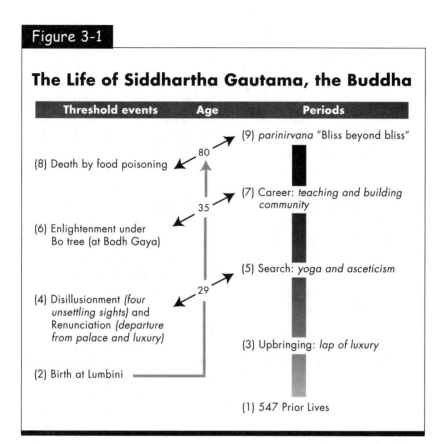

Figure 3-1

The Life of Siddhartha Gautama, the Buddha

Threshold events	Age	Periods

(9) *parinirvana* "Bliss beyond bliss"

(8) Death by food poisoning

80

(7) Career: *teaching and building community*

35

(6) Enlightenment under Bo tree (at Bodh Gaya)

(5) Search: *yoga and asceticism*

(4) Disillusionment *(four unsettling sights)* and Renunciation *(departure from palace and luxury)*

29

(3) Upbringing: *lap of luxury*

(2) Birth at Lumbini

(1) 547 Prior Lives

are quite incredible, he was almost certainly an historical person. As presented by the "Bible" of Buddhism (the *Tripitaka* or "Three Baskets") and some early biographies, Siddhartha's life consisted of five major periods punctuated by four threshold events (see Figure 3-1). Together, the periods and events are widely agreed upon by Buddhists of all schools and sects, though as with any ancient religious tradition some of the details are contradictory or contested.

The first period in the celebrated chronicle of the Buddha's life comprises his prior incarnations, is of indeterminate length and fantastic proportions, and presents the most difficulties for Western non-Buddhists to accept as having any authenticity. For Easterners conditioned to believe in reincarnation, however, the stories are at least somewhat more plausible, though not even all Buddhists take them as factual. Be that as it may, by tradition this preparatory period consisted of 547 previous lives, some human and some animal, the stories of which are meant both to reflect and to teach virtues like wisdom, selflessness, generosity, and above all compassion. In one, for example, the Buddha-to-be was a young monk who sacrificed his own life to feed a hungry lioness with his remains. In another, he was a man of such generosity that he voluntarily gave away his fortune, his children, and his wife merely because someone asked for them. Some would regard such a response as being charitable to a fault.

Interesting as they are, those legendary accounts are eclipsed in importance by the story of the first great threshold event, the miraculous, immaculate conception of Siddhartha while his mother, Mahamaya, sleeping alone, dreamed of a white elephant. More than that, she gave birth to her son in an extraordinary way: he emerged painlessly from her right side as she stood in a grove of trees. At birth, he could already walk and talk, and his first utterance was a declaration that he would become a Buddha. He bore some thirty-two physical marks suggesting the accuracy of that prediction, including golden skin, a protrusion on his head, forty teeth, webbed fingers and toes with wheel-marks on his palms and soles, a birthmark on his forehead permanently marking his spiritual third eye, and extremely long earlobes and arms. It is reported that Mahamaya died within days of her son's birth (perhaps of shock). At his naming ceremony, an old seer told Siddhartha's father, who is remembered as a powerful *raja* or king, that the child would be great: either a mighty ruler like him or a renowned spiritual master. The father, desiring to steer his child in his own footsteps and keep him from anything that would lead him to a spiritual vocation, resolved to protect him from any and all disturbing sights, but especially disease, old age, death, and—perhaps above all—holy men.

Thus began the second phase of Siddhartha's life, his upbringing. To say that he was reared in the lap of luxury and was spoiled rotten would constitute a remarkable understatement. He was kept behind the high walls of his father's three palaces, and presumably was shuttled between them from season to season in a heavily curtained vehicle that prevented him from seeing the sorrows of life that would have been all around him. The palaces were filled day and night with every distraction imaginable, including food, drink, entertainers, sporting events, friends, and—last but not least—legions of concubines. At the appropriate age, Siddhartha was married to a beautiful (and, one would hope, broad-minded) young woman named Yashodara. Given its intricacy, cost, and consistent attention to detail, his father's plan for sheltering his son worked remarkably well for nearly three decades, keeping Siddhartha blissfully ignorant of the many distresses of normal human life.

At age 29, however, a second threshold event led him to make what amounted to a dramatic escape from the sumptuous prison that his father had created for him. Siddhartha's curiosity took him outside the palace walls and into the real world. There he saw precisely those things his father had tried to shield him from: a sick person, a decrepit old person, a corpse, and a totally destitute holy man who nevertheless seemed blissfully happy, even in the face of such harsh and disturbing realities. These four disturbing encounters proved to be life-changing for Siddhartha, for he resolved on the spot to make a clean break with his life of ease and to embark on a quest for peace of mind and spirit—a decision called "The Great Renunciation."

From Search to Sangha

Siddhartha was obliged to sneak out of the palace, for his father would surely have prevented him from leaving otherwise. He thus entered the third phase of his personal journey: his search for spiritual well-being. First he studied two different systems of yoga under the two most revered masters in India, and quickly mastered both. Still not satisfied, however, he decided to embrace asceticism, and did so with a zeal that almost killed him. After six years of such spiritual rigors and self-deprivation, and having starved himself almost to death, he realized the utter futility of this approach. Thereupon, he broke his fast with a good meal, and resolved to sit under a tree—later called the *Bo* Tree ("Tree of Enlightenment")— until he reached Enlightenment. He did just that, but reports of precisely what happened under that tree vary. Some say that via concentration and reflection he gradually came to a realization of the basic ideas that would become the heart of his message and career. But others say that what he really did was clear his mind and achieve a state of awareness so pure that whenever he opened his mouth thereafter, not just wisdom but nothing less than eternal Truth (what Buddhists call the *Dharma*) poured forth naturally and effortlessly from his lips.

The fourth stage of his pilgrimage was his itinerant career, which consisted of teaching, working miracles (including some healings), and gathering and organizing his disciples into a monastic fellowship (*Sangha*) surrounded by lay supporters. His inaugural message—called by Buddhists "The First Turning of the Wheel of the Dharma"—was delivered in a deer park at Sarnath, near Varanasi, Hinduism's holiest city. There he enunciated the Four Noble Truths that would be the basis of all his teachings in a way so compelling that he won many followers. Eventually all of his family, including his wife, son, father, stepmother, cousins, and even his father-in-law were won over to his spiritual path. A long career of teaching followed, perhaps the most noteworthy event of which was his famous wordless sermon delivered on Vulture Peak. Before an audience of 5,000, he simply held up a flower. Four thousand nine hundred ninety-nine of the crowd scratched their heads in puzzlement. Only one, his beloved disciple Kashyapa, smiled knowingly, thus revealing that he alone had understood the apparently ineffable point. In response, the Buddha appointed him his successor on the spot. After some forty-five more years of preaching and community-building, the Buddha's ministry finally culminated in the last great event of his life: his death.

From Death to Destiny

The founders of most of the world's religions lived reasonably long lives and died rather unremarkable deaths. The first is certainly true of the Buddha, for he lived until his 80th year. Certain aspects of his death, however, are noteworthy, despite the fact that the cause of his death was rather unspectacular, even mundane: food poisoning. Just what the fatal dish was remains a mystery: some say bad pork, others say spoiled truffles. In any case, his death was an accident, the result of a bad meal served by a well-meaning admirer. Though ostensibly dying of diarrhea—a protracted and undoubtedly terrible way to go, so to speak—he continued to teach and to attract followers to his spiritual path. Having said all he had to say, he reportedly told his disciples to rely upon themselves and work out their own salvation, putting their faith in the Truth (*Dharma*) alone in a world where all things are transitory. Then—according to tradition, lying on his right side and cradling his head on his hands held palm-to-palm—he died, in a peaceful setting (a grove not unlike his birthplace) and a posture of repose often depicted in Buddhist art.

That final event led to the last phase of the Buddha's life-story, one that is just as difficult to document and describe as his previous lives: his ultimate bliss called *parinirvana*. More will be said about the meaning of *nirvana* shortly. For now, let us just say that it is roughly equivalent to the liberating *moksha* in Hinduism; for whatever else it might be, it is release from the endless cycles of birth-life-death-rebirth, which Buddhism, like Hinduism, calls *samsara*. It may also be added that the Buddha reportedly had already achieved this release at his Enlightenment; but as the prefix *pari*-indicates, the complete and final liberation from *samsara* came only with death. It is in this state of *parinirvana*—rather than, say, some heavenly abode—that most Buddhists believe their founder to be, both now and forever.

Scripture and Beliefs

As with most of the religions of the world, scriptures are extremely important in Buddhism. To the faithful they are valuable not only for information about the founder and inherent inspirational value, but also because they provide the basis for the faith's system of belief (which we shall treat in this section) and practice (which we shall reserve for the next). Buddhism's scriptures are many and varied, and their teachings form the heart of what may well be the most radical religious philosophy the world has yet seen.

The Buddhist Bible and Sundry Sutras

As already indicated, the "Buddhist Bible" is the *Tripitaka* (Sanskrit) or *Tipitaka* (Pali, which many Buddhists believe to be the Buddha's native tongue). The title literally means "Three Baskets," a reference to the major divisions, each of which is a collection of writings distinct in type from the others. (See Figure 3-2.) The first is the *Sutrapitaka* or *Suttapitaka* ("Discourses Basket"), comprises five parts called *Nikayas* ("Collections"), and constitutes not only the oldest writings in the canon, but those most focused on the Buddha and his teachings. Included in these *Nikayas* are the *Dhammapada*, the most famous of all the Buddha's

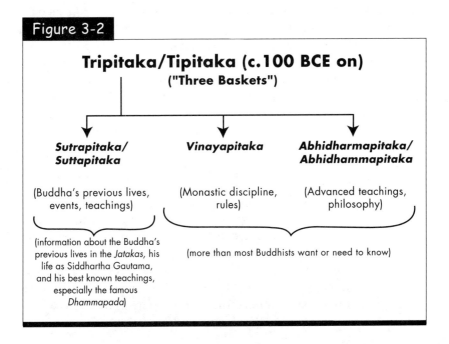

Figure 3-2

Tripitaka/Tipitaka (c.100 BCE on)
("Three Baskets")

Sutrapitaka/ Suttapitaka	Vinayapitaka	Abhidharmapitaka/ Abhidhammapitaka
(Buddha's previous lives, events, teachings)	(Monastic discipline, rules)	(Advanced teachings, philosophy)

(information about the Buddha's previous lives in the *Jatakas*, his life as Siddhartha Gautama, and his best known teachings, especially the famous *Dhammapada*)

(more than most Buddhists want or need to know)

teachings, and the *Jatakas*, which relate fascinating tales of his 547 previous lives. The second basket, the *Vinayapitaka*, consists of monastic rules and discipline, while the third, the *Abhidharmapitaka* or *Abhidhammapitaka* contains just what its name indicates: advanced (*abhi-*) teachings (*Dharma*). These last two "baskets" offer more than most Buddhists really care to know, for they do not aspire to be either monks or philosophers. (Likewise most Catholic Christians would not care to read a manual explaining the rules that a priest is to follow, except perhaps in cases where he is suspected of having transgressed them, any more than they would sit down to read Aquinas' *Summa Theologica*. But they are no doubt glad to know that such writings exist for those who appreciate or need them.) Most Buddhists, then, are likely to be far more familiar with the *Sutrapitika*, though all three baskets are generally regarded as *Buddhavacana* ("Buddha words"), and thus of course inspired—but not divinely so. For the one who uttered them, however enlightened, was still human, even in the eyes of his most ardent and admiring followers.

In addition to the canonical *Tripitaka*, most Buddhists accept a profusion of extra-canonical scriptures, primarily *Sutras* ("Discourses" or "Lessons") from the Mahayana school (see below). Most of these purport to be the actual words that Siddhartha Gautama shared only with his brightest and best students. Thereafter, they were allegedly either recorded by gods and guarded by dragons (*nagas*) or passed on orally until the world was ready for them. Whatever their source, miraculous or mundane, these *Sutras* appeared about four centuries after the Buddha's death. Best known among them is the voluminous *Prajnaparamita Sutra* ("Perfect Wisdom Discourse"), which contains two of the three most popular *sutras*, the *Heart Sutra* and the *Diamond Sutra*. The third circulated separately as the *Lotus Sutra*. Much of Mahayana Buddhist belief and piety, as well as most Buddhist philosophy, is based on these *sutras*.

Holdovers from Hinduism

In view of its Hindu origins, one should not be surprised that Buddhism maintained a style of spirituality conducive to an experience of the Ultimate within, and retained virtually unaltered a number of the parent religion's basic concepts. The everyday world and our experience of it through multiple successive rebirths, for example, are called *samsara* in both faiths. The Hindu word *karma* is also retained, but because Buddhism rejected the traditional Indian caste system, the word comes to have a broader moral connotation detached from any consideration of one's social position and its corresponding *dharma*. That latter term took on a distinctly Buddhist hue: whereas it usually means "duty" in Hinduism, the Buddhist definition of *dharma* is almost invariably "teaching," "doctrine," or "truth." *Dharma* is, in fact, one of the Three Refuges that Buddhists of every school and sect utter as a kind of statement of faith: "I take refuge in the Buddha. I take refuge in the *Dharma*. I take refuge in the *Sangha*." Precisely what a Buddhist *means* by these three statements will depend on what school he or she follows, that is, what part of the Buddhist world he or she inhabits.

Despite their shared beliefs, concepts, and practices, Buddhism deviated from its parent Hinduism in several important ways. First, it identified as its foundation the Four Noble Truths first taught at Sarnath rather than the ancient *Vedas* or any subsequent Hindu scripture. Second, it established as a basis for all of its claims two assertions that on the surface, at least, appear to pit pessimism against optimism: on the one hand, the *impermanence* of all things and, on the other, their intimate *interconnection* in a vast matrix of mutuality sometimes called "interbeing." Third, Buddhism radicalized the Hindu idea of the Ultimate as *Brahman nirguna*, and claimed that it was not simply an unknowable, inconceivable, and ineffable Something bereft of qualitites, but an utter and absolute Void. Buddhism further maintained that the experience of one's own corresponding emptiness was not only blissful, but a realization of one's oneness (or *noneness!*) with everyone and everything. In what must strike the Western mind as a *non sequitur*, such a seemingly negative realization was also presented as the basis of a radical compassion for all sentient beings or, as some Buddhists maintain, for everything that is.

Since these are perhaps the strangest and most difficult claims of any living religion, they deserve a detailed account. But before we proceed to that, it should be noted that the Buddha himself was not a philosopher *per se*, but a teacher of fairly simple and straightforward spiritual tenets. And since these had nothing to do with a god or gods, he can hardly be regarded as a theologian, either. Over the centuries, however, many schools of Buddhist philosophy emerged to provide both conceptual substance and systemization to his ideas, especially in the Mahayana tradition. The most famous and influential of these was the Madhyamika school of Nagarjuna, who lived around 150–200 CE. Nagarjuna and other philosophers believed that they were merely articulating the philosophy implicit in the teachings of the Buddha. Whether or not that is so, his systematic version of the Buddha's teachings became the normative expression of Buddhist doctrine.

The Four Noble Truths

At the heart of the Buddha's teachings, and the subject of his very first sermon, were the Four Noble Truths. (See Figure 3-3.) These are often said to revolve around the idea of "suffering" or "pain," but the operative Pali word (*dukkha*; or *duhkha* in Sanskrit) actually means something closer to "unsatisfactoriness." In any case, the Noble Truths are a combination of good news and bad news, with the latter delivered first: (1) *Life is painful* or *unsatisfactory* (depending on how one translates *dukkha*). We're never satisfied or completely happy, even—and perhaps especially—when we get exactly what we want. We never stop wanting. We are all, therefore, in deep *dukkha*. (2) *The cause of suffering/unsatisfactoriness is craving* (*tanha* in Pali and *trishna* in Sanskrit, both meaning "desire" or "clinging"). We forever desire what we don't have, and if we get it, it is never as good as we imagined or as something else we think is better. The "grass is always greener" and "be careful what you wish for" maxims of the Western world would apply here in spades.

That's the bad news. But before we look at the more encouraging third and fourth of the Noble Truths, an example will help to clarify these first two. Consider the case of the famous figure skater, Tonya (Tanha?) Harding. In the mid-1990s she was the second greatest female skater in the world; of the over three billion women alive, she could skate better than all but one. Was she satisfied? No! She allegedly had her ex-husband and his thuggish friends "knee-cap" her rival, Nancy Kerrigan, in a sneak attack. Nancy suffered, of course—not just once, but evening after evening on the news via videotape, which made TV audiences suffer repeatedly as well. When the perpetrators were caught, tried, convicted, and imprisoned, they also suffered. Tanya suffered, too, because when her credentials as a figure skater were revoked, she was no longer able to do the one thing she excelled at. Therefore she took up acting and singing, and everyone who watched and heard her suffered. That is precisely the message of the first two of the Noble Truths: it is craving or desire that makes life unsatisfactory and us miserable, and because we are so interconnected, a single act of craving can send ripples of wretchedness far and wide.

Our own lives bear testimony to this fact. We have all known the frustration and ache of wanting an unattainable piece of property or even a person, and suffering as a result. Let's say we want a Jaguar automobile, but just cannot afford one. Our brand new Ford or Honda just doesn't make us happy. Or perhaps we want a particularly attractive person as a

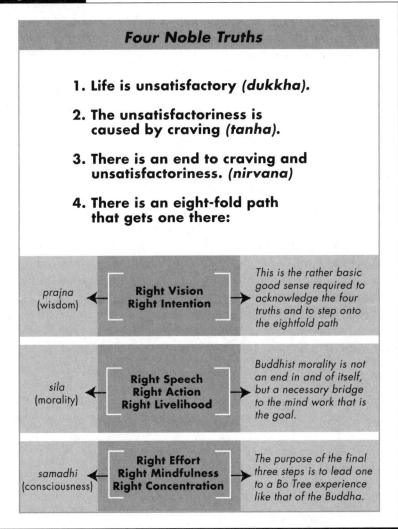

Figure 3-3

Four Noble Truths

1. **Life is unsatisfactory (dukkha).**

2. **The unsatisfactoriness is caused by craving (tanha).**

3. **There is an end to craving and unsatisfactoriness. (nirvana)**

4. **There is an eight-fold path that gets one there:**

prajna (wisdom)	**Right Vision** **Right Intention**	This is the rather basic good sense required to acknowledge the four truths and to step onto the eightfold path
sila (morality)	**Right Speech** **Right Action** **Right Livelihood**	Buddhist morality is not an end in and of itself, but a necessary bridge to the mind work that is the goal.
samadhi (consciousness)	**Right Effort** **Right Mindfulness** **Right Concentration**	The purpose of the final three steps is to lead one to a Bo Tree experience like that of the Buddha.

lover, but really haven't a chance. No other partner will suffice, so we suffer. But the fact is that even if we were successful in fulfilling our desires, the reality would never be as good as the anticipation and fantasy. Say you won a super lottery, and could afford that Jaguar, just where could you drive or park your dream automobile that you would not be afraid of dings, dents, scratches, theft, or the tarnishing effects of the sun, rain, air pollution, and road salt? And how long would it be before you found yourself coveting someone's Ferrari or Lamborghini? Or suppose you found yourself in a relationship with a real dreamboat. You would probably soon be miserable with jealousy or suspicion, which would lead to the kind of possessiveness and controlling behavior certain to drive the person off and make you even more miserable than you were in the first place. The Second Noble Truth thus exemplifies the source of all stalkings and most abductions, not to mention insecurity, greed, envy, jealousy, and a host of other debilitating qualities.

The good news comes in the last two of the Four Noble Truths. (3) *There is an end to suffering/unsatisfactoriness.* It is called *nirvana.* That concept will be discussed shortly, but it will suffice for now to call it "bliss"—namely, the bliss of non-attachment, which brings an end to craving and therefore to suffering. (4) *The way to this end is the Eightfold Path.* The steps of this path are right vision, right intention, right speech, right action, right livelihood, right effort, right mindfulness, and right meditation. They take the faithful from a simple perception of the wisdom of the Four Noble Truths (right vision) to the full realization of the awakened mind achieved by the Buddha himself (right meditation). These eight steps are often divided into three groups: *prajna* ("wisdom," the first two), *sila* ("morality," the next three), and *samadhi* ("concentration," the last three). What this division makes explicit is that in Buddhism morality is not an end in and of itself, as it is in some commandment-based religions. Rather it is a necessary stage on the way to achieving the kind of mindfulness that is the ultimate objective of all Buddhist piety and practice. In any case, the steps are not as linear as they appear. They are probably best seen as marking off vertical meridians extending up a mountain, each of which the climber encounters again and again as she or he follows a spiraling upward path.

Impermanence and Interbeing

Underlying these Noble Truths is the notion of the *impermanence* (*anitya* in Sanskrit; *anicca* in Pali) of all things. This is what the dying Buddha meant when he said that "all things are transitory." Buddhism excludes nothing from this sweeping claim, with the possible exception of the eternal *Dharma*, which is not a "thing" and cannot even be said to "exist" in the way that the stuff of phenomenal reality does. (The closest thing to the *Dharma* in Western philosophy is the eternal ideas or forms of Plato, which likewise are non-existent but profoundly real.) The clear meaning of *anitya* is that nothing in the realm of *samsara* is permanent. (The urge here to match my Tonya example with a reference to the faded career of former singer-actress "Anitya" Bryant is almost irresistible here, but I am above that.) But neither is there in Buddhism a changeless deity or anything that another religion would recognize as a stable and lasting Ultimate Reality.

Another staple of Buddhist philosophy is the *dependent co-origination of all things (pratitya samutpada* in Sanskrit; *paticca samuppada* in Pali). This is a very complex idea, but basically it means that all constituent entities in the cosmos are dynamically related to and interconnected with one another in such an intimate way that everything is both the cause and the effect of everything else. This picture of reality includes neither a first cause nor any excluded entity, such as a transcendent God. There is only interbeing. This means that if any part of the cosmic picture—and in Buddhism it is a *motion picture*, a vast and kaleidoscopic process— changes even a tiny bit, the whole picture changes. Everything is affected. As counterintuitive or simply nonsensical as that may seem to the Western mind, it should give us pause to know that it was not a Buddhist philosopher but Albert Einstein who said, "A falling leaf affects the farthest star." And he meant it! Today that same sentiment is echoed by systems theorists who claim that a butterfly flapping it wings in Tallahassee affects the weather in Tokyo, and *vice versa*.

Essential Emptiness

The most difficult concept in Buddhist philosophy—and perhaps in all of philosophy—is its view of Ultimate Reality. It may help to recall that Hindu philosophy had identified it as *Brahman*, the Supreme, and that *Brahman* was non-personal, utterly inconceivable, and (as *nirguna*) completely without qualities. But at least it was something. In Buddhism, the Ultimate is *Shunyata*, which means "The Void," "Emptiness," "Nothingness," "Nihility," or "Zilch." Yet, that equation is not really negative, much less nihilistic; for paradoxically, it bespeaks a very full Emptiness.

In order to make sense of such a strange claim, just think of common things in everyday life that are nothing. For example, the emptiness between walls, floor, and ceiling is what we call "a room." Except for the hollowness of glasses and bells and flutes, they would produce no sound. A hole in anything is nothing at all, yet it has many practical applications, and in some cases may pose a danger. The hole in the center of a wheel is nothing, but without it the wheel won't fit on an axle. A hole in a shirt is nothing, but when well-placed, it makes buttoning possible. A vacuum is by definition an emptiness, but we certainly find it useful in cleaning our carpets and sealing our jars. Similarly, the numeral 0 in the binary system is essential in the construction of the bits and bytes on which computers run. Indeed, the list of things in everyday experience that consist of nothing at all is nearly endless: apertures, spaces, slits, slots, gorges, gulches, gullies, notches, hollows, intervals—and so forth. The closest analog to Shunyata, however, is the utter Nothingness from which—according to modern theoretical physics—emerged the primal Singularity that exploded some thirteen and a half billion years ago (give or take a week) to produce our entire universe, including space and time.

Another way of approaching the positive sense of the Buddhist idea of Emptiness is to recall a distinction made by the Greek philosopher Aristotle between *actuality* and *potentiality*. To him, an actuality is any existing thing; and all actualities have potentiality in that they are potentially something else. A piece of wood, for example, is potentially light, heat, and ashes. An acorn is potentially an oak tree. But Aristotle also posited something he called Pure Potentiality, which he identified as the primal matrix out of which all actualities emerge. Aristotle called this "God," but he did not have in mind anything like the God of Christianity or any other world religion. For one thing, this Pure Potential God was not personal, though as the Source of everything it had to be that from which all personality sprang. And by definition this Pure Potentiality could not exist; for if it did, it would be an actual entity like everything else and thus lose its purity. As far as it is from the traditional religious thought of most Westerners, Aristotle's Pure Potentiality may help to convey some sense of the positive quality of Buddhism's *Shunyata*, not as nothing special, but as a very special Nothing.

Yet another way of understanding *Shunyata* might be to recall that the mysterious depths of *Brahman* in Hinduism were also given a negative designation: *nirguna*, that is, "without qualities." Something without any qualities or attributes would be closer to nothing than to something; and if infinite (as Hindus believe Brahman to be), this Something would be not just Nothing-like, but Nothingness itself. After all, they claim that the best language about *Brahman* is negative: *neti neti* ("not this, not that"). Perhaps Shunyata is simply *neti neti* taken to its logical extreme: the Infinite Not. As one Western philosopher put the matter to me in conversation: "If Nothingness truly were pure and absolute Negation, sooner or later it would negate even itself and produce Something." (I am a bit embarrassed to admit that his explanation almost made sense to me.) I think the real bottom line on the matter, however, is that if philosophy has a metaphysical "brick wall," the idea of Nothingness—which has been of great interest in Western philosophy as well—is it. And Buddhism hits it not so much with a vengeance as with vigor, then presses ahead into conceptual territories where most mortal minds dare not go—at least without a guide!

The Vacuous Self

But in Buddhist philosophy the need to wrestle with seemingly negative terms does not end with *Shunyata*, for the inner spiritual essence of everyone and everything—what was called *atman* in Hinduism—is here called *anatman* (the "un-self"). This is the Buddhist doctrine of the "No Soul" or "Not Self," which says that at our very core, we are empty. (See Figure 3-4.) A human being is thought of as consisting of five constituents called *skandhas*: body, mind, feelings, perception, and will. These are dynamically interrelated in such a way that like the cosmos itself we are, in effect, processes. Also like the cosmos, whose core is Emptiness, we are correspondingly empty. Yet here again this is an

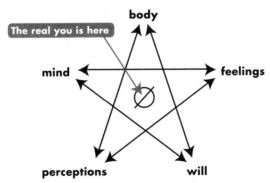

Figure 3-4

The No-Soul or Not-Self (Anatman) in Buddhist Thought

THE FIVE *SKANDAS* (bundles):

body

The real you is here

mind ← → feelings

⊘

perceptions   will

(This model suggests that a human being is a process rather than an entity. Continuity from existence to existence, then, is like that of a flame passed from candle to candle. It is the same flame with respect to process, but with respect to substance.

overflowing emptiness, fraught as it is with all possibilities for actualization or realization.

Of all of my students, the ones who understand this difficult concept of *anatman* the quickest and best are the theatre majors. That is because they are taught in acting classes that deep within them is the mysterious source of all possible characters. Their methods instructors have encouraged and taught them to dig down, far beneath the surface of their ego selves, into this inner "place" or "space," which is one of pure potential. The great actors, they are told, are the ones with the discipline to tap into this infinite reserve. That is how a Dustin Hoffman, for example, can find inside himself such utterly disparate characters as a Graduate, a Ratso Rizzo, a Lenny Bruce, a Raymond (in *Rain Man*), a Captain Hook, *and* a Tootsie. Acting classes and exercises are really all about how to access this depth dimension—this overflowing emptiness— and that makes acting, along with all true art forms, an inherently spiritual discipline.

One may wonder how Buddhism can teach reincarnation or transmigration when there appears to be nothing to be disembodied in the first place, much less re-embodied later. The answer to that question is sometimes given by lighting a candle, then using that candle to light another, and so on, blowing out each candle as soon as the next is lit, so that only one remains lit at the end of the line. Is that the same flame we started with five or six candles ago? The answer is "yes and no": there has been continuity, but nothing *substantial* remains because flames are *processes.* Indeed, Buddhism has what might be deemed a process philosophy, for everything and everyone are seen to be nothing but connected and interactive processes and patterns. It might also be called a non-essentialist or existentialist philosophy; for if all things are empty, they can have no definable essences, but only their existence.

Bliss and Benevolence

For Buddhism, as we have seen, the termination of suffering is achieved by *nirvana*. (See Figure 3-5.) That word literally means "self-extinction" and bears the connotation of having been blown out like a candle, as in the illustration above. Here again the challenge is to find a positive connotation for such a notion. What *nirvana* amounts to is an experience of one's inner emptiness (*anatman*), which is nothing other than the inner emptiness of all things (*Shunyata*). *Nirvana*, therefore, is a profound sense of the Oneness (or is it the "Noneness"?) of all things in the cosmos. (See Figure 3-6.)

Figure 3-5

The Four Linchpins of Buddhist Philosophy

Ultimate Reality = *Shunyata*
(Nothingness, the Void, Emptiness)

Temporal Reality = *samsara*
(all things as interconnected and impermanent)

Human spiritual essence: *anatman*
(the no/not soul/self)

Human spiritual goal: *nirvana*
(bliss, the extinguishing of self)

Note: While *Shunyata* and *samsara* are usually seen as very different kinds of reality and contrasted with one another, advanced Buddhist teaching maintains that they are identical precisely because both are empty. That is why the famous *Heart Sutra* can say, "Form is emptiness, emptiness is form."

Figure 3-6

Correcting an Old Joke

It may be surprising to learn that in Buddhism this experience of the unity of all things gives rise to what may be the most radical view of compassion (*karuna*) of any known religion. This compassion is not mere sympathy. Nor is it even empathy. It is far more profound. It stems from the conviction that all sentient beings (at least) are essentially the same. If anyone hurts, all hurt. It's not a matter of "I feel your pain," but rather that your pain *is mine*. Buddhist compassion even transcends the neat and comfortable distinctions we like to make between good and bad people, victims and victimizers. It is to be applied equally to all. Why? Because we "inter-be" with all human beings. *Nirvana* therefore inevitably leads to a sense of social and even political responsibility. But we also "inter-be" with all beings everywhere, sentient and non-sentient, which means that compassion should be extended to nature as well—a conviction that spurs many modern Buddhists to work for the protection of the whole environment. All such activism in the name of radical compassion operates today under the banner of "Engaged Buddhism."

Buddhists believe that on the path to realization or *nirvana*, assistance is available in the form of what they call "skillful means" (*upaya*). This term can apply to most anything: a person (a teacher perhaps, though not necessarily), a place, a writing, a picture, a piece of music, a chant, a slap, a dead animal, and so forth *ad infinitum*. We supposedly encounter these skillful means often, and in the most unexpected forms and serendipitous situations; and we usually recognize them as such only in hindsight. Nonetheless, they are considered important and perhaps even essential aids on the Buddhist spiritual path.

Historical Development

Any religion that endures for any time at all—in my cynical moments I say, "longer than two weeks"—is bound to experience complications and controversy. Once the founder (if there is one) is gone, the disciples struggle to make sense of who he or she was and what he or she was about; the almost inevitable result is disagreement about those important issues, and it is often profound. On top of that, the followers generally evince an irresistible urge to codify and reify the faith in the form of complex doctrines that stand in stark contrast to the founder's relatively simple teachings. In addition, they typically seem driven to create formal institutions and offices that contrast markedly with the informal and sometimes rag-tag community that surrounded the departed leader, and rules and regulations that either far exceed or completely contradict his or her own vision and values. If that were not enough, a religion that

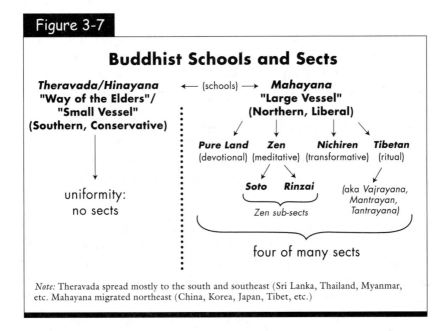

Figure 3-7

Buddhist Schools and Sects

Theravada/Hinayana ← (schools) → *Mahayana*
"Way of the Elders"/ "Large Vessel"
"Small Vessel" (Northern, Liberal)
(Southern, Conservative)

Pure Land *Zen* *Nichiren* *Tibetan*
(devotional) (meditative) (transformative) (ritual)

uniformity:
no sects

Soto *Rinzai* (aka Vajrayana,
Mantrayan,
Zen sub-sects Tantrayana)

four of many sects

Note: Theravada spread mostly to the south and southeast (Sri Lanka, Thailand, Myanmar, etc. Mahayana migrated northeast (China, Korea, Japan, Tibet, etc.)

develops a successful missionary impulse will invariably pick up foreign ideas and practices from every new culture and spirituality it encounters, and these only generate further complication and controversy. Everything in this paragraph accurately characterizes the history of Buddhism.

The Two Schools

When religions split, it is almost invariably along the fault line of conservative vs. liberal. This is not a matter of politics, but of how closely the generations after the founder's departure believe that his words and deeds should be followed. This is certainly the case with Buddhism, which early on divided sharply into two schools. (See Figure 3-7.) The more conservative, Theravada, held that insofar as possible the Buddha's words and deeds should be followed to the letter. The more liberal Mahayana school maintained that his words and deeds should be followed in principle, but with allowance for the development of new forms as the faith evolved and expanded its sphere of influence. Not surprisingly, such flexibility all but guaranteed the rise of a wide variety of Mahayana interpretations and institutional expressions, the latter in the form of sects.

Theravada means "Way of the Elders," a designation that already sounds conservative. It is also called *Hinayana* ("The Little Vehicle" or "The Small Vessel") by its detractors in the other school, precisely because of its narrow interpretation of just about every aspect of Buddhist life. Theravadans insist, for example, that the canon of scripture, the *Tripitaka*, be read in the Pali language, which was the Buddha's native tongue. And they apply the term "Buddha" almost exclusively to Siddhartha Gautama after his Enlightenment, and limit the attribution of *bodhisattva* ("Buddha-to-be" or "budding Buddha") to his previous lives. Further, Theravada is very monk-centered because its adherents believe that the Buddha's teachings and actions indicated this to be the way things should be. Indeed, most Theravadans believe that only a monk (*bhikkhu* in Pali) can achieve full spiritual realization and the status of *arahant* ("worthy one"), at which point they consider his work finished, for he bears no responsibility for helping others to their realization. Laypersons are important, but only in supporting the *Sangha* (community of monks) with gifts of food, cloth, and other basic necessities of life, and thus freeing the monks to concentrate on their goal of enlightenment. In so doing, the layperson gains merit and perhaps a measure of good fortune, and positions herself or himself for a better incarnation next time—perhaps as a (male) person fit for the monastic life and a chance to achieve *nirvana.*

The Mahayana ("Big Vehicle" or "Great Vessel") School is much more flexible, broad, and inclusive than the Theravada at every turn. It not only allows but encourages the use of any of the various versions of the *Tripitaka*—for example, the Sanskrit, Chinese, Korean, and Tibetan translations—despite the fact that they diverge from and contradict one another on many points. Mahayana Buddhists also have a fondness for extra-canonical scriptures, particularly the *Sutras* ("Lessons"), and most especially the *Heart Sutra, Diamond Sutra,* and *Lotus Sutra,* all of which they regard as inspirational, if not inspired, and depending on their sect, more or less authoritative, despite their lack of antiquity. Mahayanans also recognize a wide variety of Buddhas, some earthly and some eternally celestial, as well as a host of compassionate *bodhisattvas* who serve humanity as something like benevolent angels or saints. In fact the word *bodhisattva* has a number of meanings in Mahayana. As in Theravada it can refer to the previous lives of Siddhartha Gautama, but it may also apply to any sentient being as rightfully a "budding Buddha." It can also denote a person who has actually earned *nirvana* in life, but who at death—rather than seizing the *parinirvana* to which she or he is entitled—wills herself or himself back into *samsara* in order to help others in their spiritual quests. Finally, Mahayanans generally regard the *Sangha* to include monks and laypersons, males and females, and thus all Buddhists everywhere. Indeed, most sects in this tradition recognize female monks or nuns.

A part of Mahayana Buddhism's rationale for this kind of flexibility is that the Buddha left with his disciples secret teachings that have been passed on and only gradually revealed over time. Be that as it may, one thing is certain: if a religious tradition allows for flexibility, it will get it. In the case of Mahayana, that flexibility has produced a variety of expressions called "sects." This stands in sharp contrast to the conservative Theravada tradition which, by employing the Buddha as a litmus test or plumb line, has remained a single school and a single sect.

The Two Regions

Though both schools originally spread and enjoyed success in all directions from their native India, Theravada gradually came to dominate South and Southeast Asia, including Sri Lanka (Ceylon), Myanmar (Burma), Thailand (Siam), Kampuchea (Cambodia), and parts of Vietnam and Indonesia. Mahayana, by contrast, prospered most toward the north and in the vicinity of the eastern portion of the ancient trade route called "The Silk Road," which took this particular school to China, Korea, and Japan. (See Figure 3-8.) Tibet and its neighbors had long been isolated from Indian Buddhist missions by virtue of their location high in the Himalayas, and so received the new missionary religion relatively late and from the more accessible northeast, well after the territorial lines between Theravada and Mahayana had crystalized.

As might be expected of a conservative school, Theravada exhibits a remarkable uniformity across the part of the world it dominates, for all of its followers emulate the same standard: the founder himself and his words and deeds. Moving from country to country and culture to culture in the Theravada region, therefore, one would see little difference in Buddhism in terms of appearance, practice, and beliefs. The shared pattern would be monks begging for food, living simply, and meditating in little isolated communities or alone, with laypersons supporting them and awaiting a more auspicious future life. Mahayana, by contrast, has issued forth in seemingly countless sects that exhibit a mind-boggling range of beliefs and practices. Japan alone recognizes no fewer than thirteen major sects of Buddhism, and that does not include a number of smaller and newer expressions that despite their originality and idiosyncrasies, still identify themselves as Buddhist.

One more thing should be added about the Buddhist missions of both schools: unlike those of Christianity and Islam, they were accomplished

Figure 3-8

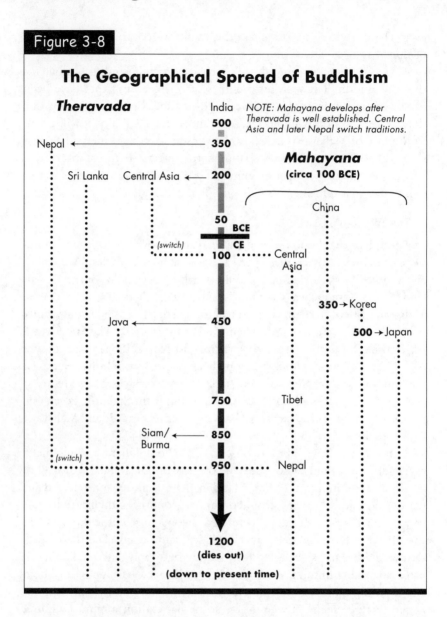

The Geographical Spread of Buddhism

utterly peacefully and with no connection to imperialist expansion or colonialism. Buddhists have fought wars, of course, and sometimes as the aggressors. But they have never advanced their faith by that means: there have never been Buddhist *conquistadors* or *jihadis*. From the start, in fact, Buddhists have taken the approach of gentle persuasion coupled with a non-exclusive attitude. They have never marched into a new region, con-demned the existing religion or spiritual beliefs and practices as inferior or wrong, and pronounced their own as the one true faith. Instead, they have observed and affirmed the existing beliefs and practices, then offered Buddhism as a supplementary or complementary system. One of two pat-terns has invariably resulted: either Buddhism learned to coexist with what was already there, sometimes in a remarkable symbiosis, or it mixed with the existing beliefs and practices to take on an altogether new and synthetic form. The former occurred in Sri Lanka and Japan, and the lat-ter in Tibet.

Buddhism in the West

Like Hinduism, Buddhism arrived in earnest in the West only with the opening of the World Parliament of Religions in Chicago in 1893, where it was represented by Rinzai Zen teacher (*roshi*) Soyen Shaku of Kamakura, Japan. Lacking the fluency in English and the flashy style of his counterparts representing other religious traditions, Shaku did not make much of an impression on his largely Western audience; but he met a publisher there who asked him to stay in the United States to translate Buddhist works. Although unable to do so himself, he recommended one of his students, Daisetz Teitaro Suzuki, whose many books on Buddhism over the next fifty years or so helped to spread the Buddhist *Dharma* in America. Another of Soyen's students founded the Buddhist Society of America in 1931.

Books by the Englishman Alan Watts in the 1950s and '60s and by Philip Kapleau in the 1960s and '70s helped to popularize Buddhism in the West even further. Like Hinduism, Buddhism also was advanced by the beatnik and hippie countercultural movements of the 1950s and '60s, finding clear expression in the works of Jack Kerouac and Gary Snyder. Robert Pirsig's *Zen and the Art of Motorcycle Maintenance* reached a wide audience in the 1970s, and further raised the West's consciousness of that most paradoxical form of Buddhism. Traditions other than Zen have also gained significant followings in recent years, a process helped by the influx of Asian people in the decades following the relaxed Immigration Act of 1963.

One measure of Buddhism's increasing popularity in this country is the huge and growing number of books in print on the subject, includ-ing a large number sporting the title *The Zen of.* ... The books of Thich Nhat Hanh have become especially popular, as have those of His Holiness the Dalai Lama and a host of American-born Buddhists, including some

female luminaries to be mentioned later in this chapter. Buddhist period-
icals like *Tricycle: The Buddhist Review* and *What is Enlightment?* have
gained wide circulation, and Buddhism has been the subject of a number
of popular movies, including *The Karate Kid, Golden Child, Little
Buddha, Seven Years in Tibet, Kundun*, and even appears in the opening
scenes of the sequel to *Ace Ventura, Pet Detective*. (All but the first of
these films feature Tibetan Buddhism, no doubt because it is so colorful
and photogenic.) More and more actors and other entertainers, it seems,
are openly professing the Buddhist faith, and Buddhist congregations of
one sect or another are springing up all over the country—even in the
Midwestern heartland—thereby changing the religious topography of
America dramatically and, one would suspect, permanently.

Distinctive Practices

To say that Buddhist practice takes on a wide variety of forms would
be an understatement. Because of its concern to emulate the founder of
the faith as closely as possible, Theravada observance is quite uniform
across the entire region of South and Southeast Asia that it dominates.
But being monk-centered, it has had little appeal in the West beyond its
distinctive style of meditation called *vipassana*, which involves a focusing
on thought, feelings, and actions in order to realize the impermanence of
all things, including the self—in other words, to match the Buddha's
achievement. Mahayana, by contrast, not only diverges greatly from
country to country, but even from sect to sect within the countries in
which it thrives; and some of its forms have made a great impression on
the West. Since an overview of all or even very many of the Mahayana
sects is beyond the scope of this book, let us focus on only four, chosen
because of their diversity and because to date they have influenced the
West more than any of the others. These are the devotional Amida or
Pure Land, the contemplative Zen, the reformist Nichiren, and the mag-
ical-mystical Tibetan. It is perhaps ironic that only one of them might be
recognizable to the religion's founder, Siddhartha Gautama.

Pure Land Buddhism

Pure Land or Amida Buddhism was founded in China, but imported to
Japan in the thirteenth century by a Japanese man named Honen, who
raised it to a new level there. It is based on the belief in a celestial Buddha
named Amida, whose infinite compassion is often pictured as the warming
rays of the setting sun. Amida Buddhism teaches that people who put their
faith in this particular Buddha will be reborn in the Pure Land (*Sukhavati*),

a Paradise in the Western sky. As a way of practicing their faith, Pure Land Buddhists are encouraged to utter a *mantra* called the *nembutsu*: "*Namu Amida Butsu*" (I revere the Amida Buddha). In fact, Honen advised saying this 70,000 times a day—approximately the number of daily heartbeats of someone in extraordinary physical shape or deep in a meditative state. That observation suggests that Honen may have meant that prayer should be autonomic and ceaseless.

In addition to the Amida Buddha, Pure Land Buddhism recognizes important compassionate beings called *bodhisattvas* (*bosatsu* in Japanese), who are, in effect, extensions of Amida and his infinite compassion. Foremost among these is Kannon, who is generally portrayed as a female, and who may well be the most popular object of Japanese religious affection, devotion, and piety. Images of her are seen everywhere in Japan, and one Buddhist temple in Kyoto, the Sanjusangendo, houses 1,000 nearly life-size, standing, wooden statues of Kannon, plus one more large one seated in their midst. Kannon, in turn, has helpers. Chief among them is the *bosatsu* Jizo (pronounced, no kidding, "Jeez-OH"). This bald little fellow specializes in caring for the souls of dead babies and aborted fetuses in the underworld of the dead. In fact, at his many little shrines found all over Japan, including on busy city streets, parents drop off messages and toys for him to deliver to their deceased offspring. In appreciation, mourning moms make little hats, bibs, and other garments to keep their bald little benefactor warm. Jizo statues are often found in groups. In fact, in Japan I saw one grotto that had hundreds of them, many with prayers from parents attached to them, and some draped with folded-paper (*origami*) cranes for good luck and healing.

Pure Land (or Amida) Buddhism exists in Japan today in two principle bodies. *Jodo* traces its lineage back to Honen, but the revisionist *Jodo Shinshu* or "True Pure Land," which originated with Honen's somewhat disgruntled disciple and reformer, Shinran, has the largest number of followers of any form of Buddhism there. The best explanation for why this is so is that like any religion that encourages its followers to put faith in the gracious saving efforts of another, Pure Land is relatively easy, exerting minimal demands and requiring very little of its followers beyond an occasional expression of faith and devotion. For that reason, it is difficult to imagine that the original Buddha—who counseled his disciples to be self-reliant—would recognize, much less endorse, Pure Land. Of course, that fact does not necessarily disqualify it as a valid spiritual expression, since Amida Buddhism may just meet an affective need (at least for some) that the Buddha's teachings cannot.

Zen Buddhism

In comparison to Pure Land Buddhism, Zen (*Chan* in Chinese) is much more challenging and time-consuming, for it calls upon its practitioners to work out their own spiritual liberation by engaging in regular and rigorous meditation. It is also far more complicated, and thus requires more explanation than the comfortable, devotional Pure Land. Zen also deserves a bit more attention than the other three because it is so unlike anything found in the mainstream expressions of the three major Western religions. And it may be precisely because of its distinctive spirit and style that Zen has had such an appeal to some American Christians and Jews, who just may have found something important there that they were missing in their own traditions.

The word *zen* means "meditation" in Japanese, and meditation is the foundation of Zen. Its origination is credited to an Indian man named Bodhidharma, who carried his meditation technique to China in the late fifth or early sixth century CE, where it absorbed some elements of Taoism before arriving in Japan centuries later. The core practice is called *zazen*, which in Japanese means "seated meditation," something that a very serious student will do many hours a day for many years—and perhaps for a lifetime. *Zazen* aims at a state of consciousness called *satori*, which Zen adherents believe to be the same clear-minded awareness that Siddhartha Gautama achieved as he sat under the Bo tree. Followers of Zen sometimes refer to *satori* as the cleansing of the mind's "mirror" of all of the accumulated dust, smoke, and smudges (that is, thoughts, ideas, information, knowledge, and preconceptions) that it has accumulated since birth, when it was perfectly clean and truly reflective of reality. This is the "beginner's mind" that Zen practitioners hope to achieve in order to see things the way a newborn baby might: on their own terms and as they really are, rather than as society and culture and parents and teachers have dictated. To use another favorite Zen image, the objective is to slow down the "monkey mind" that is always grasping greedily for more, more, more to fill—and, as it turns out, to clutter and obscure—it.

Different Zen sub-sects place their own unique wrinkles on the practice of *zazen*. Soto Zen, for example, commends "just sitting" (*shikan taza*), facing a relatively drab wall, keeping eyes slighty open but soft-focused, concentrating on nothing in particular (except perhaps one's own breathing), and allowing the mind to clear itself of its accretions. Soto teaches that *satori* is a gradual attainment, and that whether or not results are perceptible, one is making progress as long as one is engaged in the practice. Rinzai ("RINZ-eye") is a bit more active. It adds to the mix riddles or brain-stumpers called *koan* (which is both singular and plural and pronounced "KO-ahn"), the answers to which are expected to grow out of the meditation experience. Rinzai students don't really meditate on the *koan*, but rather endure its peripheral presence as a nagging, seemingly insoluble problem that must nevertheless be solved, but indirectly. For one can't really figure out a *koan*, but only meditate and wait for the moment of clarity when the answer will pop spontaneously out of the cleansed mind. A possible answer will be offered by the student in a private conversation with a *roshi*, a Zen Master who functions as a kind of demanding personal trainer whose concern is spiritual fitness and whose attitude is one of tough love. It is he who determines intuitively whether or not the solution presented comes out of the student's clear mind (or "empty middle," as Zen folks often put it) rather than from the novice's ingenuity, cleverness, or memory. An acceptable answer must be a-rational, may be non-verbal, and will inevitably seem strange and incongruous by logical standards. (Not surprisingly, the *koan* experience has been known to make students physically and mentally ill through frustration.) Rinzai also understands *satori* not as a gradual achievement, as the Soto tradition holds, but as a sudden acquisition that comes as a flash of insight after a long period in which progress is imperceptible or non-existent.

The most famous *koan* is probably "What is the sound of one hand clapping?" Another is "Why did Bodhidharma come from the West?" The last thing that a Zen master wants to hear from a student in response to that one is a history lesson: "To spread the meditative tradition of India to China and beyond, of course!" In fact, one student who answered, illogically but spontaneously, "The banyan tree in the garden"—as though the Indian sage had been a kind of Johnny Appleseed—was declared a Master on the spot. Yet another of the nearly 2,000 classic *koan* is this one: "Does a dog have Buddha nature?" Japanese Zennists regard the most famous answer to that riddle as that offered by a monk named Joshu (Chao-Chou in Chinese), and it appears as impertinent as the banyan tree was to Bodhidharma's trek eastward: "*Mu!*" That is Japanese for "No," a puzzling response, given the fact that the Buddha is remembered as having said that even grass has Buddha nature. But Joshu, too, was pronounced enlightened. Had the next student been eavesdropping and tried to use that "right" answer, however, the Zen Master would probably have been sorely tempted to slap him or hit him with a stick for his indolence and insolence.

Clearly, Zen focuses not on discursive, rational, logical thought, but on *experience*. Proponents insist that you cannot think your way into Zen, but must rather practice the techniques that will open you up to the desired *satori*. For the intellect will not get you there, nor will it serve you very well to articulate the experience to others even if you manage to attain it. In fact, Zen maintains a healthy contempt for conceptualization and theorizing. Nevertheless, it has produced a noble tradition of philosophy, almost in spite of itself. That may seem paradoxical, but because it doesn't trust the mind or intellect very much, the Zen tradition is quite fond of paradoxes. Here's one: Zen talks a great deal about "mindfulness" as the goal that it strives for. The trouble is that "mindfulness" bespeaks a state of consciousness or awareness that ideally is empty of thoughts, knowledge, facts, concepts, and preconceptions—a mind that is, in effect, full of emptiness!

Pervasiveness vs. Popularity

It surprises many Americans to learn that Zen is actually one of the least popular forms of Buddhism in Japan today. In fact, lay people there who practice it (as opposed to those who study for the Zen priesthood) are considered a bit eccentric. As should be evident by now, however, in both its Soto and Rinzai forms, Zen practice (if done right) is arduous and demanding. It is anything but an easy way. No wonder that Pure Land in both its major expressions is far more popular! But this is not to say that Zen has not deeply affected Japanese culture. It can be seen subtly present in a host of customs and folkways, as well as in some more overt institutions, such as the traditional tea ceremony (*chado*), martial arts (*kendo*, *judo*, etc.), flower arranging (*kado*), archery (*kyudo*), calligraphy (*shodo*), ink drawing (*sumi*-e), and poetry, especially *haiku*.

The last mentioned of these art forms is the well-known three-line, seventeen-syllable distinctively Japanese poem that has no metaphor or hidden meaning, but is a kind of verbal "snap-shot" of the poet's pure awareness of something. The most famous haiku of all is this one by the seventeenth century Japanese poet Basho: *Furuike ya;/Kawazu tobikomo—/Miso no oto*, which translates, "Old Pond;/Frog jumps in—/Sound of Water" (or simply "Splash"). Typical of a true *haiku*, nothing in that poem represents anything else. The pond is just a pond. The frog is merely a frog. And the splash is only a splash. The poem simply encapsulates a pure experience. In the same vein are the Zen rock gardens that are found at Rinzai temples all over Japan. Tour books pretend to tell you what all of the rocks and gravel symbolically "mean." In fact, these gardens are like *koan* and *haiku* in the sense that they don't "mean" anything, but are expressive of and conducive to the direct experience of a quiet mind.

The closest Western experience to Zen awareness is probably an athlete's experience of being "in the zone," where everything simply flows together for a "can't miss or lose" moment. This phenomenon is probably best seen in the relatively confined and fast-moving sport of basketball: on rare occasions, a player (or all five), the court, the ball, and the goal are all one flowing process, and every shot seems magically to score. Athletes testify that the surest way to lose this state of "mind"—Buddhists call it "no-mind"—is to think about it or what you're doing. Mindless mind. Effortless effort. This sort of thing perhaps happens for us non-athletes in less spectacular activities, as when we manage to be completely "in the moment" while engaged in activities like dancing, listening to music, or looking at art for the pure joy of them. These probably come very close to being Zen experiences. Perhaps a subliminal sense that we Westerners need to pay more attention to such "mindless" but fulfilling activities is what accounts for the enormous current popularity of books with "Zen" and some common activity like driving, sailing, fishing, or skiing linked in the title.

Nichiren Buddhism

Yet another sect of Mahayana that is gaining significant visibility and attracting many followers is Nichiren, which today has a number of subsects and offshoots, the largest being Nichiren Shoshu. Unlike Pure Land and Zen, Nichiren is a home-grown Japanese sect, and is second in adherents only to True Pure Land. Nichiren ("Sun Lotus") bears the symbolic adopted name of its founder, who was a thirteenth century contemporary of both Honen and Shinran. Initially he was a follower of the centuries-older Tendai school, which extolled the virtues of thousands of Mahayana Buddhist texts (particularly the *Lotus Sutra*), arranged them in categories by difficulty, and struggled to understand all of them rationally. But Nichiren found the number of texts offered in Tendai overwhelming, and—in a kind of minimalist fit—declared the *Lotus Sutra* a complete and sufficient compendium of all essential Buddhist doctrine. In a further departure from his Tendai precursors and contemporaries, who counseled a rational interpretation of that scripture (among the many others), Nichiren believed that because his era was so corrupt and decadent, most people were powerless to do that, even if they focused on his favorite. He therefore suggested that it would suffice to sing the virtues of the *Lotus Sutra* by simply intoning its title in the form of a *mantra* called the *daimoku*, which consisted of the simple phrase *Nam Myoho Renge Kyo* ("Hail to the Holy Law of the Lotus Sutra"). He proposed that devotees would thereby internalize the power of the *Dharma* contained in the book without having to open it, much less read or wrestle with it.

So far, this approach looks a great deal like that of the devotional Pure Land sect, and it certainly began that way and still bears a strain of devotionalism. But Nichiren went beyond that by declaring that if his followers were conscientious in their chanting, the power of the *Lotus Sutra* would transform not only them, but the entire social and political order as well. In fact, it would not only guarantee personal and material success, but also bring about a kind of Buddhist heaven on earth, full of peace and abundance. In other words, Nichiren and his followers were not so much venerating the *Lotus Sutra* as tapping into its power. The essential dynamic of the form of Buddhism named for this revisionist, then, is much less devotional than transformative, and not so much theoretical as practical. Both in Japan and worldwide, it and its offshoots are arguably the most materialistic expression of Buddhism. Not surprisingly, these groups have also been linked to Japanese nationalism and political activism, a connection that would be inconceivable for either the meditative Zen or the devotional Pure Land sects.

To a degree highly uncharacteristic of Buddhism, Nichiren (the man) was sharply critical of these and other Buddhist sects. For example, he called Pure Land Buddhism "hell" because of its other-worldly orientation and Zen "a devil." He was also quite aggressive in his promotion of what he touted as the one true Buddhism, an approach and attitude that got him into a great deal of social and political trouble. His modern followers, especially of the Shoshu variety, have gone far beyond their founder and his own claim to be the incarnation of a minor Buddha; they proclaim him the *only* Buddha worthy of attention. In effect, they have placed him on a par with the *sutra* that he so extolled and elevated.

A relatively recent offshoot of Nichiren is the modern lay movement founded in the 1930s called Soka Gakkai ("Society for the Preservation of Values"). Like Nichiren himself, this organization has stirred up a great deal of controversy within the Nichiren community and among the general public, largely because of its exclusivism and aggressive proselytizing techniques. (These are called *shaku baku*, which practically begs to be translated "Shake 'n' Bake evangelism.") Soka Gakkai's self-promotion outside Japan, however, has been low key and yet quite effective; claiming over two million followers in the United States alone, it rivals in success the more orthodox Los Angeles based Nichiren Shoshu of America. The advancement of Nichiren in the West is due in part to such famous followers as jazz pianist and composer Herbie Hancock and rock-and-roll diva Tina Turner. The latter, in fact, is depicted chanting the *daimoku* just before a crucial scene toward the end of the film *What's Love Got to Do with It*.

Tibetan Buddhism

The fourth sect of the Mahayana school we'll look at is Tibetan Buddhism, also known as *Vajrayana* ("The Lightning Vehicle"), *Mantrayana* ("The Chant Vehicle"), and *Tantrayana* ("The Action Vehicle"). These three alternative names reflect the belief of some scholars that this style of Buddhism is sufficiently different from the others to qualify as a School in its own right. Others argue that the flexibility and breadth of Mahayana are adequate to encompass what I affectionately call this "weird, wild, wacky, and wonderful" expression of Buddhism.

What makes Tibetan Buddhism so much more colorful than other forms is the fact that when Buddhism arrived in Tibet, shamanism (called *Bon* there) was well established, and Buddhism simply merged with it. As a result, we find beliefs, practices, and objects in Tibetan Buddhism that are found nowhere else in the Buddhist world. Only in its Tibetan branch, for example, are priests called *lamas*. The most prestigious and famous of these is His Holiness The Dalai Lama, who has lived in exile in northern India since the Chinese communists invaded and annexed his country in 1959, and cruelly suppressed the faith and its leaders. Unlike their counterparts elsewhere, Tibetan *lamas* wear very ornate robes and masks, perform ritualistic dances, and blow haunting notes on conch shells or large alpine-style horns. Prayer wheels generate prayers and blessings when spun by the devout (or anyone, actually, believer or skeptic), and prayer flags generate positive spiritual energy and blessings simply by flapping in the wind. And no other form of Buddhism uses chants or mantras more than Tibetan Buddhism or employs the distinctive sound produced by throat-generated intonations that enable a single voice to produce haunting overtones that amount to a chord. The most distinctive Tibetan *mantra* is *Om mani padme hum*, which means "the Ultimate in the heart of the lotus," though its power arises from the sound, not the meaning. This phrase can be seen inscribed on prayer wheels and even rocks in Nepal, Bhutan, and those places in northern India frequented by Tibetans. Tibetan Buddhism is also famous for its extremely intricate and beautiful patterns (*mandalas* or *yantras*), which take *lamas* days and sometimes weeks to design and construct from grains of colored sand. The priests then ceremonially sweep up the sand, place it in a container, and pour it out into the nearest stream or river, thereby demonstrating one of the last teachings of the Buddha: "All things are transitory."

Perhaps the most distinctive thing about Tibetan Buddhism is its belief system, especially as regards deities, demons, and death. Unlike other forms of Buddhism, Tibetan Buddhists have deities and demons that they portray in art and appeal to in their meditation, though some—ostensibly the most sophisticated—claim that these are only metaphors for inner states of consciousness. Tibetan Buddhism also displays a fascination with the state of the soul between incarnations—what they call the *bardo* state—and in fact embraces a unique scripture, the so-called *Tibetan Book of the Dead*, which is supposed to guide people through this uncertain and sometimes treacherous interval.

Given its many idiosyncrasies, it is no wonder that many regard Tibetan Buddhism as too odd to fit even the broadly inclusive Mahayana School, and therefore assign it to a separate school: the *Vajrayana*. It is not alone in this regard: the Shingon sect in Japan resembles Tibetan Buddhism in many respects and is generally included in the Vajrayana school as well—if indeed that is accepted as a separate school. Though both sides offer persuasive reasons and arguments, I tend to side with those who find the definition of Mahayana broad enough to include even the eccentric Tibetan style, though I find the counter-arguments almost equally sound and compelling. Whether or not one finally consigns Tibetan Buddhism to a separate school, however, the real point is to recognize and acknowledge just how *outré* it truly is.

Sorting the Sects

These four types of Buddhism—devotional, meditative, transformative, and ritualistic respectively—are obviously quite different from one another; and three of them appear to depart dramatically from what the meditative Siddhartha Gautama supposedly intended. One wonders, for example, what that ancient Indian monk, who counseled simplicity among his disciples, would make of the many intricate trappings and rituals of Tibetan Buddhism. It is also difficult to imagine that a man whose last words were about self-reliance and taking refuge in the Truth alone would recognize as Buddhist, let alone endorse, any movement that taught reliance on another, whether Amida's celestial Buddha or a sacred scripture like Nirichen's *Lotus Sutra*. Still more difficult, perhaps, is the prospect that he would accept Nichiren Buddhism's goals of worldly power and success as anything even resembling his message about eliminating all desires and the suffering they bring.

Such observations, of course, beg the question of whether—as conservative or fundamentalist voices would maintain—a religion's perhaps inevitable departure from the intention of its founder is necessarily a bad thing. Indeed, it could be argued that a religion can and does survive only by meeting people's needs, and those are bound to vary from individual to individual, as well as from time to time, place to place, and situation to situation. Had Buddhism remained pristine and true to the teachings of its founder, its appeal might well have been so time-stamped and culture-specific that it would have withered and died. It would have thus consigned to obscurity or oblivion the very teachings and values that the various schools and sects have preserved, ironically, even as they were busily engaged in breaching them.

Be that as it may, the four Mahayana Buddhist sects discussed above—and perhaps all human religious expressions—can usefully be divided into what the Japanese call *jiriki* and *tariki*. *Jiriki* denotes a sect that teaches that "salvation" (broadly defined) comes by one's own efforts, while *tariki* characterizes one that teaches reliance on another (for example, the Amida Buddha and his compassion). The former, which certainly would include the arduous practice of Zen, is sometimes described as "monkey faith," referring to the effort that baby simians must exert to hold onto their mothers' fur as they move together from place to place. *Tariki*, by contrast, is called "marsupial faith," alluding to the fact that babies of this species are carried effortlessly in their mothers' pouches. Nothing in this distinction suggests that one style is better than the other, though it must be said (for whatever it is worth) that Siddhartha himself would probably have chosen the little monkeys as the more appropriate symbol of his own self-reliant Middle Way—and would have encouraged them to let go of their moms and wend their own ways as soon as possible.

Women in Buddhism

Buddhism is typical among the world's religions in conveying a mixed message about the role and status of women, but this ambivalence is unique because it is traceable to the founder of the tradition. It is said that the Buddha believed women to be fully capable of achieving enlightenment and *nirvana*, but was reluctant to ordain them into the monastic Sangha because they would be distractions—that is, objects of *desire*, the cause of all suffering—to the male monks (*bhikkhus*). Importuned by his step-mother-aunt Mahaprajapati and his favorite disciple Ananda, however, he finally agreed to form an order of *bhikkhunis* (nuns), but imposed on them over a hundred additional rules (338 as opposed to a mere 221 for the monks). These extra regulations were supposedly intended to protect them from the monks within the Sangha and from outside suspicions and rumors. Ironically, the conservative Theravada school, which claims to follow the founder's teachings and deeds more strictly than other Buddhists, eventually allowed the sisterhood to all but die out—or discouraged it into virtual extinction. The result is that in most Southeast Asian countries where Theravada dominates, there are no *bhikkunis* today, though Thailand has an estimated 20,000 unordained nuns called *jis*. (A small number of these have sought and received ordination abroad, mainly in China, where Theravada is weak but still recognizes *bhikkhunis*, but their new status is not acknowledged by the Thai monks.) The one bright spot in the picture for women is that the *vipassana* meditation style that originated in Theravada is now being taught to men and women alike, at least in American meditation centers.

The story in Mahayana is much different. This school typically gives both women and lay people a far greater role even as it de-emphasizes and even discourages both monasticism and celibacy in most of its sectarian expressions. In the very popular varieties of Pure Land Buddhism, the priesthood is admittedly male dominated; but women are very active and, since the home is the primary locus of this form of spirituality, mothers and grandmothers are especially honored as purveyors of the warmth of the Amida Buddha's love. Indeed, Amida's most popular *bodhisattva* (enlightened helper) is Kwan Yin (China) or Kannon (Japan), a beloved figure and object of intense devotion who is found in iconography all over the Far East. Also, if my experience is any indication, most of the routine religious activity at Pure Land temples in Japan appears to be conducted by women. For its part, the Zen tradition has long recognized the ability of women to achieve the enlightened mind (*satori*), and has ordained and honored outstanding female teachers (*roshis*). Whether regarded as a form of Mahayana or a separate "vehicle," the Vajryana tradition has traditionally held women and the feminine spiritual dynamic in high esteem, though it too has a male-dominated priesthood. In addition, one of Tibetan Buddhism's most honored deities is the goddess Tara; and not only have some women attained such a high level of spiritual realization as to be recognized as *siddhas* ("perfected beings"), but others are regarded as either *tulkus* (reincarnated lamas) or even *lamas* in their own right.

As was the case with Theravada, the more liberal Buddhist traditions of China, Korea, Japan, and Tibet are finding whatever regard they have for women magnified in the West. Indeed, by most accounts, the majority of Western Buddhist adherents and practitioners are females in the Mahayana and Vajrayana traditions; and from these ranks come some of the most popular writers on Buddhism today, such as Ane Pema Chödrön (nee Deirdre Blomfield-Brown), Charlotte Joko Beck, and Sylvia Boorstein. All of this has led many to conclude that Mahayana and Vajrayana Buddhism have surpassed the world's major religious expressions in their liberated attitude toward and opportunities for women.

Conclusion

What Christians should know about Buddhism above all is that it exhibits the same kind of diversity found in their own faith and most of the other great religions of the world. In the case of Pure Land Buddhism, we have a spiritual style that in Hinduism would be called *bhakti marga*, because of its devotionalism. It thus exhibits much the same dynamic as evangelical Protestant Christianity, which emphasizes "loving the Lord" and trusting God's mercy to secure a place in a heavenly paradise. Tibetan Buddhism and its ritualism, by contrast, can be seen as an expression of the "hands-on" practicality and activism of *karma marga*. With its priests, colorful vestments, sacraments, candles, symbolic gestures, chants, and striking visual art, it is reminiscent of Catholic and Eastern Orthodox Christianity. Nichiren also represents *karma yoga*, though with a different slant, for its activity is more concerned with social and political *ethics* and personal success of a worldly sort than with *ritual*, which is kept to a minimum. Zen, then, reflects a thoroughgoing *jnana marga* because of its determination to use the mind to pursue clarity, albeit in some strange ways, even by Eastern standards of mental discipline. The closest thing in Christianity to the religious dynamic presented by Zen is the largely suppressed mystical subtradition found mostly in Catholicism and Eastern Orthodoxy. But a similar impulse can also be seen as well in Protestant and Sectarian Christianity: formerly in the introverted spirituality of the early Quakers, and recently in the principles (if not always in the practices) of the most Christian expression of the New Thought movement, Unity.

All four of these expressions of Mahayana Buddhism have something to offer Christianity. Pure Land Buddhism would seem to have little to offer Christian devotionalism, except perhaps to declare that Christians were focusing their faith and love on the wrong Lord, and should turn instead to Amida. But its contention that the Amida Buddha is so thoroughly compassionate that all people everywhere will eventually be received into the Pure Land might stir some useful reflection among Christians about some of their own most cherished doctrines. It might lead Christians to wonder, for example, whether the same universalist attitude shouldn't follow as logically from their New Testament's message of radical grace, its claim that Christ died *for all*, and its stark assertion that God *is* love. The social-political vision of Nichiren might likewise help Christians to recover a lost or repressed enthusiasm for the Reign of God that was the heart of Jesus' teachings, and that seems to call for a radical transformation, not just of individuals, but of the power-structures within which they live.

But Theravada and Zen—the two forms of Buddhism whose emphasis on meditation most authentically recaptures the experience of Siddhartha Gautama—probably have the most to offer Christians. The reason is that Christianity's monotheistic stance, which typically looks to a celestial God rather than one who dwells within, has made little room for introverted spirituality and thus produced only a meager mystical tradition. The growing popularity of Buddhism among active and former Christians, and especially of *vipassana* and *zazen* meditation, suggests that people intuitively sense that something is missing in their own traditional religion, something that needs to be recovered—or, failing that, imported. The adoption of these or similar introspective spiritual techniques could well lead inevitably to a rethinking and reenvisioning of the Ultimate so experienced.

Again, we postpone the full exploration of all that might be involved in Christianity's encounter with Buddhism and the other world religions until Chapter 5, when the fruits of our journey of Orientation will be examined and evaluated in terms of their attractiveness and applicability. Meanwhile, let us turn our attention to the noble religions of China that were founded during the same busy sixth century BCE that saw the rise of Buddhism: the polar opposite but nonetheless complementary expressions, Confucianism and Taoism.

Questions for Reflection and Discussion

1. Buddhism, like many religions, began as a reform movement within another major religion. What do you make of this pattern? What, if anything, does it say about (1) human nature, the human spirit, or human spirituality; and (2) the relative value or worth of the parent faith?

2. How do you account for the similarities between the lives of Siddhartha Gautama and Jesus of Nazareth? Are these merely coincidental or archetypal in some way? Do these similarities add to or detract from the importance of each man? Why? What would be the principal argument for the opposite view?

3. What do you think is the reason behind the conflicting tendencies to follow the founder strictly and to do so only in principle? Do you think it purely an historical accident that the more conservative form of Buddhism prevailed in Southeast Asia, while the more liberal caught on and became dominant in the northern part of the continent? How do you suppose adopting one or another school of Buddhism affected the subsequent history of these areas? What might you do to test your theories in this regard?

4. Of Pure Land, Zen, Nichiren, and Tibetan Buddhism, which is most like the religious tradition you were reared in or near? How so? Which one seems most appealing or most suitable to your personality type? Why?

5. What if anything in your experiences or activities would be most Zen-like in the sense that it is best done intuitively, spontaneously, and with the rational mind disengaged? How so? How do you account for the apparent popularity of Zen, as evidenced by the many book titles about it? Recall (or rent and review) the movie *The Karate Kid*. What in that film makes more sense now that you have an idea of what Buddhism in general and Zen in particular are about?

6. What do you think about the notions that Ultimate Reality is empty and that human beings have no substantial self or soul? How would you explain those notions to a family member or friend in a way that would give it a positive spin?

Recommended Reading

Charlotte Joko Beck with Steve Smith, *Nothing Special: Living Zen*. San Francisco: HarperSanFranscisco, 1993.

Samuel Bercholz and Sherab Chodzin Kohn, *Entering the Stream: An Introduction to the Buddha and His Teachings*. Boston: Shambhala, 1993.

Sylvia Boorstein, *That's Funny, You Don't Look Buddhist: On Being a Faithful Jew and a Passionate Buddhist*. San Francisco: Harper San Francisco, 1997.

Michael Carrithers, *The Buddha: A Very Short Introduction*. Oxford/New York: Oxford University Press, 1996.

Richard Causton, *Nichiren Shoshu Buddhism*. San Francisco: Harper and Row, 1989.

Pema Chödrön, *Start Where You Are: A Guide to Compassionate Living*. Boston, Shambala Publications, 2001.

Edward Conze, *A Short History of Buddhism*. Oxford: Oneworld, 1993.

Heinrich Dumoulin, *Zen Buddhism in the 20th Century*. Trans. Joseph O'Leary. New York: Weatherhill, 1992.

Malcolm David Eckel, *Buddhism: Origins, Beliefs, Practices, Holy Texts, Sacred Places*. Oxford: Oxford University Press, 2002.

Rick Fields, *How the Swans Came to the Lake: A Narrative History of Buddhism in America*. 3d ed., rev. Boston: Shambhala Publications, 1992.

Joseph Goldstein, *Insight Meditation: The Practice of Freedom*. Boston/London: Shambhala, 1994.

Steve Hagen, *Buddhism Plain and Simple*. New York: Broadway Books, 1997.

Thich Nhat Hanh, *The Heart of the Buddha's Teaching: The Four Noble Truths, the Noble Eightfold Path, and Other Basic Buddhist Teachings*. Berkeley, CA. Parallax Press, 1998.

Damien Keown, *Buddhism: A Very Short Introduction*. Oxford/New York: Oxford University Press, 1996.

Sherab Chodzin Kohn, *The Awakened One: A Life of the Buddha*. Boston/London: Shambala, 1994.

David Scott and Tony Doubleday, *The Elements of Zen*. Rockport, MA, et al.: Element, 1992.

Robert A. F. Thurman, *Inside Tibetan Buddhism: Rituals and Symbols Revealed*. San Francisco: CollinsPublishersSanFrancisco, 1995.

Helen Tworkov, *Zen in America: Profiles of Five Teachers*. San Francisco: North Point Press, 1989.

Chapter 4

China's Two-Way Street

Confucianism and Taoism

Objectives of this Chapter

- to survey the ancient Chinese religious beliefs and concepts that predated and influenced Confucianism and Taoism

- to explain the ancient Chinese classic, the *I Ching*, its use in divination, and the belief in a synchronous cosmic order that underlies it

- to examine the troubled social and political situation of the Chou dynasty in which Confucianism and Taoism emerged

- to sketch the contemporaneous and in many ways parallel lives and careers of K'ung-fu-tzu (Confucius) and Lao-tzu

- to explore the largely divergent, but finally complementary spiritual philosophies of Confucianism and Taoism

- to suggest some practical implications and applications of these two great philosophies for modern Western life

Our spiritual journey now takes us once again to China. This time, however, we are not following the trail of a foreign-born religion, but searching out two home-grown faiths, Confucianism and Taoism. The term "faiths" may not be quite appropriate, however, for from their inception through their early development—which is the phase that will most interest us in this chapter—the traditions in question were much more like pure philosophies than vehicles of devotion and ritualism. Both of these thought systems were rooted in a compelling notion of Ultimacy that is both literally and figuratively foreign to the Western thought found in mainstream Judaism, Christianity, and Islam. Nevertheless, these three great faiths, and Christianity especially, may acquire spiritual insight and gain conceptual enrichment from these two most unlikely sources.

Overview and Origins

As we observed in Chapter 1, the sixth century BCE was a time of such widespread religious innovation and creativity as to suggest, at least in retrospect, that a vast wave of inspiration had suddenly swept over the whole world. In India alone, Hinduism was experiencing no fewer than three religious revolutions. The Vedic period was coming to a close, and its polytheism, ritualism, and priestly religion were being displaced by a newer interest in the mysticism and philosophy of the *Upanishads*. But while this Vedantic religiosity was being assimilated by the ever-inclusive Hinduism, two other reform movements, Jainism and Buddhism arose to become religions in their own right. Meanwhile, in the Middle East, a youthful Zoroastrianism was spreading through Persia and nearby lands. Under the harsh constraints of exile, Jews were beginning to transform their tribal tradition into the Judaism we know today by defining their scriptures, rituals, and observances over against the spirituality of their captors. In Greece, a new philosophical tradition was generating ideas that radically challenged and would soon displace the Homeric worldview and its Olympian deities.

According to tradition, it was just then that in China two great, contemporaneous spiritual masters were laying the foundations of what would later be known as Confucianism and Taoism. As already indicated, the teachings attributed to these two men, though clearly spiritual in essence, were so thoroughly philosophical in expression that it is a stretch to call them "religious" at all, at least in their earliest stages of development. And yet, like most of the other major living religions of the world, both of the resulting systems of thought had (and indeed shared) an Ultimate Reality—one that greatly resembles the *Brahman* of Hinduism and the *Shunyata* of Buddhism. Furthermore, both were concerned to define humanity's relationship and responsibility to that Ultimate. But the two systems were otherwise so incompatible that they appeared to be operating at cross-purposes. Though both certainly have had a tremendous impact on Chinese thought and culture over the centuries, Taoism has demonstrated a wider appeal and has more to offer the West in general and Christianity in particular. Still, it is impossible to understand Taoism fully without reference to its counterpart, over against which it consciously forged a distinctive view of the nature of the Ultimate and Its proper role in individual and corporate human existence. And to understand both Taoism and Confucianism, we must first turn our attention to the even more ancient backdrop of Chinese spiritual belief and practice from which they emerged.

Ancient Chinese Religion

To modern Westerners, the sixth century BCE no doubt seems ancient indeed. But because China's culture is so very old, the phrase "ancient Chinese religion" here refers to the hodge-podge of animism, polytheism, and a dizzying array of diverse religious beliefs and practices that predated Confucianism and Taoism. As we shall see, a few key ideas from this early period became important building blocks in those two great philosophical religions. But it is also the case that many of the elements of ancient Chinese belief and practice live on today in what is widely identified as "Chinese traditional religion" or "Chinese folk religion." These labels denote a popular, widespread, amorphous, and unsystematic amalgam that has come to include not only elements of the Confucianism and Taoism that emerged later, but also components of the Buddhism that was imported later still.

Ancient Chinese religion recognized countless favorable spirits (*shen*) that needed to be nurtured, as well as bad spirits, demons, or ghosts (all connotations of the word *kuei*) that needed to be kept at bay. It also included a plethora of deities (also called *shen*), both great and small, chief among whom was Shang-ti ("Father Heaven," also known as Yü-huang, "The Jade Emperor"). This luminary may have been an actual patriarch of the Shang dynasty who was posthumously promoted to divine status by the Chou family that superseded them as rulers. Shang-ti ruled the high court of Heaven (*T'ien*), and was responsible for the creation of humans from clay. He kept the cosmos orderly, rewarded good and punished evil, and yet remained quite remote and aloof, relying upon his intermediaries to take care of earthly matters on a day to day basis.

More accessible and therefore more popular were the *ch'eng-huang*, local deities of limited power and dominion, but who might be supplicated for such vital things as good weather and crops, and the still more subordinate and amenable *t'u-ti*, who oversaw the welfare of specific areas, streets, buildings, and households. These lesser deities, mostly kindly, made human affairs run smoothly. Perhaps the most popular deity—even today in Chinese folk religion—was the god of the hearth and family, Tsao-chün, better known as "The Kitchen God." To this day, every traditional Chinese household has its own shrine where incense is burned daily to him and his wife. Special devotion is paid to him at the beginning of the year, when he is to make his annual report on the family to the Jade Emperor, who in turn sends good or bad luck according to what he has heard. At the New Year, therefore, devotees presented to him either honey and other sweets to make his report nicer, or candy so sticky as to cause his tongue to cleave to the roof of his mouth, thus preventing him from reporting at all.

The One Way

In addition to such popular and enduring beliefs and practices, there arose in this ancient period some concepts that would have a lasting effect, not just on the hearts and minds of the Chinese people, but on the two great philosophical systems of Confucianism and Taoism. The most important was notion of the *Tao*, which is sometimes spelled *Dao* in English and always properly pronounced "Dow." (See Figure 4-1.) *Tao* is usually translated as "Way," but can mean "Concept" and "Word" as well; and for good measure, in all of these connotations it can be used as a verb as well as a noun. The word originally referred to the paths of the heavenly bodies, but eventually came to denote the mysterious Ultimate that was both the Source of all things and the immanent, dynamic Force that subtly infused and empowered everyone and everything. This *Tao*, like the *Brahman Nirguna* of the Hindus and the *Shunyata* of the Buddhists, was a pure Unity—Simplicity Itself, as it were. For that reason, it was sometimes called *Ta'i-i* ("Supreme One") and treated as an absolute Mystery. As an utter Unity, *Tao* contained no differentiation (that is, "this versus that" distinctions) or duality ("either-or"), much less multiplicity. It was simply and unequivocally One, and was originally symbolized by an empty circle very much like the *enso* that represents *Shunyata* in Zen Buddhism.

In contrast to this primordial Unity, the Chinese ancients recognized that the everyday world is a study in differentiation and multiplicity,

Figure 4-1

English Pronunciation of Chinese Terms & Names

The English spellings of Chinese words are confusing because two different systems are used to convert Chinese sounds into English equivalents. The older Wade-Giles system, which gave us "Peking" as the capital of the People's Republic of China, is gradually being displaced by the simpler and more accurate *pinyin* system, which changed our spelling and pronunciation of that great city to "Beijing." In a perfect world everyone would use the *pinyin* spellings, which would render *Tao* as *Dao*, the way it actually is pronounced. In the field of religion, however, we have grown so fond of seeing *Tao* as such, the older Wade-Giles spellings persist for the most part except in technical scholarly writing. For this reason, this chapter uses the more familiar Wade-Giles system. Listed below, however, are important names and terms as they are rendered in both systems.

Wade-Giles	Pinyin	Identity/Meaning
Lao-tzu	*Laozi**	• by tradition, Taoism's founder
Chuang-tzu	*Zuangzi*	• Lao-tzu's alleged interpreter
K'ung-fu-tzu	*Kongfuzi*	• founder of Confucianism
Chou	*Zhou*	• a Chinese dynasty
I Ching	*Yijing*	• classic book of divination
Tao Te Ching	*Dao De Jing*	• classic Taoist text
Tao	*Dao*	• path, Way
T'ien	*Tian*	• Heaven
Ch'i	*Qi*	• life force, vital energy
Kuei	*Qui*	• ghost, avenging spirit
Shang-ti	*Shangdi*	• Lord on High
Chün-tzu	*Junzi*	• True Gentleman, a cultivated person

*Or *Lao zi* or *Lao Zi*. There is some further disagreement among those who prefer the *pinyin* system about whether to divide the syllables of newly spelled names and titles and, if so, whether to capitalize the first letters of all syllables. Note, for example, the inconsistency between *Dao De Jing* and *Yijing* in this list, which might as easily be written *Daodejing* and *Yi Jing*, respectively. Likewise, in the Wade-Giles schema there is inconsistency in hyphenation and capitalization, making either *Tao-te Ching* or *Tao-te ching* also permissible. If all of this weren't confusing enough, the *tzu* that appears at the end of the names of many important persons can also be spelled *tsu*. Thus *Lao-tzu* may be written *Lao Tzu*, *Lao-tsu*, and *Lao Tsu* (in addition, of course, to the *pinyin* options, *Laozi*, *Lao zi*, and *Lao Zi*). The best policy in using these names, then, is to choose one of the two systems and use spacing, hyphens, and capital letters consistently. It's not easy.

which is simply to say that it consists of innumerable things. It is also rife with dualistic distinctions like big-small, fat-thin, hot-cold, hard-soft, high-low, light-dark, in-out, up-down, etc. For that reason they were persuaded that our everyday language, which works so well for everyday things, simply could not do justice to *Tao*. "The *Tao* that can be uttered is not the true *Tao*," the *Tao Te Ching* (*Way-Power Book*) would later say, adding that even to call it *Tao* or give it any name is misleading. That leaves either total silence or the most abstruse and arcane mythopoetic language as the only appropriate vehicles for expressing this mysterious One. As our treatment of Taoism will show, the latter is the approach of the *Tao Te Ching*.

Inevitably, the most ancient of Chinese philosophers dealt with two questions. First, what was the source of this primordial Unity called *Tao*? Their answer seems ludicrous on the surface: *Tao* arose out of *T'ai-hsu* ("Great Void"), which was also known as *Wu-chi* (literally, the "No Power" or "Pinnacle of Nothingness"). By either name, the point of reference is the Primordial Void that is the source of everything. For most of us schooled in the idea that "you can't get something from nothing," this seems impossible. But if we recall our discussion of Buddhism's notion of *Shunyata* (Emptiness as Pure Potentiality) in the preceding chapter, it becomes clear that the Chinese are saying virtually the same thing with respect to *Tao*. So, we again recall, are modern Western physicists when they tell us that the Singularity that exploded in the Big Bang to produce the whole cosmos was, in effect, merely a wrinkle or warp in a primordial Nothingness.

The second question that the ancient Chinese thinkers faced was how such a primal Unity could be the source of the multiplicity of the everyday world in which we live—what Chinese philosophers called *wan-wu* ("the ten thousand things" or "myriad creatures") and Western philosophers term "phenomenal reality." The answer was that obviously (though for no discernable reason) the simple and unified *Tao* had expressed itself, and had done so in three stages. (See Figure 4-2.) First *Tao*—itself an extraction of Something from Infinite Nothing (*Wu-chi*)—had manifested as *T'ai-chi* ("Great Ultimate"), which consisted of the dynamic interactive opposites *yin* and *yang*. From these two came the first three elements: earth, which was *yin*; air, which was *yang*; and water, which was the perfect balance of *yin* and *yang*, since it can be hard like the earth (*yin*), gaseous like the air (*yang*), or liquid (*yin* and *yang* blended). Although later Chinese thought would posit five elements (Metal, Wood, Water, Fire and Earth), for the ancients it was from these three that

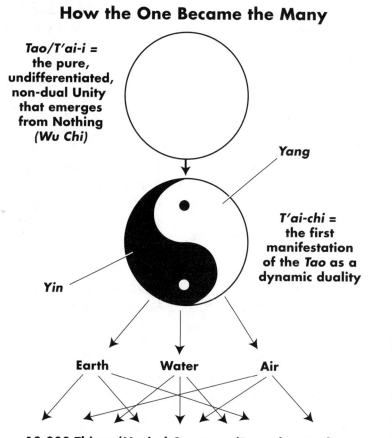

Figure 4-2

How the One Became the Many

Tao/T'ai-i = the pure, undifferentiated, non-dual Unity that emerges from Nothing *(Wu Chi)*

Yang

T'ai-chi = the first manifestation of the *Tao* as a dynamic duality

Yin

Earth　　**Water**　　**Air**

10,000 Things/Myriad Creatures/Everyday Reality

This ancient Chinese view of reality is referred to in chapter 42 of the *Tao Te Ching*, which declares that the one became two, the two became three (the elements), and the three became the 10,000 (or myriad or countless) things, which is to say, the phenomenal world of everyday, ordinary experience.

everything came into existence, including humans—who are physically, after all, a mixture of dust, breath, and water. This is the process referred to in chapter 42 of the *Tao Te Ching* when it says: "The one became two, the two became three, and the three became the innumerable." The most crucial moment in the process, however, was the initial movement that led from the Unity (*Tao*) to the manifestation of the penultimate duality (*Ta'i-chi*), for thereafter the process was all downhill. That is true in more than one sense, since Taoism regards the everyday world as qualitatively inferior to (though ever in essential continuity with) its Source, the *Tao*.

Yin and Yang

Because of the important part that *yin* and *yang* play in the scheme of things as the link between infinite, absolute Simplicity (*Tao*) and finite, thoroughgoing multiplicity (*wan-wu*), it is worth pausing to look at them a bit. The two terms originated in ancient Chinese meteorology, with *yang* referring to a bright, sunny day and *yin* to a dark, cloudy one. Gradually, however, the connotations of these terms expanded exponentially to include everyone and everything. Since the Chinese thinkers noticed that bright days tended to be warmer and drier than cloudy ones, warm and dry became attributes of *yang*, and cool and moist of *yin*. These inventors of the hot air balloon also noticed that warm, dry air rose, while cool, damp air tended to settle into valleys; so *yang* took on the connotation of lightness and height and predominance, while *yin* was associated with heaviness and lowness and subordination. Eventually, *yang* came to connote aggressiveness and males, and *yin*, passivity and females.

One might understandably jump to the conclusion that what we have here is just one more philosophical system produced by a cabal of male chauvinists bent on subjugating women, but two mitigating factors should be noted. First, *yang*, *yin*, and their attributes were intended to be value-free. High was not seen as better than low, for example, nor superior regarded as better than inferior. As Alan Watts, the late scholar and popularizer of Buddhism and Taoism in the West was fond of saying, people don't praise mountains for being high or blame valleys for being low. They complement one another. In fact, as we shall see, Taoism actually preferred the lowly and passive to the high-placed and assertive, and ironically treated them as much more powerful than their male counterparts. The other thing to note is that the ancient Chinese recognized that hardly anything was pure *yang* or *yin*, an observation indicated by the dots of contrasting colors in each side of the familiar *T'ai-chi* symbol. All things reflected a dynamic combination of the two. Had these people developed a formal discipline of psychology, they probably would have propounded something much like Carl Jung's notion that all human beings have two "souls"—a male *animus* and a female *anima*—and that these need to be in balance for good mental health.

According to ancient Chinese thought, then, in humans and everything else the relationship between *yin* and *yang* is one of opposites, but the component elements are not at odds with one another. They are in tension, certainly, but creatively and powerfully so—much like the negative and positive terminals of a battery that, in effect, need each other to produce an electrical current. *Yin* and *yang* are similarly complementary and mutually reinforcing, and everything in the everyday world bears aspects of both in a dynamic and ever-evolving balance. For example, no hot, sunny day (*yang*) is ever without some humidity (*yin*), even in a desert; and it may actually rain (even more *yin*) and turn cold there. Eventually any weather is going to change— indeed, *is* changing from moment to moment, however imperceptibly. *Yin* and *yang* are therefore dynamically complementary, forever and inextricably linked, in perpetual and cyclical motion, interpenetrating and dissolving into one another. The traditional symbol of this relationship (See Figure 4-3.) is often mistakenly called *Tao* or the *Yin-Yang*, but is actually most appropriately identified as the *T'ai-chi*, which is to say, the mysterious *Tao* in its initial manifestation. The symbol is drawn in such a way as to suggest not stasis, but motion, and circular motion at that. (It has been suggested that the symbol was inspired by the observation of two goldfish chasing each other's tails.) And again, the way it is drawn, with a spot of the dark (*yin*) in the light (*yang*) and vice versa, suggests that each has the seed of the other within it. To capture more accurately the movement of the manifest *Tao* and the blending of *yin* and *yang* in everyday reality, the symbol would better be presented as a spinning disk. In fact, some computerized animations of the *Ta'i-chi* now do just that.

The Synchronous Ming

Another important and durable ancient Chinese concept is *ming*. Often translated "fate" or "destiny," *ming* has often been confused with the *karma* of Hinduism and Buddhism and the *kismet* of Islam. It is probably best understood, however, as *synchronous order* or simply *synchronicity*, a term coined by the great psychoanalyst Carl Jung to denote the acausal underlying interconnectedness of all things that routinely produces "meaningful coincidences." The venerable Chinese notion of *ming* similarly and perhaps even more radically suggests that despite appearances to the contrary, there are no pure accidents or meaningless coincidences. Why? Because the *Tao* flows through all things and events, not only directing them, but connecting them inexorably to one another in a complex pattern of mutual causation. Synchronicity, then, is not unlike the dependent co-origination and interbeing of Buddhist philosophy that

Figure 4-3

Yin and Yang

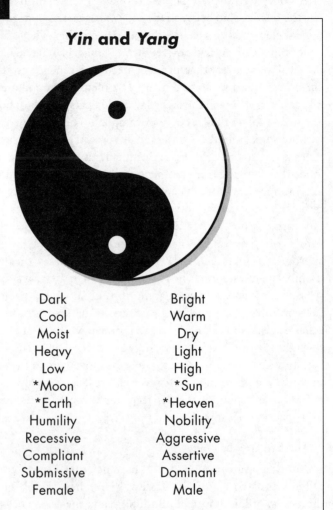

Dark	Bright
Cool	Warm
Moist	Dry
Heavy	Light
Low	High
*Moon	*Sun
*Earth	*Heaven
Humility	Nobility
Recessive	Aggressive
Compliant	Assertive
Submissive	Dominant
Female	Male

Even foods are considered *yang* (e.g., meat, poultry, onions, carrots), *yin* (e.g., fish seafood, tofu, bean sprouts, eggplant, cucumber, or balanced (nuts, grains, legumes, veggies, miso soup).

With the notable exceptions of these two pairs, nothing is seen as purely yang or yin.

we saw in the preceding chapter. The resulting conception is that everything is dynamically interrelated to everything else or, as a popular Chinese saying puts it, "things like to happen together." Even the seemingly random toss of a coin in truth produces an inevitable if unintended and unpredictable result, simply because the same *Tao* is flowing through the hand, arm, coin, wind, and gravity.

Thus, in the Chinese mind, both ancient and modern, *ming* is as philosophically and scientifically sound and reliable a principle as cause-and-effect was to Sir Isaac Newton. It represented a form of natural determinism based on an impersonal, unconscious principle or law, rather than on a Western sort of a transcendent deity who intentionally predestines or otherwise directs events. *Ming* was and is as automatic, effective, and natural to the Chinese mind as gravity is to ours, however difficult that may be for the modern Western mind to grasp. Yet, the concept of *ming* might be enlisted to explain such all-but-universal "coincidences" as a phone call from an old friend we "just happened" to be thinking about, or an idea for a current project triggered by a casual word overheard in a nearby conversation or TV program. To the traditional Chinese mind, these are not examples of mere happenstance, but manifestations of *ming* at work—or better, in motion. We have all seen coins tossed prior to football games to determine who will have the choice to kick off or receive the ball. If the notion of *ming* is correct, the team that wins the toss is not just the luckier of the two, but the one who is *supposed* to have the option, given the movement of the *Tao* at that particular time and place. It also means that the person who hits a Super Lotto or slot machine jackpot is the one that was *supposed* to win, not because of a prior divine decision, but in accordance with a patterned flow of natural events. How often have we heard losers in any given competition say "It just wasn't meant to be"? To the ancient Chinese ear, that would sound like a very *ming*-tinged assertion.

Prevalent Ancient Practices

Over the centuries a profuse array of religious practices arose in ancient China, including shamanism, necromancy (contact with the dead through mediums), spirit and deity possession, and exorcism. Sacrifices to the various deities of such things as fruit, grains, wine, incense, animals, and (early on at least) humans were also common. Of particular importance was the practice of filial piety (*hsiao* or *xiao*) and its ultimate expression, ancestor worship. Chinese tradition has always taught the importance of children's respect for their parents, and by extension that of subjects for their rulers and the young for their elders (which in China means everyone over the age of 60). As we shall see, Confucius formalized and systematized these relationships, but they greatly predate him. Chinese ancestor worship (or, more accurately, *veneration*) is a conceptual stretch

Figure 4-4

The Chinese Zodiac

If you were born in: You are a:

1906, 1918, 1930, 1942, 1954, 1966, or 1978 . . . . HORSE

1907, 1919, 1931, 1943, 1955, 1967, or 1979 . . . . SHEEP

1908, 1920, 1932, 1944, 1956, 1968, or 1980 . . . . MONKEY

1909, 1921, 1933, 1945, 1957, 1969, or 1981 . . . . ROOSTER

1910, 1922, 1934, 1946, 1958, 1970, or 1982 . . . . DOG

1911, 1923, 1935, 1947, 1959, 1971, or 1983 . . . . BOAR

1912, 1924, 1936, 1948, 1960, 1972, or 1984 . . . . RAT

1913, 1925, 1937, 1949, 1961, 1973, or 1985 . . . . OX

1914, 1926, 1938, 1950, 1962, 1974, or 1986 . . . . TIGER

1915, 1927, 1939, 1951, 1963, 1975, or 1987 . . . . RABBIT

1916, 1928, 1940, 1952, 1964, 1976, or 1988 . . . . DRAGON

1917, 1929, 1941, 1953, 1965, 1977, or 1989 . . . . SNAKE

for Westerners, inasmuch as its proponents apparently had no clear concept of an immortal soul, much less of a heavenly destination for the dear departed. They seem to have believed that the living had two souls. The first, *po*, was a spiritual energy that returned to the earth at death. The other, *hun*, was a cognitive energy that could live on in wooden tablets placed on a household altar and thus remain a part of the family for as long as its deceased bearer was remembered and honored with rituals. In at least a vague sense, then, the dead somehow lingered, if only as ghosts (*kuei*).

The two ancient practices that most directly drew upon the concepts of *Tao*, *T'ai-chi*, yin-yang, and *ming* were the use of animal symbolism and divination. As anyone who has read the place mat at a cheap Chinese restaurant knows, a recurring set of twelve animals (that is, a zodiac) served to identify calendar years (See Figure 4-4.). Perhaps the most spiritually powerful of these creatures is the one most associated with Chinese culture and celebrations, the dragon. The Chinese dragon was a ground-hugging serpent with functional wings, and thus represented a perfect balance of earth (*yin*) and air (*yang*). Likewise reflective of *yin* and *yang* was divination, which was developed to a high art *and* science in Chinese culture with the emergence of the *I Ching*, the "Book of Changes" (or

---

Figure 4-5

A Hexagram

Kwei Mei
("Fire-Water")
Connotes a father's marrying off a younger daughter
before her older sister, or putting the cart before the
horse. Both mean inauspicious beginnings
—a task that cannot turn out well

This is only one of the 64 diagrams of the *I Ching*. If properly generated, the bottom line was determined first either by drawing or shaking a stick marked *yin* or *yang* out of a container, or tossing coins or some other traditional method. Once the diagram is in place, one may consult the *I Ching*, or, if one is serious, a Master of the *I Ching*. But not so fast! Lines two and five, counting upward, are unstable "moving lines," and could go either way. Thus there are several other phantom hexagrams always in play.

"Transformation," or "Process"), a text that was already ancient when Confucius edited it. It presented a system based on sixty-four diagrams called *hexagrams*, representing every possible six-line combination of solid (*yang*) and broken (*yin*) lines. (See Figure 4-5.) Each had a name and a meaning, and could be used by a skilled practitioner to tell the future toward which current events were tending.

In using the *I Ching*, the first task was always to generate a master diagram one line at a time, usually by tossing coins or randomly selecting sticks made of the stalks of the herb yarrow, which were then marked to represent the two kinds of line. In the West, we consider such a process to be based strictly on chance. In Chinese thought, however, everything is an expression of *Tao*, and thus dynamically interconnected to everything else. And since the movement of the manifest *Tao* produces *ming* ("synchronicity"), one automatically and inevitably gets the correct hexagram, naturally generated by the grand scheme of things. Once the hexagram is determined (in more ways than one), then the proper chapter in the *I Ching* can be consulted and interpreted, but again only by a professional diviner, a Master of the *I Ching*.

The *I Ching* still is widely consulted in modern China, for it is an integral component of the multifaceted folk religion there. It has also drawn a following in the West, if book sales are any indication. Of course, the very idea that an American could simply buy an English version of the *I Ching* and perform valid divination would be as absurd to Chinese people as the image of a Chinese layperson's purchasing *Gray's Anatomy* with the intention of doing successful self-surgery would be to us. Much more plausible and promising to the Chinese, perhaps, would be the proposition that intelligent and inquiring Westerners might profitably read the works of Confucius and Lao-tzu, and come to understand and benefit from the key concepts gleaned from those two philosophical giants.

Two Masters

Both Confucianism and Taoism arose in the historical and cultural milieu that marked the declining years of the Chou Dynasty. It was a time of social unrest and upheaval: a combination of internal problems and external threats from hostile neighboring people caused such instability and uncertainty that the fabric of society itself seemed to be unraveling. Especially unsettling was the obvious breakdown of the old feudal system that had made a clear distinction between nobility and peasants (with no middle class at all), and presupposed the unquestioning obedience of the latter to the former. The dissolution of that neat pattern was producing a chaotic situation in which those who had traditionally been respected and obeyed were now being ignored or downright disdained. But it was also a time of religious and spiritual richness, with many ancient practices and beliefs to appropriate and build upon. According to tradition, both K'ung-fu-tzu and Lao-tzu did just that, but from very different perspectives and with quite divergent solutions to the social and political problems they saw around them.

In contrast to the supernatural claims made for many of the world's religious leaders, the founder of Confucianism was conceived and born in a perfectly natural fashion in the year 551 BCE. His given name, now often forgotten, was K'ung-ch'iu, and his family belonged to the nobility of the two-tiered feudal Chinese society. Early in his childhood, however, his father died, leaving him to be reared by his single mother in rather difficult economic circumstances. This personal experience of impoverished nobility no doubt left the young K'ung yearning for "the good old days," when feudal society was intact and all nobles were wealthy and only peasants were poor. When he was 23, his mother died, and K'ung went through a traditional period of mourning that lasted over two years. During this time of fasting and grief, he steeped himself in the writings and lore of the ancient sage-masters of China and came to espouse the values they represented: education, morality, virtue, tradition, and social stability.

Not long after his period of mourning and study, K'ung Ch'iu went into civil service, eventually becoming what today might be called a free-lance city manager who was hired by princes to improve the living conditions and stability of their respective states. By all accounts, he was so good at his work that wherever he was employed, the social situation was quickly and vastly improved. Over time he gained a further reputation as a learned man and fine teacher. He not only taught his evolving philosophy, but edited ancient spiritual classics like the *I Ching*, an activity that eventually earned him the honorific title K'ung-fu-tzu, meaning "Master K'ung." He is also regarded as the author of the *Lun Yü* ("The Analects" or "Select Sayings"), despite the fact that this work is really a later compilation of his students' recollections of his sayings regarding proper social behavior, ethics, character development, and other related subjects.

The other master, known as Lao-tzu ("Old Man"), is so shrouded in mystery and lore as to appear purely legendary. Some speculate that he was a later invention of a school of thinkers who felt the need for a prestigious (even if fictitious) founder to match the reputation and counter the views of K'ung-fu-tzu and his disciples. This view is reinforced by the existence of conflicting versions of Lao-tzu's given name, and the incredible account of his birth. He is said to have been miraculously conceived when his mother, sleeping alone, dreamed of a shooting star. Thereafter, we are told, he was in the womb for 62 years, and thus was born a white-haired elder. Not to be robbed of a long life by having spent so many years in gestation, he is supposed to have lived to the ripe old age of 160 or beyond—yet another detail that suggests a fictional rather than historical figure.

Other reported aspects of Lao-tzu's life, however, are so mundane—or at least plausible—as to make him seem authentically historical. For example, nothing is particularly remarkable about Lao-tzu's purported vocation. Like K'ung-fu-tzu, he is remembered as a minor government appointee, an archivist who as a sideline sifted the ancient Chinese traditions and texts for wisdom applicable to the sorry state of society, developed a philosophy, taught it, and gained a following. When he retired, Lao-tzu is said to have mounted an ox and left China for some unspecified mountainous destination to the west, and disappeared from history. At the border, however, a guard supposedly recognized him and impelled him to record all of his wisdom for posterity. Lao-tzu did this in a mere 5,000 or so Chinese characters, and the result was his only book, the *Tao Te Ching* ("The Way-Power Book"), whose original title was simply *Lao-tzu*. Remarkable though it may be, it is conceivable that it is in fact the work of a single genius rather than (as some claim) a product of a school of thinkers.

Unlike K'ung-fu-tzu's prosaic and practical advice about tradition and social interaction in the *Analects*, the ideas attributed to Lao-tzu in the *Tao Te Ching* are poetic, abstract, metaphorical, counter-intuitive, and often downright puzzling assertions about the nature of things. The difference in the two writings is one not just of form and style, however, but of focus and substance, an observation that brings us to a closer examination of the writings and teachings of the respective religious traditions that these two great spiritual luminaries (whether real or fabricated) engendered.

Scriptures and Beliefs

Because of its name, one might suppose that Taoism is about the *Tao* and that Confucianism is not, but the truth is that the concept of the *Tao* was central to the teaching of both systems. Predictably, however, the two founders gave very different applications to the idea. K'ung-fu-tzu believed that by bringing social behaviors and relationships into alignment with the *Tao*, order and peace would be restored and, as a kind of secondary effect, individuals would be spiritually fulfilled. Lao-tzu, by contrast, believed that society necessarily corrupts and compromises the *Tao*, and that only if individuals were attuned naturally and mystically to the *Tao* would they be spiritually fulfilled and society cured of its many ills. Another way to put the difference between the two sages and their systems is this: K'ung-fu-tzu's *Tao* was fundamentally approached objectively, while Lao-tzu's was accessed subjectively. This difference in dynamic runs through the respective scriptures and beliefs of the two traditions they spawned.

Confucian Canon and Concepts

Confucianism recognizes two sets of scriptures. First are the Five Classics (*Wu Ching*), which were said to have predated K'ung-fu-tzu and to have been edited by him: *The Book of Changes* (*I Ching*), the *Book of History*, the *Book of Songs*, the *Spring and Autumn Annals*, and the *Book of Rites*. Much later, the so-called neo-Confucians of the twelfth century CE raised to canonical status the *Four Books* (*Se Shu*): the aforementioned *Analects*, the *Book of Mencius*, the *Great Learning*, and the *Doctrine of the Mean*. None of these is regarded as the result of revelation, a notion utterly foreign to the thoroughly rationalistic K'ung-fu-tzu, and, for that matter, to Chinese religions in general.

K'ung-fu-tzu gave the ancient concept of *Tao* a social-political connotation, for in his view *Tao* was most at work and visible in the fabric of society. He spoke about the social structure in terms of *li*, which literally means the sorts of patterns found in jade or wood, though it traditionally referred to such rituals as ancestor veneration as well. When K'ung-fu-tzu used the term, however, he meant it to denote the broader patterns and actions that comprise the very warp and woof of the social fabric: traditions, mores, customs, manners, and propriety. These he saw played out in five basic relationships: ruler-subject, father-son, husband-wife, elder sibling-younger sibling, and older friend-younger friend. In each case, the latter member was to be obedient, and the former was to be benevolent. Kung-fu-tzu's schema, therefore, was inherently elitist and male-dominated because, in the manner of a good conservative or traditionalist, it harked back to traditional Chinese ways. Yet the seemingly reactionary social reciprocity that he was advocating was oddly innovative for Chinese society of the chaotic Chou era, for all of Master K'ung's supposedly normative social relationships had come to be regarded passé and irrelevant. His reformist teachings, by contrast, spoke to what by his standards was a degenerate social-ethical situation in which the only obligation was for the lower party to yield to the higher; and in the current troubled time, even that expectation was being ignored more and more.

K'ung-fu-tzu's system, therefore, was all about re-establishing traditional social patterns of behavior through deliberate and concerted *cultivation* of what his fellow Chinese citizens generally knew (but typically ignored) as *te* (virtue or moral power). For K'ung, the cardinal human virtue and mainstay of character was *jen* (or *ren*), a difficult term to translate, because it connotes so many traits: goodness, benevolence, kindness, love, empathy, charity, compassion, thoughtfulness, humaneness, and human-heartedness. He saw *jen* as rooted in self-respect and self-affirmation, and the cultivation of it as leading to *yi* (morality, righteousness, or character). To put it succinctly and in K'ung's own terms: *yi* was a state of being achieved by the practice of *te* in the social matrix entailed in the idea of *li*. In other words, Master K'ung regarded *yi* as the inner dynamic or spiritual counterpart of the much more behavioral *li* that he valued to such an extent that his religion often appears to be purely a matter of ethics. The fact is, however, that in the Confucian system, ethics is important mainly because *yi* cannot be cultivated in isolation, but only within the context of social relationships. Thus self-development, self-fulfillment, and self-realization—the main personal goals of Confucianism—would be realized through an ongoing process of internalizing one's own actions and interactions. In this process, which he called "rectification of names," people would manifest their true natures and achieve their full potential. They would thus become what they were supposed to be: rulers would again become real rulers, fathers would once more become real fathers, and so forth.

For K'ung-fu-tzu, the development of character (*yi*) was not easy. It meant cultivating (there's that word again) not only personal power or virture (*te*) in general, but a host of specific virtues as well. We have already seen two: *jen* ("benevolence") and *li* ("propriety," that is, the proper way to behave in social relationships). In addition to these was *chung*, which meant doing one's best, especially in the intentional and active development of one's own character. Equally important was *shu*, which meant selflessness, altruism, or reciprocity. K'ung-fu-tzu often expressed *shu* in terms of what has sometimes been called the "Negative Golden Rule," despite the fact that its intent and meaning are clearly positive: "Do not do to others what you wouldn't want them to do to you." *Hsin* (loyalty, faithfulness, trustworthiness) was another treasured Confucian virtue, as was the filial piety (*hsiao*) that had been an integral part of Chinese values from time immemorial.

Underlying the definition of Confucian virtues and the advocacy of their development were two important presuppositions. The first was that a human being cannot properly be defined or understood as an individual in isolation, but only as a thoroughly social animal—in effect, as the sum of his or her interrelationships. That is why none of the cardinal virtues of Confucianism has an internal reference point in some isolated spiritual essence to be found and cultivated mystically. Instead, they are all defined by and directed toward others. The second and equally important assumption is that although people are not by nature virtuous, they do have the capacity for self-improvement and even self-perfection, and are malleable to that end. This is a rather optimistic view of human nature, especially as compared to a third century BCE successor of K'ung named Hsün-tzu, who taught that humans are basically selfish in motive and action. Still, K'ung-fu-tzu was not nearly as optimistic about human nature as his (perhaps purely legendary) contemporary Lao-tzu, who (as we shall see shortly) is remembered for his view that human beings needed no cultivation at all, being perfect in their natural state. K'ung's view was more reserved: he believed that people are *potentially* good, but that goodness needed to be developed—one might again say "cultivated." Not surprisingly, he was a strong advocate of education.

In the Confucian system the goal was to mold oneself into a *Chün-tzu*, a truly cultivated, even noble-minded person—the best human being possible. Indeed, the very purpose of his *Analects* was to provide specific guidelines for the attainment of this lofty status. (See Figure 4-6.) The idea that one could achieve nobility by effort rather than by birth was a real innovation on the part of K'ung-fu-tzu, and perhaps his greatest; for indeed much of the rest was, by his own admission, simply an ordering, structuring, and transmitting of ancient ideas and values. To be sure, he was not optimistic that the majority of people could ever exhibit true *yi* (spirit), for he believed that only a relatively few would be intelligent and motivated enough to do so. (Yes, classical Confucianism is elitist, not to mention paternalistic.) For the masses, therefore, external controls in the form of rules and rulers provided the *li* (structure) needed to stabilize society on their behalf. (And yes, this is an inherently conservative viewpoint, politically speaking.) "The *Chün-tzu* understands *yi*," he once said, "the little people understand *li*."

Confucianism in America?

If any of this has a ring of familiarity, it may be because our modern American society is steeped in the same spirit: "Mind your manners," we tell our children; "Sit up straight," "Act like little ladies and gentlemen," "You've got to make something of yourself." Those all express a Confucian attitude. "Be all that you can be" urges the U. S. Army's recruitment ad with its perfect prescription for creating a *Chün-tzu*! But we start much earlier than that: the Cub Scout motto is "Do your best"

Figure 4-6

SAYINGS OF K'UNG FU TSU
FROM THE *ANALECTS*

(Laughlin's renderings)

On the Tao:
"To hear in the morning that the Way (*Tao*) still prevails is to be able to die that night without any regrets." 4.8

On the *Chün-tzu*:
"The truly cultivated person (*Chün-tzu*) yearns for virtue, while the petty yearn for wealth. The truly cultivated person yearns for the law, while the petty yearn for privilege." 4.11

"The truly cultivated person (*Chün-tzu*) studies literature extensively, is tempered by the rites, and is unlikely to lose the Way (*Tao*)." 6.25

On *jen (ren)*:
"If a person is without benevolence (*jen*), then what good are the rites (*li*)?" 3.3a

"To hang out with people of benevolence (*jen*) is good. To choose not to associate with such people is to me unthinkable." 4.1

"Simple meals, water to drink, an arm for a pillow: that's happiness. To me, wealth and status without righteousness (*jen*) are like floating clouds." 7.15

On *shu*:
"Worry not that others don't appreciate you. Worry instead that you are not appreciating others." 1.16

On *ruling*:
"A ruler should treat subjects in accordance with the rites (*li*). Subjects should serve their ruler with loyalty." 3.19

"To rule with virtue (*te*) is like taking the place of the North Star, with all others revolving around it in homage." 2.1

On filial piety *(hsiao, xiao)*:
"Today, merely providing for parents is considered filial piety. But even dogs and horses do that! Without respect, what's the difference?" 2.7

(*chung*). All this is far from accidental. Military and para-military organizations are perfect examples of Confucian ideals. The clear distinction between officers and enlisted people is the very kind of ancient feudal society that K'ung-fu-tzu wanted to recreate, and the expectation that the latter must dutifully obey the former who must treat them fairly in return is Confucian through and through. Indeed, governments, most large companies, and even universities maintain a two-tiered hierarchy of power, and whether it is government versus governed, management versus labor, or administration versus faculty, the dynamics are thoroughly Confucian, and rules and regulations abound. Moreover, permeating all such institutions is an ethos that individuals should bring out the best in themselves (which is to say, achieve personal success) by working within the given system to meet its goals. For better or for worse, the spirit of Confucius is alive and well in the West.

And why shouldn't it be? After all, for much of its early history our country was shaped in large part by Puritans whose well-documented "Protestant work ethic" was nothing if not Confucian in nature. The subsequent pioneers, unlike the Native Americans they encountered and subdued, were bent on getting nature under control, cultivating the land, and imposing their idea of social order on an otherwise unruly frontier. From them, and their successors in the economic sphere, emerged the ideal of the "self-made man," which is but a variation of the *Chün-tzu*, the truly cultivated person. Is it any wonder that for so many of us, much of life revolves around the drive to make something of ourselves, and to do so within traditional social structures and their inherently conservative values? If Master K'ung were alive today, he would feel quite at home in mainstream America, *and* he would be fighting aggressively against the same kind of creeping social disorder that he saw as a threat in his own time and place. Whether his approach would be deemed correct or appropriate depends on how compelling one finds the opposing views of K'ung's contemporary, Lao-tzu.

Taoist Texts and Teachings

The main scripture of Taoism, of course, is the aforementioned *Tao Te Ching*, traditionally attributed to Lao-tzu himself. Of nearly equal status is the later *Chuang Tzu*, whose title bears the name of its purported author, supposedly a successor of Lao-tzu. Among Taoists, this text has achieved a level of prestige and authority almost on a par with the *Tao Te Ching*; indeed, some consider it far superior to the earlier work in both style and substance. Some, as we shall see, also claim that it actually predates the more famous work. Unlike the major Western scriptures and some Eastern ones, but like the *Analects* of K'ung-fu-tzu, neither of these books claims divine inspiration or anything other than human authorship. Their authority is self-validating: they have struck generation after generation of readers as delivering not just a plausible, but an authentic and compelling account of how the universe works and how human life should be lived accordingly.

Yet even a brief perusal of these three writings attests that Lao-tzu's and Chuang-tzu's interpretations of *Tao* were much more individual-centered and mystical than those of K'ung-fu-tzu, whose enormous attention to behaviors amounted to working on oneself (as actors sometimes put it) "from the outside in." Lao-tzu took the opposite approach: he believed that a person should approach self-realization from the inside out, directly experiencing her or his individual spirit, aligning it with the universal *Tao* (the Way of nature), and letting behavior and society be naturally and positively affected as a result. Such a stance would have social and political consequences, of course, and Lao-tzu occasionally pointed these out, especially as regards the role of a ruler. Thus, while K'ung-fu-tzu's main concern was the cultivation of the individual in a social context, Lao-tzu's was allowing the naturalness of the individual to shine through. The Chinese word for "naturalness" is *tzu-jan*, and it permeates all of Taoist philosophy. It connotes—among many other things, but above all—simplicity and spontaneity.

According to Lao-tzu, the way to achieve such a state is to do little or nothing at all. In place of the active or even aggressive Confucian advice entailed in *chung* ("best-doing"), Taoism counsels *wu wei* ("not doing"). "The Tao does nothing, yet leaves nothing undone," says the *Tao Te Ching*. Although the phrase *wu wei* is sometimes translated as "inactivity," Lao-tzu did not intend people to be catatonic, but rather nonassertive, non-aggressive, and non-manipulative. He simply believed that in meeting life's challenges, less is more—that going with the flow naturally rather than slam-jamming artificial solutions into place was always the best policy. That "flow," of course, was the *Tao* itself, which the *Tao Te Ching* suggests is "like a river flowing back to the sea." (See Figure 4-7.) A better translation of *wu wei*, therefore, might be "forbearance" or "effortlessness" or, with a more positive spin, "spontaneity." The cautions "Take it easy" and "Easy does it" are expressions of the Taoist approach. So is the punch-line of an old country music tune: "All I gotta do is act natur'ly."

The eventual outcome and highest goal in Taoist philosophy is for one to become a *P'u*. That word is usually translated "uncarved block" of wood or stone, but that rendering is misleading because a *block* of anything *is* carved (or otherwise artificially shaped) by definition. Nature

Figure 4-7

Selections from the *Tao* Te Ching
(The Laughlin Version)

The *Tao* is the core of all things. (62)

The *Tao* is hidden and has no name.
And in that anonymity provides for and perfects everything. (41)

The *Tao* does nothing
Yet leaves nothing undone. (37)

Receding is the motion of the *Tao*.
In its weakness is its power. (40)

The supreme good is like water,
Which benefits all things effortlessly,
And occupies the lowly places that people despise.
In this way is it like the *Tao*. (8)

The softest thing in the world
Subdues the hardest.
The insubstantial enters where there is no opening.
Thus I know the advantage of effortless action. (43)

Therefore it is possible to align one's actions with the *Tao*,
And thus to become one with it. (23)

Do nothing, and nothing is left undone.
You can gain the world only by not trying to. (48)

Do without "doing."
Live effortlessly. (63)

Nothing in the world is softer than water,
Yet nothing can match it at conquering the hard and strong. (78)

Take Emptiness to the limit.
Guard stillness assiduously. (16)

All existing things arise from being.
Being arises from non-being. (40)

The person who knows does not speak.
The person who speaks does not know. (56)

does not produce blocks, and *p'u* means "in its natural state," that is, before a carver (woodworker or stonemason) has manipulated it into some desired shape. "Uncarved *chunk*," therefore, would be more accurate; and a fallen limb, a piece of driftwood, or a rock found lying at the foot of an outcropping (but not a quarry!) provide good examples. Taoism says that it should be every person's aim to become just such an unshaped—or, in Confucian terms, uncultivated—entity: to achieve plainness, simplicity, humility, gentleness, spontaneity, and above all naturalness, and to do so effortlessly. "*Make* something of yourself," "Just do it," and "Get going," urges the Confucian. "Just *be* yourself," "Let it be," and "Let go," responds the Taoist. The Confucian, yells "Charge!" The Taoist whispers, "Chill."

A Dash of Displaced Taoism?

As we noted earlier, modern Western society has a decidedly Confucian feel about it. We are goal-oriented, structured, hierarchy-conscious, and subject to all kind of norms, expectations, traditions, customs, mores, manners, rules, and regulations that determine not only our behavior but our very self-image. We honor or even idolize people who are "go-getters" and "self-made." From a Taoist perspective, however, such people are simply role-players, or even phonies: they are inauthentic. Far more authentic and admirable are poets, artists, gardeners, underachievers, and dropouts from society and its structures and strictures—the very sorts of people that our society typically regards as weirdos, idlers, nonconformists, failures, or losers.

And yet even in the West we find examples of Taoist sentiment. We may enjoin our children to be polite and obedient, and to behave and succeed in accordance with societal standards and values, but we nonetheless encourage them to be self-expressive and inner-directed. We also read them "Little Bo Peep," which suggests that the best way to "find" lost sheep (solve a problem) is to "leave them alone" and let their natural instincts lead them home (let it resolve itself). We also take young people to Sunday School and church to learn about Christianity, which would appear to be the last place you would find a trace of Taoism. Yet, Matthew 26 pictures Jesus praising the natural beauty of wild lilies that never did a lick of work over that of King Solomon, a wise, successful, accomplished, wealthy, and yes, cultivated man. The same chapter has Jesus advising his listeners to "take no thought for tomorrow." Elsewhere, he reportedly counsels non-aggression with his famous "Turn the other cheek," blesses the meek and poor, and issues warnings both to and against the high placed, rich, and reputable. "The last will be first, and the first will be last," he reportedly declared. All of that sounds very Taoist! So, by the way, does his approval of his disciples' spontaneous act of casually plucking and eating food in a field on the Sabbath despite the fact that their actions were in violation of the Jewish Law and the strict standards of the bystanders who criticized them on that score.

As for adults, we see companies observing Friday as a "dress-down day," ostensibly as a mitigation of the Confucian uniformity of dress generally required of the workplace. We also read and hear—often with understanding and sometimes with grudging admiration—of people for whom such concessions are not enough, and who leave the nagging demands of the business world for a life that promises to be more leisurely and closer to nature. Occasionally we learn of successful businesses that operate with a minimum of rules and complete flexibility of work schedule. One recalls, for example, the famous and wildly successful computer companies started and run by unkempt and casually dressed non-conformists, many of whom are now wealthy beyond belief, and all because they did what they loved to do in the way and at the pace that suited their dispositions. Perhaps there is something to this Taoist stance toward life after all.

Contrasting or Complementary?

To all appearances, there could hardly be two more contrasting philosophies than Confucianism and Taoism. Confucianism is predominantly *yang*, active, hands on, and even aggressive in its approach to life, with an eye always on the social context and propriety. Taoism favors the *yin*, and is thoroughly nature-oriented, passive—or better, laid back—and introspective in style. The contrast is evident in two very public arenas of our lives: politics and popular culture.

Confucianism advises political leaders to be benelovent but firm, ruling insofar as possible by moral example rather than by force. But if that approach fails, they are to be authoritarian and strict with their subjects in order to keep them in line. Taoism, by contrast, says that rulers should *always* govern with a gentle hand. "Rule a country as you'd cook a small fish," says the *Tao Te Ching*, for this will allow people's natural goodness to find expression. This contrast was never clearer to me than while attending college and graduate school from the mid-1960s to early '70s. These were the years that simultaneously marked the height of our country's involvement in the Vietnam War and the peak of popular opposition to it. When Richard Nixon came to the Presidency in 1968, he brought with him Vice President Spiro Agnew, who quickly became the point man—many said "hit man"—for Nixon's firm (and thus Confucian) law and order stance. Whatever anyone thought about Agnew, it could not be denied that he was always perfectly groomed and nattily dressed in a very traditional, neatly tailored suit—to all appearances, a truly cultivated man. (Not coincidentally, Confucius is always portrayed by artists as having perfectly groomed hair and beard and nicely pleated, expensive robes.) Agnew's archenemies were, of course, the scruffy and simply, barely, or carelessly (but colorfully) attired young hippies and student radicals. (Lao-tzu is generally shown clad simply and casually, in the ancient Chinese equivalent of jeans.) Whether or not they recognized it, these idealistic young people were Taoists, especially in their antipathy toward authority, traditions, and social structures and norms. This was the "sex, drugs, and rock and roll" and "let it all hang out" generation, and from the vantage point of the White House, they were an utterly lawless bunch. These two political (and, I would add, spiritual) poles were captured nicely by a classic news photo of that era. It showed a scene from a campus demonstration to which soldiers of the National Guard had been assigned. A uniformed, helmeted, and armed young soldier stood at tense attention with his rifle held close to his chest, while a seemingly carefree, tie-dyed, and long-haired young woman gently put a flower in the muzzle of his gun. *Yang* and *yin* converge. Confucius meets Lao-tzu.

Most recently, one can detect more than a modicum of Taoism in the activities of the Sierra Club, the Green Party, and other nature-friendly environmentalist organizations. Sitting quietly in a tree for days on end to keep it from being chopped down is a striking depiction of *wu wei*—especially in the face of time-is-money-conscious loggers impatiently wielding chain saws and revving the engines of their eager bulldozers. A similar case might be the ongoing debate between those favoring gun control and the National Rifle Association, with the former representing a much less aggressive and thus essentially Taoist approach to the problem of crime. Of course, even if Taoist in spirit, *activist organizations* also have almost by definition at least of touch of Confucianism. Indeed, some would argue that the opposing sides on any political issue—almost invariably conservative traditionalists and radical reformists—really need each other in a well-ordered *and yet* free society. Perhaps with their ancient *T'ai chi* symbol the Chinese are right: when all is said and done, it finally comes down to a matter of balance.

Three of the most popular TV shows of the 1970s and '80s also reflected the interaction of the dynamics of Taoist *yin* and and Confucian *yang*, albeit in a more confrontational mode. In *All in the Family*, the two generations living in the Bunker household were a *yang* and *yin* combination: archconservative, macho-minded, and controlling Archie (unknowingly Confucian) and his liberal, sensitive, and feminist son-in-law, Michael, aka "Meathead" (unwittingly Taoist). In fact, most of the situations that the characters found themselves in on that show were *yin-yang* confrontations. Similarly, in the play, movie, and TV show *The Odd Couple*, the tidy, natty, punctual, and always well-mannered Felix found . himself forced by circumstances to room with his messy and irresponsible slob of a friend, Oscar. And again the comedy sprang in large measure from the clash of the former's *yang* to the latter's *yin*. (An irony in both the show and the Neil Simon play on which it was based, was that the *yin* character was an uncharacteristically manly sports writer, while the *yang* character was a commercial photographer—stereotypically, at least, a sensitive artistic type.) The popular *M*A*S*H*, both as a movie and on TV, was likewise based on a *yang-yin* premise. On the one hand, here was a military unit exemplified by the right-wing sticklers for discipline, Frank Burns and Hotlips Hoolihan (quite *yang*, despite her gender and appearance). On the other hand, we had the antics of such anti-authoritarian goof-offs as Hawkeye and Trapper John, who were expressing the spirit of *yin*, going with the flow (*wu wei*), and marching to their own drummers (*tzu-jan*) rather than going by the book and military protocol (*li*). Other shows that followed the pattern were *Family Ties* (ex-hippy, liberal parents versus a conservative, yuppy son), and more recently *Dharma and Greg*, who together with their respective sets of parents follow the same *yin* and *yang* pattern of Taoism and Confucianism, respectively.

A popular movie that attests to our culture's fascination with the Confucian-Taoist clash is *Dances with Wolves*. In it a spit-and-polish military man who obeys his superiors in a good Confucian way by chance finds himself alone at a remote outpost surrounded by Taoists. They don't know they are Taoists, of course. They think they are Sioux Indians. But in their unstudied life of harmony with nature, and even in their imaginative and idiosyncratic dress and hairstyles, which suggest anything but uniformity or conformity, they manifest the spirit of Taoism. Gradually the young soldier becomes just like them, as evidenced by the slow disintegration of his uniform, the waning of his spit-and-polish habits, and his increasing inattention to grooming. And didn't we boo his fellow soldiers, Confucians all, who eventually showed up to retrieve their colleague in arms, found him way out of uniform in every respect, and tried literally to whip him back into shape? In the end, the part of us that wanted the Taoists to win was not disappointed.

Taoist Parenting?

The difference between Confucianism and Taoism may also be visable in our private lives—for example, in our parenting attitudes and activities. Died-in-the-wool Confucian parents must be strict, constantly urging the child to walk the straight and narrow and toe the line, and always strive to establish themselves as role models. Taoist parents, by contrast, would be much more relaxed and far less demanding, affording a child a great deal of latitude to explore and experiment, and even to make mistakes on the road to self-discovery. Instead of encouraging the youngster to *make* something of herself, the Taoist parent would urge her to *be* herself.

A personal example might clarify this seemingly counterintuitive Taoist approach. Years ago, a female friend of mine was going through a very tense time with her adolescent daughter, a situation that today appears typical, perhaps even normal. This case was quite severe, however. As the mother once put it, "My daughter went to bed one night as Cinderella and woke up the next morning as Godzilla." This young woman had suddenly become mean, nasty, disrespectful, and verbally abusive. I saw her on one occasion storm into her house cursing, throwing and breaking things, slamming doors, and so on, all for no apparent reason. Yet her mother remained remarkably calm, sitting relaxed in the midst of this shattering emotional outburst. When I asked how she could possibly remain so placid in such chaotic circumstances, she replied that if she responded to her daughter just then and in kind—with shouted criticisms, demands, or threats of punishment—it would only make matters worse. "She's right where she needs to be just now. I have learned that I just have to let go of the situation and remain confident that things will get better and work themselves out." And, in fact, they did. The girl eventually outgrew this disruptive phase and evolved into a charming young woman with a very close and loving relationship with her mother, whose attitude of compassionate inaction is the very heart of Taoism. It is also thoroughly Buddhist, for the Buddha's Second Noble Truth, a key component of his fundamental teaching, was that the root of all suffering is clinging or grasping. Thus "letting go" is pivotal to both traditions, and probably offers excellent though often difficult advice not only in parenting, but in many of life's most challenging circumstances.

Of course, that approach may not work in every conflict situation. In fact, if applied consistently on a society-wide basis, it could well lead to complete anarchy and utter chaos. What would likely make more sense, and in fact reflect the ancient Chinese penchant for balance symbolized by the *T'ai-chi*, would be to rule or parent with a healthy dose of both Confucianism and Taoism. In my own parenting, for example, I established rules like a good Confucian, but like a Taoist I also understood that it was my son's job to test, bend, and break those rules in the natural process of maturation and self-discovery. Now a young adult, he seems to have turned out just fine—more than likely (says the Taoist in me) in spite of anything that I did or did not do. Had he not, of course, society had provided the Confucian mechanisms to shape him up: military school, the Marines, and—worst case—various more severe rehabilitation options, including prison.

Historical Developments

In their original forms, both Confucianism and Taoism were thoroughly philosophical. Neither founder had much to say about specifically religious rites, practices, priesthoods or, for that matter, gods. They were either atheistic (disbelieving in gods) or transtheistic (believing in gods but having no use for them). But like any enduring religion, both of these systems experienced the effects of change and conflict, resulting in a variety of interpretations and sects. The most profound thing that happened to them, however, was that both eventually took on the priestly and ritual trappings inevitably developed, either sooner or later, by all religions.

Confucianism in Confusion?

When Confucius died in 479 BCE, he apparently had only a small following. Subsequently, two great figures (among other lesser lights) were successful in carrying on and building upon his thought, thereby elevating his visibility and stature among the intelligentsia and eventually the general public. These two, whose lives bridged the fourth and early third centuries BCE, took the Confucian view of human nature in very different directions and in the process created competing Confucian schools.

Meng-tzu (better known by his Latinized name, Mencius), who died in 289 BCE, is generally regarded as the more orthodox of the two. Unlike Confucius, who taught that human beings were potentially but not naturally good, Mencius held that human beings were naturally good, and committed evil acts only because of environmental influences. Following Confucius, however, he maintained that the social and political context most conducive to the promotion of proper behavior would be a traditional feudalism under control of the nobility. The other figure who tried to carry on the Confucian tradition was Hsün-tzu, who died in 238 BCE. He gained the reputation of being the most pessimistic and heterodox interpreter of Master K'ung by denying the basic goodness of human beings. People, he maintained, were fundamentally evil in nature, and goodness could be achieved only through proper moral training, laws, and above all the observance of *li*. Not coincidentally, Hsün-tzu was a great military strategist, and is best known in the West as the author of *The Art of War*. He also introduced religious (as opposed to merely social) rites into Confucianism. As different as they were in their thinking, however, both Meng-tzu and Hsün-tzu agreed with the fundamental premise that personal development and realization, worked out in a social context, constitued the proper way to live a healthy, happy, productive, and peaceful life.

It was the Han Dynasty, which ruled China from 206 BCE until 220 CE, that afforded Confucianism its first major opportunity to exert significant influence across Chinese society, and at the same time marked the beginnings of its evolution from an almost purely philosophical to a more fully developed religious system. Not only did Confucianism (which in China is called *Ru-chia*, "the teachings of the scholars") become the state religion, but Confucian texts were adopted as a basic part of Chinese education and popular reverence toward K'ung-fu-tzu himself began to grow. By the mid-second century BCE, temples were being built in his honor, and sacrifices and other ceremonies directed to him, but still merely as "The First Teacher." For a time after the fall of the Han dynasty, Confucianism was somewhat eclipsed, though certainly not eliminated, by both Taoism and Buddhism. The latter had been introduced into China in the first century CE, and thereafter Confucianism began to develop similar ceremonial practices, and thus to become more religious in the ritual sense, with Master K'ung elevated to divine or quasi-divine status.

Thus transformed and revitalized, Confucianism regained its prominence during the Sung dynasty (960–1279 CE). This period also saw a return to philosophy with the emergence of Neo-Confucianism, which incorporated Taoist and Buddhist elements in an effort to produce a fully developed Confucian metaphysics—that is, a comprehensive view of the nature of reality. Religious Confucianism prevailed at the popular level, however, and continued uninterrupted on the mainland until the early twentieth century, when the creation of the People's Republic of China curbed all religious practice. It was preserved on Taiwan, however, where Confucian temples and monasteries abound. Now, early in the twenty-first century, with a relaxation of the religious ban in the People's Republic, religious Confucianism appears to be making a comeback on the mainland as well.

Developments in Taoism

According to tradition, Taoism followed a path similar to that of Confucianism, though its fortunes tended to wax and wane in inverse proportion to how the latter was faring. Like Confucius, Lao-tzu is said to have had his own orthodox successor in the person of Chuang-tzu (c. 300 BCE), who was mentioned earlier in connection with the important Taoist scripture he wrote. Together these two men and their works constitute the fountainhead of what came to be called *Tao-chia* ("Philosophical Taoism"). Eventually, this strain of Taoism also developed its own "Neo-" variety, which mixed in a heavy dose of Confucianism and went on to produce a panoply of schools.

But elements of mystery and controversy surround whatever may have been the real historical relationship between these two Taoist sages and their writings. As we have seen, the story of Lao-tzu's life is sufficiently extraordinary to render it suspect as reliable biography. Furthermore, we find no mention of the *Tao Te Ching* itself until about 250 BCE. That leads some scholars to conclude that this *magnum opus*, supposedly written in the sixth century BCE could not possibly date earlier than the fourth, and more likely is a century later than that. All of this raises the distinct likelihood that Lao-tzu, even if he was an actual, historical person, was not the original source of Taoism after all.

A Phantom Founder?

If our redating is correct, then a century prior to Lao-tzu or his scholarly inventors, a truly great and seminal thinker had appeared in the person of Chuang-tzu (c. 350 BCE). That would mean that he, rather than Lao-tzu or the philosophers who invented him, would be the true founder, foundation, or fountainhead of Taoism. Indeed, similarities of themes and styles suggest that these hypothetical creators of both Lao-tzu and the *Tao Te Ching* may have incorporated some of Chuang-tzu's ideas into their work; and if so, what has long appeared to be the cart of early Taoist history is truly the horse.

The credibility of this scenario is enhanced by an analysis of Chuang-tzu's work. Modern scholarship has determined that only the first part of it, the seven so-called "Inner Chapters," can be reliably attributed to that sage, and this suggests that the remaining twenty or so are merely commentary and elaboration. Chuang-tzu's thinking is quite different in tone from that of the *Tao Te Ching*, which, though focusing on the individual, hurls a number of criticisms at Küng-fu-tzu's view of how rulers should govern. The *Chuang-tzu*, by contrast, is not simply non-political in its agenda, but downright anti-political. It also appears clearly concerned (some would say preoccupied) with subjects the *Tao Te Ching* largely or totally ignores: for example, Chuang-tzu cheerfully accepts death, a topic absent from the *Tao Te Ching*, as a natural and even welcome aspect of life. On the other hand, the two works share a central controlling theme. Both maintain that while everything else in nature is in tune with the *Tao*, humanity is encumbered by a lack of spontaneity and a predisposition to run counter to the flow of nature and its processes. Both works are also poetic in style, humorous in tone, and fraught with nature imagery; neither has much use for Confucian tradition or ceremony. Thus, though the historical connection between Lao-tzu and Chuang-tzu may have been invented in retrospect on the basis of faulty historical assumptions, assigning the two works ascribed to them to a single school of thought labeled "Philosophical Taoism" was not without justification.

Religious Taoism

Whatever its exact origins, Philosophical Taoism (*Tao-chia*) contrasts markedly with Religious Taoism (*Tao-chiao*), a movement whose most important figure was Chang Tao-ling (c. 150 CE). He injected into Taoism both belief in and worship of deities, two elements that were completely foreign to Lao-tzu's worldview. He also stirred in a motley assortment of shamanistic chants, spells, dances, alchemy, talismans, and a variety of magical techniques aimed either at warding off evil or at strengthening and preserving the individual's *chi* ("vitality" or "life force") and prolonging life. Finally, Chang—who by some accounts lived to the age of 132 as a result of his dabbling in magic and medicine—created an order of priests call *Tao-shih* ("Masters of the Way"). He also named himself the first *T'ien-shih* ("Heavenly Master"), a quasi-papal office that has been passed down to the present incumbent, who resides in Taiwan. Though Heavenly Master Taoism, as it is called, is the dominant form of religious Taoism today, more than 80 other sects that have proliferated over the centuries still remain active today. The fastest growing of these appears to be Complete Perfection Taoism, which draws heavily from Confucianism and Buddhism.

Like Confucianism, therefore, Taoism evolved from a pure spiritual philosophy and adopted the trappings of deification, devotion, and ritual. Indeed, it went even further than its counterpart by embracing shamanistic magic. It is tempting to treat this as a regrettable devolution and to disparage Religious Taoism as a bastardized form of the original, pristine, philosophical purity of Lao-tzu, Chuang-tzu, or both. Indeed many scholars and students of Taoism have done and continue to do just that. From the standpoint of Chinese culture itself, however, it must be admitted that religious Taoism's popular religious practices have a purpose and integrity of their own and would not have persisted and evolved, much less thrived, unless they served human spiritual needs in some important ways. Also, had it not been for the dogged viability of this religious form of Taoism, the more thoroughly philosophical *Tao Te Ching* so cherished by critics of Taoism's later religiosity would probably not have survived.

Taoism and the West

That said, it is probably not surprising that in the West, and particularly in America, far removed from the cultural milieu that supports Chinese folk religion, the pristine philosophical form of Taoism has made the greatest impression. The *Tao Te Ching* has been extremely popular here for nearly a century, with no fewer than a dozen English translations of it in print at any given time. Purist defenders of Chinese history and culture sometimes object that a Westerner who reads that masterpiece— especially in translation and with no clue about Chinese patterns of language and thought—cannot hope to gain an authentic understanding of it. Yet despite the considerable measure of truth in that objection, the persistent Western interest in this admittedly puzzling work suggests its inherent power to speak in a compelling and even inspiring way across cultural and linguistic lines. In this regard, the *Tao Te Ching* is like a great poem from any culture or age: it has a life and power of its own which, readily assimilated by the reader or hearer, brings new meaning that somehow transcends the original intent of its author.

That perhaps helps to explain why, in addition to the many English translations of the *Tao Te Ching* that are always available, nearly a hundred books currently in print have titles beginning with the phrase "The Tao (or Dao) of...." These include *The Tao of Motherhood* and *The Tao of Music*; *The Tao of Eating*, *The Tao of Food*, and *The Tao of Cooking*; *The Tao of Immunology* and (failing that) *The Tao of Dying*; *The Tao of*

Psychology and *The Tao of Physics*; *The Tao of Sales* and (come vacation time) *The Tao of Sailing*; *The Tao of Love*, *The Tao of Love and Sex*, and (cutting to the chase) *The Tao of Sex*; *The Tao of Meow* and *The Tao of Bow-Wow*; *The Tao of Bruce Lee* and *The Tao of Muhammad Ali*; *The Tao of Jung* and *The Tao of Pooh* (as in Winnie the); *The Tao of Jesus*, *The Tao of Islam* and *The Tao of Zen*; and last and maybe least (no kidding) *The Tao of Elvis*. Major booksellers stock such titles, not to sponsor or promote a shift in American spirituality, but simply because they sell.

I suspect that such books are in demand because even in watered-down forms Taoism resonates with Westerners and perhaps even fills a need in our society. From childhood, it seems, we are driven to succeed and conform in educational, business, and professional structures that are hierarchical and rule-based, and thus not all that different from the feudal society for which Confucius was so nostalgic. The pattern extends even to our dominant institutional religions, which seem only to reinforce the already rampant cultural Confucianism that tells us to work hard and to make something of ourselves. If book sales are any indication, Taoism's exhortation to spend less time doing and more time being is a message that many in our society are ready and perhaps even longing to hear. These books on Taoism may well be supplying an antidote for the Confucian imbalance that we sense pervades our culture and society. We Americans seem intuitively aware that today we need a bigger dose of Taoism than of Confucianism.

Distinctive Practices

As already indicated, neither Confucianism nor Taoism was originally conceived as a religion in the usual sense. Each was a worldview and a way of life that obscured or obliterated such neat distinctions as sacred and secular. Living a spiritual life, accordingly, was simply living life to its fullest. Nevertheless, the seemingly inevitable human urge to draw a spiritual line of separation between heaven and earth, and then to create religious bridges to span the gap, transformed two largely philosophical belief systems into religions with ritualistic practices and all the customary trappings.

Confucianism in Action

Despite the contemporary Chinese government's waning but nonetheless palpable antipathy toward religion in general and religious Confucianism in particular, it has in recent years maintained and even promoted Confucius as a moral example. It has also reclaimed

Confucianism—not as a religion, but as a pedagogical method and a model for cultivating the spiritual side of Chinese culture. At the popular level, many obviously religious forms of Confucianism also persist unofficially and perhaps all the more profoundly, especially in rural areas of China and among Chinese expatriates in Southeast Asia.

Chief among the most distinctive practices of religious Confucianism are the six ceremonial rituals called the *Li Ki*: capping, marriage, mourning, sacrifices, feasts, and interviews. The first three of these mark major transitional moments in life. Capping refers to a father's ceremonial bestowal of a squarish cap upon his twenty-year old son to mark his maturity. The wedding ceremony is the culmination of a marriage arranged by the families of the parties involved. It establishes a state of matrimony in which a wife is required and a man is encouraged to be monogamous, though the latter is allowed to keep concubines, especially when the wife appears unable to bear male children. Mourning rites for the dead, and especially for the head of household, are quite elaborate, involving weeping, wailing, sackcloth, fasting, and for the surviving son a period of self-deprivation lasting over two years. Sacrifices are also very important; today they are mostly food offerings directed to a variety of spirits and lesser deities, with ceremonies at which the male head of household officiates, since there is no priesthood in Confucianism. Worship of the high gods was traditionally left to the emperor or others of high rank, and so plays little part in popular Chinese piety; feasts, by contrast, are usually directed to the ancestors, and are the main form of expression of the so-called ancestor worship mentioned earlier. Virtually every Chinese household has a closet-like ancestral shrine featuring wooden tablets inscribed with the names of deceased family members. Before these tablets, which are deemed to be the temporary residences of their spirits, food offerings are set. This is the context in which, as previously indicated, Confucius himself has come to be worshipped as a kind of Super-ancestor of the Chinese people: they worship at his tomb, erect temples to him, and grant him a quasi-divine status far above that of a familial ancestor. Finally, the rites pertaining to interviews inculcate the demeanor required in meetings between two parties, especially when they are of unequal status or rank.

Nevertheless, due in large part to Confucius' failure to distinguish between sacred and secular, the major expressions of Confucian practice are the ways in which the founder's appreciation for education, morality, and social stability have become staples of Chinese society and politics. Though Confucianism initially fell out of favor with the Chinese government after Communism dissolved the dynastic system and took over power in the mid-twentieth century, its profound effects proved to be enduring. Some have pointed out that Chairman Mao, who expressed utter disdain for Confucius, was in fact profoundly Confucian in his own ideals and style, even down to the format and content of his famous *Red Book*. More recent decades have seen the Chinese government not only expressing an appreciation for Confucius, but reintegrating his ideas into the state-run educational system. Given his durability, it is no wonder that K'ung-fu-tzu is still remembered today as "The First Teacher" of China.

Taoist Inaction?

We have noted that Religious Taoism is the variety most evident in China today, and its many embellishments suggest anything but the gentle effortlessness (*wu wei*) of its philosophical forerunner. In fact, were a Westerner whose interest in Taoism derived from the *Tao Te Ching* and perhaps the *Chuang Tzu* to go to China to learn more about Taoism, the experience would probably be very disappointing, if not utterly shocking. What she or he would find is a dazzling and dizzying array of shamanistic and magical practices being conducted under that banner. Encountering a Taoist funeral there, for example, one should not be surprised to see a colorfully costumed priest—perhaps fresh from conducting an exorcism or two—dancing wildly around an elaborately constructed scaffold, fireworks being set off, and acrobats performing skillful antics all around. (Not all Taoist funerals are this elaborate, however.) It is perhaps because of such paraphernalia, none of which seems to be traceable to Lao-tzu or the *Tao Te Ching*, and all of which are more prevalent in Taoism than in Confucianism, that most Chinese people today consider Confucianism a philosophy and Taoism a religion. The truth of the matter is that both originated as philosophies, and both responded to the seemingly uncontrollable human urge to introduce ritualistic worship, deities, and spirits, as well as to divinize the founder.

But just as in the case of Confucianism, Taoism's most pervasive influence today is not in religious ritual and ceremony, but in daily life. It is said that whereas Confucianism has been manifest in the politics, morality, and educational goals of the Chinese establishment, Taoism has been an important philosophical underpinning for the arts and other such counter-establishment activities as healing, exorcism, and unconventional sexual practices. In other words, Taoism has had an enormous impact on specific areas of Chinese culture. And in a more general way, it has provided the Chinese people with a healthy strain of gentleness that can be seen in the exercise technique called *T'ai chi chuan*, whose movements mimic both the continuous movement of the *Tao* and the balance of the *yin* and *yang*.

This is but the best known of a number of Taoist practices that, like the books mentioned earlier, have become quite popular in the West, and especially in the United States. T'ai Chi is taught for physical education credit at many colleges and universities, as well as in community centers and churches. It was even featured in some recent TV ads for pharmaceutical and dietary products. A similar physical-spiritual technique is found in the increasingly popular *Chi K'ung* (*Qigong*), which literally means "the skill of generating vital energy." Many architects, interior decorators, and homeowners are paying attention to the Taoist art of environmental modification called *Feng Shui* (pronounced "Fung shway" and meaning literally "wind-water"), which is supposed to improve one's overall well-being and good fortune. Many of these techniques probably predate Taoism, but their interpretation and practice today are almost invariably rooted in or read through Taoist philosophy.

Women in Chinese Religions

The role and status of women for most of China's history can be epitomized by a single term: "foot-binding." That inhumane practice was outlawed in 1911, fortunately, but it still stands as a symbol for the traditional Chinese estimation and treatment of women as inferior, weak, stupid, conniving, dangerous, and in some cases even sub-human. What little worth, respect, and power they have been accorded has derived from their only acceptable roles—as wives and mothers. Much of the blame for this situation has been laid (and properly so) at the feet of tradition-affirming Confucianism and its later variant, Neo-Confucianism, both of which have exerted tremendous influence on Chinese life and culture. That is especially true with respect to their consignment of women to a position of subservience to fathers, husbands, and even sons. Among the few positive results of China's turn to Communism in the twentieth century have been the suppression of Confucianism's malevolent attitude toward women and the granting of certain political rights irrespective of gender. In such areas as reproductive freedom, however, it seems that women have merely traded one master (husbands) for another (the state). To be sure, in recent years Western feminist currents have been felt in China, especially in urban areas, but only in spite of the tenacious effects of Confucianism.

In this matter as in so many others, Taoism presents a very different and much more positive picture. In its original philosophical form, it not only honored femininity (*yin*), but actually exalted it above masculinity (*yang*). The *Tao Te Ching*, for example, declares that the female conquers the male through stillness (or submissiveness, depending on the translation of Chapter 61), and counsels male readers to know their masculine strength, but to claim and cling to their feminine side (Chapter 28). It is not surprising, therefore, that the later and more ritualistic "Religious Taoism" has continued to recognize the propriety and legitimacy of female priests (*Tao shih*), though over the centuries they have been largely eclipsed by their male counterparts.

In light of the long tradition of the subjugation and suppression of women in Chinese society and the ascendancy of Confucianism through most of Chinese history, it is understandable that their clerical role in religious Taoism has waned. But the fact that women had an exalted status at all reflects Taoism's unprecedented and unparalleled appreciation of the feminine in the face of enormous opposing social and cultural pressures. Quite simply stated, *no other religious tradition as firmly incorporates the feminine dynamic in its formative principles as does classical, philosophical Taoism.* Indeed, if any religion can be called quintessentially feminist, it is this one.

Conclusion

The original versions of Confucianism and Taoism offer open and inquisitive Christians two diametrically opposed yet ultimately complementary approaches to life, both worthy of consideration. Confucianism advises us to be orderly, well-mannered, and aggressive, while Taoism counsels us to go with the flow and let go. We almost seem to be looking at "The Odd Couple" of religions here, which in the end need each other for the balance that together they offer. Both teach us to attune ourselves to an Ultimate Reality, the eternal Tao, though in different ways: Confucianism is rationalistic and behavioristic, and prods us to realize our full potential, while Taoism tells us to look to our inner nature (or spirit) and simply to be ourselves. Confucianism hopes to put society in tune by the efforts of individuals to achieve full self-cultivation through the observation of traditional social conventions. Taoism aims at bringing individuals into a conscious realization of their true selves and harmony with nature. In light of their very different approaches and goals, all of which appear salutary for a well-rounded life, combining these two philosophical religions might provide a prescription for harmony *and* wholeness, rigor *and* relaxation.

Christians can find three important lessons here. The first is that it is possible for more than one religion to coexist and to complement one another in the hearts and minds of individuals. Most Chinese today are not exclusively Taoist or Confucian, but a combination of both. In fact, they are likely to identify with what they call "The Three Doctrines," which adds Buddhism to the mix. Such an attitude might set a precedent for those Christians who, sensing something spiritually lacking in their own faith but unwilling to abandon it altogether for another, might simply supplement it with beliefs and practices drawn from other traditions. A second lesson is that an understanding of these two faiths might help to clarify the relation between Jesus and the institutional churches that were spawned by people who perceived him as the Christ. If, as suggested in this chapter, the purported teachings of Jesus exhibit clear parallels to Taoism, a recognition of these might foster a new and compelling understanding of him and his message. It might also serve as a corrective to those clearly Confucian (traditionalist, structured, cultivated, proper) institutions called churches, denominations, and the like operating today in his name. The third and perhaps most important thing to be gained from Taoism is yet another new way to think about Ultimate Reality, an approach that is not surprisingly quite compatible with what we found earlier in Hinduism and Buddhism. Great attention will be paid to this important issue in the following and final chapter.

Our mental backpacks should now be quite full of information and ideas. "*Too* full!" some might protest; but in any case, we have certainly collected enough to make it advisable to begin our journey home, where our Orientation of Christianity will move from its task of collection to the more daunting challenge of *construction*. Once we have arrived, therefore, we shall unpack and sort through our mementos to see which of these treasures will enrich us the most, which we might set aside for possible use later, and which we might want to discard altogether. To that task we turn in the next chapter.

Questions for Reflection and Discussion

1. What do you think (or how do you feel) about the fact that the very ancient Chinese believed in numerous, various kinds, and indeed different sizes of deities (e.g., the cosmic *Shang-ti* versus the more local and limited *t'u-ti*)? What would be the advantages or disadvantages of such a religion? Do you see any similarities with Christianity, say, in the veneration of saints in Catholicism, or even in the creation and adoration of American idols in the form of popular musicians and movie stars? Explain why or why not.

2. Does the ancient Chinese explanation for the emergence of the material world from an undifferentiated Unity make any sense to you? Do you find it more, less, or equally cogent and compelling than the Western religious belief in a transcendent, personal God who consciously created the universe out of nothing (*ex nihilo*) or the scientific view that the cosmos emerged from a Singularity that itself emerged from Nothing? Why?

3. Compare and contrast the kind of determinism that is implicit in the notion of *ming* with the doctrine of predestination promoted by some Christian theologians and groups, which holds that God determined who would be saved "before the foundations of the world." Do the same thing with congenital and genetic determinism, which strongly suggests that the nature we are born with is far more determinative of who we are and what we become than any of us care to admit. What do all of these ideas imply about human freedom?

4. Do you see any plausibility in the use of the *I Ching* to prepare for one's future? How is this similar to and different from the Western use of astrological signs and charts? Do you find one more sensible than the other? Why or why not?

5. Evaluate Confucianism and Taoism in comparison with one another. Which one do you find to be the better approach to life in general? Which is more characteristic of your actual lifestyle and values? What do you think about this chapter's contention that modern Western life is disproportionately Confucian and could use a higher dose of Taoism?

6. Were your parents more Confucian or more Taoist in their child-rearing practices? How so? How effective were they in this regard? How might your childhood or adulthood have been different had they taken a different approach? Which philosophical stance did you (or would you) adopt as a parent yourself? Why? Give some practical examples of what you would do to reflect that approach.

7. Take a modern controversial issue, such as abortion, human cloning, or the treatment of convicted criminals. How do you suppose a thoroughgoing Confucian would view those issues, in comparison with an equally doctrinaire Taoist? Does your answer change the way you think or feel about either philosophy? How and why? Can anything be said for a more balanced Confucian-Taoist approach? Why or why not?

Recommended Reading

Wing-Tsit Chan, *A Sourcebook in Chinese Philosophy*. Princeton, NJ: Princeton University Press, 1963.

Julia Ching, *Chinese Religions*. New York: Macmillan, 1993.

Chuang Tzu, *The Book of Chuang Tzu.*, Trans. Elizabeth Breuilly and Chang Wai Ming. London: Arkana Press, 1996.

Confucius, *The Analects*. Trans. D. C. Lau. New York, et al.: Penguin Books, 1979.

Herbert Finagrette, *Confucius: The Secular as Sacred*. New York: Harper and Row, 1972.

Benjamin Hoff, *The Tao of Pooh*. New York, et al.: Penguin Books, 1982.

Lao-tzu, *Tao Te Ching.*, Trans. Gia-Fu Feng and Jane English. New York: Vintage Books, 1989.

Donald Lopez, ed., *Religions of China in Practice*. Princeton, NJ: Princeton University Press, 1999.

Jordan Paper, *The Spirits are Drunk: Comparative Approaches to Chinese Religion*. Albany: State University of New York Press, 1995.

Isabelle Robinette, *Taoism: Growth of a Religion*, Trans. Phyllis Brooks. Stanford, CA: Stanford University Press, 1997.

Lawrence G. Thompson, *Chinese Religion: An Introduction*, 5th ed. Belmont, CA: Wadsworth Press, 1996.

Holmes H. Welch with Anna Seidel, Ed. *Facets of Taoism*. New Haven, CT: Yale University Press, 1979.

Yao Xinzhong, *An Introduction to Confucianism*. Cambridge: Cambridge University Press, 2000.

Chapter 5

Return and Reflection

Toward an Enlightened Christianity

Objectives of this Chapter

- to move beyond the informational "Getting Oriented" stage to the constructive task of creating an enlightened form of Christianity that draws on insights from the Eastern religions that we have reviewed

- to identify mysticism as the dynamic in Eastern religions that shows the most promise as a foundation for such an enlightened version of the Christian faith

- to recast four key topics in Christian doctrine in an Eastern light: God, Human Nature, Jesus Christ, and the Bible

- to offer enlightened, unorthodox interpretations of such distinctive Christian doctrines as the Trinity, the Incarnation, and the Atonement, as well as the pivotal concepts of grace and faith

- to make a case for an Eastern-style mysticism, not just as a useful interpretive tool, but as a viable alternative Christian spirituality with great potential for reviving Christianity in its third millennium

aving now surveyed the three great religious traditions of the East—the Hindu, Buddhist, and Chinese—we have fulfilled the first of the purposes set forth in the Introduction, which was to "Orient" ourselves, as people with a Christian heritage, by learning more about these exotic faiths. For many readers, that may be enough and for them the journey may well end here. But I also suggested early on that beyond simply becoming better educated as a result of our virtual journey, we might also use our new-found knowledge to enrich the Christian faith itself. For the more adventurous among us, therefore, this is a time not to rest, but to forge ahead, into a new and exciting process of reconstruction. The first task in this enterprise will be to sort through the many diverse treasures we have obtained *en route*, and to identify those that show the most promise for reformulating the Christian faith in some enlightened and enlightening way. Once that is accomplished, the next step will be to draw up a provisional sketch of a viable and refreshing new reformulation of the faith. Rather than press the book's quirky use of the adjective "Oriented" in its title any further, however, we shall henceforth refer to our proposed revision of the faith using light obtained from the East as an *enlightened* Christianity.

Toward an Enlightened Christianity

A crucial first step in the direction of an enlightened Christianity is to determine precisely which of the Eastern riches to draw upon. As we have seen in the preceding three chapters, Hinduism presents us with a complex mixture of polytheism, monism, and henotheism; a plethora of gods and goddesses in addition to an Ultimate Reality; and a panoply of ideas and practices from which to choose. Buddhism provides, among many other fascinating things, the devotionalism of its Pure Land variety, the meditation and paradoxical thinking of Zen, and the colorful ritualism and trappings of its Tibetan permutation. Not to be outdone, China offers us a rich ancient tradition of beliefs, symbols, concepts, and practices, as well as such contrasting later expressions as philosophical Taoism, religious Taoism, and the socio-political ethics of Confucius. Which of these riches might we find most useful?

Why Bother?

At this point an important preliminary question might be whether any purpose will be served by such a re-envisioning of the Christian faith. To some extent, we addressed this in the Introduction, where we pointed out that large and growing numbers of Christians have been drifting away from their faith tradition, not just in the United States but in the entire Western world. This phenomenon has many causes, of course, but perhaps the most important is that religious ideas in general and Christian doctrines in particular have been severely challenged by the modern era—the shift in worldviews that we chronicled in Chapter 1. New ways of looking at and thinking about the cosmos, the world, and ourselves have rendered the traditional biblical, doctrinal, and theological arguments and answers untenable for many thoughtful Christians. The result is that untold thousands have abandoned what they have come to regard as an outmoded system of theological thought and spiritual practice; and they have fled the faith in droves. As one way of resisting this discouraging trend, let me suggest that ideas gleaned from some of the Eastern religions that we have explored in this book may offer a basis for transforming Christianity into a more relevant and meaningful option. They may even help to rescue the faith for a number of the disaffected—or even some who have already defected.

Discerning and analyzing worldviews is a tricky business. For the most part any worldview—that is, any tacitly shared understanding of the nature and workings of reality—is transparent. It is so much a part of a person's acculturation and environment that she or he simply does not realize that what appears to be "just the way things are" is in fact an assortment of objects and events perceived through an invisible interpretative lens. As we noted in Chapter 1, for several centuries and for most people in the West that largely transparent refractive medium has been primarily the post-Enlightenment, modern scientific worldview, the chief components of which are naturalism, empiricism, and rationalism. (I say "primarily" because some aspects of pre-scientific thinking persist, particularly in superstition and popular religion.) Philosophically speaking, our worldview also tends to embrace some kind of *material monism*—the view that the fundamental or perhaps only reality is matter. This particular metaphysics (that is, conception of the basic structure of reality) reflects the fact that sense perceptions and reasoning processes, the Western Enlightenment's co-arbiters of knowledge and truth, deal most effectively with hard, measurable data. Since the emerging modern scientific worldview was also inclined to notice and appreciate natural, lawful, and predictable processes, it almost inevitably produced a mechanistic picture of the universe and its workings. The resultant materialistic-mechanistic cosmos was seen as a single closed system that not only operated on automatic pilot, but also excluded any serious notion of transcendence.

Of course, with the advent of the so-called New Physics—first propounded by such luminaries as Einstein, Bohr, Planck, and Heisenberg—science has been expanding the perimeters and rewriting the parameters of the very worldview with which most of us in the West have grown so comfortable. Indeed, we appear to be edging toward a new or radically revised worldview in which the basis of reality may be neither time, nor space, nor matter, but energy—probably arranged at its most basic level in what physicists are now calling "strings." Consequently, scientists themselves have had to move beyond their strict empiricism and rationalism to test such alternative ways of knowing as intuition and imagination, the perennial staples of religious discourse. The most challenging search among theoretical physicists now is for a Unified Field Theory that they hope will interrelate the major forces of nature already identified, including those that operate at the seemingly surreal sub-atomic quantum level.

To put it bluntly, the emerging view of the cosmos is mind-boggling. In the famous dictum of British biologist and geneticist J. B. S. Haldane, "The universe is not only stranger than we imagine, but stranger than we can imagine." The cosmos described by current physicists is not the Newtonian one that your parents or grandparents knew; and theirs in turn was already far removed from the ancient worldview that informed the authors of the Bible. Surprisingly, a number of enthusiasts of this emerging post-scientific worldview have offered detailed attestations of its remarkable compatibility with the spiritually-based, monistic philosophies produced by Hinduism, Buddhism, and Taoism. The exploration of this connection began in earnest with Fritjof Capra's *The Tao of Physics* and Gary Zukav's *The Dancing Wu Li Masters*, both first published in the 1970s. Their insights, though still worth considering, already seem dated, and have been eclipsed by such extraordinary and more scientifically current works as *Quantum Physics* and *A Brief History of Everything* by Ken Wilber, a philosopher with clear Buddhist roots *and* a background in chemistry and physics. Also noteworthy are Michael Talbot's *The Holographic Universe* and *Mysticism and the New Physics*. Such investigations suggest that Christians who find a bridge to Eastern religions may just discover clues to reconciling their newly enlightened faith with the very cutting edge of scientific thinking as well.

To Bolt, Or Not to Bolt?

Another important question at this point, and a very fair one at that, is why Christians attracted to Eastern religious traditions should bother revising their own faith rather than abandoning it for one or more of the others. That is, of course, an option; and many Christians have already exercised it. Some of our fellow travelers may well have found in Hinduism, Buddhism, Taoism, or Confucianism elements so attractive and compelling as to render their former Christian faith totally outmoded and completely irrelevant. Accordingly, their best choice might be to stay in the East: to adopt or synthesize a faith from the treasures found there, and perhaps to look for even more riches from that region. In some ways, that might be the simpler option.

But the fact of the matter is that however difficult and daunting the work of revising one's own faith might be, it is always easier than adopting another one wholesale. That is because the distinctive cultural imprinting of the alternative religious tradition and of the person considering it inevitably produces cognitive and existential dissonances that are difficult for would-be converts to overcome. Some people do, of course, transfer successfully from one religion to another, and even adopt such trappings as foreign robes, hairdos, languages, chants, and even names. But they spend more time, effort, and energy doing so than most people, even those vitally interested, arc willing or able to invest. Tweaking one's existing faith, even as extensively as this chapter may suggest, is a much less formidable task, if only because the concepts and images encountered remain comfortably familiar even when spun in sometimes radical ways.

A case in point is a former colleague, who was (and remains) a devout Southern Baptist minister and a gifted and widely respected Old Testament scholar. As often happens at a liberal arts college, over the course of a decade or more he found himself repeatedly teaching the basic comparative religions course. Such an experience is bound to impress any open-minded professor (as it sometimes does exceptional students in only a single encounter) with the nobility and integrity of the world's great faith traditions. I teased him one day by suggesting that he had gotten so immersed in that subject matter, he had become a Zen Baptist. He responded with a hearty laugh of acknowledgement. After he left the college to take a position elsewhere, I assumed the teaching responsibilities for that same course, and within a few years found that I had become a Metho-Taoist—yet another way of saying "an enlightened Christian." I suspect that many others have fashioned similar syntheses for themselves as a result of their forays into other faith traditions, and have found the eclectic result, however tentative, more satisfying than the wholesale adoption of any foreign faith could possibly be.

Sorting, Selecting, and Setting the Stage

But it is difficult to decide precisely what to appropriate from the Eastern faiths for incorporation into a re-oriented, enlightened Christianity, for the bounty is so rich that the possibilities are virtually endless. It is conceivable, for example, that the Confucianism presented in Chapter 4 could be used to fashion a new Christianity that would be predominantly social-ethical, and thus—ironically—more in line with the Torah-based Judaism from which it emerged. Much less likely, but still possible, evangelical Christians might look to such exotic traditions as Sectarian Hinduism, Amida Buddhism, and religious Taoism for inspiration and practices useful in the cultivation of their own devotion to Jesus Christ and worship of the God they believe he uniquely incarnated.

I intend to suggest something much more radical than either of these alternatives, however. I propose that in the spirit of true adventure and for the sheer fun of pushing the envelope and thinking outside the box, we draw upon the aspect of those faiths that is furthest removed from the dominant spiritual dynamic of mainstream Christianity. By this I mean the *mystical* dimension that has been merely a minority expression in the Western monotheistic faiths generally and Catholic and Protestant Christianity in particular, but a thoroughly valued, explored, and developed spiritual tradition in the East. One important consequence of this choice is that we shall need to pay no further attention to Confucianism, whose overwhelmingly ethical orientation is not only inimical to mysticism, but extremely culture-bound. Although it has been of service to us in clarifying philosophical Taoism, whose inherent mysticism is much more amenable to our present purposes, it will be of little use henceforth. Nor shall we find of further use the various devotional forms of the East that might enhance popular Christian piety—Hindu sectarianism's *bhakti*, Pure Land Buddhism's faith in its celestial Amida and *bodhisattvas*, and religious Taoism's adoration of deities. These are, to be sure, respectable styles of religiosity with their own integrity, and have served millions of devotees well for centuries; but they offer little that can transform Christianity's well-established and most familiar manifestations.

By way of quick review, let me simply remind the reader that mysticism is always the search for the Ultimate—or, in the case of Christian mysticism, for God—as the eternal, infinite Self that resides at the depths of the temporal, finite ego-self. This is the sort of thinking about Ultimacy that we found in the teaching of philosophical Hinduism: the notion that one's inner spiritual energy-essence (*atman*) is identical to the Ultimate Spirit of the universe (*Brahman*). Seen in such a light, the relationship of one's soul to God would be very much like that of *atman* to *Brahman*, which we saw as comparable to that between a droplet of seawater and the ocean itself: undeniably part and parcel of the whole despite its apparent separateness. In a similar vein, Mahayana Buddhism teaches that we all have an essential Buddha-nature identical to that possessed by Siddhartha Gautama (the aforementioned Sakyamuni) some 2500 years ago, an inner quality that he called upon his followers to realize within themselves. In China, the classical (philosophical) Taoism of Lao-tzu and Chuang-tzu used different terms, but said pretty much the same thing: one's Inner Nature (*tzu-jan*) is the Way (*Tao*), which is both the Source of all things and their immanent Essence. Existing things and persons, then, are not so much creations of this Way as extensions, emanations, radiations, or effluences of it.

My choice of the mystical dimension means that I shall be exploring the implications of that dynamic for Christian thought. (Eventually attention to Christian *practice* will be necessary, of course, but the primary concern here will be the conceptual side of the faith.) The choice of this particular spiritual alternative virtually dictates that I focus on Vedantic Hinduism, Madyamika Buddhism, and the earliest forms of Taoism, all of which are primarily philosophical in character and, more to the point, grounded in mystical insight. In particular, I shall be exploring their shared monistic view of Ultimate Reality, which the mystical experience seems inevitably to generate. Also important will be the correlative idea that the Ultimate must be understood as an integral part, indeed the very core and essence, of human nature. That conviction, if it proves attractive and is taken to heart, should at the very least improve the self-image of individual Christians, especially those most affected by the traditional assertion that they are fundamentally sinful. What is more, the suggestion that they are essentially divine might well alter their understanding of the human predicament, the way it is to be ameliorated, and the very identity and function of Jesus Christ in the teachings of the faith and lives of the faithful. Finally, because of their mystical predisposition we shall attach special value to particular scriptures within these three preferred Eastern traditions, and in particular Hinduism's *Upanishads*, Mahayana Buddhism's *Sutras*, and Taoism's *Tao Te Ching*. These works will be of special interest as we attempt to reorient and enlighten Christianity and search for resonant writings in that tradition.

Four Key Tenets Transformed

Since we are proposing to recast Christianity in an Eastern mystical light at the end of a book devoted mostly to personal edification, it makes no sense to attempt a systematic or comprehensive presentation of all of the key Christian teachings. Such an undertaking might prove desirable at some point in the future. For the time being, however, I propose to take four of the most basic doctrinal elements of traditional Christianity— its view of God, human nature, Jesus Christ, and the Bible—and to adapt them to the mystical teachings of the Eastern faiths. The first two of these address what I take to be the fundamental issues of any viable religious system: first, the nature of Ultimate Reality, and second, human nature and its relationship to that Ultimate Reality. The other two will render our refashioned faith specifically Christian, for they deal with the role of Jesus Christ and the place and purpose of the Bible.

Viewing these four doctrinal topics from the standpoint of the great mystical traditions of the East, I intend to generate four working tenets of an enlightened Christianity. These will not, of course, be exhaustive; for like any religious perspective, a fully developed enlightened Christianity would necessarily entail many additional beliefs and concepts, some of which might appear as essential to other observers as the four just mentioned. For the present purposes, however, such will be treated as subsidiary correlates of the four propositions that I shall presently identify as crucial. A fully developed enlightened Christianity will also have practical aspects and applications which, though beyond the scope of the present volume, will at least be suggested in the Conclusion of this chapter.

For now let me present for consideration four basic constituent doctrines of an enlightened Christianity: God as the Immanent One, Human Nature as Essentially Divine, Jesus Christ as Mythical Archetype, and the Bible as Inspiring Metaphor. Besides its brevity, this list differs from traditional topical presentations of the Christian faith in four significant ways. First, the very wording of these beliefs sets them at odds with Christian orthodoxy, which sees God as transcendent Creator, humans as distinct and innately sinful creatures, Jesus Christ as a uniquely divine atoning Savior, and the Bible as the Word of God in some straightforward if not literal sense. Second, a number of elements usually considered essential to the Christian faith seem to be missing: the doctrines of the Holy Spirit, the Virgin Birth, and the Trinity, along with the notions of grace, faith, atonement, salvation, prayer, ethics, church, ritual, and social action. Again, these are all important but ancillary, and will either be subsumed under one or more of the four tenets or, if matters of religious practice, largely ignored in the present conceptually-focused exercise. A third curiosity is the characterization of Jesus Christ not so much as an historical person (though that aspect will hardly be ignored) as a mystical-archetypal figure. That is a move almost certain to rankle both traditional Christians and liberal scholars of Christianity, for both groups value what they perceive as the historical Jesus, though for different reasons, in different ways, and with varying results.

But perhaps the most controversial thing about the list of doctrinal supports is placing the topic of Humanity ahead of both Jesus Christ and the Bible. That unusual and seemingly impious order is quite intentional for two reasons. First, no Christian belief system can adequately define the respective roles that this key figure and focal scripture play in the overall scheme of things until some clarity is achieved about that scheme and the place of human beings in it. Second, a mystically based doctrinal system will necessarily elevate humanity—and especially the personal experience of the individual—to a level of importance that relativizes not only the putative founder and uncontestable foundation of the faith tradition, but the scriptural tradition that attests him. In other words, in an enlightened Christianity, the religious or spiritual experience of the believer will determine both the image of Jesus Christ and the importance of the Bible—rather than the other way round, as traditional Christianity has always maintained. *If an enlightened Christianity poses one primary stumbling block for traditional Christians, this may well be it.*

As concerns God's nature and human nature, however, the order of treatment is quite arbitrary in such a system. This is because mysticism aims, expects, and sometimes claims to lead to an experience of the deep point at which the Ultimate and the individual self blend indistinguishably into one another. There, in a kind of chicken-and-egg fashion, the spiritual experience of the individual determines the very image of God, which in turn attests the divinity of the particular individual and, by extension, of humanity in general. Only for the sake of convenience, then, does our discussion of the key tenets of an enlightened Christianity begin with divine rather than human nature.

God as the Indwelling One

"...the kingdom of God is within you." (Luke 17:21b, KJV)

The first and most important lesson for an enlightened Christian individual or the faith as a whole to learn from the Eastern faiths is a theological one. It is to be humble, cautious, and reserved rather than reassured and absolutist with respect to assertions about God. The main reason that such reticence is advisable is something Eastern religions know well: that God—or the Ultimate Reality by whatever name—is utterly unique and therefore incomparable. It is, above all, Mystery. Thus our normal modes of discourse and description, which rely so heavily on commonplace frames and points of reference, quickly prove inadequate. That is why the religions of the East recommend silence in response to experiences of the Ultimate or, failing that, an intentionally indirect, elliptical, or paradoxical use of language. "The Way that can be spoken is not the true Way" we may recall as the famous opening disclaimer of the *Tao Te Ching*, which later adds, "Those who speak don't know, and those who know don't speak." Under such circumstances, we who cannot refrain from speaking about the Ultimate should recall with appreciation the Hindus' recommendation of the *neti neti* ("neither-nor") approach. We might also recall that when speaking of *Shunyata*, Buddhists often just tell strange stories or pose and ponder impenetrable riddles.

Conceptualizing Immanent Being

Having said that, we may cautiously assert that because it builds upon an introverted, mystical spirituality, an enlightened Christianity will follow the general thinking of the East about Ultimate Reality by holding that *God is the indwelling One, the Spirit inherent in all things, including nature and human nature.* That is because the Ultimate Reality that we sense at the heart of our introspection will inevitably be the Divinity abiding in us as our very spiritual essence—in other words, a profoundly immanent Deity rather than the heavenly sky God of our fathers and mothers. This God will not be understood as transcendent (that is, "above," beyond," or "other"), except perhaps in the weak sense of being for the most part elusive of our everyday, ordinary powers of perception, comprehension, and articulation. "Transcendence" of this sort says more about our limited abilities than about the qualities inherent in God. With respect to basic nature, however, an enlightened Christianity's God must be profoundly *immanent* (literally, "abiding within") in nature, infusing or permeating the cosmos and everything in it. All existing beings, therefore, will be seen as possessing (as opposed to being possessed by) this pervasive Spirit as their very essence. Spiritual reality will be understood as involving not so much a Higher Power or Supreme Being, as a Deeper Presence or the quality of Being Itself. The One will be regarded as indwelling and energizing everyone and everything in the cosmos as the universal dynamic Source, driving Force, and abiding Essence. An important implication here will be that everyone and everything in the universe—indeed, the universe itself—is essentially divine, a notion that will be developed shortly.

In conceiving of and referring to this God, the word "Power" would be acceptable (though, like all theological language, provisional) so long as it be understood as driving, invigorating, edifying, and transforming people—and perhaps things and events—from *within*, rather than impinging upon them from without. Other possible appellations for the newly conceived Ultimate would include Absolute, Being Itself, Cosmic Consciousness, Divine Mind, Energy, Essence, Great Spirit, Ground of Being, Holy, I AM, Infinite, Inner Nature, Mystery, One, Reality, Sacred, Source, Ultimate, Universal Soul, Way, and Within—or any combination thereof, with or without the definite article "The." (The *Star Wars* movies, which were heavily influenced by Eastern thought, called this pervasive Something "The Force.") Because of their Western heritage and lifelong habit, most enlightened Christians will no doubt continue to use the word "God." But the term will have a meaning very different from that found in traditional Christianity, in which it bespeaks a monotheistic Deity, personal Being, and supernatural Creator of the natural order who is utterly distinct from it while yet being actively involved in its operation. Enlightened Christian thinking, by contrast, will follow the Eastern pattern of conceiving the Ultimate in largely non-personal or transpersonal (neither of which is quite to say "impersonal") terms as *the dynamic, intranatural, spiritual aspect of the cosmos.*

The alternative conceptual model that I am suggesting here is the kind of *monism* that we have found in the Eastern conceptions of the Ultimate, or perhaps one of its close philosophical or theological relatives. Philosophically, monism always suggests that reality basically involves one sort of "stuff," either matter (material monism), or mind (idealistic monism)—or as in the case of the Eastern religiously-based philosophies, spirit (spiritual monism). If the name "God" is retained, then we are probably embracing some variety of *pantheism*, which is the view that the "one something" that everything consists of is God or essentially God. A popular model endorsed by some prominent Christian theologians in recent decades is *panentheism*, which maintains that everything is contained in God in such a way that everything contains "Godness" as well. Though its affirmation of divine immanence certainly makes it more attractive than traditional theism from a mystical standpoint, panentheism still maintains a measure of metaphysical transcendence for God that is unattested by the most respected mystics or, for that matter, by practitioners of any other discernable spiritual discipline. This or other theological and philosophical models might be suggested and adopted, however, as long as they were based on the idea of divine immanence. Conceptual systems will be negotiable in an enlightened Christianity; the quality of immanence will not.

Omnipresence and a Geometric God?

In a way, this notion of the immanence of God is merely a radicalization of the traditional Western attribution of omnipresence, which holds that God is everywhere. If that is true in its most profound sense, then God is not just hanging out in the proximity of all things, but permeates every molecule, atom, and subatomic particle or wave. Indeed, if God is utterly everywhere, there is nothing that is truly distinct from God. In other words, it is a short conceptual leap from omnipresence to monism or pantheism—from "God is everywhere" to "God is everything." An old pantheistic aphorism puts it this way: "There is no spot where God is not."

Because it is both non-personal and highly expressive of this kind of immanental omnipresence, I have found a particular metaphor for God to be helpful: "God is a circle whose center is everywhere and whose circumference is nowhere." Though variously attributed, its most likely source is the ancient Greek philosopher Empedocles, who certainly did define God as the "sphere of perfect Love" from which every existing thing originated. And from ancient times, religions have used circles and spheres to symbolize infinity, perfection, completeness, inclusiveness, and unity—witness the solar disk of ancient Egypt, the *T'ai-chi* (*yin-yang*) of Taoism, the Wheel of the *Dharma* in Buddhism, and the calligraphic empty circle (*enso*) of Zen. The particular beauty of the image of a circle with a ubiquitous center and a boundless circumference is that it is at the same time a suitably non-personal metaphor for the Ultimate *and* a paradoxical and confounding one (in a Zen sort of way). Circles and spheres, then, are excellent images for God, the life of the spirit, and the spiritual journey. They recall the cyclical thinking that we noted in Chapter 1 as characteristic of Eastern faiths, and they will have significant implications for both an enlightened Christian spirituality and spiritual practices which, whatever their precise forms, will be all about *centering*.

An enlightened Christianity, then, suggests a kind of conceptual conversion for those reared in traditional Christian circles and cultures: from monotheism to monism, pantheism, panentheism, or a similarly immanentalist model. The only good reason to make such a trade of one view of God for another, of course, is that the old and familiar ways of thinking are no longer plausible or convincing on rational or experiential grounds. A new conceptualization should be entertained, accepted, and adopted only if it makes more sense in terms of the way one understands and experiences oneself and the world. An enlightened Christianity will probably come to realize that a God of the immanentalist sort is not just a "neat" notion that is fun to play with and kick around, but an image made commendable by the fact that it comports with one's spiritual experience. An added benefit may be that it is more amenable to the prevailing and still evolving modern scientific worldview than is the traditional God, who is portrayed as an essentially transcendent, supernatural, and personal being who intervenes in nature and worldly affairs from a distant, imaginary realm.

The Question of Personality

As already suggested, given the broad spectrum of thought in the Eastern religions, an enlightened Christianity will leave plenty of room for a variety of ways of thinking and speaking about God. But because Ultimate Reality in the East is generally conceived in non-personal terms, a Christianity illuminated by such thinking will be prone to use the kinds of non-personal terms and concepts that were suggested earlier. Water and Light imagery for the Divine, both of which are found throughout the Bible, might prove especially attractive and helpful in this regard, since both are so dynamic, all-pervasive, and familiar. Since more than seventy percent of the human body consists of water, that element is profoundly immanent with respect to our physical composition. Yet that simple fact largely transcends our awareness, for we neither look nor feel like water. Light is another useful image, for it always implies a source, and the energy shared by both the light and its source is essentially the same. The sun and the photons that it emits (or that emanate from it) are at once a single energy process; *and* both are in continuity with the life that they engender and energize. No wonder, then, that the ancient Gnostics—whose thinking was largely Eastern in style if not origins, and for whom God was therefore an immanent presence in the form of "divine sparks"—were inclined to use light imagery for both the Source and Its spiritual emanations.

Attractive as such metaphors may be, however, allowances must be made for the fact that the abstract ideas and entities they represent simply leave some people cold. Hinduism makes an obvious concession to this problem by providing a huge variety of very personal gods and goddesses to serve as "expressions" or "faces" of the Absolute that simple folks can comprehend and even adore. Mahayana Buddhism, too, produces a host of personal Buddhas and *bodhisattvas* with endearing human traits that attract and fuel devotion. Accordingly, an enlightened Christianity might do well to leave room for the use of personal images, metaphors, and language with respect to God so as to accommodate those who find meaning and comfort in such things or who are disposed neither to mysticism nor to abstract intellectualizing. An enlightened Christianity might even find a renewed role for mediating saints. Ultimately, however, such personifications can be only be regarded as concessions and compromises, since the real and whole truth is that only One Absolute exists, and that It is nameless and faceless.

But however useful at the popular level, personal images for God pose a double danger. Not only are the most common ones—like "Father," "Lord," and "King"—gender exclusive and in two cases culturally irrelevant to citizens of Western democracies, but if used by enlightened Christians, they might invite a relapse into the old notions of transcendence and monotheism. The first of these problems could be overcome with some less traditional personal metaphors, such as Creator, Lover, Mate, Friend, Partner, Mother, Mother Nature, Coach, Programmer, or —just for fun—Inner Child. Two of those are also gender exclusive, but they are so non-traditional and well counterbalanced by standard male imagery in Christian circles as to be innocuous, while at the same time so universal in terms of human experience as to be inviting. (We do manage, for example, to speak of Mother Earth and Mother Nature without really personifying either.) But the danger with nearly all of these is that they imply an Other Reality rather than an Inner One, and thus reintroduce transcendence of being and its baggage of otherness, beyondness, and aboveness. All things considered, then, it might be a good idea for enlightened Christians to exert every possible effort to avoid personal imagery for God. If and when employed, it should be recognized as strictly metaphorical and far less theologically sound than nonpersonal metaphors.

The Persistent Problem of Evil and Suffering

The greatest challenge for any religion, theology, or philosophy that posits a single God or Ultimate Reality of any sort is to give an adequate explanation for the evil and suffering that afflict undeserving people. In traditional Christianity the problem is that somewhere along the way God was envisioned, presented, and widely accepted as omniscient (completely knowledgeable), omnipotent (capable of anything), and omnibenevolent (totally good)—all abstract attributes that, strictly speaking, were neither biblical nor essential to monotheism. This convergence—or collision!—of alleged divine qualities inevitably begged a highly inconvenient question: "If God knows the evil that is happening or is about to happen, and has the power to do something about it, but clearly doesn't, can God really be said to be good?" (Wrestling with this kind of quandary is called *theodicy*, "justifying God.") Since none of the stock and sometimes glib answers to this perplexing and persistent problem of evil has proven satisfactory, Christian (as well as Jewish) theologians who have tackled it have generally been obliged to make concessions with respect to God's knowledge, power, beneficence, or some combination thereof.

An enlightened Christianity will likewise be called upon to account for evil and suffering, of course, and will likewise find it a challenge to do so. The problem will be different from that faced by the mainstream Western faiths, however, since a monistic starting point does not posit a personal Supreme Being Above whose knowledge, actions, qualities, and abilities are quasi-human but exaggerated. Enlightened Christianity's God will no doubt look more like Hinduism's *Brahman*, which possesses the quality of *sat* ("consciousness") not as an all-pervasive awareness, or vast storehouse of knowledge, or massive thought process about this and that, but as a kind of energy source that fuels thought. As for omnipotence, an enlightened Christianity might do well to adopt Taoism's paradoxical conviction that the Ultimate *does* nothing, yet leaves nothing undone. It might even redefine omnipotence as *omnipotentiality* in light of Buddhism's idea of *Shunyata* ("Emptiness") as the Grand Matrix of Pure Possibility out of which things come to be and the backdrop against which actual things exist and happen.

With respect to the problem of evil, however, the best approach may be to join Hinduism and Buddhism in viewing evil and suffering as regrettable but natural and unavoidable elements of human existence. One way to do this would be to adopt some amalgam of the interrelated doctrines of *samsara* and *karma*. *Samsara* suggests that all existing beings are in a cyclical process that, however chaotic and tragic, is still superficial: the roiling and sometimes engulfing surface of the Spiritual Sea, at whose depths all is calm. The notion of *karma* interjects the view that suffering not only has meaning and purpose, but manifests overall fairness and balance as well: it all comes out right in the end (but only in a manner of speaking, of course, since an eternal process has no absolute end). Such thinking, of course, exposes the idea of *karma* to the charge of being nothing more than a vehicle of wishful thinking and denial in the face of tragedy. A stronger argument for the concept would be that *karma* bespeaks a cyclical process consonant with the patterns and processes of nature—perhaps, as we have seen, comporting with the very nature of God—and only *happens* to account for the existence of evil and suffering.

One thing is certain, however: a monistic, pantheistic, or other cognate theological variation on the God Within of an enlightened Christianity will not accept a separate Power of Evil. Since by definition monism allows for only one Deeper Reality, what is commonly called "Satan" and conceived in traditional Christianity as a real and god-like power, simply cannot exist. That would seem to leave only two possibilities. The first is that God, like The Force in *Star Wars*, has a dark side (though mystics have rarely if ever reported experiencing such a thing, except perhaps as a temporary "Dark Night of the Soul" on the way to full spiritual realization). The other is that evil emerges (like everything else) from the Pure Potentiality (God) as a neutral element in the grand scheme of things, but one that unfortunately but unintentionally affects human beings (including the innocent) negatively. The latter might seem easier for enlightened Christians to accept, given their traditionalist conditioning to think of God as pure Good and Love. But whether God (as Pure Potentiality) has a dark side will probably have to remain an open question, if only for the sake of intellectual honesty. The bottom line, then, is that like all theologies and philosophies, an enlightened Christianity will continue to struggle with the nagging problem of evil—its nature and its relationship to an immanent, all-pervasive God. At all costs, however, it will avoid the naïve conclusion, common to many New Age and other "feel good" spiritualities, that the lack of an Evil Power (Satan) necessitates a denial of evil itself, and that suffering merely is a matter of faulty thinking or self-delusion.

The Trinity Transformed

One might assume that a monistic or pantheistic or similarly immanentalist theology would have no room for a doctrine of the Trinity, but
that is not necessarily the case. We have already acknowledged the necessity of using such flexible modes of discourse as metaphor and allegory
when speaking about Ultimate Reality; and we have even cautiously
allowed for the use of personalistic language, as long as it is not taken to
imply that the Ultimate Reality is a person. It is a short step, then, to
allowing the figurative or symbolic use of Trinitarian language for God,
provided that one is aware that it does not represent a literal characterization of the way things really are, much less were or ever shall be.

Outright rejection of a doctrine like the Trinity because it is not logical—that is, to say that God is both One and Three makes no sense—
falls into the same trap that Fundamentalism does: literalism. An
enlightened Christianity, by contrast, will have learned from Hinduism
that it is entirely possible to think and talk about a One and a Several—or
even a Many—that are finally identical. It might also appreciate the use
in Zen and Taoist traditions of paradoxical and other seemingly self-con-
tradictory discourse when speaking of things spiritual, including the
Ultimate. For some enlightened Christians, therefore, the "One is Three
is One" Trinitarian language might prove useful. But they would be
mindful of its being merely another feeble attempt to speak of "That
Which Cannot Be Spoken" (to borrow a phrase from the *Tao Te Ching*),
or (as Zen puts it) simply one more frail finger pointing to the moon.

In an enlightened Christianity, for example, the Godhead might represent the primal, undifferentiated Divine Depth, the Ultimate-as-
Mystery/Matrix—the equivalent of *Brahman Nirguna* in Hinduism,
Shunyata in Buddhism, and the pure, simple, undifferentiated *Tao* of
Taoism. (See Figure 5-1.) The traditional designation of "Father" might
connote the Ultimate-as-Manifest, though for reasons already indicated,
an enlightened Christianity might want to use a less gender-exclusive
image: perhaps "Father-Mother" or "Great Parent of us all," or better
yet, such a wholly non-personal one as "The Force." The Eastern precedents for this include the *Saguna* aspect of Brahman in Hinduism; the
Tathata ("Suchness") that manifests *Shunyata* in Buddhism; and the *T'ai
Chi* that is the result of the first movement of *Tao* toward the multiplicity
of existence in the Chinese tradition. "The Son," then, might be seen as
the Ultimate-as-Male-Personal, assuming a role resembling that of Ishvara

Figure 5-1

An Enlightened Christian Trinity?

The Ultimate-as-Mystery/Matrix (The Godhead)
(Brahman nirguna, Shunyata, Tao)

The Ultimate-as-Manifestion ("Father-Mother")
(Brahman saguna, Tathata, Ta'i Chi)

The Ultimate-as-Male-Female/Person ("Son-Mother")
(Ishvara-Mahadevi, Buddhakaya, Tzu-jan)

The Ultimate as Multiplicity ("Holy Spirit")
(samsara, the 10,000 things)

(*Note:* What makes this a Trinity rather than a Quaternity is the identity of the Mystery-Matrix as Pure Potential, which is to say, Nothing-at-all. This Trinity does indeed have a different dynamic from that of the traditional Trinity, with its three co-eternal Persons constituting a single Godhead. Here we have something of a process Trinity, with each of the three consequent elements emerging—progressively but eternally—from a single, unconditional, ultimate, absolute, and utterly mysterious Matrix.)□

("Lord") in Hinduism, the primary male personal expression of *Brahman Saguna*. In keeping with the Hindu tradition at this point, however, an enlightened Christianity might also want to recognize Mary as the image of the Ultimate-as-Female-Personal (*Mahadevi* in Hinduism), thus raising her to a status coequal to that of the Son. (Jesus-Mary as the Ultimate-as-Personal would also echo Genesis 1:27 in recognizing the creation of humanity as male and female in God's image. It also recalls the image of the Hindu God Shiva as *Ardhanarishvara*—"Lord Half-Woman.") "The Holy Spirit" might then represent the Ultimate-as-

Multiplicity, that is, the Absolute expressed as the wildly differentiated physical universe and everyone and everything in it. In any such conceptual play, however, enlightened Christians will remain aware that they are employing metaphors for That which cannot be adequately conceived or expressed. This observation brings us—how appropriately!—full circle in our discussion of God as the Immanent One that is best known in the silence of the mystical moment.

Humanity as Inherently Divine

"... Christ in you, the hope of glory." (Colossians 1:27, RSV)

Whether explicitly or implicitly, every religion includes a view of human nature. Indeed, one might argue that the less conspicuous that view, the more insidious it is likely to be. For example, relatively few Christians recognize that the traditional Catholic and Protestant expressions of their faith have the most negative view of human nature of any religion, present or past. That is simply another way of saying that they have the most radical view of sin. Sin in traditional Christianity is not just a bad act or an accumulation of wicked deeds, but the congenital condition that causes such things. Hence, the often-heard claim, found in no other religion, that we are "born in sin." An enlightened Christianity will not only utterly reject such a notion, but assert its very opposite.

Universalizing Incarnation

An enlightened Christian view of human nature will be based upon the conviction that *God (or the Ultimate) dwells innately in every person in such a way that everyone is essentially divine.* This is, of course, a radical departure from the traditional Christian doctrine of sin and the resulting negative view of human nature. It also parts company with the *unique* Incarnation ("enfleshment") of God's own divinity in the person of Jesus, and affirms a *general* or *universal incarnation*, a concept that resonates with Eastern mystical religious traditions. Something like this is suggested in several of the teachings of the biblical Jesus (who is not to be confused with the historical Jesus, as we shall further see below). In the gospel portraits he not only exhibits divinity himself, but utters sayings that strongly suggest the existence of this same quality at the very core of *our* being. (Some non-traditional Christians have referred to this quality in a quasi-Buddhist fashion as the universal "Christ-nature.") Another possible designation would be "Word Within," an allusion to the divine *Logos* that the opening lines of the Gospel of John claim as primordial, divine, and creative (John 1:1-4), and that is traditionally identified with the second Person (Son) of the Trinity. By whatever name, this quality not only bears a strong resemblance to, but is actually identical with the inner spiritual essence called *atman* in Hinduism, the "Buddha-nature" in Mahayana Buddhism, and *tzu-jan* ("Inner Nature") in philosophical Taoism. All of these concepts define the human essence as identical with that of the Ultimate Reality (*Brahman*, *Shunyata*, and *Tao*, respectively), and thus strongly assert that we are *not fundamentally sinful*, but in fact *innately and inherently divine* (though, for reasons articulated below, capable of hurtful and even heinous acts).

An enlightened Christianity will therefore maintain that the dwelling place (Kingdom, Domain, or Realm) of God really and truly is *within*, as Luke 17:21 reports Jesus to have said. (Some English translators reveal their own non-mystical, Western orientation by translating the common Greek adverb and preposition *entos* as "among," even though its common meaning is clearly "in," "within," or "inside.") The biblical Jesus also implies that we are all equally divine offspring by his many reported suggestions that we regard and address God as "Father." Whether the historical Jesus actually said either of these things is, as we shall see, beside the point; the real issue is that they have a ring of truth in the light of a mystical spirituality. An enlightened Christianity certainly will appreciate the essential continuity suggested by what might be called the "spiritual-genetic lineage" entailed in this parental metaphor. To avoid any misunderstanding, however, instead of the image of a father's children, some such non-personal terminology as *emanations, emissions, extensions,* or *expressions* of the Supreme One might be more appropriately Eastern. Thus an enlightened Christianity would recognize that when the Johannine Jesus says "I and the Father are One" (John 10:30), he is not making an exclusive claim for his own unique status, divinity, or incarnation. Rather, he (or, more likely, the evangelist) aims at bringing his audience to a consciousness of their own indwelling Christ-Nature or Word-Within, and to that end asserts their oneness with the One by presenting an affirmation clearly reminiscent of Hinduism's *aham Brahmasmi* ("I am the Absolute"). With this in mind, a favorite scripture of enlightened Christians (as it was for the founders of the Eastern-tinged New Thought movement mentioned earlier) will likely be Paul's declaration in Colossians 1:27 that "Christ in you" is "the hope of glory."

In view of the earlier suggestion that God be imaged as "a circle whose center is everywhere and whose circumference is nowhere," it is noteworthy that the eminent psychoanalyst Carl Jung modified that statement by substituting the word "Self" (*das Selbst* in German) for "God." Jung was very familiar with and appreciative of Eastern faiths, and especially Hinduism and its affirmation that *atman* (the individual self) is *Brahman* (the Ultimate Self). In fact, his concept of the Self, which he characterized as one's Ultimate Nature beneath even the Collective Unconscious, profoundly resembles *Brahman Nirguna*. It is no wonder, then, that he tweaked the circle metaphor to suggest that the human essence has the same ubiquitous center and boundless circumference hitherto attributed to God. God and the Self—the latter not to be confused with the ego—are simply one and the same. Absorbed into an enlightened Christianity, such a view would nudge us from the two central traditional Christian reservations about humans—that we are at best merely "in the image and likeness of God" and at worst "damned sinful"—toward a much more positive view. For it would strongly suggest that we have a full share in the very being and goodness of God, and that we are all incarnations of the divine. Such a position, by the way, would by no means be incompatible with humanistic beliefs; indeed, it might appropriately be characterized as a "deep" or "spiritual" humanism!

The Holy Spirit Revisited

In traditional Christian thought, the Holy Spirit is conceived in the context of the Trinity as one of the three distinct, co-eternal Persons contained in the Godhead. Though a Person by definition, it is safe to say that the Holy Spirit's personality is at best ambiguous in comparison with those of the Father and Son, whose very titles suggest familiar human roles, and therefore *bona fide* persons. In contrast to the Father, who is connected in the Christian imagination with the image of a King enthroned on high, and the Son, who is inevitably identified with the man Jesus, the Holy Spirit seems more vaguely ethereal. It is often represented by such things as a bird and the wind, or in the words of one modern creed, as simply a "Divine Presence." No wonder that Christians find it difficult to know whether to speak of the Holy Spirit as "He" or "It," and generally opt for the latter pronoun.

One thing that traditional Christians seem to agree upon, however, is that the Holy Spirit can affect people. Indeed, it is said in the New Testament to be able to "come upon" individuals and even "enter" them. Pentecostal Christians not only personally attest this possibility, but build their spirituality around the idea of being "filled with the Holy Ghost." Such a claim would seem to blur the sharp distinction that the theist model otherwise draws between God's divinity and humanity. As we shall see, such a compromise actually does occur in the doctrine of the Incarnation, which effectively fuses divinity and humanity. But the idea of the Holy Spirit does not similarly attenuate the divine transcendence of theism, for it is commonly agreed that It (or He) can come and go—blow into and out of people's lives, as it were—and this means that It is not essential to human nature. It is for that reason that even when It is present, the affected human, though changed or transformed, is still regarded and treated as distinctly human. Not even Pentecostals would think of bowing to one another with prayerful hands and acknowledgments of one another's inner divinity, as Hindus routinely do.

It has already been suggested in this chapter that an enlightened Christianity might refashion the Holy Spirit to represent the Ultimate-as-Multiplicity, which is to say it might envision the universe and its plethora of contents as expressions and manifestations of an indwelling, self-emanating God. Another possibility, by no means incompatible, would be to reconceive the Holy Spirit as the essential divinity of human beings—in other words, as identical to the Christ-nature described above. Accordingly, the Holy Spirit would truly be a Divine Presence, but it would be *innate* and would constitute the fundamental and true identity of all people, including non-Christians, whether or not they recognized, believed, or manifested it. It would bespeak the essential spiritual continuity between God and humanity. It would therefore be both a birthright and an abiding fixture of the spiritual life—something to be discovered within, rather than an ephemeral visitor that might be expected to arrive occasionally from above and then depart sooner or later for its heavenly home. For an enlightened Christian, the Kingdom of God will be truly within, and the Holy Spirit its permanent resident.

The Human Predicament

If human beings are not inherently sinful but in fact essentially divine, one would think that the world would be a paradise. Of course, that is not the case. As we have already recognized, evil is an undeniable element of human existence; and despite the fact that evil is not a Power, satanic or otherwise, it nevertheless brings pain, suffering, and death—and sometimes a great deal of tragedy in the process. How might an enlightened Christianity account for this predicament?

We have already admitted that an enlightened Christianity will not pretend to have solved the problem of evil any more than any other religion has, but will tend to understand it at the level of existence rather than attribute it to an Evil Power or the Divine Essence. Following Eastern religions, an enlightened Christianity would likely assign the willful evil caused by human agents—as opposed to the suffering and loss caused by natural disasters—as a mental problem: ignorance or insanity. It would hold that while human beings do indeed incorporate a divine essence, they fail to recognize and therefore to manifest it; and it would propose that even if they intellectually accept the notion of their essential divinity, they do not comprehend it at the deeper spiritual level of Wisdom. Thus failing to grasp their true nature, they act out of their superficial ego-selves, and thus commit wrongful acts that yield unfortunate consequences.

Of course, even with such an acknowledgement of the possibility of ignorance and misdeeds, this view of human nature as essentially divine is counterintuitive. We don't look in the mirror or at one another and behold divinity. Instead we see egos with all of their frailties, flaws, and failures. On top of that, we daily learn of individuals who have assaulted, tortured, molested, raped, terrorized, and murdered without guilt or remorse. We know also of the Hitlers, Stalins, and Husseins of the world, who have wrought unspeakable evils on such grand scales that to regard them as essentially divine seems absurd. In our most lucid moments of self-awareness, we may even recognize and admit that we ourselves are capable of despicable behaviors, given the right (or wrong!) circumstances. Nevertheless, an enlightened Christianity, like the Eastern faiths, will tend to account for such evil acts as the terrible effects of either profound ignorance or insanity, either of which can leave us utterly unaware of, unconnected to, and unaffected by our deepest divine nature. And the consequence of living at the level of ego rather than spirit is that we lead superficial and sometimes even despicable lives. That, rather than any inherent condition of sin, would serve to explain why human lives so often go awry and wreak such havoc on others and on the planet itself. In short, most of us are in need not of redemption, but of enlightenment; the rest need psychological or psychiatric help.

Salvation, Atonement, Grace, and Faith

If the basic human existential predicament is caused by ignorance or insanity, then it stands to reason that the solution is to overcome one or the other mental deficiency or defect. In the comparatively rare cases of insanity, both the problem and the solution are probably more physical and medical than spiritual. For the vast majority who suffer from mere ignorance, however, the answer would seem to lie in spiritual practices that can lead us from our superficial level of awareness toward our "center," where the real truth and good news about ourselves resides. Experiencing that center and the Pure Potentiality that is there should transform our individual lives for the better. An enlightened Christianity will probably be reluctant to use the word "salvation" here because of its traditional connection to sin. Rather, the concept of salvation will be replaced with that of enlightenment or awakening.

Yet the notions of atonement, grace, and faith might still be useful, though the words would take on quite different connotations. Atonement (reconciliation, but literally "at-one-ment") would not bespeak a restored relationship with an Ultimate Other obtained for us by the sacrifice of a uniquely divine God-Son, but would affirm the innate human condition of identity with the Ultimate One within. We could, therefore, never lose it, but only our sense of it. Grace would refer to the fact that our essential divinity is not something to be achieved or earned, but inherent—a given and most salutary fact of life. Faith would not be blind belief in anything; nor would it mean giving assent to any proposition or doctrine or sets thereof. It would instead be a profound *trust*—an inward assurance based on intuitive personal experience—that we ourselves and our world are part of a Unified Something that is more than meets either the eye or the rational mind. Thus understood, therefore, faith would be an empirically-based conviction that we are participants in an Underlying Power or Presence that energizes and enriches existence, usually in subtle but sometimes in spectacular ways. (Acts of prodigious creativity and compassion would be examples of the latter.) It would be faith in yet another, more commonplace sense as well, for the existence of this mysterious Something cannot be proven, but only inferred from and attested by mystical experience.

Unlike most forms of mainstream Western Christianity, then, an enlightened Christianity will have an extremely positive view of human nature. There will be little or no talk about sin, Original or otherwise, much less of being "born in sin." Thus there will be no underlying theme of guilt, shame, or blame, or threats of a fiery Hell. "Sin"—if the term is used at all—will refer either to an alienated state of mind that keeps us from realizing our true nature and full potential for holiness and wholeness, or to the bad deeds that result from that mental state. At the same time, an enlightened Christianity will not be naïve. It will recognize that all is not "sweetness and light" with us; that humans have what Jung and his followers referred to as a "shadow side" that must be faced and dealt with. Much of what happens to us is certainly the result of the spiritual energy we generate, attracting either misfortune or blessings like a magnet. Yet bad things do happen to good people, if only because living in close proximity to so many others opens all of us to the possibility of being affected by the shock waves and fallout from their self-alienation, negative energy, and resulting harmful acts.

Eternal Life or What?

From what has been said and left unsaid here about the unitive, mystical starting point of an enlightened Christianity, it should be obvious that what is being proposed is a style of religion or spirituality that is about this life rather than death or an afterlife. It will be mainly concerned with living in the here-and-now the best possible life, one that is of spiritual depth and serves as its own reward. Insofar as an enlightened Christianity looks at death at all, it will be as a minor concern, simply a part of nature, life, and the sacred order of things. That said, however, the fact that human beings are endowed with spirits that are themselves Spirit means that they must share in some important way in Its infinity and eternality. At the same time, since the individual spirit is not identical with the ego-self, it seems unlikely that anything resembling the survival of a distinct personality or individual self-consciousness would be propounded. More likely would be the prospect that any spiritual persistence would be something akin to the recycling of one's non-personal energy-essence in other material and perhaps (but not necessarily) personal forms.

In other words, given their affinities with Eastern thought, enlightened Christians will tend to believe in—or at least be open to the possibility of—some form of reincarnation or transmigration of souls. In effect, that would amount simply to the continuation of one's essential spiritual identity (as opposed to the ego-self) into eternity or infinity. After all, as we saw in Chapter 1, everything else in nature—e.g., heavenly bodies, seasons, and even the winds—seems to move in cycles and circles (or at least ellipses) within a larger, ongoing process. Why should death break this pattern? Likewise, as we have already suggested, enlightened Christians will probably be willing to entertain some version of the idea of *karma*, as a way of explaining the mechanism for ensuring that these possible successive lifetimes are automatically regulated in some just way. Still, as was acknowledged in the Introduction, Christians enlightened by the rationalism of the West as well as by the spiritual musings of the East will likely understand both reincarnation and *karma* either as metaphors or as highly speculative notions rather than proven facts or essential tenets of the faith.

Jesus as Mythical Archetype

"Jesus Christ: yesterday, today, and forever the same." (Hebrews 13:8, translation mine)

In popular Christianity, Jesus the man and Christ the subsequent object of devotion and doctrine have always been assumed to be one and the same. Modern New Testament scholarship, however, has long drawn an important distinction between these two under the rubric of "the Jesus of history vs. the Christ of faith," and has effectively documented how early Christianity transformed the former into the latter. Most liberal theologians (and I among them) have deemed this transformation regrettable, and have tried to imagine (usually longingly) what a Christianity based on Jesus' own teachings rather than later beliefs about him would have looked like. An enlightened Christianity will likewise value the historical Jesus, and will in fact view him and his message anew in its own Eastern-enhanced mystical light. But it will also take a giant step beyond most liberal scholarship by self-consciously re-intertwining the images of Jesus and the Christ, though in a most non-traditional way. It will accomplish this first by recognizing the Jesus of scriptural narrative as having a unique integrity and appeal in his own right, not as an historical figure, but as a mythical exemplar and teacher of the spiritual quest. Second, it will reconcile this mythical-narrative Jesus with a Christ understood not as an object of faith and devotion, but as an archetype of the mystically self-realized person, a paradigm that will help clarify, articulate, and perhaps even reinforce the mystical spiritual quest.

The Historical Jesus Reviewed

However much it appreciates a mythical Jesus and the archetypal Christ he embodies, a truly enlightened Christianity will have to take into account nearly two hundred years of modern biblical scholarship. One major result of this research has been to make any discerning person duly suspicious (if not downright skeptical) of all definitive claims as to who the historical Jesus *really* was and what he was *truly* about. The scholars of the Jesus Seminar, for example, have determined that most of the words and deeds of Jesus reported by the Synoptic Gospels and virtually all of those in the Fourth Gospel were later constructions of the early church or the gospel authors themselves. The authentic material, then, consists of tidbits from the one to three years of his ministry; the rest bears indelible signs of either exaggeration or outright fiction retrospectively attributed to him.

Nevertheless, the Jesus Seminar has managed to piece together the sketchy but evocative snippets that have the stamp of reliability into something of a consensus profile, one whose broad strokes suggest—to me, at least—a spirituality with an underlying Eastern flavor. For one thing, the historical Jesus' apparent determination to see the Infinite immanent in the finite (the Reign of God operating in the human realm) recalls Hinduism's insistence that the Supreme, *Brahman*, indwells everyone and everything. It also resonates with Buddhism's teaching that *samsara* (everyday reality) and *nirvana* (the blissful realization of the Ultimate)—or form and Emptiness, as the *Heart Sutra* has it—are ultimately and paradoxically one and the same. Second, the historical Jesus appears to have lived and taught a non-assertive "trust ethic," which amounts to an easygoing confidence in the basic goodness of both the created order and humanity that stood in stark contrast to the rigid priestly legalism that dominated contemporary religious practice. This theme is highly reminiscent of *wu wei,* Taoism's relatively passive approach to life, which puts faith in nature and its underlying Way over against social structures and traditions and those who base their power, prestige, and authority upon such artifices. Likewise, Jesus' distinction-shattering "house without walls" (the Seminar's shorthand for their subject's radical inclusiveness) greatly resembles not only Hinduism's remarkable tolerance of religious diversity, but its fundamental contention that those who are one with the One are in essential spiritual unity with one another. His non-discriminating inclusiveness also reflects Buddhism's view that one's experience of *nirvana*—which amounts to one's identity with the Ultimate None (*Shunyata*)—necessarily leads to a boundary-shattering, universal compassion (*karuna*). Finally, in addition to the content of the historical Jesus' message, his often frustrating, oblique, and even paradoxical teaching style is reminiscent of the East's suspicion of direct discourse about spiritual matters. In fact, it echoes Hindu philosophy's roundabout *neti neti* approach to *Brahman*, the perturbing paradoxes of Zen stories (*mondo*) and riddles (*koan*), and the perplexing poetry of the *Tao Te Ching*. Though the evidence about the historical Jesus is admittedly thin, if a spirituality is discoverable in those of his teachings deemed authentic, one is hard-pressed to see it as anything but mystical.

However incomplete and equivocal the sketch of the historical Jesus pieced together by modern scholars may be, its lack of precision should not deeply concern those who have made the journey to the East and surveyed the great religious traditions there. Hinduism, for example, doesn't even have a nameable founder, though some of its adherents have cast the obviously legendary Krishna in this role. Few of the reported events of the Buddha's life—including his miraculous conception and birth—can be taken as literally true, and most of the teachings attributed to him are reconstructions from later centuries. The same is true of Lao-tzu: preceded by a sixty-two year gestation and culminating in an ox-mounted westward journey into a deathless retirement, the events of his life are obscure in the extreme and no doubt similarly fictitious. In all of these cases and many others that could be offered as evidence, the biographical facts about the purported founders of the major world religions are not important. Only two things really matter: (1) the *symbolic meaning* of their portraits, which ultimately derives from whatever spiritual authenticity resides in the tales told about them, and (2) the *inherent power* of the teachings attributed to them. When all is said and done, it is quite irrelevant whether those teachings originated with an historical founder or with the historical persons who imaginatively embellished that founder—or even invented him outright.

The Mythical-Narrative Jesus

Regarding the traditional Jesus story, it is safe to say that an enlightened Christianity will unabashedly understand it as mythical in the most technical and appreciative sense: as a fiction that conveys important spiritual truth. Furthermore, an enlightened Christianity will be at least as vitally interested in the inspiring and instructive life of the scriptural Jesus as in the occurrences surrounding his death, which traditional Christianity has stressed as the climactic, defining, atoning event in the story. It was hardly by chance that the cross became the main symbol of traditional Christianity, nor is it an accident that the most revered ancient creeds, the Apostles' and the Nicene, completely omit the reported experiences, deeds, and teachings of Jesus. An enlightened Christianity, by contrast, will take such details seriously, though not historically (much less literally). Jesus will be understood and embraced not as a Divine Emissary and Sacrificial Lamb, the details of whose life are incidental, but as a mythical figure whose story—the *whole* story, not just the Passion—conveys important spiritual truths, and does so without resorting to mere facts. In this regard, Jesus may be seen as what mythologist Joseph Campbell described as a classic archetypal *hero*: one whose life by its dramatic and adventurous external events actually represents a typical if not universal inner spiritual journey.

As with everything it surveys, then, an enlightened Christianity's reading of the mythical life of Jesus will reflect a self-consciously mystical standpoint. In broad strokes, it will acknowledge that his story both is and isn't ours. Like us, he is a person with two seamlessly integrated natures, one human and one divine. But as an archetype he is fully (and *seemingly* preternaturally) in touch with his inner divinity (his Christness, if you will); and he acts accordingly, teaching and manifesting love and compassion, especially to the poor and powerless. He also does amazing things that could not originate from the superficial level of humanity, the ego. He is able to bring healing (goodness and well-being) to the sick (the defeated and desperate). He can make the blind (the ignorant) to see (the Light) and the lame (disabled) to walk (the Way). He can even bring the dead (the hopeless and disaffected) back to life (hope and love). This fictionalized character is so extraordinarily compelling and transparent to the Divinity within that many people later mistook him to be not only an historical human figure, but also one who had uniquely been God in the flesh. In other words, they missed the central point of the story featuring him: that its protagonist was a prototype of themselves, and that it was really they who were essentially divine. They also failed to see in this character's occasional display of such emotions as sadness, impatience, rage, and even alienation from God (which in a mystical context would connote a lost sense of his innate divinity), their own chronic existential predicament of being out of touch with their deepest, most authentic selves.

Enlightened Christians will therefore have the highest regard for the Jesus presented in scripture. They will see him as a human being—indeed a *model* human being—in whom "the image and likeness of God" (humanity's birthright, according to Genesis 1:27) is fully (albeit fictionally) realized and expressed, as evidenced by this central character's ministry, message, and miracles. He is "The Christ" in the sense of being an incarnation or embodiment of the same Divinity that we all share, but one whose full self-realization of this universal human condition makes him a noble example to be emulated rather than a uniquely divine being to be worshipped. From the standpoint of an enlightened Christianity, then, Jesus' mythical Incarnation will be seen as only quantitatively different from that of all human beings (since he is, after all, an archetypal figure) and identical with that of such other (and equally archetypal) fully-realized spiritual masters as the Buddha and Lao-tzu. In other words (that parody the immortal Pogo), in the Jesus of scripture *we have met the Christ, and he is us.* He simply typifies our most ideal, profound, spiritual, divine, authentic selves.

The Teachings of the Scriptural Jesus

According to an ancient tradition in India, Nepal, and Tibet—widely believed but impossible to verify—the historical Jesus traveled and sojourned there sometime in the first three decades of his life, the period about which the four Gospels of the New Testament tell us next to nothing. Indeed, many natives of these countries believe that while he was there, he studied with the great Hindu gurus and Buddhist masters, and then returned to Palestine by way of Persia, where he spent time with the Zoroastrian astrologers before returning to Nazareth to begin his ministry.

No one really knows, of course, whether the historical Jesus really traveled to India or its environs; and, for reasons already indicated, it doesn't really matter if he did. What is clear is that many of the things that flow from the lips of the mythical-narrative Jesus sound curiously Eastern and mystical. "The Realm of God is within you," he says, for example (Luke 17:21). A Hindu might ask, "Well, where else would you expect to find the Ultimate?" According to Matthew (11:29), he says, "Take my yoke upon you...." That might seem an oddly weighty metaphor for a teacher to use about his own message of "good news," even if he quickly and reassuringly claims his "burden" to be "easy" and his "yoke" to be "light." But it just so happens that the Sanskrit word *yoga* literally means "yoke" and refers to any religious or spiritual discipline that explicitly connects an individual's essential self with the Supreme Spirit that is its implicitly true identity. Could it be that the narrative Jesus is really saying here, "Take my *yoga* upon you"? That would seem to make more sense. If these Orientalisms were not enough, John's Jesus tells Nicodemus that a person has to be reborn to enter God's Domain, a declaration whose most obvious implication is reincarnation (*samsara*). Jesus' frequent use of images of sowing and reaping might be seen as enhancing this interpretation by suggesting a notion of *karma*, a connection made explicit by Paul's insistence in Galatians 6:7 that people reap what they sow. The Johannine Jesus even says, "I and my Father are one" (John 10:30), the Hindu equivalent of *aham Brahmasmi* ("I am the Absolute."). He also claims to be "the Way, the Truth, and the Life" (John 14:6) These three metaphors are, respectively, the equivalent of the key Hindu and Buddhist terms *marga* (a spiritual path), *dharma* (the ordering principle of the cosmos as well as the basis of individual morality), and *ahimsa* (the conviction that all living sentient beings are inherently spiritual and should therefore be respected and protected from harm). Other examples could be offered, but the point is that the recorded teachings of Jesus (irrespective of their authorship and grounding in an historical person) take on a whole different character if viewed through monistic Eastern lenses rather than the theistic ones that the Christian tradition has provided.

Some of the sayings of the mythical-narrative Jesus of scripture take us beyond India and into China by suggesting themes held dear by Taoists. When he commends the lilies of the field for eclipsing the glory of even so accomplished a monarch as Solomon, not by doing anything but simply by being (Matt. 6:28–29 and Luke 12:27), he mirrors the principle of *wu wei*. He blesses the poor and meek above the rich and powerful (Luke 6:20–26) and declares that the last will be first and *vice versa* (Matt. 19:30 and 20:16; Mark 10:31, and Luke 13:30). He also claims that a faith the size of a mustard seed can move a mountain (Matt. 17:20) or uproot and relocate a tree (Luke 17:6) with a mere command. These and similar sayings echo Taoism's "less is more" appreciation for the lowly, the small, the unobtrusive, and the unassuming—the *yin*. In the passage from John cited in the previous paragraph, the scriptural Jesus' claim to be the *Way* suggests an identification on his part with none other than the *Tao* of Chinese thought—which, by the way, can also mean Word (*Logos*).

While the old tradition that the historical Jesus spent the formative time of his youth in the East may be purely legendary, therefore, the sayings clearly indicate that something of the spirit of the East is evident in the Jesus depicted by the gospel writers. That is especially true with respect to those of his utterances that we find most strange, puzzling, and unsettling. If Jesus did not really make the long trek to the farther reaches of Asia as reputed, perhaps Eastern ideas made their way to him along the well-traveled caravan routes. Or these notions may simply have arisen from the collective human unconscious, a shared mystical experience, or a common intuition of oneness with the One. In any case, the obvious resonance of many of the recorded sayings of Jesus with the ancient teachings of the East will provide modern enlightened Christians plenty of food for thought, as well as an incentive for further exploration of the mystical side of their own faith.

The Emerging and Evolving Archetypal Christ

In addition to reclaiming the mystical-narrative Jesus, an enlightened Christianity will lay claim to the mystical archetype born in scripture and reared to maturity in tradition. This archetype is already detectable in the "mythical Jesus" portrait of the canonical gospels, and in fact underlies and informs it, despite the fact that even in the ethereal Jesus of John's heightened Christology such a portrait was not yet fully developed. His and the other three evangelists' accounts did, of course, play an important part in the genesis of what I am calling here the archetypal Christ. So did the writings of Paul, which predated the canonical gospels by a decade or more. But it would take another three and a half centuries of conceptualization, controversy, councils, and finally creeds to hammer out the definitive version of the Christ archetype that has dominated Christian thought ever since—and that even an enlightened Christianity will find compelling, though for a much different reason.

Over the first four centuries or so of Christian history, the Christ archetype evolved from soft focus to clear delineation. (See Figure 5-2.) Paul provided the prototypical Christ, which he constructed virtually without reference to a mythical, narrative, quasi-biographical framework. Though not yet fully formed, it was nonetheless sufficiently compelling to mark the emergence of what would later be fashioned into a full-blown Christ archetype. It may well have influenced the mythical archetype that was implicit in the various gospel portraits of Jesus which, unlike Paul's, were couched in a complete story-line, though like his they were not very finely drawn. Even in the highly stylized Jesus of John's Gospel, the implicit archetype is more suggestive than definitive. Eventually, however, this underdeveloped concept evolved into the master Christ archetype that after centuries of haggling was finally forged into a finished doctrine at the Council of Chalcedon in 451CE.

The controversies that led up to the Chalcedonian Christological formula are too complicated to occupy us here. Suffice it to say that the resulting creed unambiguously affirmed that Jesus Christ was totally human and wholly divine, with two different and complete natures seam-

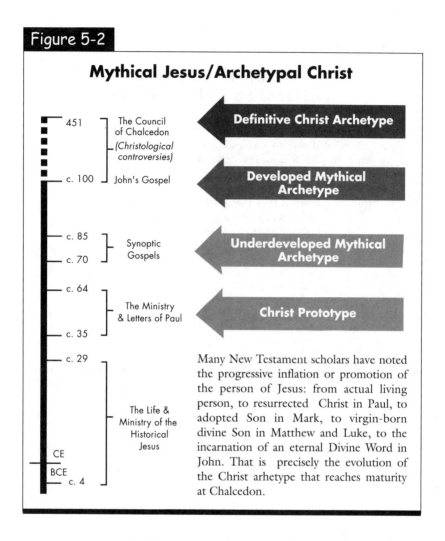

Figure 5-2

Mythical Jesus/Archetypal Christ

451	The Council of Chalcedon	**Definitive Christ Archetype**
	(Christological controversies)	
c. 100	John's Gospel	**Developed Mythical Archetype**
c. 85	Synoptic Gospels	**Underdeveloped Mythical Archetype**
c. 70		
c. 64	The Ministry & Letters of Paul	**Christ Prototype**
c. 35		
c. 29	The Life & Ministry of the Historical Jesus	
CE		
BCE		
c. 4		

Many New Testament scholars have noted the progressive inflation or promotion of the person of Jesus: from actual living person, to resurrected Christ in Paul, to adopted Son in Mark, to virgin-born divine Son in Matthew and Luke, to the incarnation of an eternal Divine Word in John. That is precisely the evolution of the Christ arhetype that reaches maturity at Chalcedon.

lessly united in one person. (See Figure 5-3.) Despite the inherent problems of this "one plus one equals one" resolution *and* its clear violation of the stipulation of monotheism that divinity is one thing (supernatural) and that humanity is quite something else (natural), the formula has clearly demonstrated a remarkable staying power. Though never fully or widely comprehended at the popular level, it has never been officially retracted or rescinded in the fifteen or so centuries since. It is explicit not only in most popular Christian affirmations of faith, but in all of the mainstream theologies enunciated since Chalcedon. One even sees depictions

Figure 5-3

The Chalcedonian
Christological Formula

"...our Lord Jesus Christ, the same perfect in
Godhead and also in manhood; truly God and truly
man ..., to be acknowledged in two natures, inconfus-
edly, unchangeably, indivisibly, inseparably; the distinction of the natures being by no means taken away by
the union, but rather the property of each nature being
preserved, and concurring in one Person and one
Subsistence, not parted nor divided into two persons,
but one and the same Son ..."

Note: The intention here was to say in every possible way (count them!), and thus
clearly and emphatically, that Jesus had two complete natures, but was one integral
person. As we saw in our first chapter (and especially in Figure 1-7), this idea was
reflected in many medieval paintings of Jesus, which show him with a hand raised
and forming what Hindus and Buddhists would call a mudra (symbolic hand position) by placing thumb on ring finger to form a circle (unity) and extending the
first two and little finger (two-in-one).

of the dual-natured Jesus Christ in genres ranging all the way from
medieval art to modern film.

The Chalcedonian formula presents us with the fully developed form
of the archetypal Christ. It is carefully constructed so as not to blur the
distinction between the divine and human; but its paradoxical "both-
and" (so reminiscent of Eastern philosophy) clearly compromises God's
transcendence, however unique and unrepeatable the alleged divine-
human convergence in Jesus Christ is claimed to be. Of course, that is a
problem only if one takes the two-in-one formula as a statement of actual
fact *and* is committed to the monotheistic theological model of mainstream Christianity. Viewed in an Eastern mythical and monistic light,
however, the Christ of Chalcedon bespeaks a profound truth not about a
unique human, Jesus, but about humanity in general. In the view of the
predominant philosophies of Hinduism, Buddhism, and Taoism, all of us
have two natures: the superficial, personal, visible ego-self, and the
deeper, spiritual, subtle, true-self. If there is any truth to that view—and
from a mystical standpoint there certainly is—then the formula of

Chalcedon would be properly understood not as an historically factual statement, but as the unintentional declaration of an eternal verity. It would constitute an assertion of *Jesus Christ as an archetype for human nature properly understood,* which is *from the perspective of its divine depth dimension.* For an enlightened Christianity, therefore, the Jesus Christ archetype affirms a *general and perhaps universal incarnation* rather than a unique one: a Divinity that resides within everyone, if not everything. Such a conceptualization both reflects and reinforces the kind of intro-verted, unitive, and mystical spirituality that we earlier identified as fun-damental to an enlightened Christianity.

Two caveats are in order about the Chalcedonian archetype. The first is that a key element of the formula has to be jettisoned for our purposes: the insistence that *only* Jesus personified the paradoxical combination of humanity and divinity. Archetypes are, by definition, timeless, ahistorical, and universal. If Jesus is uniquely *the* convergence of humanity and divin-ity, then he can't be an archetype. Second, an enlightened Christianity will forever liberate the Jesus Christ archetype inadvertently defined by Chaceldon from the sacrificial-atonement salvation schema within which (and indeed *for* which) it was originally framed, and will boldly transfer it to another, more salutary and encouraging context. Its new and more hospitable setting will be none other than the mystically derived convic-tion that divinity and humanity coincide in everyone.

The Power of the Archetype

As defined by Chalcedon and newly interpreted by an enlightened Christianity, therefore, Jesus Christ is an archetypal expression of the true human nature encountered in mystical experience and reflection. Once clearly identified as such, he provides mystically oriented readers an inter-pretative lens through which to read anew the gospel accounts and to appreciate fully the inherent spiritual depth of these writings. The arche-typal Christ that was always implicit but generally underdeveloped in the Jesus story of the gospels is thus revealed more clearly than ever as the focal point of a great myth—that is, a fictional, fanciful, and fantastic but nonetheless truth-telling story. Or, to put it another way, this Chalcedonian archetype now sets both the Synoptic teller of parables and the incarnate cosmic Christ of John's gospel in deep relief as the central character in a larger, overarching meta-parable, the Jesus Myth. In so doing, it sheds light not only on the scriptural Jesus and his story, but upon us and our lives as well. Far from taking anything away from the importance, the significance, or the reality of the Jesus portrayed in the gospels, this interpretation actually adds substance and relevance by presenting him as part and parcel of our own lives and experiences—an exemplar of and guide to our own Christ-natures.

The danger in all of this is, of course, that this rehabilitated Jesus Christ might become something of a Rorschach figure into which we can read anything we want, or even serve as a mirror for our superficial ego-selves. However regrettable, this would be nothing new. Indeed, for nearly two millennia mainstream Christians have, largely unconsciously, read and conflated the Jesus story in terms of a preconceived and largely self-serving image of its central character. That image usually has been inherited from some sub-tradition of Christianity and tacitly shared by its followers, who have then naively regarded it as a self-evident norm that "just so happened" to reflect their own (and often worst) dispositions and meet their perceived (and sometimes crassest) needs. Enlightened Christians, by contrast, will recognize and employ the image with more deliberation and intentionality; and because they will do so on the basis of a consciously embraced, mystical spirituality, it should lead them to a deep self-awareness (or Deep-Self awareness!). For them, Jesus Christ would be not so much a Rorschach or mirror as an X-ray in which to see not just their surface-selves, but their deepest and most authentic divine-selves, which are none other than the Self Itself.

The real test of the integrity of such a reading of Jesus Christ as a mythical figure and master archetype, then, will be in determining whether it leads to self-understanding, self-criticism, and self-realization, rather than merely to self-congratulation. The best measure of its authenticity will be its ability to call into question our current lives and to drive us ever deeper in search of the spiritual treasure that lies hidden within. Despite its fictitious nature, insofar as the narrative portrays Jesus Christ as operating out of a deep self that is one with the Absolute Self, the story can be affirmed as truthful. Indeed, to the extent that the New Testament writers have presented in Jesus and all of his fanciful acts and utterances a divinity-bearing person, their accounts—as well as the Chalcedonian Christological formula based upon and reinforcing them—can be regarded and embraced as conveying a great wisdom about humanity. Quite simply put, the mythical-narrative Jesus and the archetypal Christ merge in our religious imaginations to express the truth that the Christ (divinity) is innate and inherent within us all, and to elicit the experience of that most gracious and gratifying fact.

The Bible as Inspired Metaphor

"All scripture is inspired by God . . . ." (2 Tim. 3:16)

It may seem strange to some readers of this book that consideration of the Bible is placed fourth and last among tenets in a treatment that purports to be Christian, especially coming as it does well after our consideration of humanity. But as already suggested, our order of topics reflects the fact that an enlightened Christianity, being spiritually and mystically based, will ascribe more authority to the religious experience of interiority than to any external source, including scripture. It will thus relativize the Bible, just as it does the historical Jesus and the archetypal Christ rooted therein. Not coincidentally, then, what has already been said about an enlightened Christian approach to Jesus and the Christ as stimuli for spiritual interiority and self-realization contains important clues about how the Bible will be regarded as well.

Scripture in an Eastern Light

Before addressing the place of scripture in an enlightened Christianity, it might be helpful to remind ourselves of Eastern attitudes toward scripture in general. First, with the possible exception of the ancient Hindu *Vedas* (which are regarded as *shruti*, "that which is heard"), the Western notion of revelation generally does not apply in the East. Neither Buddhism nor Taoism has any notion of revelation, for the inspired quality of any scripture is considered self-evident and self-authenticating. And even in Hinduism, the later and technically less inspired *smriti* ("that which is remembered") scriptures (such as the many *Sutras*) are routinely valued more than their theoretically more inspired Vedic antecedents, which generally are more revered than read, let alone internalized, even by the most devout. All three of these religions have a kind of smorgasbord of spiritual writings, and their adherents are free to choose those that ring most true to their dispositions and situations. Especially treasured, however, are those that are most mythopoetic in form, such as poetry, epics, and other stories.

This preference reflects the fact that Eastern religions often treat religious language with extreme caution and sometimes even contempt. Earlier in this chapter we cited passages in the *Tao Te Ching* that admitted the inability to speak about the Ultimate Way and a deep suspicion of those who would make bold to do so. We saw in Chapter 2 that in Hinduism *Brahman* at its deepest, most mysterious level (*Nirguna*) is ineffable and best experienced *and* expressed in an awe-filled, reverent silence. (See Figure 5-4.) Unlike Western clergy, theologians, and other purported religious leaders, then, the most spiritual people in the East—the *mahatmas, rishis, gurus, roshis,* and other masters of the various religions and sects—are typically people of few words or avowed silence. The reason, of course, is that the kind of spiritual realities that most interest them commonly elude the human mind and expose the limitations of human language.

When it comes to articulating the Ultimate and direct experience of It, therefore, what we see in the mystically oriented scriptures of the Eastern faith traditions is a similar pattern of valuing silence over verbiage. Yet, most people who espouse these faiths—even while expressing a distrust of language in religious and spiritual contexts—nevertheless use it. They do so, however, in very odd ways, resorting to poetry, paradoxes, metaphors, myths, and even riddles with no logical or single correct answer—anything but linear, discursive, or literal language. It is largely in appreciation of this Eastern reticence concerning language in a spiritual context that I long ago developed the following axiom, which enlightened Christians might well find useful: "The best religious language is always closer to poetry than to prose; but the real language of the spirit is silence." That maxim certainly applies to the kinds of theologies and philosophies that have arisen from Eastern religious or spiritual contexts, which routinely employ metaphorical and mythopoetic language for discussing the Ultimate and related matters—and in the end, that includes everything. Here again, an enlightened Christianity will likely manifest a similar preference for indirect language, which in turn will dramatically affect how the Bible is regarded, read, and interpreted.

Inspiration, Authority, and Interpretation

Enriched by Eastern wisdom, therefore, an enlightened Christianity will view *the Bible as comprising, among other collateral material, an inspired collection of metaphors and related forms of discourse (such as myths, parables, poetry, and symbols), the understanding of which requires interpretative methods that are anything but literal.* According to this understanding of scripture, what traditional Christians refer to as the Word of God (which Hinduism and Buddhism both call the *Dharma* or Truth) will be seen as contained (and sometimes hidden) in the words of scripture. It will therefore have to be discovered by a subtly evocative reading of the Bible rather than a literal and definitive interpretation.

Figure 5-4

Silence as Sacred

"Silence is the best response to mystery."
—Kathleen Norris

"Language can only deal meaningfully with a special, restricted segment of reality. The rest, and it is presumably the much larger part, is silence."
—George Steiner

"We live in succession, in division, in parts, in particles. Meantime within man is the soul of the whole; the wise silence; the universal beauty, to which every particle is equally related; the eternal ONE."
—Ralph Waldo Emerson

"Silence is deep as Eternity; speech is shallow as Time."
—Thomas Carlyle

"Still waters run deep." —English Proverb

"Silence... is when we hear inwardly,
sound when we hear outwardly."
—Henry David Thoreau

"If you want to avoid God, don't go to the desert,
and whatever you do, don't get quiet."
—Anonymous

"Silence is the general consecration of the universe....
Silence is the only voice of our God."
—Herman Melville

"Silence alone is respectable and respected.
I believe God to be silence."
—Henry Brooks Adams

"We need to find God, and he cannot be found in noise and restlessness. God is the friend of silence. See how nature—trees, flowers, grass—grows in silence; see the stars, the moon and the sun, how they move in silence."
—Mother Teresa

"A moment of silence is not inherently religious."
—The U.S. Supreme Court

From this viewpoint, the most spiritually useful and inspiring parts of the Bible will resemble the parables of Jesus and the myths and scriptures of all the world's great mystical religions. An enlightened Christian, then, will search the Bible for its rich mythical treasures, which in turn will be interpreted and understood not literally, but metaphorically, figuratively, and allegorically. This radical approach to reading scripture might appropriately be called "depth interpretation," for it aims to release the spiritual meaning (the "treasure in earthen vessels") hidden deep within the text, far beneath the superficial words and any real or alleged facts toward which they might point. Indeed, the key hermeneutical (interpretive) principle of an enlightened Christianity may well be the Bible's own assertion that "the letter kills, but the spirit gives life" (2 Corinthians 3:6)—which is itself, of course, a metaphorical assertion.

Over the years, I have employed what I call a "proof of the pudding is in the eating" view of scriptural inspiration: *a scripture or spiritual writing is inspired if it proves to be inspiring*, that is, if it serves to encourage a higher consciousness or deeper spirituality. The corollary of this view of inspiration is that the authority of a scripture does not derive from any external source, including authorship; rather, scriptures are authoritative to the degree that they inspire persons and take them to more advanced spiritual levels (which in a mystical context are always *deeper*). Since some scriptures do this more effectively or consistently or for more people and over a longer time span than others, it seems to follow that inspiration and authority are a relative matter. The most inspired and authoritative scriptures, then, are those that have stood the test of time and crossed cultural divides in moving a great number of people over successive generations to new spiritual levels. However exotic to one's own culture, these are the writings whose titles are the most familiar: Bible, *Qur'an*, *Bhagavad Gita, Dhammapada, Tao Te Ching*, etc. It should be added that such a view of scriptural inspiration has little to do with infallibility, which is a bedfellow of literalism, but rather holds that the Absolute Spirit always speaks (metaphorically, of course) through finite, human, and therefore flawed channels.

Given the diversity of writings in the Bible, an enlightened Christianity will join the Eastern faiths in employing a number of types of interpretation, depending in large part on the genre of the writing being examined. For example, the relatively few sayings and doings in the Synoptic Gospels deemed through scholarly exegesis to be historically accurate might be amenable to a literal or historical interpretation, while the more clearly mythical passages might invite allegorical or metaphorical interpretation. Sayings whose historical authenticity could not be verified could still be found to be spiritually authentic—which is to say, inspiring and valuable—if they proved both edifying and either expressive of or conducive to mystical experience. To put it another way: in an enlightened Christianity, the *authenticity* of the saying or scripture as manifest by its ability to nurture one's spirit will always trump the question of who uttered or authored it (which is to say, its *authority*).

The Point of Origen

The identification and advocacy of diverse types of biblical interpretation is anything but new. One of the earliest and by far the most sophisticated and influential of exegetical systems was created by a controversial and thoroughly mystical Christian theologian of Alexandria, Egypt, named Origen (about whom we shall have much more to say later). He posited three levels of interpretation for biblical texts that corresponded to what he regarded as three aspects of the human being. *Literal* interpretation, which corresponded to the physical body and focused on historical events, was the least important type of interpretation, but still useful for some passages. More valuable was *moral* interpretation, which corresponded to the soul (in Greek, *psyche*). The most significant of all, however, was *allegorical* interpretation, which corresponded to the spirit (*pneuma*) and yielded the deepest, most spiritual understanding of the text. Origen believed that *every* text had a spiritual meaning, but not necessarily a literal sense. (He took great offense, for example, at the anthropomorphic and vengeful depiction of God in the Hebrew Bible and utterly rejected it as a literal portrayal of the divine nature.) But he did acknowledge that finding the spiritual meaning of a passage was not always easy, and in especially challenging cases where none was obvious, he often let his imagination run free and sometimes generated allegories from whole cloth. It should come as no surprise that his position on biblical interpretation and other alleged deviations from orthodoxy caused him to be condemned as a heretic by two church councils. He was later exonerated for his doctrinal deviances, but by an ironic twist was denied the sainthood he almost certainly deserved because he (of all people!) had taken Matthew 19:12 literally and castrated himself. Nevertheless, his hermeneutical system has influenced many biblical interpreters ever since, though mercifully rarely with the result of sexual self-mutilation and impotence.

While an enlightened Christianity will not necessarily maintain with Origen that every text has an allegorical or metaphorical meaning, it certainly will endorse the validity of such an approach to many biblical passages, and particularly to those that are the most at odds with our modern scientific worldview. Oddly enough, these tend to be the very ones that are most in harmony with mystical experience and thus most edifying for an enlightened Christian. The story of Adam and Eve in the Garden of Eden, for example, has long been seen by Judaism not as an historical account of human origins and disobedience, but as an allegory of the coming to moral awareness and maturity—and the resulting loss of innocence—experienced by all of us. Likewise, some have suggested the resemblance of Noah's Flood to an imaginative dramatization of a therapeutic purification of consciousness: cleansing divine rains wipe out negative thoughts and feelings (the wicked humans), raising a consciousness (the ark) filled with positive thoughts and feelings (the paired animals), and leaving it at a higher level (the mountain). Jesus' suggestion that his frustrated disciples cast their nets from the other side of the boat, where they met with instant success (John 21:1–14), might be a lesson about trying new approaches in the face of challenges and obstacles that accrue to the inward spiritual journey. (It might also prove to be sound advice for spiritual searchers who are disappointed with what has been obtained from their own spiritual traditions!) Last but certainly not least, an allegorical interpretation of the death and resurrection of Jesus might express the gracious truth that from even the most tragic and unjust circumstances, new possibilities of spiritual life may arise.

Of course the danger in all of this is the same one encountered with the archetypal Christ: rendering the Bible so flexible as to mean anything to anyone. In such a case, it would more than likely reveal not the inherent divinity of individuals, but the exact opposite—their most immediate and superficial desires, perhaps even their deepest perversities. The often expressed observation is absolutely true: Christian scripture can be made to support virtually any end, however heinous and destructive. (We need to remember only the medieval Crusades, American slavery, the suppression of women throughout Christendom, and the Holocaust under the avowedly Christian Third Reich.) Here again, the proof-of-the-pudding rule prevails: one's interpretation of the Bible or any of the world's great scriptures is valid if it demonstrably leads people to a fuller realization of their very best (which is to say, deepest) selves.

A Shorter Canon ...

Owing in large part to the kind of interpretation she or he favors, every person of faith embraces a shorter canon (that is, a focal, authoritative scripture) than the one officially recognized and touted by his or her faith. No Christian, for example, finds all of the biblical writings equally moving or inspiring. I don't ever recall hearing anyone claim to love the books of Numbers or Jude in the two testaments of the Christian canon; and even books that are almost universally beloved are selectively remembered or quoted. Except for numbers 1, 8, 23, 24, 150 and perhaps half a dozen others, for example, most of the one hundred fifty Psalms are widely ignored. Most Christians could quote or at least recognize chunks of the prophet Isaiah, perhaps by virtue of having sung cantatas in choirs; but few would know a word of Habakkuk or Haggai. They would also probably know and value John 3:16, if only because of the signs displayed by enthusiastic evangelical Christians in the end zone bleachers at televised football games, and perhaps a few other verses and episodes from that most beloved gospel. Biblical literalists would probably also know 2 Timothy 3:16, since most of them use (or twist) it to support their wooden understanding of verbal inspiration. But few Christians of any stamp would know a word of the rarely read Titus or equally obscure Philemon. Different people and denominations or sects will have verses, passages, and sometimes whole chapters (such as the wedding favorite, 1 Corinthians 13) that are particular favorites for a variety of reasons, and will return to them again and again. They may even string together the scriptural tidbits they do know into a pastiche of their own or (more likely) someone else's design. But they will virtually ignore the rest (which is to say, the vast majority) of scripture—while yet claiming to value the entire canon.

Enlightened Christians will be no different in this regard, except in recognizing and admitting their subjective selectivity. I would expect an enlightened Christian to appreciate the memorable portions of Genesis and Exodus (like the ones just cited) because of their richness in mythical stories that are highly amenable to metaphorical or allegorical interpretation evocative of spiritual truths. Many of the Psalms will no doubt be treasured, especially the lyrical ones that use pastoral settings, nature themes, and allusions to music to extol the Divinity inherent in nature and human nature. The other Wisdom Literature of the Hebrew Bible—Job, Proverbs, Ecclesiastes, and the Song of Solomon—will be valued for their almost Zen-like and sometimes poetic insights concerning the human condition. In the New Testament, the Synoptic Gospels (Matthew, Mark, and Luke) would continue to be valued, but less for the historical facts they provide than for the elements of the Jesus myth they contain. The Gospel of John should be especially treasured for its obvious lack of historicity, the distinctively stylized and heightened Word-enfleshed Christology, the unique "I AM" sayings, and the emerging Christ archetype mentioned above, which together signal its thoroughly mythic *and* mystical quality. (Enlightened Christians might even recognize the true mystical genius of the New Testament as the evangelist John rather than the Jesus he purports to portray!) Some of the Jesus-sayings in the non-canonical Gospel of Thomas (see Figure 5-5) and Gospel of Mary of Magdala (see Figure 5-6) might also be valued. Some of the writings of Paul would be appreciated as well, especially those that treat Jesus Christ as a cosmic reality or an indwelling presence. Oddly enough, the book of Revelation—once rescued from the absurd, literalist, futurist, and often sadistic interpretations of Fundamentalists—could prove to be a treasure trove of symbolism and imagery open to the kind of allegorical and metaphorical interpretation that might unlock its deepest spiritual truths.

Enlightened Christians, therefore, will recognize and freely admit that not all of the Bible is valuable or useful to them and that affirming its often metaphorical and symbolic language does not mean that every word of the Bible is to be so construed. As Freud is reported to have said, "Sometimes a cigar is just a cigar." Enlightened Christians will value only the books, chapters, and verses of the Christian scripture that they find compelling and spiritually edifying; and those will in effect constitute their Bible—their shorter canon. But enlightened Christians will by no means be shortchanged in this regard, for that abbreviated scripture will become the core of a much larger canon of their own construction.

... and a Longer Canon

As indicated earlier, an enlightened Christianity will not pretend that it has a corner on the Truth, but will follow the claim of the Hindu *Rig Veda*, which says "Truth is one; sages call it various names." That implies that Truth is to be found in all of the world's great religions and their holy writings, and thus follows the lead of the Hindu, Buddhist, and Chinese traditions in recognizing many scriptures as sacred. Hinduism, for example, has the *Vedas, Upanishads, Law of Manu, Ramayana, Mahabharata, Bhagavad Gita,* and a host of *Sutras.* Buddhism has the *Tripitaka* and its own dizzying array of *Sutras* (e.g., *The Heart Sutra* and *The Lotus Sutra*). *Taoism* has not only the *Tao Te Ching* but the *Chuang Tzu* and a variety of other treasured writings; while Confucianism has its *Five Classics* and *Four Books,* chief among the latter being the *Analects.* What is more, many Hindus, Buddhists, Taoists, and Confucians routinely read and profit from one another's sacred writings.

Figure 5-5

Eastern Themes in Jesus Sayings from the Thomas Gospel

(from the Scholars Version)

Here are some sayings of Jesus in the Gospel of Thomas which, despite their openness to multiple interpretations, nevertheless appear to speak to such Eastern Themes as: (1) the hidden location within of the eternal Ultimate One, the Source of all things, into Which all distinctions finally dissolve; (2) the need to bring forth That from within; and (3) the virtue of non-attachment to worldly things.

"If your leaders say to you, 'Look, the (Father's) kingdom is in the sky,' then the birds of the sky will precede you. If they say to you, 'It is in the sea,' then the fish will precede you. Rather, the kingdom is within you and it is outside you."

"Know what is in front of your face, and what is hidden from you will be disclosed to you. For there is nothing hidden that will not be revealed."

"I am the light that is over all things. I am all: from me all came forth, and to me all attained. Split a piece of wood; I am there. Lift up the stone, and you will find me there."

"Congratulations to the one who came into being before coming into being."

"Where there are three deities, they are divine. Where there are two or one, I am with that one."

"When you make the two into one, and when you make the inner like the outer and the outer like the inner, and the upper like the lower, and when you make male and female into a single one, so that the male will not be male nor the female be female . . ., then you will enter [the kingdom]."

"For this reason I say, if one is whole, one will be filled with light, but if one is divided, one will be filled with darkness."

"If they say to you, 'Where have you come from?' say to them, 'We have come from the light, from the place where the light came into being by itself, established [itself], and appeared in their image.'"

"Whoever drinks from my mouth [i.e., partakes of my teachings] will become like me; I myself shall become that person, and the hidden things will be revealed to him."

"There is light within a person of light, and it shines on the whole world. If it does not shine, it is dark."

"If you bring forth what is within you, what you have will save you. If you do not have that within you, what you do not have within you [will] kill you."

"Be passersby."

Figure 5-6

Eastern Themes in Jesus Sayings from the Mary Gospel
(from the Scholars Version)

Here are some sayings of Jesus in the Gospel of Mary (Magdalene) that clearly reflect Eastern themes:

* * * * * * *

"Every nature, every modeled form, every creature, exists in and with each other. They will dissolve again into their own proper root. For the nature of matter is dissolved into what belongs to its nature. Anyone with two ears able to hear should listen!"

This is very similiar to the assertion of Chapter 34 of the *Tao Te Ching* that all things derive from the Tao and return to It.

* * * * * * *

"There is no such thing as sin; rather you yourselves are what produces sin when you act in accordance with the nature of adultery, which is called 'sin.' For this reason, the Good came among you, pursuing (the good) which belongs to every nature. It will set it within its root."

This saying reflects the Eastern view that all things are essentially good and that sin is insubstantial and therefore not the basic problem faced by humans.

* * * * * * *

"Peace be with you!" he said. "Acquire my peace within yourselves!"

This teaching echoes the Eastern sense that all that is needed spiritually lies within the individual; or, as the Buddha put it in his final teaching: "Be your own lamps. Rely upon yourselves."

* * * * * * *

"Be on your guard so that no one deceives you by saying, 'Look over here!' or 'Look over there!' For the child of true Humanity exists within you. Follow it! Those who search for it will find it."

This saying is more than reminiscent of the Mahayana Budhist teaching that everyone possesses the Buddha-nature within themselves.

* * * * * * *

"The soul replied, saying, 'What binds me has been slain, and what surrounds me has been destroyed, and my desire has been brought to an end, and ignorance has died. . . .'"

The Mary Gospel identfies two of the four cosmic Powers that threaten to interrupt the soul's journey home to The Good (God) as desire (which the Buddha's Second Noble Truth teaches to be the cause of suffering); and ignorance, which Hinduism identifies as one of the things that keeps people in the cycles of *samsara*.

Following their lead, an enlightened Christianity will take at face value and affirm the scriptural declaration that "All scripture is inspired by God." (2 Timothy 3:16), regardless of whether the writer of that declaration intended it in such a general sense. (This, by the way, would be one of the few verses in the Bible that enlightened Christians might choose to take literally, precisely because it expresses their own experience of having been inspired by non-Christian scriptures.) An enlightened Christianity thus will maintain that there is great value in reading such Eastern spiritual classics as the *Upanishads, Dhammapada,* and *Tao Te Ching,* to name but a few. It will also value as inspired the writings of the great mystics in religious history, both Christian and non-Christian. That would include such modern spiritual luminaries as Ralph Waldo Emerson, Thomas Merton, and the Dalai Lama, of course. But enlightened Christians will also profit from such less widely known mystical adepts as H. Emilie Cady, Emma Curtis Hopkins, Emmett Fox, Krishnamurti, Ernest Holmes, Evelyn Underhill, Mary Oliver, Joel Goldsmith, Eric Butterworth, Chögyam Trungpa, Charlotte Joko Beck, Thich Nhat Hanh, Pema Chödrön, Father Thomas Keating, and Ken Wilber (again, to name but a few). Nor should congenial works of fiction and poetry be overlooked, whether or not they are overtly religious or spiritual. To an enlightened Christian, Truth will be where you find it.

For an enlightened Christian, then, the final word on the Bible is that it stands as one of a number of inspired (that is, demonstrably inspiring) scriptures that can help to inform and sustain a mystical spirituality. The kinds of biblical and other writings that will prove most edifying and susceptible to an allegorical, metaphorical understanding will be those most obviously mythical and poetic in nature. For these are the types of literature most amenable to depth interpretation; and an enlightened Christianity is all about experiencing the life of the spirit in depth.

The Case for a Mystical Christianity

"God is Spirit, and it is necessary for those who would worship to do so in Spirit and Truth." (John 4:24, translation mine)

Our treatment of the Bible as Inspired Metaphor rounds out the four basic tenets of our tentative reworking of the Christian faith in an Eastern mystical light. Before we began this exercise, the stated rationale for choosing the dynamic of mysticism as the basis for refashioning Christianity was that it was more highly developed in the East and thus promised to push the faith in a direction radically different from its dominant, orthodox forms today. That has certainly proven true. But the *whole* truth is that mysticism was selected for two other very good reasons as well. First, it comports with the spiritual orientation of the author, and without that motivating factor, this book would not have been conceived, much less written. Second, and far more important, mysticism has been a part of Christianity virtually from its inception and has manifested itself again and again in the history of the faith, usually in the form of individual religious geniuses and small, distaff communities. Having covered the highlights of this mystical Christian sub-tradition in the final chapter of *Remedial Christianity*, I need not rehearse it here in any great detail. Suffice it to say that the apparent idiosyncrasy and novelty of what has been accomplished in the present chapter ought not to be exaggerated. Indeed, in some respects, the "Orientation" that we experienced in the previous chapters, and that yielded a reformulated "enlightened Christianity" in this one, may now be seen as something of a *re-orientation* of the faith itself to its historic but often overlooked mystical subcurrents.

Historical Precedents

Not only does mysticism *per se* have a well-established place in the history of Christianity, but the idea of applying specifically Eastern perspectives and ideas to the faith is not really all that original. Indeed, this book began with an account of a band of seventh century Christian monks who traveled to China and did just that, producing the Taoist-tinged *Jesus Sutras*. But four centuries earlier, Christian theologians Clement and Origen (both of Alexandria, Egypt) had produced theologies that greatly bore the imprint of their teacher, the philosopher Ammonius Sacca (or Saccas). That sage's non-Egyptian, Latinized, and perhaps inverted name (Saccamonius?) suggests that he was a descendant—spiritually and philosophically if not genetically—of one Shakyamuni (often spelled without the "h"), better known as the Buddha. Sacca taught a very Eastern notion of God as a single Supreme Essence, Unknown and Unknowable, and of the human soul as an emanation of It that therefore shared Its very nature. The tremendous influence of his two Egyptian students on the history of Christian thought may help to explain, among other things, the non-personal and abstract view of the Godhead that provided the unifying principle for the Holy Trinity in its classic doctrinal formulation.

Origen's view of God had a significant effect on Christian thought in the Middle Ages, especially in the theology of Eastern Orthodoxy and in the mystical sub-tradition of the Western (Roman Catholic) Church. Eastern Orthodoxy's view of human nature was, like Origen's, consistently more positive than its Western counterpart, and in fact understood salvation not as the overcoming of a sinful human nature, but the perfection—indeed, the *deification*—of essentially divine persons. In other words, while this Orthodoxy was called Eastern because its Patriarchs and people were located in the eastern territories of the Roman Empire, it was Eastern in the modern sense of the word as well. Though never a dominant expression in Western forms of Christianity, a mystical sub-tradition flourished there as well, beginning as early as the late first century with Gnostic Christians and reaching its apex in the fourteenth century with the German cleric Meister Eckhart. He startled his religious superiors and others of his orthodox contemporaries by challenging their profoundly transcendent God with the claim that "Being Itself is God" (*esse est deus* in Latin) and that those who see divinity and humanity as two different things are mistaken. Obvious in such assertions are deep affinities with the East, and it is understandable that more than one Zen Master has recognized in Eckhart a kindred spirit. His mystical spirituality and theology were perpetuated—usually privately and sometimes secretly—by a number of individual Catholics, and even some religious orders. It re-emerged publicly in the Protestant Quaker movement founded in the seventeenth century by George Fox. He emphasized the divine "Inner Light" that all people possessed, and recommended a silent form of corporate worship that eliminated such things as sacraments, set prayers, sermons, and even scripture readings as potential distractions from the preferred focus inward. Not surprisingly, early Quaker worship resembled nothing so much as group *zazen*.

A more recent exemplar of an enlightened Christianity is the New Thought movement that emerged in America in the latter part of the nineteenth century as an early spin-off of Christian Science. The founders—notably Emma Curtis Hopkins, Charles and Myrtle Fillmore, Thomas Troward, Warren Felt Evans, and Emilie Cady—were all influenced by Eastern religious traditions that first gained general awareness in America at that time, and interpreted Christian teachings in their light. New Thought managed to produce a few small, relatively obscure institutional expressions, most of which gradually drifted away from Christianity to become something more akin to popular programs of positive thinking and prosperous living. But all of the New Thought organizations, including the few that remain self-consciously Christian, largely lost touch with the Eastern, mystical, and philosophical roots of their movement, and thus failed to realize the full potential, much less the spiritual depth, of the revolutionary views of their enlightened founders.

The enlightened Christianity presented in this chapter, therefore, follows in the lineage of all of these precursors and their appreciation for Eastern spirituality and thought. Like them, it offers some essential ingredients for a cogent, contemporary, and compelling style of spiritual thought and practice that synthesizes Eastern and Christian motifs; but it does so, I believe, in a bolder and more substantial way. In addition to an ever-burgeoning popular interest in and openness to non-Christian traditions, what makes this possible is the fact that contemporary Western knowledge of the Eastern religions is much more extensive and accurate today than at any other time in history. The primary motive for effecting such a synthesis, however, is the same as that of our forerunners: to produce a version of Christianity that will resonate with at least some for whom the traditional formulations of the faith are no longer convincing. What makes this task permissible, and indeed commends it, is the fact that Christianity as we know it is the result of a long history of reinterpretation and revision in light of other systems of thought and spirituality. As always, the faith continues to be a work in progress, with or without this chapter's proposals for an enlightened variation; indeed, Christianity owes its very survival to this ongoing process of rethinking and reshaping the tradition. To miss a promising opportunity to contribute creatively and meaningfully to that challenging task, therefore, would be to shirk our responsibility to our Christian heritage and to the faith itself.

A Personal Testimony

As already indicated, a major motive behind this book, its attention to the great Eastern religions, and its ultimate reworking of Christian belief in their light has been my own mystical orientation. Simply put, my version of an enlightened Christianity takes for its foundation the type of introverted, introspective, unitive, mystical spirituality that in retrospect at least, has always been a remarkably natural fit for me. Unfortunately, what for me is a most congenial religious style, and one so revered in the East, has been rare in the Western world; and as a result, I languished for several decades in a traditional Christianity whose dominant expressions—mostly devotional—simply did not touch or move me in any profound way. Alas, that remained the case long after I had been ordained into the ministry of one of that faith's major denominations. The situation began to shift only when, in my thirties, I became immersed in the Eastern faith traditions and, not long afterward, began to see important connections to minority reports in the history of my own professed Christian faith. Had I not, I might have become one of the former adherents who have left and continue to leave Christianity in despair—*and* in droves.

My basic problem (or so it seemed) was that I had both a mystical disposition and an analytical mind that thirsted for knowledge and reveled in ideas and their interplay. I have gradually come to recognize that it was precisely my own peculiar (and sometimes antithetical) mystical and intellectual leanings that had led to my initial and longstanding dissatisfaction with mainstream Christianity—and particularly its dominant devotional manifestations. But it was also this oddly bipolar disposition that eventually impelled me to undertake the quest for an East-West rapprochement. Christianity as I had come to know it through family and church had neither felt quite right nor made complete sense to me. Yet, the very dissonance that led to my discontent now appears to serve me well in seeking to overcome it. My mystical bent has allowed me to recognize certain elements in the Eastern traditions that reflect a mystical orientation and thus resonate deeply with me—and just happen to depart radically from the traditional Christian perspective I had inherited. My intellectual proclivity has permitted me to detect and understand for the first time important mystical strains in the religion of my birth and youth, and these in turn have enabled me to clarify and render meaningful the very doctrines that previously had made no sense to me.

I don't believe, however, that an enlightened Christian—that is, one who accepts a reworking of the faith like the one offered in this chapter—must combine my mystical *and* intellectual tendencies. Some may be attracted to such a version of the faith on purely rational or even esthetic grounds—because it makes sense and has a kind of beauty to it. Neither do I imply that those who *are*, like myself, of a mystical orientation need to be *accomplished*, in the sense of having achieved a level of profound insight and self-realization. Nor do I suggest that to be a mystic one must lead an *ascetic* life, renouncing and abandoning material possessions, family, and finally selfhood in search of such an experience.

By no stretch of he imagination could I regard myself as either ascetic or accomplished in this area. Such descriptives properly apply only to the great spiritual masters and aspirants who will probably always represent the religious minority—not only in Christianity, but even in the Eastern faiths that are more hospitable to such a life and quest. These adepts point the way, but simultaneously alert us less accomplished seekers to how far we fall short of a full realization of the Ultimate or God within. Fortunately for us lesser lights, there is a more common, run-of-the-mill (what I jokingly call "half-vast") mysticism that is more a matter of disposition or orientation than of achievement or attainment. It amounts to a kind of spiritual introversion—an inclination to search within the self rather than elsewhere for an Ultimate Reality or Absolute Mystery. That is the modest sense in which I identify myself as a mystic.

I am convinced that even in the West, where a more extraverted spirituality has long prevailed, a growing segment of the population similarly displays an inherent and perhaps even innate inclination to mysticism. My own experience over the years in helping students to clarify their own spiritual dispositions and orientations suggests that a greater than average representation of such folks can be found among participants in the various arts, probably because the creative process entails the expression of something deep within the artist. (It finally occurred to me in my forties that my own mystical orientation is probably due in large part to my having been since my early teens a jazz pianist, and thus a musical improviser who has always stood in awe of the mystery of the creative process.) Yet I also believe that there are people in all walks of life who are introspective by nature, and therefore perhaps naturally receptive or even prone to a mystical spirituality. I further believe that many of us have had at least some inklings of a mystical nature—subtle experiences akin to what poet William Wordsworth called "intimations of immortality." (See Figure 5-7.) I am convinced that if we learn to pay attention to these relatively low-level mystical moments and to develop the faint awareness they contain, it is possible to cultivate them into a full-fledged, intentional spirituality. Ideally, that would in turn generate an intuitive way of knowing, one that would supplement (but not supplant!) the more familiar linear, logical, discursive approach. Should that inwardly-directed intuition lead to a sense of Ultimacy abiding within, the result would likely resemble the kind of mystical spirituality that has long been honored in the Eastern faiths and now plays so central a role in our enlightened Christianity.

Figure 5-7

From "Lines Written a Few Miles above Tintern Abbey, on Revisiting the Banks of the Wye during a Tour"
by William Wordsworth (1798)

(The highlighted portion suggests an Eastern view of Ultimate Reality. It also sheds light on the title of another of his poems, "Ode: Intimations of Immortality from Recollections of Early Childhood.")

. . . For I have learned
To look on nature, not as in the hour
Of thoughtless youth, but hearing oftentimes
The still, sad music of humanity,
Not harsh nor grating, though of ample power
To chasten and subdue. **And I have felt**
A presence that disturbs me with the joy
Of elevated thoughts; a sense sublime
Of something far more deeply interfused,
Whose dwelling is the light of setting suns,
And the round ocean, and the living air,
And the blue sky, and in the mind of man,
A motion and a spirit, that impels
All thinking things, all objects of all thought,
And rolls through all things. Therefore am I still
A lover of the meadows and the woods,
And mountains; and of all that we behold
From this green earth; of all the mighty world
Of eye and ear, both what they half-create,
And what perceive; well pleased to recognize
In nature and the language of the sense,
The anchor of my purest thoughts, the nurse,
The guide, the guardian of my heart, and soul
Of all my moral being.

Conclusion

This chapter has spelled out in tentative fashion what might constitute the doctrinal basics of an enlightened Christianity. Viewing this alternative form of the faith through Ninian Smart's typology discussed in Chapter 1, we might say that for tactical purposes we began with the *experiential dimension* in the form of a mystical and unitive spirituality, a choice that we later substantiated as personal and historical as well. Second, we set forth in our four basic tenets the distinctive *doctrinal* or *intellectual dimension* of an enlightened Christianity. Third, we covered at some length the *mythological dimension* when we discussed how an enlightened Christianity would appreciate Jesus Christ as mythical-archetypal and approach scripture metaphorically and allegorically. Along the way, we also touched upon a number of the distinctive doctrines of Christianity that we did not identify as primary or definitive, but that eventually would have to be included in a fully developed system of enlightened Christian thought. Left to be examined—in a subsequent volume, perhaps—are the more practical of Smart's dimensions: *ritual, ethical, social,* and *artistic.*

The enlightened Christianity that I have envisioned in this chapter, though exhibiting a strong doctrinal dimension, does not constitute a complex or rigid body of belief, dogma, or creed. Nor does it presume to be either the last word on Christianity or the viewpoint that every Christian should adopt and embrace. I certainly hope that it will be substantial and engaging enough to inspire further theological and philosophical reflection and discussion, but it should never be considered as the definitive system of Christian thought. The last thing the world needs is yet another orthodoxy claiming to have the Absolute Truth. The enlightened Christianity that I have proposed is anything but that. It is instead much more like *a style or mode of Christian thought (and eventually practice) drawing inspiration and provisional insights from the great Eastern religious traditions.* In other words, it is *an alternative perspective on Christianity* that contrasts with traditional expressions of that faith in profound and, I believe, salutary ways. Despite its grounding in the imagination of one admittedly idiosyncratic individual, I believe that it nevertheless has the potential to speak to a wide range of people, but especially to many current and former Christians who have found traditional Christianity troublesome or downright untenable.

In setting forth the basics of an enlightened Christianity, I do not pretend to have recognized and appropriated from the East—or even from the previous three chapters— everything that might be useful. On the contrary, I have been highly selective. Readers of the preceding chapters may well conclude that in building my enlightened Christianity I have overlooked or shortchanged certain aspects of Hinduism, Buddhism, and the Chinese traditions that better suit their own spiritual dispositions. They may, for example, identify some elements of Confucianism—which I have all but ignored in this chapter—that they find as important and commendable for an enlightened Christianity as the ones that I derived from philosophical Taoism and its mystical Indian counterparts. They may even find that their own spiritual orientation is sufficiently different from mine that they have to start from scratch and repeat the sorting, selection, and synthesizing process for themselves. That is just fine, for my intent has been to present provocative ideas for others to consider, accept, customize, or reject in accordance with their own proclivities, experiences, insights, and needs. I hope only that my particular gleanings and musings will provide some helpful new ways of understanding familiar Christian beliefs and themes, and that those for whom such traditional expressions have become problematic or downright incredible will be spurred to discover other profitable Eastern connections of their own.

Questions for Reflection and Discussion

1. This chapter identifies the foundation of an enlightened Christianity as a mystical spirituality. To what extent do you or do you not identify with that kind of introverted, introspective approach to God or the Ultimate Reality? Have you had any experiences that might be identified as mystical? How do you assess the validity of such alleged experiences? If skeptical of them, how do you account for reports of such things?

2. What do you think (and how do you feel) about the following ideas presented in this chapter, all drawn from the mystical East?
    a. God is primarily immanent, indwelling nature and human nature as their very essence, as opposed to the more traditional Western notion of a transcendent God.
    b. Humans are essentially divine and only superficially sinful, doing bad acts as a result of their ignorance about their true nature.
    c. The authentic sayings of the *historical* Jesus suggest a mystical orientation on his part.
    d. Of primary importance are (1) the teachings presented in his name; (2) his mythical life story; and above all (3) the archetypal Christ-figure that represents humanity at its spiritual best.
    e. Although inspired, the Bible is largely—and at its best—mythical, and its most important passages are to be interpreted allegorically or metaphorically.

3. Now argue for the opposite view in each case, much as you would in a debate context with assigned topics and positions. Are there any fundamental issues in these assertions that you can identify? Name them and indicate their importance.

4. How do you think such ideas would play out in the church or churches with which you are most familiar? Why do you suppose that is? How do you feel about that? Why?

5. Can you identify any aspects of Hinduism, Buddhism, or Taoism that caught your interest and could well have been incorporated into the enlightened Christianity delineated in Chapter 5, but were omitted? Would you consider these as foundational principles, basic beliefs, practical considerations, or what?

6. This chapter paid no real attention to Confucianism, on the grounds that it was too ethically focused and culturally bound to be of much use in enlightening Christianity. Do you agree with that assessment, or can you think of elements of Confucianism that might offer useful contributions to a reoriented Christianity?

Recommended Reading

Masao Abe, *Zen and Western Thought*, ed. William R. Lafleur. Honolulu: University of Hawaii Press, 1985.

Karen Armstrong, et al. *The Once and Future Faith*. Santa Rosa, CA: Polebridge Press, 2001.

Marcus Borg, *Jesus and Buddha: The Parallel Sayings.* Berkeley, CA: Ulysses Press, 1997; and *The Heart of Christianity: Rediscovering a Life of Faith.* San Francisco: HarperSanFrancisco, 2003.

Joseph Campbell, *The Hero with a Thousand Faces.* Princeton, NJ: Princeton University Press, 1972.

Fritjof Capra, *The Tao of Physics.* Berkeley, CA: Shambhala, 1975.

Robert E. Carter, *The Nothingness beyond God: An Introduction to the Philosophy of Nishida Kitaro*, 2d ed. New York: Paragon House: 1998.

Harvey Cox, *Turning East: The Promise and Peril of the New Orientalism.* New York: Simon and Schuster, 1977.

H. H. The Dalai Lama, *The Good Heart: A Buddhist Perspective on the Teachings of Jesus.* trans. Geshe Thupten Jinpa; ed. Robert Kiely. Boston: Wisdom Publications, 1998.

Lynne M. Deming, ed. *The Feminine Mystic: Readings from Early Spiritual Writers.* Pilgrim Press, 1997.

Robert S. Ellwood, *Mysticism and Religion*. 2d ed. New York: Seven Bridges Press, 1999.

Matthew Fox, *The Coming of the Cosmic Christ: The Healing of Mother Earth and the Birth of a Global Renaissance*. San Francisco: HarperSanFrancisco, 1988.

Robert W. Funk, *Honest to Jesus: Jesus for a New Millennium*. San Francisco: HarperSanFrancisco, 1997; and *A Credible Jesus: Fragments of a Vision*. Santa Rosa, CA: Polebridge Press, 2002.

Thich Naht Hanh, *Living Buddha, Living Christ*. New York: Riverside Books, 1997; and *Going Home: Jesus and Buddha as Brothers*. New York: Riverside Books, 2000.

Phil Jackson and Hugh Delehanty, *Sacred Hoops: Spiritual Lessons of a Hardwood Warrior*. New York: Hyperion Books, 1996.

William Johnston, *Christian Zen*. New York: Fordham University Press, 1997.

Robert E. Kennedy, *Zen Spirit, Christian Spirit: The Place of Zen in the Christian Life*. New York: Continuum, 1995.

Karen L. King, *The Gospel of Mary of Magdala: Jesus and the First Woman Apostle*. Santa Rosa, CA: Polebridge Press, 2003.

Robert M. May, *Cosmic Consciousness Revisited: The Modern Origins and Development of a Western Spiritual Psychology*. Rockport, MA, et al.: Element Books, 1991.

Keiji Nishitani, *Religion and Nothingness,* trans. and introduction by Jan Van Bragt, with foreword by Winston L. King. Berkeley: University of California Press, 1982.

Edward Geoffrey Parrinder, *Mysticism in the World's Religions*. Oxford/Rockport, MA: Oneworld, 1995 (copyright 1976).

John A. T. Robinson, *Truth is Two-Eyed*. Philadelphia: Westminster Press, 1979.

John A. Sanford, *The Kingdom Within: The Inner Meaning of Jesus' Sayings* (rev. ed.). San Francisco: HarperSanFrancisco, 1987; and *Mystical Christianity: A Psychological Commentary on the Gospel of John*. New York: Crossroad/Herder and Herder, 1994.

Michael Talbot, *The Holographic Universe,* New York: HarperPerennial, 1991 and *Mysticism and the New Physics,* London/New York: Arkana Publishing, 1993.

Wayne Teasdale, *The Mystic Heart: Discovering a Universal Spirituality in the World's Religions*. Novato, CA: New World Library, 1999.

Alan Wilson Watts, *Behold the Spirit: A Study in the Necessity of Mystical Religion*. New York: Vintage Books, 1972.

Ken Wilber, *The Eye of Spirit: An Integral Vision for a World Gone Slightly Mad*. Boston: Shambhala, 1998; *Quantum Questions: Mystical Writings of the World's Great Physicists*. Rev. ed. Berkeley, CA: Shambala, 2001; and *A Brief History of Everything*. 2d ed. Berkeley, CA: Shambala, 2001.

Gary Zukav, *The Dancing Wu Li Masters: An Overview of the New Physics*. New York, Bantam Books, 1980 (copyright 1979).

Conclusion

The Road Ahead

"For our goal was not only the East, or rather
the East was not only a country and something
geographical, but it was the home and youth of
the soul, it was everywhere and nowhere, it was
the union of all times."
— Hermann Hesse, *The Journey to the East*

We have come a long way on our journey, not only geographically, but ideologically as well. In traveling from West to East
and returning home, we have in fact traversed the theological-
philosophical landscape from end to end and back again. In so doing,
however, we have confirmed Thomas Wolfe's famous dictum: "You can't
go home again." We have returned to the West, certainly, but because of
the treasures that we have brought back, it is no longer the same West
that we left. The appearance of its terrain has changed dramatically
because, by virtue of our exposure to a different and compelling perspective, we have changed. Our situation recalls another adage, this one
Eastern: "Before Zen, a mountain is a mountain; during Zen, the moun-
tain is no longer a mountain; after Zen, the mountain is again a moun-
tain." It is not the same mountain as before, however, for the Zen
experience has transformed the observer, and therefore the thing
observed. The mountain is viewed, as it were, once again for the first
time.

So it is with us. Having allowed Christianity to be enlightened by the
information and insights acquired in our Eastern adventures, we are no

longer bound by the traditional, theistic, devotional version of the faith that we left. Gone are the supernatural God, sinful humanity, uniquely divine Jesus Christ as atoning Savior, and factually true Bible. In their place is a mystically based Christianity, replete with an intimately indwelling Deity, divinely infused humanity, mythical Jesus evidencing an archetypal Christ, and metaphorical scripture. It is, quite simply, a faith of a different hue: more plausible, more credible, and more compatible with both the prevailing modern scientific worldview and the emerging postmodern one that is being spawned by the all-but-incredible discoveries of the theoretical sciences, and especially the New Physics. That observation points to yet another departure from the static formulations of traditional Christianity: the enlightened Christianity envisioned here will be much more open to spiritual exploration and intellectual examination—and therefore amenable to change.

In other words, an enlightened Christianity will be both revolutionary and evolutionary. This so-called "home" to which we have returned, you see, is really but a way station on a long spiritual journey that shows few signs of approaching its final destination. Indeed, in matters of the Infinite, there can never be a final destination, only a boundless and receding horizon ahead. Wherever we now find ourselves, we shall not be here long. At least the more adventurous among us will find that the journey has really just begun, and is bound to continue for the rest of our lives—and, some would say, beyond. In the future we may even find ourselves traveling back and forth between East and West on a regular basis, or setting out in new directions altogether. It is even possible that to support our metaphorical travels and efforts, we might build an imaginary "truth hostel" on this East-West route, a kind of halfway house for spiritual trekkers and sojourners, located at the metaphorical fork in the road to which we referred in the first chapter. What we then saw as a parting of the ways may now become for us a place of convergence and contemplation. From that vantage point, we might one day see the two routes reconfigured into a single path of spiritual and intellectual understanding, cut through the thickets of ignorance and provincialism and paved with the wisdom of all the great faith traditions, Eastern and Western. We might even live to see it well traveled in both directions by many pilgrims representing all of the world's religions. But we are not quite there yet.

However pleased we may be with the new vision of the Christian faith resulting from our journey, some might nevertheless feel that they will be out of place, alienated, and perhaps lonely amid those who have never ventured into such strange territories as we have. That should not be of great concern, however, for two very good reasons. First, a number of others among our Christian contemporaries—indeed, more than we might imagine—have returned from the same journey to the East similarly transformed; and many more will surely follow their tracks and ours. We already have, therefore, a substantial and growing number of enlightened Christian companions to accompany us on this continuing spiritual adventure. Second, however many traditionalist Christians we may have left by the wayside in our travels and reflections, that number is more than offset by the number of spiritual adventurers and seekers to be found the world over, whose noble company we now join. Many of them, like us, have broken free from stifling or confining religious traditions of their own. However isolated and odd we may feel now or in the future, therefore, we shall never be alone. On the contrary, we shall be in very good company, indeed!

Some might wonder, quite understandably, whether Christianity has anything unique or worthwhile to contribute to this process of clearing and paving a more accessible East-West spiritual thoroughfare. After all, our Eastern interpretations have so transformed the key doctrines of the faith that traditionalists would barely recognize it. Is it possible that in the process it has become nondescript and unremarkable, merely a lackluster imitation of its Eastern counterparts? Or is Christianity sufficiently irreconcilable with a mystical orientation that it is time for those so inclined to abandon it and adopt instead a more compatible Eastern faith? In short, could it be that Christianity no longer has anything distinctive to offer—that it has been but a stepping stone that is no longer needed or even useful and thus better left behind? Rather than returning home to Christianity, would it have been wiser perhaps to remain spiritually in the East and assimilate its mystical traditions wholesale, as others surely have done already?

In my considered opinion, the answer to all such questions is a resounding "No!" For Christianity boasts something absolutely unique and invaluable, a spiritual potential that no other tradition can match. It is none other than the archetypal Christ rooted in the Jesus myth, a tale and an image first crafted by the writers of the New Testament and later codified by the Church. Liberated from its literalist confinement, it is a grand, moving, and radically truthful piece of sacred symbolism that presents a compelling archetype of ourselves as paradoxically both human and divine, and it does so in a way that no other religious myth to date has equaled, much less surpassed. The fact is that none of the other founders or key figures of the Eastern religions can rival the metaphorical power of the fictional-archetypal character Jesus Christ: not the playful Krishna, nor the mindful Buddha, nor the enigmatic Lao-tzu, nor the wise Confucius—nor, for that matter, the Moses or Muhammad of the other Western theistic traditions. To be sure, the lives and teachings of all of these great spiritual adepts are noble, fascinating, informative, and inspiring. But none conveys the powerful and mystically derived metaphysical truth about us as incarnations of the Ultimate in the dramatic and compelling way that the Jesus Christ of narrative and doctrine does.

The uniqueness of this mythical-archetypal Jesus Christ is that he presents the image of complete divinity paradoxically suffusing an uncompromised humanity in a unified and seamless amalgam. He does this, furthermore, in a way that honors our own sacred, substantial selves without denying or minimizing the all too evident realities, deficiencies, and tragedies of human existence. From the joy and celebration surrounding his birth, through the triumphs and disappointments of his life and ministry, to the injustice of his trial and finally the grief and despair of his untimely, gruesome, and—yes—godforsaken death, this Jesus dramatically holds a mirror up to the best and the worst of human existence. More important still, as one who descends from the eternal spiritual realm into human flesh and who, in the end, ascends whence he came, he represents—in a remarkably Eastern cyclical pattern—the eternal Infinite diffused in temporal finitude for the span of a human lifetime. His particular Incarnation in myth, then, is an image of the universal incarnation that according to mystical spirituality and thought we all share. In other words, the Jesus Christ story is our story, only writ large.

The unmatched power of the biblical Jesus and doctrinal Christ suggests the special and important contribution that an enlightened Christianity might make in creating new paths that could eventually merge to form a single way in the realm of religion and spirituality. Its Jesus Christ will not be the sweet, sentimentalized Savior whose ancient atoning blood still washes away the sins of the contemporary world (or at least those of the faithful). Nor will it be the Jesus who ascended into heaven and sits there next to the Father as an object of religious devotion, waiting to come in triumphal glory and stern judgment. Nor will he be the only Way who renders all other teachers and traditions irrelevant and vacuous. He will be instead the archetypal, mythical, and mystical Jesus Christ revealed by the light we found in the East. As such, he will exemplify the life-giving—not to mention love-spreading—effects of a fully realized person, one who helps to illuminate our own true selves and the spiritual path we are carving out. A re-oriented, enlightened

Christianity, then, will offer to the spiritual seekers of the world Jesus Christ not as a sacrificial Lamb or sovereign Lord, but as a Light that leads to self-discovery and a spiritual Life to emulate.

There is much more do to, of course. This book has been involved above all with the conceptual side of an enlightened Christianity; but a purely conceptual faith will not do. It remains for another time to explore the practical implications and applications of our revised Christianity. For now, suffice it to say that an enlightened Christianity will also be an *engaged* Christianity. It will have not only a centripetal dynamic energized by the idea of spiritual *centering*, but a centrifugal impetus characterized by *compassion*. The connection between the two, of course, will be the mystical sense—expressed in many and various ways throughout this book—that the profound experience of one's oneness with the One inevitably leads to a strong identification with all who share that essential identity. As it turns out, it leads as well to an empathic experience of the existential plight of all creatures, and a determination to alleviate their suffering in every possible way, in accordance with the teachings of the scriptural Jesus.

The spiritual road, therefore, lies both behind and ahead. We have come a long way, but our journey has only just begun. The good news is that we do not have to travel in darkness. Rather, we have been to the East and we have found a great Light to illumine our path. It turns out to be not so foreign or strange after all, for it is none other than the innate Divinity that we find not only in the mythical-archetypal Jesus Christ, but in ourselves as well. It can hardly be foreign, for it does not shine *upon* us from without or above; it radiates forth from *within* us. For that reason, we shall not walk *in* this light, as many traditional Christian sermons and hymns would have it, but *as* it. It is in this vein that the dying Buddha is reported to have said to his disciples: "Be lamps unto yourselves." The mythical Jesus likewise tells his followers, "If then your whole body is flooded with light, and no corner of it is darkness, it will be completely illuminated as when a lamp's rays engulf you." (Lk 11:36, SV) He says both "I am the light of the world" (Jn 8:12a, SV) and "You are the light of the world" (Mt 5:14, SV), and in the blessed convergence of those two assertions lies the precious essence of mystical experience and reflection, the very heart of an enlightened Christianity. His promise to both enlightened Christians and seekers in other spiritual traditions who might avail themselves of his example is this: "My followers won't ever have to walk in the dark; no, they'll have the real light." (Jn 8:12b, SV)

May your light so shine!

Glossary

Abhidharmapitaka—the third part ("basket") of the Tripitaka*, purportedly containing the advanced or esoteric wisdom of Siddhartha Gautama,* the Buddha*

A.D. (abbreviation for *Anno Domini*, "Year of [Our] Lord")—the traditional way of denoting the years from the birth of Jesus (or thereabouts) to the present; now increasingly being replaced with "CE"*

Advaita Vedanta (Sanskrit, "Non-duality Philosophy")—the most influential branch of the most influential of the six traditional Schools* (*darshanas**) of Hindu philosophy; founded by Shankara*, it was also known as *Kevala Advaita* ("Absolute Non-Duality"), a thoroughgoing monism* that held that everything was finally *Brahman**

Agni—the ancient Vedic* god of fire, and therefore of the hearth and sacrifices, second only to Indra* in importance in early Hindu history

agnostic (as a noun, literally, a person who "does not know")—in the strongest sense, a person who has no answers at all, usually referring to the existence of God; in a more restricted sense, a person who has questions about specific doctrines, e.g., the Trinity or Virgin Birth in Christianity

aham Brahmasmi (Sanskrit, lit."I am *Brahman*")—one way that Hindus indicate the absolute identity of their individual spiritual essence, *atman**, and *Brahman**, the Absolute Ultimate*

Note: Cross-references to other items in the glossary are indicated with asterisks (*). In order to simplify things, cross-references have not been made to the macro-terms "Hinduism," "Buddhism," "Taoism," "Confucianism," or their cognates (e.g., "Hindu" and "Buddhist"), despite the fact that these are included in the glossary. All foreign words (but not proper names) have been italicized. For terms relating to Christian doctrines, scripture, history, and practice not contained in this list, see the extensive glossary in my *Remedial Christianity: What Every Believer Should Know about the Faith, but Probably Doesn't* (Polebridge Press, 2000).

Amida (Buddha)—the Japanese name for Amitabha, the Buddhist Celestial (Dhyani) Buddha of Compassion who is the object of devotion for Pure Land* (Amida* or Jodo*) sect as well as its Shin* variant; he is pictured as dwelling in a heavenly paradise in the Western sky called *Sukhavati**

Amida Buddhism—the form of devotional Buddhism founded in China c. 400 CE as *Ching-t'u** and imported by Honen* to Japan in the early 13th century CE as Jodo*; it teaches trust in the celestial (or Dhyani*) Buddha, Amida*; its two main branches in Japan today are Jodo* and Jodo Shinshu* (or simply Shin*)

ancient religions—an alternate name for polytheistic-ancient religions*

ananda (Sanskrit, "bliss")—together with *sat** and *cit/chit**, one of the three main attributes regularly applied to *Brahman**

anatman/anatta (Sanskrit/Pali, "un-*atman**")—the Buddhist doctrine of the "No Soul" or "Not Self" that holds that individuals at their spiritual core are empty (*shunya**), and thus manifest the utter (but potent!) Emptiness (*Shunyata**) of all things, the experiential realization of which is *nirvana**

animism—the worldview found in prehistoric and contemporary tribal religions; it views nature as teeming with spirits (as well as interrupted or possessed by *mana**), which can do harm or good and can be manipulated to some extent, especially by the *shaman**

anitya/anicca (Sanskrit/Pali, "impermanence")—the Buddhist conviction rooted in Hindu thinking but based on one of the last recorded (or attributed) sayings of the Buddha ("All composite things are transitory."); it asserts that there is nothing in the everyday (phenomenal) world that is substantial and therefore worth craving or clinging to

anthropomorphism—the practice of conceiving or depicting anything that is not human in physical human form (e.g., a cartoon animal that walks on two legs, wears clothes, talks, etc.); often applies to portrayals of a theistically-conceived Deity (e.g., "The Man Upstairs")

Ardhanari, Ardhanarishvara (Sanskrit, "Half-Woman," "Half-Woman Lord")—terms applied to Shiva* to indicate his gender-ambiguity or -inclusiveness, sometimes portrayed in art with male physical characteristics and attire on his right, and female equivalents on the left

arahant/arhat (Pali/Sanskrit, "saint," "adept," "worthy one,")—in Theravada* Buddhism, the personal goal of the *bhikkhu**, just shy of Buddhahood (which they attribute only to Siddhartha Gautama* and his forerunners)

archetype—(1) an original model upon which things are later patterned; (2) an ideal or quintessential example; (3) in Jungian psychology, a cognitive pattern or symbolic image derived from the past collective experience and residing in the deepest recess beneath the individual unconscious, a kind of repository known as the "collective unsconscious"

artha (Sanskrit, "gain")—the second highest life goal* (of four) in traditional Hindu thought and practice

Aryans (Sanskrit, "The Nobles")—the ancient people, probably from the vicinity of modern Iran, who invaded, conquered, and subsumed the settled people of the Indus Valley, and in so doing, laid the social and spiritual foundation for what would evolve into India and Hinduism

asana (Sanskrit, "seat," "posture")—in *hatha yoga**, any one of a number of physical postures for balancing and tuning spiritual energies of mind and body for meditation, health, and longevity

ascetic—one who practices asceticism*

asceticism—spiritual practice aimed at elevating the soul or spirit through unusual and sometimes intense self-denial or self-punishment, e.g., fasting, celibacy, mortification of the flesh

ashrama/ashram—(1) any one of the four life stages* recognized in Indian culture: student, householder, spiritual retiree, and solitary renunciant; (2) a Hindu spiritual retreat center

atheist—a person who does not believe either specifically in the God of theism* or generally in any sort of Ultimate Reality*

atman—in Hinduism, one's inner spiritual energy-essence, roughly equivalent to the Christian "soul" or "spirit," but non-personal, uncreated, eternal, recyclable, and totally one with the Ultimate Reality*, *Brahman**

AUM (Sanskrit)—the most sacred syllable in Hinduism (also found in Buddhism), meaning nothing in particular, but indicating the inner spiritual essence of everyone and everything, which is to say, *Brahman** itself; more commonly presented in English as *OM**

Avalokiteshvara—the Bodhisattva of Compassion in Mahayana* and Tantric* Buddhism; a manifestation of the Amida* Buddha, he reincarnates in this world in countless male and female forms (e.g., as Kwan Yin*, Kannon*, and the Dalai Lama*).

avarna (Sanskrit, "no-caste")—an alternative term for an outcaste* in Indian society; also known as *candala/chandala**, *dalit** and *pariah**; see *varna**

avatara/avatar (Sanskrit/Hindi, "descent")—the incarnation (enfleshment) of a god or goddess in human or animal form (e.g., Vishnu* manifesting as Rama*, Krishna*, and Kalki*)

avidya (Sanskrit, "ignorance")—lack of awareness of one's true, spiritual nature (e.g., mistaking one's physical or ego self for the true self, which is *atman**)

B.C.—abbreviation for "Before Christ*"; the traditional way of denoting the years before the birth of Jesus (or thereabouts); now increasingly being replaced with "BCE"*

BCE or B.C.E.—a fairly recent abbreviation of "Before the Common Era," a replacement for "B.C.*" increasingly used in deference to the sensitivities of non-Christian people

Baha'i—one of the youngest yet most widespread of the recognized world religions, with nearly six million followers; founded in the nineteenth century by the Muslim sage Baha'u'llah, its basic monotheistic* teaching is that all religions originated with God, who has sent many prophets (including Krishna*, Buddha*, Christ, Mohammed, and Baha'u'llah); that all human beings are equal; and that any form of prejudice is immoral and destructive

Banaras, Benares—alternative names for the holiest Hindu city, Varanasi*

bardo (Tibetan, "the in-between")—in Tibetan* Buddhism, the crucial intermediate state that lies between death and rebirth, usually divided into six separate events (also called *bardo*) in which one's psycho-physical disintegration occurs; its successful traverse is the subject of *The Tibetan Book of the Dead**

bhakti (Sanskrit, "divine love," "devotion")—love or devotion expressed to any Hindu deity, often in the form of *puja**

bhakti marga or *bhakti yoga* (Sanskrit, "love/devotion" plus "way" or "spiritual discipline")—the Hindu style of spiritual expression that revolves around *bhakti**

Bhaktivedanta, A. C. (aka Swami Prabhupada; died 1977)—born Abhay Charan De; a prolific modern Hindu philosopher, author of numerous commentaries on Hindu scripture, and founder of the International Society for Krishna Consciousness* (ISKCON*), whose members are better known as the Hare Krishnas*

Bhagavad Gita (lit. "Lord's Song" in Sanskrit)—a Hindu scripture, a small portion of an incredibly long epic; it tells of a strangely philosophical battlefield conversation between an Indian Prince named Arjuna and his charioteer, Krishna*, who is really an *avatar** of the god Vishnu*; a key scripture in devotional (faith-based) Hinduism

Bhagavat or *Bhagavad* (Sanskrit* for "Lord")—used by Hindus to refer to any male deity, and by Buddhists as a nickname for the Buddha

bhikkhu/bhikshu (Pali/Sanskrit, "mendicant")—a Theravada* Buddhist monk; the female equivalent, theoretically permissible, but seldom seen in modern times is the *bhikkhuni/ bhikshuni* (nun)

Bo Tree—(1) the ancient tree in Bodh Gaya that Siddhartha supposedly sat under in his attainment of enlightenment; (2) the modern tree that grows there today, said to be grown from the sapling of a sapling after the original tree died and a replacement was cut down

Bodh Gaya—the small town (and pilgrimage site) in Northeast India (in the state of Bihar) reputed to be the place where Siddhartha Gautama* attained enlightenment* under the Bo tree*, a descendant of which grows there today next to the commemorative Mahabodhi Temple

Bodhidharma—(470–543 CE) the semi-legendary twenty-eighth Patriarch of Indian Buddhism and missionary-founder of the *Zen/Chan** tradition in China

bodhisattva/bosatsu (Pali/Japanese, "one destined for enlightenment")—in Theravada* Buddhism, mainly a term for the 547 previous lives of Siddhartha Gautama*, in which he was progressing toward becoming the Buddha; in Mahayana*, (1) any individual who postpones entry into *nirvana** out of compassion for the suffering of others, and who dedicates himself or herself to assisting others in attaining enlightenment and *nirvana*; (2) one of a number of high-profile, quasi-divine, and often beloved helper-beings (e.g., Kannon* in Japan; Kwan-Yin* in China), usually attached (but subordinate) to one or another celestial Buddha* (e.g., Amida*); (3) in Tibetan* Buddhism, anyone who is seeking enlightenment and is motivated by compassion (*karuna**)

Bon—the form of shamanism* practiced in Tibet prior to the arrival of Buddhism in the late eighth century CE; Tibetan* Buddhism incorporated many of its practices and trappings, which gives that particular branch of Buddhism a distinctive and very rich, colorful character to this day *bosatsu*—Japanese for *bodhisattva**

Brahma—the creator god of India and by far the least popular of the *Trimurti**

Brahma Sutra—a first or second BCE* distillation of the *Upanishads** into aphorisms, and focusing (despite its title) on the Ultimate*, *Brahman**, rather than the creator god Brahma*

Brahman—in Hinduism, the Ultimate Reality* or Supreme Spirit; not a god or goddess, but a Power or Principle immanent* in the universe, nature, and human nature as *atman**

Brahmana (Sanskrit, "priest"; Anglicized as **Brahmin**)—(1) a priest in the Vedic* tradition; (2) the name of the highest caste* in Indian society; or (3) any person belonging to it

Buddha (Sanskrit, "Enlightened One")—the title given to Siddhartha Gautama*, the founder of Buddhism, as a result of the pure consciousness or awareness that his followers believed that he had achieved through meditation at around the age of thirty-five; aka Shakyamuni*, Bhagavat*, and Tathagata*

Buddha-nature—in Mahayana* Buddhism, the innate potential all sentient beings (at least) have for complete spiritual self-realization

Buddhism (adj. Buddhist, which is also the designation of a follower)—the religion that originated in India in the 6th century BCE* with the life and teachings of Siddhartha Gautama*, who came to be known as the Buddha*; today it consists of a variety of sects in three major Schools*: Theravada* (southern and southeastern Asia), Mahayana* (eastern and northeastern Asia), and Vajryana* (Tibet and surrounding countries), though the third is sometimes subsumed under the Mahayana

candala/ chandala (Sanskrit, "dog-eater")—an alternative term for an outcaste* in Indian society; also known as *avarna*, *dalit*, and *pariah**

canon (adj. **canonical**, the opposite being **non-canonical**)—the scripture taken by any religious tradition to be authoritative and focal (e.g, the Bible and the Qur'an)

Cao Dai—a Vietnamese religion founded in 1919 by Ngo Van Chieu on the basis of a series of claimed revelations; doctrinally, a blend of elements of Christianity, Buddhism, Taoism, Confucianism and Western nineteenth-century Romanticism; centered in South Viet Nam, it has an estimated 8 million members there and as many as 30,000 among expatriates elsewhere in the world, including the United States

caste, caste system (*varna** in Sanskrit)—the spiritually-based stratum and structure found in traditional Indian society and consisting of four major levels (*varna**) and innumerable sub-divisions (*jati**)

CE or C.E.—a fairly recent abbreviation for "Common Era," a less Christian-specific way of designating the years of the era earlier known as A.D.*

chakra (Sanskrit, "wheel")—(1) any one of seven loci of intense spiritual energy along the spine (from sacroiliac to the crown of the head) recognized by the *yoga** tradition; (2) in iconography, a disk-shaped weapon especially associated with Vishnu* and Ganesha*, and representing the sun and the mind (and therefore enlightenment*)

Chalcedon—the fourth great ecumenical* Christian council that, in 451 CE*, finally established the compromise formula that Jesus was one person with two complete natures (human and divine)

chan (Chinese, lit., "meditation")—the Chinese mispronunciation and shortening of the Sanskrit *dhyana**, and the source of the Japanese equivalent, *zen**

Chang Tao-ling—(c. 150 CE) a key figure in the development of Religious Taoism (*Tao-chiao**); he introduced deity-worship and shamanistic-magical practices, as well as an order of priests (*Tao-shih**) and a quasi-Pope (*T'ien-shih**)

chi (Chinese, "vitality," "life force")—an innate power in humans widely recognized in ancient Chinese religion and philosophy as a guarantor of health and longevity, if only tapped by the proper spiritual techniques

Chi K'ung or **Qigong** (Chinese, "vital-energy skill")—a Chinese physical-spiritual exercise technique for unleashing the power of *chi**

ching or *jing* (Chinese, "book")—the equivalent of the Sanskrit *sutra**, and therefore a sacred or spiritual writing (e.g., the *I Ching** and *Tao Te Ching**)

Ching-t'u—the original Chinese form of Amida* or Pure Land* Buddhism, founded c. 400 CE by Hui-yüan or c. 500 CE by T'an-luan

cit/chit (Sanskrit, "consciousness")—together with *sat** and *ananda**, one of the three main attributes regularly applied to *Brahman**

Chuang Tzu—the title of the scripture attributed to the fourth century BCE Chinese sage of the same name (Chuang-tzu) that is the virtual canonical equal of the venerable *Tao Te Ching** and may, in fact, have predated it and served as its inspiration

Chün-tzu (Chinese, "True Gentleman" or "Cultivated Person")—a fully cultivated, noble-minded person; the personal ideal and goal in Confucianism*

Classic Religions—an alternate name for the perennial-archetypal religions*

Clement of Alexandria—early (c. 200 CE) Egyptian Christian theologian, one of the so-called "Greek Fathers" because of the language in which he wrote; known for his grafting of Greek philosophical ideas onto Christian doctrine and for influencing a notable student, Origen*

Code of Manu/Law of Manu, The—an Indian (Sanskrit) scripture written sometime between 200 BCE and 100 CE and named after and attributed to the first (mythical) man of the current age; containing, among much mythology and guidelines for social and religious life, excellent information about some of the constituent elements of Hindu society, such as the caste system* and life stages*

Confucianism (adj., **Confucian**)—the popular English name for the philosophical system laid down by K'ung-fu-tzu*, which the Chinese call *Ru-chia**

Confucius—the Latinized form of the name of K'ung-fu-tzu*

conservative/conservatism—in a religious context and a general sense, a designation for the insistence that the words and ways of the founder be followed as closely and strictly as possible, with no allowance for flexibility in response to changing historical or cultural settings

cult—originally, any group that "cultivates" any distinctive spirituality*; in recent years, a pejorative term for any small, new religious group sufficiently out of the mainstream to be perceived (rightly or wrongly) as dangerously heretical or fanatical (often misconnected to the word "occult," which has an entirely different Latin root)

Dalai Lama—the spiritual head of the dominant sect of Tibetan* Buddhism and widely revered as the spiritual and political leader of the Tibetan people; the current is the 14th, His Holiness Tenzin Gyatso

dalit (Sanskrit, "crushed," "oppressed")—an alternative term for an outcaste* in traditional Indian society; also known as *avarna**, *candala/chadala**, and *pariah**

darshana/darshan (Sanskrit, lit. "seeing" or "viewing"; "viewpoint")—(1) in Hindu devotional* practice, the deep, spiritual exchange of glances between the devotee and the god encountered in a physical representation (e.g., a statue) that is believed to produce a special blessing for the practitioner; (2) any one of the six major philosophical schools* of Hinduism

deity/Deity—a god or a goddess or the fundamental quality of such a being; capitalized, a synonym for "God"

Dependent Co-Arising or **Dependent Co-Origination**—See *pratitya samutpada/paticca-samuppada**

devotion (**devotional, devotionalism**)—the religious orientation or style of spirituality* that emphasizes faith in and/or love of a particular object (e.g., a god, saint, Buddha*, or *bodhisattva**); in Hindu terms, *bhakti**

Dhammapada—the most famous collection of the Buddha's teaching, consisting of 423 verses in Pali* compiled into one book of twenty-six chapters arranged according to subject matter; found in the *Nikayas** of the *Sutrapitaka** of the *Tripitaka**

dharma or ***Dharma*** (Sanskrit, "order," "duty")—in Hinduism, cosmic-social order and one's responsibility toward it, mostly as defined by one's social status (by *caste** and stage of life*); in Buddhism, the Eternal Truth or Teaching channeled by the Buddha* and maintained by the tradition he spawned; one of the Three Jewels/Treasures/Refuges* of Buddhism

Diamond Sutra—See *sutra**.

Dimensions of Religion—a well-established and widely-used schema for analyzing and understanding the complexity of religion and religions devised by famed historian of religion Ninian Smart, who came to recognize seven aspects that could be found in varying degrees in the world's religions; slightly restated, they amount to: (1) doctrinal-intellectual; (2) ceremonial-ritual; (3) moral-ethical; (4) mythical-narrative; (5) experiential-psychological; (6) social-communal; and (7) material-artistic; some would expand on these to include, for example, an historical-developmental dimension

divination—a form of magic (that is, spirit-manipulation) widely practiced in prehistoric-animistic* tribal religions (and in their modern tribal counterparts), involving reading patterns of such things as thrown pebbles, heat-cracked bones or shells, flights of birds, tea leaves, etc., in order to discern future prospects; seen in fossil form, perhaps, in astrological signs and charts, and the tossing of a coin just prior to the start of a football game to determine who will (is supposed to?) kick off or receive the ball first

divine/divinity/Divinity—as an adjective, of or relating to a god or goddess; as a noun, the defining quality of a deity*; [capitalized] a synonym for "God" and "Deity*"

doctrine (adj. **doctrinal**)—a teaching, tenet, or belief derived from certain principles, whether religious or otherwise

dogma (adj. **dogmatic**)—a teaching, tenet, or belief promulgated by some authority as true and therefore non-negotiable (i.e., a doctrine*, but more "carved in stone")

dorje—The Tibetan word for the Sanskrit *vajra**

dukkha/duhkha (Pali/Sanskrit), "sorrow," suffering," "pain," "discomfort," "unsatisfactoriness")—the heart of Buddhism's Four Noble Truths*, the first of which is that life is unsatisfactory, and the second of which is that the root of that situation is *tanha/trishna**

Durga—the red-dressed consort* or Shiva* who is armed to the teeth and rides either a lion or a tiger into battle against evil

Dvaita Vedanta (Sanskrit for "Dualist Philosophy")—the dualist wing of the *Vedanta** School* of Hindu philosophy; it was founded by Madhva*, who held that reality consists of two absolute, eternal, and irreducible principles: one independent, eternal, and unitive (Divinity*, which Madhva called "Lord Sri Hari"); and the other dependent, created, and plural (finitude), with the spiritual goal as the enjoyment of God-as-Krishna*, which he called *moksha**

dhyana (Sanskrit for "meditation")—the Sanskrit (Hindu and Buddhist) word that became *channa* or *chan** in Chinese and *zenna* or *zen** in Japanese

Eastern religions—the perennial-archetypal religions* that were founded to the east of an imaginary line running between Iran and India, characterized by a monistic* view of Ultimate Reality*, a belief in an eternal universe, a cyclical view of time, an understanding of human nature as essentially divine, a unitive spirituality*, and an appreciation for meditation and mysticism*

Eckhart, Meister Johannes (c.1260–c.1327)—a German Dominican monk and theologian*, and arguably the most radical of all Christian mystics* in his claim of absolute essential identity with God; his radically monistic* views of God led his being declared (posthumously) a heretic by his Roman Catholic Church and a spiritual master by later practitioners and students of Zen* Buddhism

Eightfold Path—the way of escaping suffering (*dukkha**) commended by the Fourth Noble Truth of Buddhism, it includes: right vision and intention (*prajna**); right speech, action, and livelihood (*sila**); and right endeavor, mindfulness, and meditation (*samadhi**)

empiricism (adj., **empirical**, when referring to data or evidence; **empiricist**, when referring to a viewpoint or person)—(1) broadly, reliance on sensory-input-based experience or observation; (2) specifically, a philosophical theory that all knowledge originates in experience (as opposed to being innate, as Plato had maintained, or intuition-based); its chief proponent was John Locke (1632–1704)

enlightenment/Enlightenment—(1) in Eastern religions*, the goal of the spiritual* life: the overcoming of ignorance (*avidya**) of one's true, essential nature; (2) in the Western world, a philosophical movement of the 17th and 18th centuries that emphasized empiricism* and rationalism*

enso—the Japanese calligraphic empty circle that symbolizes *Mu** or *Shunyata**

feng shui (Chinese, "wind-water," pronounced "Fung SCHWAY")—a Chinese technique of modifying one's environment for the purpose of improving the overall well-being and fortune of oneself and others

fetishism—a form of magic (that is, spirit-manipulation) widely practiced in prehistoric-animistic* religions (and in their modern tribal counterparts), involving an object (*fetish*) believed to be useful in the control of spirits that impinge on human life, especially in the hands of a *shaman**

Four Noble Truths, The—the supposed content of the very first sermon of Siddhartha Gautama* delivered at Sarnath* (near Varanasi*) soon after his enlightenment*; they revolved around the idea of *dukkha**, its pervasiveness in life, its cause as *tanha**, the possibility of its elimination in *nirvana**, and the Eightfold Path* that leads to that desired end

Ganapati—an alternative name for Ganesha*

Gandhi, Mohandas K. ("Mahatma")—(1869–1948) an Indian lawyer-turned-holy-man and non-violent political reformer credited with improving the lot of oppressed Indian immigrants in South Africa, and later with ending Bristish colonial control of his country, both accomplished through non-violent, passive resistance based on his principle of *satyagraha**

Ganesha, Ganesh (Sanskrit/Hindi)—the elephant-headed son of Shiva* and Parvati*, and the "remover of obstacles" (which is to say, the god of good luck) who is (for obvious reasons) a special favorite of business people in India

Ganga, Ganges—the holiest and most spiritually pure (despite its abject chemical pollution) river in India today and regarded as a goddess who is associated with Shiva*; the holiest city in India, Varanasi*, sits on its banks

Gautama (Gotama)—the family name of the man who became the Buddha* and founded Buddhism

Hanuman—the name of the monkey general who plays a key heroic role in the Hindu epic, *Ramayana**, and is now treated as a deity* ("Lord") in his own right

Hare Krishnas—the popular name of ISKCON*, the devotional Hindu spiritual movement founded by A. C. Bhaktivedanta*; it derives from their favorite utterance (and hymn) of praise for their Lord, Krishna*

hatha yoga (Sanskrit, "union-of-opposites")—the physically-based Hindu spiritual discipline that is the source of the postures (*asanas**) familiar to Westerners, which in turn facilitate the integration of body, mind, and spirit.

Heart Sutra—See *sutra**.

henotheism (adj. **henotheistic**; an advocate is a **henotheist**)—the worship of one god without denying the existence of other deities; a kind of blend of practical monotheism* and theoretical polytheism*

Hinayana (Sanskrit, "Little Vessel," "Small Vehicle")—a pejorative term for Theravada* School* of Buddhism that nevertheless reflects its generally narrow interpretation of the Buddha* and his teachings

Hinduism (adj. **Hindu,** which is also a noun that refers to a person)—the poly-theistic-ancient*, cultural religion of India (called there *Sanatana Dharma**, dating back at least 3500 years (but with roots much earlier); it combines a vast array of practices and beliefs, including polytheism*, monism*, and henotheism*

Honen—13ᵗʰ century Japanese sage who imported Ching-t'u* to his own country and established it there as Amida* or Pure Land* Buddhism

humanism—the view (often said to have originated with Erasmus of Rotterdam in the sixteenth century, but with clear roots in Greek antiquity) that human beings are basically good, full of potential, and capable of self-improvement (as opposed to the orthodox Christian view that they are grievously con-stricted or disabled by sin); taken to extreme (sometimes referred to as "sec-ular"), it denies the existence of God and takes humanity as "the measure of all things" (Protagoras)

hsiao (Chinese, "filial piety")—an ancient Chinese virtue and practice involving extreme respect for elders and parents, living and dead; also valued in Confucianism

hsin (Chinese, "loyalty," "faithfulness," "trustworthiness")—one of the cardinal virtues of Confucianism in its set standards for proper social interaction

Hsün-tzu or **Sün-tzu**—(died 238 BCE) the most heterodox and pessimistic of the successors of K'ung-fu-tzu*, denying as he did the basic goodness of human beings; best known, not surprisingly, for his *The Art of War*

I Ching (Chinese, "Book of Changes" or "Process Book")—an ancient Chinese scriptural classic that predates Confucianism and Taoism; it comprises 64 chapters, and serves to this day as a kind of manual for divination*

idealistic monism—See monism*

imitation—a form of magic (that is, spirit-manipulation) widely practiced in prehistoric-animistic* religions (and in their modern tribal counterparts), involving doing on a small, symbolic scale (e.g., in dance or paintings) what one wants to transpire on a larger scale later (e.g., in a battle or a hunt)

immanence (adj. **immanent,** when applied to God; **immanental** or **immanen-talist,** when talking about an idea, theology, or philosophy, all from the Latin *immanere,* meaning "to dwell within")—the theological* quality whereby the Ultimate Reality* can be said to abide within the universe, rather than in some removed or remote, separate realm; in the strongest, ontological* sense, it means that the essence of the Ultimate and the essence of the universe and its components are the same—as in pantheism* and panentheism*; in a weaker sense, an ontologically transcendent* Ultimate can be said to be immanent as *active* "in" (but not really *within*) the uni-verse, while still remaining distinct (or "Other") in being or essence—as in theism*

Impermanence—See *anitya/anicca**.

incarnation, Incarnation (adj. **incarnational**)—in its most general sense, an embodiment or enfleshment of a god or goddess—what in Hinduism is called an *avatar**; in traditional Christianity, [capitalized] it refers to the orthodox belief and doctrine* that Jesus (and he alone) was God "in the flesh" (Latin, *in carne*)

Indra—the chief of the ancient Vedic* gods of Hinduism, a sky-thunderer resembling Zeus of Greek mythology

Indus—the most sacred Indian river in ancient times, the cradle of one of the earliest civilizations in the world, and the birthplace of both India and Hinduism; now located mostly in Pakistan

Inner Light—what Englishman George Fox (1624–1691 CE), founder of the Society of Friends or Quakers, called the spark of divinity* that he believed everyone possessed within themselves and that they therefore needed to experience and tap for spiritual power

Interbeing—See *pratitya-samutpada/paticca-samuppada**.

International Society for Krishna Conciousness, The (also known as **ISKCON***)—the modern organization founded by A. C. Bhaktivendanta* and better known as the Hare Krishnas*

intranatural—a term coined in this book to describe the ontological* immanence* or profound pervasiveness of the Ultimate in monistic*, pantheistic*, and panentheistic* religious and spiritual systems (in contrast to the supernatural Deity* in transcendence*-dominated theism*)

ishta deva or *ishta devta* (Sanskrit, "chosen deity")—in modern Hinduism's henotheistic* sectarian* form, the god or goddess one selects (or, more likely, inherits as a family tradition) from the multitude of options as the object of one's devotion* (*bhakti**)

Ishvara (Sanskrit, "Lord")—in Hinduism, the non-personal Ultimate* (*Brahman**) as manifested as a god; in common usage, the term is applied to any male deity* in the Hindu pantheon, though the name Mahesh* (Maha + Ishvara, "Great God") is used almost exclusively by *Shaivas** and others for the god Shiva*

ISKCON—the International Society for Krishna Consciousness founded by A. C. Bhaktivendanta* and better known as the Hare Krishnas*

Jainism—an Indian religion founded in the sixth century BCE by Nataputta Vardhamana (aka Mahavira), originally based on a strict ascetic* ethic, and most widely known for its principle of protecting all life forms (see *ahimsa**)

Jatakas—the subsection of the *Sutrapitaka** that contains the moral-conveying stories of the previous lives of Siddhartha Gautama*

jen or *ren* (Chinese, "humane" or "humaneness")—perhaps the quintessential virtue in the system of K'ung-fu-tzu*, connoting humanity's innate potential for consideration, forbearance, patience, and kindness

Jesus Sutras, The—a collection of seventh-century CE writings produced by Persian Christian missionaries to China and reflecting an innovative Oriental interpretation of the core teachings of and about Jesus

jiriki (Japanese, "self-power")—a designation used in Buddhist circles for forms of spirituality* (mainly devotional*) that place trust in other beings or objects to achieve the spiritual goal (e.g., the counsel of Pure Land* Buddhism to place one's faith in the Amida Buddha*)

jnana (Sanskrit, "knowledge," "insight")—in Hinduism, the pursuit of an understanding of the true nature of things and oneself in order to connect one's own true spiritual essence (*atman**) with the Ultimate*, *Brahman**, and thereby to achieve *moksha**

270 Glossary

jnana marga or *jnana yoga* (Sanskrit, "knowledge," "insight" plus "way" or "spiritual discipline")—the Hindu style of spiritual* expression that revolves around *jnana**

Jodo—the Japanese name for the devotional* Ching t'u* or Pure Land* sect of Buddhism imported to Japan by Honen* in the early 13th century CE

Jodo Shinshu (or simply **Shin**)—the variation of Jodo* promoted by Shinran*, the chief (but reformist) disciple of Honen*, and the most popular form of Buddhism in Japan today

Juche (Korean, "self-reliance")—the only officially recognized philosophical, religious, or spiritual* ideology in North Korea, rooted in dialectical materialism as articulated mainly by Kim Il Sung; founded in 1955, it stresses nationalism, personal industry and frugality, social unity, and the revolutionary tradition of North Korea

Kalki—the tenth and final *avatar** of the Hindu god Vishnu* who appears just before the end of an age and the accompanying destruction of the world in the endless succession of cosmic cycles

Kali (Sanskrit, "The Black One")—a popular Hindu goddess, the "Devourer of Evil" who is one of the principal consorts of Shiva*; she is generally depicted as having ink-black skin, an extended bloody tongue, a necklace of human skulls, and the severed head of a man, and as standing on her reclining (and seemingly carefree and sometimes even sexually aroused) mate

kama (Sanskrit, "pleasure")—the first life goal* of traditional Hinduism, often associated (not incorrectly) with imaginative sexual indulgence

Kama Sutra (Sanskrit, "Love Text")—a Hindu scripture attributed to an obscure author named Vatsyayana, generally dated around the fourth century CE, and constituting a scholarly treatise and guide on the subject of sexual pleasure as a form of spiritual realization

Kannon/Kwan Yin (Japanese/Chinese)—in Buddhism, a *bodhisattva** and the principal feminine form of Avalokiteshvara*, generally regarded as a compassionate, motherly guardian of living and deceased children

Kapilavashtu—the supposed location of the principal palatial home of Siddhartha Gautama* during his luxuriant childhood and youth; it was then within the borders of India, but today lies in southern Nepal

karma (English adj. **karmic**)—in both Hinduism and Buddhism, (1) deeds, (2) the consequences that they bring upon the doer, and (3) the universal law that "you reap what you sow" and "what goes around, comes around"—i.e., that all get their just deserts eventually

karma marga or *karma yoga* (Sanskrit, "deed-path" or "deed-discipline")—in Hinduism, one of the three principle ways of attaining spiritual* realization, namely, through ritual or ethical works rather than through faith-love (*bhakti marga**) or knowledge (*jnana marga**)

karuna (Sanskrit, "compassion")—in Buddhism, the deeply-felt empathy that arises from the experience of a profound spiritual* connection with all sentient beings or even all composite things, triggered by the mystically-realized sense that all are essentially One in their (and the universe's) Emptiness (see *Shunyata**)

Kashi (Sanskrit, "City of Light")—an alternative name for Varanasi*

kathenotheism—the serial worship of individual deities* in a polytheistic* system; in Hinduism, the worship of one god or goddess after another, sometimes according to a set schedule (e.g., by devoting one day a week to a specific god or goddess) or perhaps the Shakti* as a whole

kensho (Japanese, "seeing into one's own true nature")—in the strictest sense, one's abruptly-experienced first taste of awakening or enlightenment in the Zen* Buddhist tradition, considered dangerous by some because it might be mistaken for full self-realization; for others, however, a virtual synonym for *satori**

kinhin—the Japanese term for the walking meditation used in Zen* to break up long sessions of *zazen** and restore circulation to the legs

koan—the illogical, mind-boggling puzzle used in Rinzai* Zen* to neutralize the mind; its answer is almost invariably irrational, and sometimes non-verbal

Krishna—the most popular *avatar** of the Hindu god Vishnu*, star of the epic *Bhagavad Gita**, and the object of devotion for Hare Krishnas*

Kshatriya (Sanskrit, "sovereign," "governing")—the second Indian caste* from the top, traditionally comprised of rulers, lawmakers, law-enforcers, and the military

kundalini (Sanskrit, "coiled one")—in Hinduism, an intense concentration of potential spiritual power envisioned as lying like a coiled serpent at the base of the spine (in the vicinity of the lowest *chakra**), which—when loosed by *yogic** practice—will invigorate a person both spiritually and physically

K'ung-fu-tzu (Chinese, "Master K'ung)—the title given to the man born in 551 BCE as K'ung-ch'iu and better known in the West as Confucius*

lama (Tibetan, "priest")—a Tibetan Buddhist priest

Lakshmi or **Laxmi**—a Hindu goddess and the main consort of Vishnu*, she is a patron of luck and wealth, and is usually pictured with gold coins showering from the palms of her hands

Lao-tzu (a Chinese honorific title meaning "Old Man")—the perhaps-legendary 6th century BCE* Chinese author of the *Tao Te Ching** and supposed (and perhaps actual) founder of Taoism

Law of Manu, The—See *Code of Manu, The**.

li (Chinese, "natural patterns")—the Confucian ideal of proper behavior, with reference to both religious rituals and social propriety, but with an emphasis on the latter; it connotes manners, mores, courtesy, propriety, and respect for traditional social roles and relationships

Li Ki (Chinese, "Six Rituals")—traditional Confucian ceremonials: capping, marriage, mourning, sacrifices, feasts, and interviews

liberalism (adj. **liberal**, which may also refer to an advocate)—in general, the tendency of any religion to develop a religious tradition of interpretation that applies the principles of its founder with some degree of flexibility, as opposed to following that person's example and teachings to the letter and simply accepting traditions about him; also known as "progressivism"*

life goal—See *purusartha**.

life stage—See *ashrama/ashram**.

lila (Sanskrit, "play," "frivolity")—a term applied (along with *maya**) by Hindus to *samsara** in order to indicate the superficiality and triviality (but not the utter unreality) of the everyday world and human affairs in comparison with the substantiality and eternality of *Brahman** and *atman**

linga (Sanskrit, "penis")—the primary phallic symbol of the god Shiva*, usually cradled in a *yoni** and kept moist and often flower-decked for ritual and devotional purposes

lotus—a flower popular in Eastern religions* and art as a symbol of spirituality* because it roots in mud (cf. the body, consisting of dust and water) but produces a glorious blossom (cf. *atman** or Buddha-Nature*)

Lotus Sutra—See *Sutra**.

Lumbini—the purported (and perhaps actual) birthplace in northern India (modern Nepal) of Siddhartha Gautama*, the Buddha*

Lun Yü (Chinese, "Analects" or "Selected Sayings")—the collected wise utterances of K'ung-fu-tzu* that constitute his only preserved direct teachings

Madhva—(1238–1317 CE) a *Vaishniva** and Indian philosopher, who founded the Vedantic* school's* dualistic expression called *Dvaita**, which held that reality consists of two absolute, eternal, and irreducible principles: one independent, eternal, and unitive (Divinity*, which he called "Lord Sri Hari"); and the other dependent, created, and plural (finitude), with the spiritual* goal being the enjoyment of God-as-Krishna*, which he called *moksha**

Madhyamika—the most famous of all of the Buddhist philosophical schools*, founded by Nagarjuna (c. 175 CE), whose systematic presentation of the ingredients and implications of the teachings of the Buddha became normative in the Mahayana* tradition

Mahabharata—an ancient epic India poem containing over 100,000 stanzas, and describing a family feud of cosmic proportions; a mere eighteen of its chapters constitute the devotional* classic, *Bhagavad Gita**

Mahadevi (Sanskrit, "The Great Goddess")—one of two terms (see *Shakti**) widely used in India to denote the Divine Feminine, of which the various goddesses are but refractions; her devotees sometimes underscore their high regard for her by referring to the three gods of the *Trimurti** as but the legs of her footstool

Mahamaya (Sanskrit, "Great Illusion")—the honorific form of the name of the mother of Siddhartha Gautama*, the Buddha*

Mahatma (lit., "man with a great soul")—a common Sanskrit* appellation for any Hindu holy man, e.g., a *sadhu** or *sannyasi**

mahatmya (Sanskrit, "praise")—the kind of holy exaggeration one finds among henotheistic* practitioners in Sectarian* Hinduism when they begin to attribute many or all of the distinctive traits of the most popular deities* to their own (as when a *Vaishniva** praises Vishnu* as Creator and Destroyer—the respective roles of Brahma* and Shiva*—as well as Preserver); hence, a kind of virtual monotheism*

Mahayana (Sanskrit, "Big Vessel," "Great Vehicle")—the larger (or largest) of the two (or three) Buddhist schools*, characterized by a broader interpretation and greater inclusiveness than the Theravada*; sometimes distinguished from, but sometimes regarded as inclusive of, *Vajrayana**

Mahayana Sutras—later and technically non-canonical scriptures (because not part of the *Tripitaka**) (see *sutra**.) valued in the Mahayana* School* because they are believed to be based on advanced teachings of the Buddha* passed on by disciples via oral tradition; the most important are the *Heart Sutra, Diamond Sutra,* and *Lotus Sutra.*

mahayuga (Sanskrit, "great age," "eon")—a unit of cosmic time in Hinduism, amounting to four *yugas** of varying lengths and a total of 432 million years; 1,000 *mahayugas* constitute a *kalpa* (432 billion years), which represents one day in the life of the Creator, Brahma*, who lives 100 years of such days (or about 311 trillion years)—which is the length of a single breath for the Preserver god, Vishnu*

mana (Melanesian, "power")—generically, the sort of free-floating spiritual power recognized in prehistoric-animistic* religions (and their modern tribal counterparts) and believed to be able to possess people, places, and things (usually temporarily and for very short periods), rendering them useful in rituals but dangerously *tabu** if mishandled

mandala—a geometric design (also known as *yantra**) used in Hinduism and Buddhism (and especially the Tibetan* branch) for expressing the spiritual* dimension of reality and enhancing meditation

mantra (Sanskrit, "chant")—any one of a number of incantations used in various sects of both Hinduism and Buddhism; the most popular have a seven-beat cadence (e.g., *Namu Amida Butsu*), with the first syllable often absorbing two beats for emphasis (e.g., *OM ma-ne pad-me hum* and *NAM myo-ho ren-ge kyo*)

marga (Sanskrit, "path")—any particular spiritual discipline in Hinduism, the most important being *karma**, *jnana**, and *bhakti**; a virtual equivalent of *yoga**, though the latter term is often said to include a *raja** variety (mystical* in nature) in addition to the three recognized as *margas*

materialistic monism— See monism*.

maya ("illusion")—the Hindu notion that the everyday world (*samsara**) is not what it appears—not that it is totally unreal, but that its apparent and assumed substantiality is illusory, especially compared to the eternality of *Brahman**; capitalized, the name of the mother of the Buddha*

Maya—the given name of the mother of Siddhartha Gautama*

Meister Eckhart—See Eckhart, Meister.

Mencius—Latinization of the name of the Chinese sage Meng-tzu*

Meng-tzu—(d. 289 BCE) the most orthodox and optimistic of the successors of K'ung-fu-tzu*, teaching that human beings were not just potentially good by nature, as his venerable predecessor had maintained, but truly (naturally) good

metaphysics (adj., **metaphysical**)—(1) in its most precise sense, the branch of philosophy that addresses the nature of reality, whether that be seen as material, spiritual, or something else; (2) in a more popular, modern sense, a reference either to a spiritual* realm believed to be beyond the everyday, physical one, or to the belief itself

Metaphysical Christianity—a type of Christianity that arose in America in the mid-to-late nineteenth century, emphasizing the immanence* of God, the essential divinity* of humans, the metaphysical* nature of scripture, and the power of positive thinking, especially in healing; included in this category are Christian Science, Theosophy*, and various New Thought* sects*

Middle Way, The—an ancient nickname for Buddhism, indicating its attempt to avoid the extremes of self-indulgence and asceticism*

ming (Chinese, "law," "order," "destiny," "fate")—the ancient Chinese idea that the physical order of the universe is completely out of human control, moving in determined (though not predetermined) ways; while not exactly "fate" in any predeterminist or predestinarian sense, there is the suggestion here that cosmic order itself dictates that there are no accidents, a view affirmed and conveyed by C. G. Jung by his term "synchronicity"

modern scientific worldview—the worldview* in the Western world ever since (and as a result of) the Enlightenment*; it is based on empirical evidence, reason, an appreciation for cause-and-effect, and a fundamental belief in natural law

moksha (Sanskrit)—in Hinduism, the longed-for "liberation" or "release" from the nearly endless cycles of rebirth (*samsara**) achieved via one or another spiritual discipline (*yoga**)

mondo (from the Japanese, *mondai*, "to question," but also connoting "gateway")—a short, rapid-fire, and seemingly nonsensical question-answer dialogue between Zen* Master and student intended to elicit a spontaneous, intuitive response that short-circuits the intellect and hastens enlightenment; it evolved eventually into the *koan**

monism (adj. **monistic**)—(1) in philosophy, the metaphysical* belief that all reality is essentially of one kind of substance, whether matter (materialistic), mind or spirit (idealistic), or something else altogether (neutral); (2) in Eastern religions* especially, the belief in an Ultimate Reality* that is a non-personal Something—e.g., *Brahman** or *Tao**—but definitely *not* a god

monotheism (adj. **monotheistic**; a proponent is called a **monotheist**)—a belief in only one God of the theistic* type, or a theology* based on such a belief

mudra (Sanskrit, "gesture")—in the Hindu yoga* tradition, any symbolic body position; in Buddhism, a symbolic hand gesture used in meditation, devotion, or artistic representations of Buddhas* and *bodhisattvas**

Mystery—one of the many possible appellations for an Ultimate Reality*, especially One conceived in a monistic* way and connoting not simply something that is not known, but That Which Cannot Be Known

mysticism (adj. **mystical** or **mystic**, which is also a noun that refers to a person)—the introspective spiritual* orientation that seeks an experience of one's essential identity with the Ultimate Reality* or God; though found in Western religions* as a kind of sub-tradition, it is much more common in Eastern religions* precisely because it is far more compatible with a monistic* theology* than a theistic* one; some identify a kind of "relational mysticism" in the West, but it is really only an intense form of devotionalism*

myth—a story that couches a deep religious or spiritual* truth, but—as with a parable—at a level well below the superficial facts, and therefore requiring allegorical or metaphorical interpretation

Nataraja (Sanskrit, "Dancer-Royal")—the Hindu god Shiva* in his dancing pose; also, the name of one of the more rigorous postures (*asananas**) in *yoga**

nembutsu—a chant (*Namu Amida Butsu*, "Reverence to the Amida Buddha") used by Buddhists of the Pure Land* variety

Neo-Confucianism—the name of a variation of Confucianism that arose in China during the Sung Dynasty (960–1279 CE) and that incorporated Taoist and Buddhist elements into a comprehensive metaphysics*

neti neti (Sanskrit, "neither-nor")—in Hinduism, other than merely chanting OM*, the safest way of talking about *Brahman**, namely, by indicating what that Ultimate Reality* is not; best expressed in English as in- and un- words (e.g., infinite, invisible, unimaginable)

neutral monism—See monism*.

New Physics, The—a common appellation for the post-Newtonian scientific approach to understanding the properties of matter at the atomic and sub-atomic levels (and therefore the cosmos itself); triggered by the early twentieth century work of the likes of Planck, Einstein, Bohr, de Broglie and Heisenberg, it is also known as quantum theory or quantum mechanics

New Religions (*Shin Shukyo*), **Japanese**—a term used for the 3,000 or so religions founded in Japan since 1800, the most popular of which were founded after World War II

New Thought—a late 19th century movement in American Christianity that took a self-consciously metaphysical* approach to scripture and doctrine, viewing God as immanent* in humanity, and Christ as one who realized his own inner divinity ("the Kingdom of God within") and who set out to put others in touch with theirs; it produced such sects* as Divine Science, Religious Science, Science of Mind, and Unity

Nicea or **Nicaea**— the first truly great Christian Council, which was convened by the Emperor Constantine in 325 CE* and established the theoretical basis not only for the doctrine of the Trinity, but for the full divinity of Christ as well

Nicene Creed—together with the Apostles' Creed, one of the two classic affirmations of the Christian faith, based on the findings of the Council of Nicea* concerning the relationship of God the Son to God the Father, but probably finalized at the Council of Constantinople in 381 CE.

Nichiren (Japanese, "Sun-Lotus")—(1) the adopted name of a thirteenth-century CE priest in the Japanese Tendai Buddhist sect, which focused on the rational understanding of the *Lotus Sutra**; he concluded that his era was so degenerate that people could not understand that (or any) text, but should instead simply pay devotion* to it by chanting its title; (2) the name of the sect* that he founded; it is best known for its signature chant: *nam myoho renge kyo* ("Reverence to the *Lotus Sutra of the Good Law*")

Nikayas (Pali, "Collections")—the five parts of the Buddhist *Sutrapitakas/ Suttapitakas**, containing the *Dhammapada**

nirguna (Sanskrit, "without attributes/qualities")—a term used in Hindu philosophy to denote the most mysterious depth-aspect of *Brahman**, about which nothing can properly be conceived or uttered

nirvana/nibanna (Sanskrit/Pali, "extinction")—in Buddhism, the blissful realization of one's *anatman** and its identity as *Shunyata**, roughly equivalent to Hinduism's *moksha**

non-dualism—a synonym for monism*, especially in its most radical expressions; See *Advaita Vedanta**

ontological (from the Greek, *ontos*, "being")—a term used by philosophers to refer to the very being or true essence of anything (e.g., to declare that something has "no ontological status" means that it has no basis in reality)

OM—an English variant of *AUM**

Origen—(185–254 CE) a most influential Egyptian Christian theologian who resided in Alexandria and who, like his teacher Clement*, articulated a Neoplatonist philosophical version of Christian doctrine and devised a very sophisticated system of biblical interpretation

orthodoxy (adj. **orthodox**; from the Greek for "right opinion")—officially correct belief, as determined by any religious authority

outcaste—any person who is officially excluded from the four castes* of traditional Indian society and relegated to such ritually unclean acts as the handling of excrement, blood, and corpses; variously designated by the Sanskrit *avarna**, *candala/chandala**, *dalit**, and pariah*, but redefined by Gandhi* as *harijan* ("child of God") as a way of raising consciousness of such a person's worth

Pali—the original Indian language in which the *Tripitaka** was composed; alleged by many (especially in the Theravada* Buddhist tradition) to have been the native tongue of Siddhartha Gautama* himself

panentheism (adj. **panentheistic**; a proponent is called a **panentheist**)—the notion (from the Greek *pan*, "all" or "every," *en*, "in," and *theos*, "god") that everything is in God in such a way that God is immanent* in it, while God yet retains a large measure of ontological* transcendence*

pantheism (adj. **pantheistic**; a proponent is called a **pantheist**)—(from the Greek *pan*, "all" or "every," and *theos*, "god") the notion that everything is God or is *essentially* God

pariah (from the Tamil, "festival drummer")—a term often used for the outcastes* of India, and taken over into English to denote a person who is socially shunned for any reason

parinirvana—in Buddhism, the ultimate experience of *nirvana** associated with death; also the name of the reclining pose of the dying Siddhartha Gautama* frequently portrayed in Buddhist iconography and art

Parsees or **Parsis** (Hindi and Old Persian, "Persians")—Zoroastrians* living in India (especially in the states of Maharashtra and Gujarat, and most especially in and around Bombay/Mumbai), having fled their native Persia over the centuries under the threat of Islam

Parvati—the kindest, gentlest, and most beautiful of all of the consorts* of Shiva*, and the mother of Ganesha*

perennial-archetypal—(1) a description of the type of religions that emerged between 700 or 600 BCE and 600 or 700 CE and that exhibit a unity of focus (monism or monotheism) and a universal appeal; they include Zoroastrianism*, Buddhism, Jainism*, Taoism, Confucianism, Christianity, Islam, and Judaism (at least in its modern recognizable form, though its roots are certainly earlier); (2) [Capitalized] a designation of the period in which these religions emerged

Philosophical Taoism—See *Tao-chia**.

Pinyin or *pin yin*—the newer, less familiar, but far more accurate system of transliterating Chinese words and names into English, gradually replacing the older Wade-Giles* method of representing them

pluralism (adj. **pluralist** or **pluralistic**)—(1) in philosophy, a metaphysics* that holds that reality consists of a multiplicity of different elements, the exact numbers and names varying from philosopher to philosopher; (2) the phenomenon, increasingly common in modern times, of competing and often conflicting religious views coexisting in a way that their adherents cannot ignore one another; (3) the view (of Gandhi*, for one) that religious or spiritual truth (or Truth itself) is partially grasped by many traditions

polytheism (adj. **polytheistic**)—belief in many gods and goddesses, characteristic of ancient religions worldwide—e.g., Indian (Hinduism), Japanese (Shinto*), Mesopotamian, Chinese, Egyptian, Greek, and Roman

polytheistic-ancient religion—(1) a description of the type of religions produced by ancient civilizations (e.g., Mesopotamia, Egypt, India, Japan, Greece, and Rome) between 1500 and 600 BCE or so, and characterized by polytheism, ritual, priests, temples, scriptures, and a lack of missionary interest or activity; all except Hinduism (India) and Shinto (Japan) were displaced and destroyed by later religions of other cultures that conquered their native lands; (2) [Capitalized] a designation for the era that produced these religions

post-classical religion—another name for prolific-alternative religions*

prajna (Sanskrit, "wisdom")—a term used especially in Buddhism to connote various levels of spiritual wisdom rather than intellectual knowledge, from the insight and intention that constitute the first two steps of the Noble Eightfold Path* to the advanced wisdom of fully-realized spiritual adepts (sometimes dubbed *prajnaparamitra*, "perfect/perfected wisdom")

Prajnaparamitra Sutras (Sanskrit, "Perfect/Perfected Wisdom Texts")—one of the most important of the non-canonical, but nonetheless important collections of scriptures of Mahayana* Buddhism, containing the popular *Heart Sutra** and *Diamond Sutra **

pratitya-samutpada/paticca-samuppada (Sanskrit/Pali, "dependent co-origination," "dependent co-arising," "interdependent genesis," "all-embracing togetherness")—the Buddhist philosophical idea that everything in the universe is intimately interrelated to everything else, in a complex and dynamic pattern and process in which everything is both cause and effect of everything else—the implication being that to change any one thing anywhere changes everything everywhere; sometimes referred to as "Interbeing"

prayer flag—colorful, inscribed cloths left to blow in the wind to generate prayers or positive spiritual* energy; one of the distinctive features of Tibetan* Buddhism

prayer wheel—inscribed wheels of varying sizes, containing prayers that are generated in the spinning; one of the distinctive features of Tibetan* Buddhism

prehistoric-animistic—(1) a descriptive term for the religions that existed before the invention of writing and the rise of the ancient civilizations around 3000 BCE, as well as the animistic-tribal religions that still endure among the pockets of surviving tribal peoples around the world today; (2) [Capitalized] a designation for the era that originally produced these religions

progressivism (adj. **progressive**)—an alternative term for liberalism/liberal*

prolific-alternatives—(1) a descriptive term for the prodigious number of new religions and sects* (or other spinoffs) of older ones produced from about 700 CE to the present; (2) [Capitalized] a designation for the period that produced these religions

puja—the Sanskrit term for the kind of worship of an *ishta deva** found in devotional (*bhakti**) or Sectarian* Hinduism; it may be either private or public (and, if the latter, it can be an actual festival)

pundit or *pandit* (Sanskrit, "learned")—a Hindu scholar

Puranas—a collection of post-Vedic* (*shriti**) Hindu scriptures that combine a preponderance of mythology with a bit of history in narratives about ancient gods, sages, and kings; the best known are those named for the *Trimurti**: *Brahma* Purana*, *Vishnu* Purana*, and *Shiva* Purana*

Pure Land (Sanskrit, *Sukhavati**; Japanese, *Jodo**)—the dwelling place in the western sky of Amitabha or Amida*, the Buddha of Compassion, and the heavenly home sought by his followers on the basis of his love and mercy

Pure Land Buddhism—See Amida* Buddhism.

purushartha (Sanskrit, "male-goal")—in Hinduism, any one of the four controlling motivations of life, roughly paralleling the four recognized life stages*; in order of importance, the goals are (1) *kama**, "pleasure," (2) *artha**, "gain," (3) *dharma**, "duty," and (4) *moksha**, "liberation" (spiritual*); as the name suggests, traditionally reserved for males of the three highest castes

Quakerism (adj. **Quaker**)—a left-wing Protestant Christian movement (later a denomination) also known as the Society of Friends, founded in England by a radical Puritan named George Fox (1624–1691 CE); a basically mystical* expression, whose original focus was on the Inner Light* of divinity within each person, its most distinctive features were its rejection of clergy, scripture, music, sacraments, creeds, and confessions, and its practice of silent worship—all in order to direct spiritual attention inward

Radha—the favorite consort or mate of Krishna*, though he is often surrounded by many other *gopis* (female tenders of cows)

raja yoga (Sanskrit, "royal spirituality")—a fourth spiritual* style added to the more traditional three *margas** to denote the mystical* path; the name suggests a certain level of prestige for this *yoga**

Rama, King—one of the more popular of the *avatars** of Vishnu*, and regal star of the epic, *Ramayana** (not to be confused with another *avatar* of Vishnu bearing the same name, but with no regal status)

Ramakrishna (1836–1886 CE)—popular Indian holy man revered for his deep spirituality and conviction that all of the great religious traditions of the world lead to the same goal ("As many faiths, so many paths," he declared.); his ecumenical views greatly influenced Swami Vivekananda*, the first great Hindu missionary to the West

Ramanuja—(1017–1137 CE) a *Vaishniva** and the first major innovator of the *Vedanta** philosophical school* (*darshana**) after Shankara*; he promoted a much less radical non-dualism called *Vishishtadvaita* ("qualified [or complex] non-dualism"), which referred to *Brahman** as "God" and rejected Shankara's *Brahman nirguna** as an empty abstraction, asserting instead that *Brahman*-God has qualities (*saguna**), including personhood, and that both matter and souls are ultimately as real as God, having been created out of "His" eternal substance to form, in effect, "His" body; the spiritual goal for individuals, therefore, was seen as communion rather than union with *Brahman*; if there is any of the mysticism* of Shankara* left here at all, it (along with non-dualism*) is deeply compromised

Ramayana—an extremely popular Indian epic poem by Valmiki (circa 100 BCE) and starring Rama* as a King whose wife, Sita, is kidnapped, taken to the island of Lanka, and eventually rescued

rationalism (adj. **rationalistic**)—the recognition of reason, usually in conjunction with empirical* data, as the only source of true knowledge (an implicit rejection of revelation)

reincarnation—the term generally used by Westerners to convey the Hindu-Buddhist idea of *samsara**, though its general limitation to the recycling of souls from lifetime to lifetime within the human sphere is less accurate in this regard than the more comprehensive idea of *transmigration**

relational spirituality—the religious style especially associated with theism*, henotheism*, kathenotheism* and the devotion to an "Other" Deity* entailed in these models

Religious Taoism—See *Tao-chiao**.

Rinzai—the more active sub-sect of Japanese Zen*, characterized by the use of *koan** in addition to the practice of *zazen**

rishi (Sanskrit, "seer")—in Hinduism, one who has extraordinary powers of spiritual* insight

rita or *rta*—in Hinduism, the eternal cosmic Law, both natural and moral, managed by the Vedic* god Varuna*

roshi (Japanese)—a Zen* master and teacher

Ru-chia (Chinese, "the teachings of the scholars")—the proper name for the tradition (or traditions) that trace their lineage back to K'ung-fu-tzu*, what the West calls Confucianism

sadhu—a Hindu practitioner of extreme asceticism*, probably having dropped out of society and the caste system* as a youth to seek spiritual* realization through celibacy, fasting, and some sort of rigorous physical discipline

(which can include seemingly masochistic forms of self-punishment and even self-mutilation)

saguna (Sanskrit, "with attributes or qualities")—a term used in Hindu philosophy to denote the more accessible, manifest-aspect of *Brahman**, about which concepts and language can be used, if due humility and restraint are exercised

samadhi ("concentration")—refers to the last three steps in the Eightfold Path*

samsara (Sanskrit)—in Hinduism, (1) the nearly endless cycles of rebirth that an *atman** goes through on its way to *moksha**; and (2) the everyday world in which these cycles are lived out

Sanatana Dharma (lit., "Eternal Truth")—the Indian name for Hinduism, usually indicating the philosophy or worldview of that religion rather than its practices

Sangha (Pali, "community," "fellowship")—originally, the community of ordained Buddhist monks, but extended by many in the Mahayana* to include all Buddhists, including laypersons

sannyasi/sannyasin (Sanskrit, "renunciant")—a person, traditionally a male of advanced years, who has reached the fourth and last of the four stages of life* in Indian society by achieving *moksha**, and who therefore has renounced personal name, family and societal ties, and worldly possessions

Sanskrit—the most important ancient language of India, located in the Indo-European family (and therefore related to Latin and the Romance languages), and used today by Hindus only for scholarly-philosophical and liturgical purposes

sanzen—in Rinzai* Buddhism, a private meeting between a *roshi** and an *unsui** to discuss the latter's progress in solving his designated *koan**

Saraswati—a Hindu goddess, mate of Brahma* and patron of learning, music, and penmanship (and thus a favorite of school children)

Sarnath—an ancient town and modern Buddhist holy site near Varanasi* where the Buddha* is said to have preached his first sermon on the Four Noble Truths*

sat (Sanskrit, "being")—together with *cit/chit** and *ananda**, one of the three main attributes regularly applied to *Brahman**

satori (Japanese, "enlightenment," "self-realization")—in Zen* Buddhism, the same clear-minded, pure-consciousness awareness that the original Buddha* is believed to have achieved under the Bo Tree*

satyagraha (Sanskrit, "truth-force," "holding onto the truth")—the technique of non-violent social-action practices promoted by Mahatma Gandhi*; it entails defeating the oppressor by simply being morally steadfast and appealing to the conscience of the adversary

savarupa (Sanskrit, "form")—in Hinduism, the physical or superficial make-up of any entity, as distinct from its *svabhava* (ontological* essence or substance)

schism (most properly pronounced "**SIZZ-um**")—in religion, a major institutional split, usually over a difference of opinion in interpretation or practice

school—mostly a Western designation for one of the two or three major divisions of Buddhism, a smaller sub-division of these generally being referred to as a *sect**; also, any one of the six traditional types (*darshanas**) of Hindu philosophy (e.g., *Advaita Vedanta**)

Se Shu—the *Four Books* raised to canonical status in China by the so-called neo-Confucians of the twelfth century CE: the *Analects**, the *Book of Mencius*, the *Great Learning*, and the *Doctrine of the Mean*.

sect (adj. **sectarian**)—(1) in Eastern religions, a smaller division of a larger branch (often called a "School*") of a dominant religion (e.g., Hinduism, Buddhism), regardless of the antiquity or size of the group in question; (2) in Christianity, a smaller, newer, and somehow idiosyncratic branch, at least in comparison with the more established, larger, and more mainstream denominations that derive from European Protestantism

Sectarian Hinduism—a designation for type of Hinduism that has thrived in India from about 800 to the present, in which henotheism* and *puja** have been directed to one or another of a relative handful of popular deities* (namely, the *Trimurti** and *Shakti**)

sectarian religions—a synonym for prolific-alternatives* religions

*Shaiva/***Shaivism**—a follower/the sect* of the Hindu god Shiva*

Shakti (Sanskrit, "Power")—(1) a reference to the creative power of *Brahman**; (2) an alternate name for Mahadevi*; and (3) a collective name for the various goddesses, but especially applied to the consorts of Shiva* or his own feminine side as Ardhanari/Ardhanarishvara*

*Shakta/***Shaktism**—Hindu devotee of/devotion to the Divine Feminine as Mahadevi* or Shakti*, often treated as a sect* alongside Shaivism* and Vaishnivism*, and sometimes associated with sexual-spiritual practices and related expressions

Shakyamuni (Sanskrit, "Shakya-sage")—one of several titles applied to Siddhartha Gautama*, this one referring to his membership in the Shakya clan of northern India

shaman—in prehistoric-animistic* religion (and surviving modern tribal counterparts), the person born with the gift to manipulate the spirits for the general good

shamanism—a virtual synonym for animism*

Shang-ti—in ancient (and modern folk) Chinese religion, "Father Heaven" òr the "Jade Emperor"; the remote ruler god of high heaven who keeps cosmic order and rewards good and punishes evil through intermediaries

Shankara—(788–820 CE) the most influential and best known Hindu philosopher, and founder of the most influential School* (*darshana**) of Vedantic thought, *Advaita* ("Non-duality," also known as *Kevala Advaita*, "Absolute Non-Duality*"), a thoroughgoing monism* that held that everything was finally *Brahman**; his mystically-based understandings of such important concepts as *Brahman**, *atman**, *samsara**, *nirguna**, and *maya** became definitive for later Hindu thought

sheng jen or *sheng ren* (Chinese, "birth," "life," "innate nature" plus "humaneness")—the Taoist ideal of the natural goodness that people are born with, in contrast to the Confucian *jen/ren**, which suggests only the potential for such a virtue

shikan taza (Japanese, "just sitting")—the distinctive, comparatively passive style of *zazen** practiced by the Soto* subsect of Zen*

Shin—a shortened form of Jodo Shinshu*

Shinran—(1172–1263 CE) the most brilliant (but reformist) disciple of Honen* and founder of the Jodo Shinshu* or "True Pure Land"* sect

Shinto, Shintoism—the indigenous, ancestral, polytheistic-animistic*, cultural religion of Japan, well-established before the arrival of Buddhism from continental Asia in the sixth century CE

Shiva—the Destroyer, one of the principal gods of Sectarian* Hindu devotion*, and overseer of the natural processes of disease, decay, destruction, and death as well as music, dance, sexuality and (oddly enough) asceticism*

shruti (Sanskrit, "that which was heard")—a designation for the earlier and most inspired of Hindu scriptures, and especially the *Vedas**, in contrast to the *smriti**

shu (Chinese, "altruism," "selflessness," "reciprocity")—a cardinal virtue of Confucianism, often stated as "The Negative Golden Rule": "Do not do to others what you would not want them to do to you."

Shudra (Sanskrit, "Servant")—the fourth caste* from the top, traditionally consisting of laborers

Shunyata (or **Sunyata**, Sanskrit for "Emptiness" or "Nothingness")—Ultimate Reality* in Buddhist philosophy, conceived in seemingly negative terms in order to (1) capture a sense of its utter mysteriousness; (2) underscore its total dissimilarity to existent beings and things; and (3) convey its role as the infinitely potential Source of all actualities (existing entities)

siddha (Sanskrit)—in Buddhism, a highly realized and powerful spiritual being

Siddhartha Gautama (or **Gotama**)—the Indian prince who lived, according to tradition, sometime around 580–460 BCE (or 583–463, though some put him a century or so later), and who became known as the Buddha* after an experience of enlightenment* around age 35

Sikhism—an Indian religion founded in the early sixteenth century CE by Nanak (1469–1539 CE), as a way of synthesizing the two major competing religions in India at that time, Hinduism and Islam

sila (Pali, "virtue," "morality")—in Buddhism, a reference either to the various lists of moral precepts expected of Buddhist monks and laypersons, or to steps three through five of The Noble Eightfold Path*

skandhas/khandhas (Sanskrit/Pali, "components," "bundles," or "aggregates")—in Buddhism, the five dynamic constituent components of a human being: (1) body or physical form; (2) feeling or sensation; (3) perception; (4) will or disposition; and (5) consciousness; none of these is a root phenomenon, for at the center a human is *anatman/anatta**, which is to say "without soul or self" or simply "empty"

smriti (Sanskrit, "that which was remembered")—a designation for the later, less inspired of Hindu scriptures, and especially the *Vedas**, which are considered *shruti**

Soto—a Japanese Zen* sub-sect imported from China by Dogen in the thirteenth century CE and distinguished by its practice of *shikan taza**

spirituality (adj. **spiritual**)—the way in which one orients oneself toward life, existence, the universe, and any Ultimate Reality* that might be perceived therein or thereabouts; with respect to a belief in an Ultimate Reality, there are, broadly speaking, only two patterns of spirituality to be found in the world's religions: (1) *relational-devotional*, which aims at a *communication* or *communion* with a transcendent* Other; and (2) *unitive-mystical*, which has as its goal total *absorption* into or *union* with an immanent* One

Sukhavati—the Sanskrit name for the Pure Land* (heavenly abode) in the western sky where the Amida Buddha resides; it is called *Ching-t'u* in China and *Jodo* in Japan

supernatural (from the Latin for "above nature")—a term properly applied in a theological* sense only to the Deity* of the *theistic* type, underscoring as it does divine transcendence* (that is, the ontological* discontinuity between the Creator, on the one hand, and the Creation and its creatures on the other)

sutra (Sanskrit, "thread," "lesson")—a later, non-canonical, but nonetheless important scripture in either Hinduism (e.g., *Kama Sutra*) or Mahayana* Buddhism; (e.g., the *Lotus Sutra*, *Heart Sutra*, and *Diamond Sutra*)

Sutrapitaka/Suttapitaka (Sanskrit/Pali, "Lesson-Basket")—the first of the three sections ("baskets") of the Buddhist "Bible," the *Tripitaka*; it contains many stories about and teachings of Siddhartha Gautama*

svabhava (Sanskrit, "substance," "essence")—in Hindu and Buddhist philosophy (metaphysics*), a way of talking about what makes anything what it is; some philosophers, East and West, deny that there is any such thing, maintaining that "what you see is what you get" (See "materialist monism*.")

taboo or *tabu*—in prehistoric-animistic* religions (and among surviving contemporary tribal peoples), the condition of being possessed by *mana* and therefore being off-limits to the uninitiated (that is, the non-*shaman**)

T'ai-chi (Chinese, "Great Power")—(1) the *Tao** in its primordial manifestation, from which all other manifest multiplicity (that is, the variegated stuff of cosmos itself) derives; (2) the proper name for the familiar *yin-yang** symbol

T'ai-chi chuan—a Chinese martial art based mainly on Taoist principles, and best known in its "soft" form, which resembles a gentle, rhythmic cross between ballet and calisthenics

tanha (Pali, "craving," "clinging," "desire")—in Buddhism, the cause of *dukkha** (suffering) and therefore the basis of the second of the Four Noble Truths*

Tantra/Tantrism (Sanskrit, "loom," "treatise," "text" "action"; adj. **Tantric**)—(1) an esoteric Hindu or Buddhist text/movement; (2) a Hindu or Buddhist (especially Vajrayana*) spiritual expression that promises sudden enlightenment* in a single lifetime; especially in its so-called "left-hand" expressions, it often associates (in symbol, iconography, and practice) the ultimate spiritual union with sexual intercourse between male and female

Tao or *Dao* (Chinese, "Way," "Word," or "Idea")—an ancient Chinese term connoting the paths of heavenly bodies; later adopted and adapted conceptually, but in very different ways, by both Confucianism and Taoism; in its later, fully developed form it refers to the Absolute and Undifferentiated Non-Personal One that is both the Source of the cosmos and the inner (immanent*) Force that motivates it, but in a most gentle, unobtrusive, natural, and fluid way

Tao-chiao (Chinese, "Way-religion")—the religious form of Taoism that developed from the original philosophical variety (see *Tao-chia**)

Tao-chia ("Way-philosophy")—the philosophical form of Taoism that predated and undergirded its later, more religious expressions (see *Tao-chiao**)

Tao-shih (Chinese, "Way-master")—a priest of Religious Taoism (*Tao-chiao**)

Tao Te Ching/Dao De Jing—an ancient Chinese book of esoteric wisdom attributed to Lao-tzu*; a cautious, poetic, and self-effacing description of the Ultimate Reality* as the Mysterious One that is immanent* in nature and human nature; the key scripture of Taoism*, though rivaled in the minds of some by the *Chuang Tzu**

Taoism—the ancient Chinese religion said to have been founded in the sixth century BCE* by Lao-tzu* and based on the *Tao Te Ching**; its basic principles are naturalness, non-assertiveness, simplicity, and spontaneity—all expressing a fluid and effortless harmony with the *Tao**

tariki (Japanese, "other-power")—a designation used in Buddhist circles for forms of spirituality (mainly devotional*) that place trust in other beings or objects to achieve the spiritual goal (e.g., the counsel of Pure Land* Buddhism to place one's faith in the Amida* Buddha*)

Tat (Sanskrit, "That" or "That One")—a nickname of sorts for *Brahman**

tat tvam asi (Sanskrit, "That thou art" or "That's you")—one of several ways in which Hindus indicate the absolute identity of their individual spiritual essence, *atman**, and *Brahman** (aka *Tat**), the absolute Ultimate*

tathata (Sanskrit, "thusness," "suchness")—in Buddhism, a term used for the unconditioned nature of things, and thus a more positive-sounding version of *Shunyata**; presumably, the world as truly beheld by the enlightened or awakened mind

Tathagata (Sanskrit/Pali, "The Thus Gone")—one of the many titles for Siddhartha Gautama*, its meaning being something like "Pathfinder" or "Guide"

te (Chinese, "virtue," "strength," "power")—an important value in the Chinese tradition, though variously understood (e.g., as something natural and innate in Taoism versus a quality that requires cultivation in Confucianism)

theism (adj. **theistic**)—the theological* model that holds that God is transcendent* in the strong, ontological* sense (i.e., that God's essence is fundamentally different from that of the universe and its contents) and immanent* in the weaker sense of being its Creator and *active* in worldly events, human lives, and history in an ongoing way; in Western religions*, theists—such as traditional Jews, Christians, and Muslims—are *monotheists**, claiming that only one such Deity* exists

theodicy—any effort to offer an explanation for evil and suffering, especially among the apparently helpless and innocent, within the context of belief in an omniscient (all-knowing, including prescience or foreknowledge), omnipotent (all powerful), *and* omnibenevolent (thoroughly loving) God

theology (adj. **theological**; a person who does theology is a **theologian**, all from the Greek *theos*, "god," and *logos*, "word," "thought," or "reason")— (1) informally, any idea or statement concerning God or Ultimate Reality*; (2) more strictly, a formal intellectual discipline that engages such matters as the existence of God, the nature of God, and God's relevance to humanity in some kind of deep, intentional, and perhaps even systematic, philosophically grounded way (though not *all* formal theologies are systematic or philosophical)

Theosophy/Theosophical Society—an eclectic American metaphysical* religion founded in the late 19th century by Madame Helena P. Blavatsky (1831–1891 CE), blending elements of Christian theology* with ideas drawn from Eastern religions* and their philosophies—hence, "Theosophy"

Theravada—one of the two (with Mahayana*) or three (if one includes Vajrayana*) major Schools* of Buddhism; it is strongest in Sri Lanka and Southeast Asia (Thailand, Myanmar/Burma, Campuchea/Cambodia, and environs)

Three Doctrines, The—Confucianism, Taoism, and Buddhism as they are traditionally recognized and practiced in China, which is as complementary and mutually reinforcing traditions

Three Refuges, The (also known as "Treasures" or "Jewels")—the most basic and widely accepted creed or affirmation of faith in Buddhism: "I take refuge in the Buddha*, I take refuge in the *Dharma**, I take refuge in the *Sangha**."

Tibet—formerly a sovereign nation bordering Nepal, Bhutan, and China; now a part of China, having been forcibly and violently annexed in the late 1950s, sending the Dalai Lama* and many other practitioners of Tibetan* Buddhism into surrounding countries

Tibetan Book of the Dead—the best-known and most distinctive scripture of Tibetan* Buddhism, providing tips for a successful spiritual excursion through the *bardo** experience between the present life and the next

Tibetan Buddhism—the distinctive form of Buddhism found in the formerly sovereign Tibet* and surrounding countries (especially Nepal, Bhutan, and northern India); the most widely recognized form of *Vajrayana**

T'ien or **D'ien**—in ancient and modern Chinese folk religion, "Heaven" as (1) a celestial place where Shang-ti* resides; (2) an impersonal Power after the fashion of *mana**

T'ien-shih (Chinese, "Heaven-master")—the quasi-papal spiritual leader of Religious Taoism (*tao-chiao**)

totem—a form of magic (that is, spirit-manipulation) widely practiced in prehistoric-animistic* religions (and their surviving tribal counterparts), involving the identification of a tribe or clan with something in nature (usually a "power animal") for the purpose of drawing upon its strength in a spiritual sense, often by ritually killing and consuming it; seen in fossil form, perhaps, in team mascots, national symbols (e.g., the American eagle), and the eat-drink-body-blood language of the Christian Mass/Lord's Supper

transcendence (adj., **transcendent**, when applied to God; **transcendental** or **transcendentalist**, when applied to an idea, theology,* or philosophy, all from a Latin verb meaning "to go beyond")—a word important in theology in two distinct senses, one strong and one weak: (1) *ontological* transcendence*, which is the divine quality of being prior to, above, beyond, and other than (or any combination of these) in such a way that the being or essence of the Deity* in question is clearly and qualitatively different from that of the universe and its constituents, so that "God is not the cosmos, world, or humanity and they certainly are not God."; and (2) *perceptual* or *conceptual transcendence*, which speaks more to human limitations than to the nature of God, holding that whatever God's own nature is (whether immanent* *or* transcendent), it is *beyond* the powers of human perception, conceptualization, and verbalization (See Transcendentalism*.)

Transcendental Meditation—a Hinduism-derived *yoga** designed for and promoted among Western laypersons beginning in the 1950s by Maharishi Mahesh Yogi*

Transcendentalism (adj. **Transcendentalist**, which is also used as the designation for a follower of this view)—an American spiritual* and literary movement of the early 19th century (most associated with New Englanders Henry David Thoreau and Ralph Waldo Emerson) that was closely related to Romanticism in its appreciation of intuition over reason, and—despite its name—its vision of a Divinity* of essential or ontological* *immanence** rather than transcendence*

transmigration (of the soul)—the passing of a soul or spirit from one mortal body (at its death) to another, the distinction from reincarnation* usually but not universally being that the latter requires the bodies involved to be human, while transmigration embraces the possibility of non-human recipients, at least theoretically

Trimurti (Sanskrit, "Three Forms")—traditionally, the three main (male) gods of Sectarian* Hinduism: Brahma*, the Creator; Vishnu*, the Preserver; Shiva*, the Destroyer; in popular piety and actual practices, the female *Shakti** have eclipsed Brahma in importance

Tripitaka/Tipitaka (Sanskrit/Pali, "The Three Baskets")—the Buddhist "Bible," though more highly regarded in the Theravada* than in the Mahayana* School*, which has a preference for later *Sutras**; it comprises the *Sutrapitaka/Suttapitaka**, *Vinayapitaka**, and *Abhidharmapitaka/Abhidhammapitaka**

trishna—the Sanskrit equivalent of the Pali *tanha**

tulku (Tibetan, "incarnate priest")—in Tibetan* Buddhism, a person recognized (usually early in life) as the reincarnation* of a great *lama** or spiritual teacher, the best-known example being the Dalai Lama*

tzu-jan or *zi-ran* (Chinese, "self-so," "of itself," "nature," "naturally")—a term used in Taoism to connote its appreciation for things in their natural (uncultivated), plain, simple state

Ultimate, The/Ultimate Reality—a generic term used in religious studies for the Supreme Spirit or Being in any system of monotheism* or monism*; what various religions call "God," "*Jahweh,*"* "*Allah,*"* "*Brahman,*"* "*Tao*," and the like

unitarianism (adj., unitarianism)—the view that God is integral rather than Triune, as the traditional Christian doctrine of the Trinity holds; when capitalized, the term refers to the ultra-rationalist (and therefore non-doctrinal) religious organization founded in America in the early nineteenth century, which later merged with another likeminded group to form the Unitarian-Universalist Association

unitive spirituality—a phrase coined in this book to refer to a religious or spiritual* orientation appropriate to a monistic* understanding of the Ultimate Reality* and the mystical* practice generally deemed as the best way to approach it

Universal Religions—an alternative name for the perennial-archetypal religions*

universalism—the idea, found in some religions as the majority position and others as a minority view, that whatever the ultimate religious or spiritual* pay-off is conceived to be, everyone gets it sooner or later; the notion is invariably grounded *either* in the thoroughgoing love, mercy, or grace of a god or other compassionate spiritual being or power (such as a Buddhist *bodhisattva**), who simply could not permit any to perish or be otherwise punished or lost forever, or in a sense of the benevolence of the universe itself

unsui—a novice Zen* student, studying under the guidance of a *roshi**

Upanishads, The—a collection of ancient Hindu philosophical writings antedated only by the venerable *Vedas*, to which they are sometimes considered appendices and called *Vedanta* ("the *Vedas'* end-parts"); the main theme is the proper relation between—indeed, the unity of— *atman** and *Brahman**

upaya (Sanskrit, "skillful means," "expedients")—in Buddhism, anyone or anything that can nudge one in the direction of enlightenment* or actually help them to achieve it

Vaishya—the merchant-farmer-entrepreneur caste* in India, situated just below the *Kshatriya** and just above the *Shudra**

Vaishniva/Vaishnavism—a Hindu follower/the sect of the god Vishnu*

vajra/dorje (Sanskrit/Pali, "diamond," "thunderbolt")—in the Tibetan* or Vajrayana* Buddhist tradition, a symbol of the preciousness, purity, and power of the enlightenment* or self-realization experience, as well as of the suddenness with which this esoteric tradition claims it can come upon the spiritual seeker

Vajrayana (Sanskrit, "thunderbolt vehicle" or "diamond vessel")—according to some, the third major School* of Buddhism, reflecting a more esoteric and exotic variation on that faith, and including Tibetan* Buddhism and the Shingon sect in Japan; also known as *Mantrayana* (because of its extensive use of chants) and *Tantrayana* (because of its employment of esoteric texts), its so-called "left-hand" expression is especially noted (and criticized) for its indulgence (for spiritual purposes) in things otherwise forbidden to lay or monastic Buddhists (e.g., sex, gluttony, and intoxication)

Varanasi—a city on the River Ganges* (or Ganga) considered by most Hindus to be the most sacred site of all, and a goddess in its (her) own right; closely tied in lore and sentiment to Shiva*; also known as Banaras/Benares* and Kashi*

varna (Sanskrit, "color")—any one of four major castes or social strata in India: Brahmin* (*Brahmana**), Kshatriya*; Vaishya*; and Shudra*; see caste system* and outcaste*

Varuna—the ancient Vedic* Hindu god whose task is to manage cosmic order (*Rita**) and who therefore guarantees the smooth workings of nature and morality

Vedanta (Sanskrit, "end of the *Vedas**")—a virtual synonym for the *Upanishads*, denoting (1) that they were originally attached to the end of each of the four *Vedas** and (2) eventually came to be regarded as the "end" (as in *goal*) to which the *Vedas* and their rituals were pointing; also (3) one of the six major Schools* (*darshanas**) of Hindu philosophy

Vedanta Societies—the pioneer Hindu missionary organization in the West, founded in the late nineteenth century in New York City by Swami Vivekananda* and administered from India by his Ramakrishna* Order (1897); its nearly twenty centers in the United States are known for their humanitarian and educational efforts

Vedas (from Sanskrit *vid*, "to know"; adj., **Vedic**)—the most ancient and revered (though not always the most read and regarded) of Hindu scriptures; considered *shruti**; four in number; compiled sometime between 1500 and 500 BCE, and consisting mostly of ritual-related materials (hymns and such), but including the philosophical *Upanishads**, which eventually took on a life of their own and became the basis of all Hindu philosophy

Vinayapitaka (Sanskrit/Pali, "monastic rule basket")—the second of the three "baskets" of the Buddhist canon*, *Tripitaka**, consisting of rules to be followed by monks and nuns, and therefore of little interest to most Buddhists (who are laypersons)

vipassana/vipasyana (Pali/Sanskrit, "insight")—the principal form of meditation taught in the Theravada* School* of Buddhism, emphasizing attention to the transitoriness of composite, conditional reality; in Mahayana, it connotes meditation that focuses on the ultimate emptiness of that reality

Vishishtavaita (Sanskrit, "qualified [or complex] non-dualism")—the moderate expression of the *Vedanta** philosophical school* (*darshana**) proposed by Ramanuja* (1017–1137 CE), injecting a measure of transcendence* into the monism* of his predecessor, Shankara*, by insisting that while *Brahman** is the only Absolute Reality, it is best thought of as God (called either *Brahman*-God or *Ishvara**) and the creator of matter and souls, which constituted his body; and that the spiritual goal of individuals was to achieve communion (rather than union) with this now-personal Ultimate*

Vishnu—the Preserver God of Sectarian* Hinduism, known for his incarnational appearances in human history as *avatars** (e.g., Rama*, Krishna*, and Kalki*)

Vivekananda, Swami—the first great Hindu missionary to the West, whose palpable spiritual presence and spectacular performance as a speaker at the World Parliament of Religions* in 1893 gave his religion its first real foothold in America, and led to the establishment of Vedanta Societies* there

Wade-Giles—the older and more familiar system of transliterating Chinese words and names into English (e.g., Peking and *Tao*), gradually being supplanted by the more correct *pinyin** (with its Beijing and *Dao*)

wan-wu (Chinese, "the ten thousand things," "myriad creatures")—what philosophers call "phenomenal reality" and everyone else thinks of as the everyday world and the multiplicity and dualities that it comprises

wat (Thai, "monastery")—a Theravada* Buddhist monastery, mostly found in Southeast Asia

Western religions—the perennial-archetypal religions* that were founded to the west of an imaginary line running between Iran and India; they are characterized by a monotheistic* view of Ultimate Reality*, a belief in a created universe, a linear view of time, an understanding of human nature as essentially distinct from the divine, a predominantly relational spirituality*, and an appreciation for devotion* and prayer

World Parliament of Religions, The—an extraordinary and unprecedented gathering of representatives of many of the major world's religions (including Hinduism and Buddhism) in Chicago in 1893, in conjunction with the Columbian Exposition there; many of the featured speakers (e.g., Swami Vivekananda*) either established institutional footholds in or cultural ties to America themselves or later sent influential representatives to do so

worldview—the way people of any society or culture of any era implicitly agree on what reality is and how it works

Wu-chi (Chinese, "Infinite Nothingness")—the mysterious Void from which the *Tai-chi** emerged, and thus the equivalent of the Buddhist *Shunyata**

Wu Ching—the so-called "Five Classics" of ancient Chinese religion and philosophy, supposedly edited by K'ung-fu-tzu* himself: *The Book of Changes* (*I Ching*), the *Book of History*, the *Book of Songs*, the *Spring and Autumn Annals*, and the *Book of Rites.*

wu wei (Chinese, "not doing")—the Taoist attitude and ethic, not of total passivity, but of "going with the flow" with respect to life and its challenges rather than assertively or aggressively imposing meanings and solutions upon them

yang (Chinese, "bright," "lighted")—the side of the primal duality of the *T'ai-chi** (and indirectly the *Tao** itself) that reflects such attributes as brightness, warmth, dryness, height, assertiveness, and maleness, but always and only in balance with its counterpart, *yin**

yantra—See *mandala**.

yi—(Chinese, "morality," "righteouness," "character")—in Confucianism, a state of being achieved by practicing *te** within the major human relationships; the spiritual counterpart of *li**

yin (Chinese, "shadowy")—the side of the primal duality of the *T'ai-chi** (and indirectly the *Tao** itself) that reflects such qualities as darkness, coolness, dampness, lowliness, non-resistance, and femaleness, but always and only in balance with its counterpart, *yang** *yoga* (Sanskrit, "to yoke")—(1) any one of a number (usually three, four, or countless) of spiritual disciplines recognized in Hinduism as effective in making the crucial (and inevitable) connection between one's *atman** and *Brahman**—also sometimes called a *marga* (path); or (2) a specifically physical practice or technique associated with *hatha* (i.e., bodily exertion) *yoga*

yogi (Sanskrit)—a practitioner of *yoga**

Yogi, Maharishi Mahesh—(1911?–) Mahesh Prasad Varma; founder of the Transcendental Meditation* self-help method in the mid-1950s; guru of the Beatles a decade later; promoter of the *Ayurveda** method of holistic health; and founder of Maharishi University of Management (formerly Parsons College) in Fairfield, Iowa

yoni (Sanskrit, "vagina")—in Hinduism, the symbolic feminine counterpart to (and iconographic cradle of) the *linga** of Shiva*, representing the awesome power of the feminine

yuga (Sanskrit, "age")—in Hinduism, any one of four periods of cosmic time amounting (by some estimates) to 10,800 human years; the general agreement is that we are living in the last of these, the *Kali** *Yuga**, which is a dark time of surging materialism and declining spirituality*, at the end of which the universe will be returned (in good cyclical fashion) to the best and brightest of times

zazen (Japanese, "sit-meditate")—the seated meditation that constitutes the core practice of Zen* in all of its various forms

zen, Zen (Japanese corruption of the Chinese *chan** and the Sanskrit *dhyana**, both of which mean meditation)—the Mahayana* sect said to have been founded in the sixth century CE by the eccentric Indian sage Bodhidharma*; it emphasizes meditation as the most effective spiritual path

Zoroastrianism—an ancient Persian, profoundly dualistic, but somehow quasi-monotheistic religion founded, probably in the sixth century BCE, by the prophet Zoroaster (or Zarathustra); most of its followers there later fled an emergent and hostile Islam for asylum in India, where they live today as Parsees*

Index